Rapidex

Dictionary of Phrases

English & Hindi

अंग्रेज़ी-हिन्दी अभिव्यक्ति कोश

Rapidex
PUBLICATIONS

Published by:

Rapidex PUBLICATIONS

An Imprint of

Pustak Mahal®

Administrative office and sale centre

J-3/16 , Daryaganj, New Delhi-110002

☎ 23276539, 23272783, 23272784 • *Fax:* 011-23260518

E-mail: info@pustakmahal.com • *Website:* www.pustakmahal.com

Branches

Bengaluru: ☎ 080-22234025 • *Telefax:* 080-22240209

E-mail: pustak@airtelmail.in • pustak@sancharnet.in

Mumbai: ☎ 022-22010941, 022-22053387

E-mail: rapidex@bom5.vsnl.net.in

Patna: ☎ 0612-3294193 • *Telefax:* 0612-2302719

E-mail: rapidexptn@rediffmail.com

Rapidex Trade Mark Registration No. 318345//dt. 6.9.76

ISBN 978-81-223-1415-1

Is Edition: 2014

Printed at: **AR Emm ınternatıonal, Delhi**

Part-I

Dictionary of Phrases with Meaning in English & Hindi with Usage

1. Advice, Suggestions and Rebuke

- Remember you are **swimming upstream**:
  You are going against the normal practice and will have a tough time.
  आप मुख्यधारा के विपरीत जा रहे हैं, आपको मुश्किलों का सामना करना पड़ेगा।

- You must learn to **hold your tongue**:
  You must learn to be silent.
  आपको चुप रहना सीखना होगा।

- You will have to **live in harmony** with:
  You will have to live peacefully with.
  आपको मिल-जुलकर रहना होगा।

- She will have to **tread her ground** carefully:
  She has to be watchful.
  उसे सँभलकर चलना होगा।

- **Where do you think this road will carry you?**
  This kind of life is dangerous.
  तुम्हें क्या लगता है कि ऐसा करके तुम क्या पाने वाले हो?

- **The results could be utterly disastrous:**
  The results will be bad.
  नतीजा ख़राब होगा।

- **Here each one is on his/her own:**
  It's a disorganised place.
  यह एक अव्यवस्थित स्थान है।

- **I had better be on my way:**
  I cannot wait any longer.
  मैं तनिक भी इंतज़ार नहीं कर सकता।

- Ensure that you stay within the **letter of the law**:
  Follow the rules and regulations.
  नियमों का पालन करें।

- He doesn't **have the vision** and is likely to blow it up:
  He can't think big and will mess up things.
  उसमें दूर की सोच नहीं है, उससे भी गड़बड़ हो जाती है।
- You can become an **agent of change**:
  You can start changing the system.
  आप कार्यप्रणाली में परिवर्तन ला सकते हैं।
- To **go with the flow** is not always desirable:
  You have to take a stand against the system.
  हमेशा भेड़-चाल चलना ठीक नहीं।
- You need **to create a framework** for your success:
  You must make a proper plan to succeed.
  सफलता प्राप्त करने के लिए आपको सुनियोजित योजना बनानी चाहिए।
- **You are in the cockpit,** so control things:
  You are in charge, so learn to handle the situation.
  आप इंचार्ज हैं, तो स्थिति को नियंत्रित करना आना चाहिए।
- You have to write the new script; **accept the change**:
  Don't get upset if things are not as per your wishes.
  अगर परिस्थितियाँ आपके अनुकूल नहीं हैं तो हताश न हों।
- You have **to reassert** what is truly important:
  Find out and stress the correct priorities.
  अपनी महत्त्वपूर्ण प्राथमिकताओं को पहचानकर कार्य कीजिए।
- Think **outside the box** and be open-minded:
  Accept new ideas.
  नए विचारों को स्वीकार कीजिए।
- You should not **get consumed** by self-focus:
  Think about others also.
  दूसरों के बारे में भी सोचें।
- You have **to chart your own course**:
  You will have to make your own plans.
  अपनी योजनाएँ आपको स्वयं बनानी चाहिए।
- You must always **be on guard**:
  Be careful and alert.
  आपको हमेशा सावधान रहना होगा।

- You will be **walking into a minefield**:
  You will encounter a lot of difficulties.
  आपको बहुत सारी कठिनाइयों का सामना करना पड़ेगा।
- Kindness goes a long way in **building a relationship**:
  Kindness is beneficial in forming relationships.
  रिश्ता बनाने में उदारता की बहुत आवश्यकता होती है।
- **Don't harbour bad feelings against her**:
  Don't think badly about her.
  उसके ख़िलाफ़ कोई भी बुरी भावना मन में मत रखो।
- **Tap into your conscience**:
  Ask your soul.
  अपनी अंतर्रात्मा से पूछें।
- **Look into your collar**:
  You are also not clean.
  अपने गरेबान में झाँकें।
- Do a little bit of **soul-searching** and you will find the answer:
  Look at your own self critically and you will realise you are not flawless.
  अपने अंदर झाँककर देखो, आपको अपनी कमियाँ नज़र आ जाएँगी।
- Try not to become **narcissistic**:
  Don't be obsessed with your looks.
  स्वयं के सौंदर्य पर मोहित न हों।
- Be open – **nurturing grievances** would do more harm:
  Forget the past, it will do no good.
  दिल बड़ा करो, पुरानी बुरी यादों को मन में रखने से नुकसान ही होगा।
- **If you don't improve, you may regret it**:
  If you don't mend your behaviour, you will pay the price.
  यदि आप अपने व्यवहार में सुधार नहीं लाएँगे तो आपको उसका मूल्य चुकाना पड़ेगा।
- Kick them where it **hurts the most**:
  Attack their weak points.
  उसकी कमज़ोरियों पर वार करो।

- **You will see him in different light once you know more details**:
You will know his real worth once you have the facts.
जब आपको उसकी असलियत का पता चलेगा, तो आपका उसके प्रति दृष्टिकोण बदल जाएगा।
- **Don't be daft**:
Don't behave senselessly.
मूर्खतापूर्ण व्यवहार मत करो।
- **Be patient, the apple will fall in your lap**:
Be patient, you will succeed.
धैर्य रखें, आप अवश्य सफल होंगे।
- Don't let your husband **off the hook**:
Don't let your husband get away without facing the consequences.
अपने पति की लगाम कसकर थामो।/अपने पति को अपने नियंत्रण में रखो।
- Time is **running out**, so talk business:
There is no time to waste, so come to the point straightaway.
समय कम है, काम की बात करो।
- Are you looking to **shoot the moon**?
You are being too ambitious.
आप अत्यधिक महत्त्वाकांक्षी बन रहे हैं।
- **Keep your trap shut or I'll rearrange your teeth**:
Shut your mouth or I will thrash you.
चुप रहो वरना मार खाओगे।
- I hope you won't **breathe a word of** this:
I hope you won't disclose this.
मुझे आशा है आप यह बात हमारे बीच ही रखेंगे।
- If the case is not solved, your name will **be covered in mud**:
If the case is not solved your reputation will be badly affected.
यदि आपका केस नहीं सुलझा तो आपकी साख समाप्त हो जाएगी।
- Don't **make a big deal out of it**:
Don't get upset about a minor thing.
छोटी-सी बात के लिए दुखी मत हों।

- Don't ask me to **fight your war**:
  Don't expect me to handle your problems.
  तुम अपनी समस्या को सुलझाने हेतु मुझसे आशा मत रखना।
- Do not use me as **a front** to do your dirty work:
  Don't take undue advantage of me.
  अनुचित कार्यों के लिए मेरा सहयोग लेने का प्रयास मत करना।
- **If I do this I will get nailed badly by the boss**:
  The boss will deal sternly with me if I do this.
  अगर मैंने ऐसा किया तो बॉस मेरी बखिया उधेड़ देगा।
- **Don't give me this crap**:
  Don't tell me all this rubbish.
  मुझसे फालतू बातें मत किया करो।
- Watch out or you will be in **dire straits**:
  If you are not careful you will be in a very serious trouble.
  यदि आप सावधानी से काम नहीं करेंगे तो बहुत बड़ी मुश्किल में फँस जाएँगे।
- No **buck passing**, please!
  Own up and take responsibility.
  अपने कार्य को दूसरे पर मत थोपो।
- **Don't hedge the issue**:
  Face the issue like a man.
  समस्या का सामना बहादुरी से करो।
- **Don't beat a dead horse**:
  Don't waste time with a person who can't do anything.
  ऐसे व्यक्ति के साथ समय बर्बाद मत करो जो कुछ भी करने में सक्षम न हो।
- **Don't leap on the back of a shaky horse**:
  Don't expect support from a weak person.
  कमज़ोर व्यक्ति से कभी सहायता की आशा मत करो।
- **Please don't shut me out**:
  Please include me in the plans.
  कृपया योजना में मुझे भी सम्मिलित कीजिए।

- You must **put your shoulder to the wheel**:
You must work very hard.
आपको कठोर परिश्रम करना चाहिए।

- **It is none of your business**:
Don't interfere in my affairs.
आप मेरे काम में दख़ल मत दीजिए।

- **My patience is at an end**:
I am losing patience.
मेरे सब्र का बाँध टूट रहा है।

- **You must learn to say please**:
You should be more polite.
आपको सभ्य और शिष्ट होना चाहिए।

- **It is too soon to give up the game**:
Don't lose hope but continue your efforts.
निराश न हों, अपना प्रयास जारी रखें।

- **You seem to be in a state of pique**:
You look irritated.
आप क्रुद्ध लग रहे हो।

- **What made you say yes?**
How did you agree to this?
क्या आप इससे सहमत हैं?

- **Button your lip**, only then will we proceed:
Shut up so that we can move ahead.
अगर चुप नहीं हुए तो काम यहीं रोक देंगे।

- We should **double-check**:
We must reconfirm this.
हमें यह दुबारा सुनिश्चित करना चाहिए।

- We will have to **cut corners**:
We will have to control expenses.
हमें खर्चे कम करने होंगे।

- **Don't act like the Gestapo**:
Don't spy on me.
मेरी जासूसी मत करो।

- **What hope is there?**
  Everything is lost.
  अब कोई उम्मीद नहीं है।
- Don't be **snappy**:
  Don't get angry/irritated.
  गुस्सा न करें।
- You have to **come to terms** with it:
  You have to accept the reality.
  आपको परिस्थितियों से समझौता करना होगा।
- **You should have dropped a hint:**
  You should have given me some clue.
  आपको मुझे कोई संकेत देना चाहिए था।
- **Where does that get you?**
  How does it benefit you?
  आपके लिए यह कितना लाभदायक है?/आप इसका लाभ कैसे उठा सकते हैं?
- **Don't ask me to be rational in this situation:**
  How can I tolerate this nonsense?
  मुझसे इस हाल में उदारता की उम्मीद न करें।
- You must get to the **heart of** the matter:
  You must find out the real truth.
  आपको इस मामले की तह में उतरकर सच्चाई का पता लगाना होगा।
- **What kind of stakes are we playing for?**
  What are the benefits and risks of this venture?
  इस काम के क्या-क्या फायदे और नुकसान हैं?
- **Are you itching for a thrashing?**
  Are you looking for trouble?
  क्या आपको मार खानी है?/क्या आपका सिर खुजला रहा है?
- **You have done more than your share to prevent it:**
  You couldn't have done more than this.
  इस परेशानी को सँभालने में आपने अपनी क्षमता से अधिक प्रयास कर लिया है।

- **Mind your blood pressure:**
  Take care that your blood pressure does not rise.
  अपने क्रोध पर नियंत्रण रखें वर्ना रक्तचाप बढ़ जाएगा।
- **How come you got mixed up with that rogue?**
  How come you are involved with that crook?
  आप उस धूर्त के साथ कैसे फँस गए?
- **We will have to rush or someone will beat us to it:**
  Hurry up or someone else will get the benefit.
  जल्दी करें, कहीं कोई और फ़ायदा न उठा ले जाए।
- **We will first test the waters:**
  We will first judge the situation.
  हम पहले परिस्थिति को समझेंगे।
- **Be wary of him:**
  Be careful of him.
  उससे सावधान रहें।
- **Any disaster now will be on your head:**
  You will be held responsible for any future problem.
  भविष्य में किसी प्रकार की समस्या के लिए आप जिम्मेदार होंगे।
- **Your head seems to be out there in the stars when there is enough trouble here:**
  It seems your mind is somewhere else, unconcerned about this problem.
  ऐसा लगता है आपका दिमाग इस समस्या को छोड़कर कहीं और है।
- **You are not going to make decisions that are mine:**
  Don't interfere in my work.
  मेरे काम में दखलंदाजी न करें।
- Prevent him from going **down under**:
  Help him so that he does not get into serious trouble and collapse.
  उसे परेशानियों के महासागर में डूबने से बचाओ।
- It's time you **cut him loose**:
  It's time to give him freedom to act.
  अब वक्त आ गया है जब आप उसे आज़ादी से काम करने दें।

- **Don't pursue bottomed-out hopes:**
  Don't waste time on useless ventures.
  अनावश्यक कार्यों में समय बर्बाद मत करो।
- He is **a diamond in the rough**:
  He has hidden talent / potential but is outwardly rude and uncultured.
  उसके भीतर अपार क्षमता छिपी है। / वह गुदड़ी का लाल है।
- **The queen can't hold a candle to you:**
  You are much better than the queen.
  आप रानी से बहुत बेहतर हैं।
- **Just keep a normal friendship going:**
  Don't break up the relationship completely but remain friends.
  पूर्णरूप से संबंध मत तोड़ो कम-से-कम दोस्ती का रिश्ता तो रहने दो।
- **You have tremendous responsibility up the road:**
  You will have great responsibilities in the future.
  भविष्य में आपको बहुत-सी जिम्मेदारियाँ उठानी हैं।
- **Try to unfold your mind:**
  Think clearly and forget about the past.
  दिमाग से पुरानी बातें हटाकर सोचना शुरू करो।
- I need **one more crack** at it:
  I must try once again.
  मुझे एक बार और प्रयास करना चाहिए।
- **Latch on** to him at the first opportunity:
  He is an important man so keep in touch with him whenever you have the chance.
  वह एक महत्त्वपूर्ण व्यक्ति है, उसके सम्पर्क में रहें।
- Do **have a word** with your dad before you take a decision:
  Discuss it with your dad before deciding.
  निर्णय लेने से पहले अपने पिता से अवश्य सलाह ले लें।
- **Don't treat them as if they are cattle:**
  Give them some respect.
  उनके साथ जानवरों जैसा व्यवहार मत करो।

- **Keep out of his way for a few days:**
  Avoid him for a few days.
  उससे कुछ दिन दूर रहो।
- **Don't buckle under:**
  Be strong and don't give in.
  परिस्थितियों के दबाव में आकर हार मत मानो।
- Beware! Or you **will be led** up the garden path:
  Be very careful or you will end up being cheated by false promises.
  सावधान रहें वरना आपके साथ धोखा हो सकता है।
- I am **cheesed off** with you:
  I am put off by you.
  मुझे आप पर गुस्सा आ रहा है।
- **Don't mess around with me:**
  Don't interfere with me or you will be sorry.
  मुझसे न उलझें वरना पछताना पड़ेगा।
- **You simply mind the store:**
  You just do the routine work.
  आप दैनिक कार्य में ध्यान दें।
- Stop this **monkey business:**
  Stop these silly pranks.
  ये बेवकूफ़ी भरे खेल बन्द करो।
- **Stop nit-picking:**
  Stop finding faults.
  छोटी-मोटी गलतियाँ निकालना बन्द करो।
- You will be **out of line** if you say 'No':
  It will be improper on your part to disagree.
  आपका मना करना उचित नहीं होगा।
- **Don't play games with me:**
  Be honest with me.
  मेरे साथ चालाकी मत कीजिये।
- **Play it cool:**
  Relax.
  आराम से करो। / इसमें परेशान होने की ज़रूरत नहीं।

- Please **pull up your socks:**
  Be more careful and improve your performance.
  सावधान होकर बेहतर करने का प्रयास करें।
- **Rap his knuckles:**
  Scold/beat him.
  उसे डाँट लगाओ।
- **Stop badmouthing her:**
  Stop spreading negative stories about her.
  उसके बारे में नकारात्मक बात फैलाना बंद करो।
- **Grin and bear it:**
  Accept and live with the situation.
  परिस्थितियों से समझौता कर लो।
- I suggest you **get it off your chest:**
  I suggest you open out and share your grief.
  मेरी सलाह है कि दिल खोल के हमें सब कुछ बता दो।
- **Take the bull by the horns:**
  Face the issue and fight it out.
  समस्याओं का सामना करें और उनसे लड़ें।
- **Don't get miffed with me:**
  Don't be angry/upset with me.
  मुझ पर क्रोधित न हों।
- I suggest you **patch up** with him:
  Forget the past and revive the friendship.
  पुरानी बात को भूलकर दोस्ती बनाए रखो।
- **Rise and shine!**
  Get up and act.
  उठो और काम करो।
- You must be **on your toes**:
  You must be active and alert.
  आपको हमेशा सतर्क और सचेत रहना चाहिए।
- If you don't know the answer, **duck it**:
  Avoid answering the question if you don't know it.
  अगर आपको इसका जवाब मालूम नहीं तो चुप रहो।

- **Let's get cracking:**
  Let's begin work.
  चलो काम शुरू करें।
- Go and meet them **eyeball to eyeball**:
  Be brave and fight it out.
  साहसी बनो और सामना करो।
- **Keep tabs on him:**
  Keep watch on him.
  उस पर नज़र बनाए रखें।
- **Slip him a buck and get your job done:**
  Bribe him to get your work done.
  उसे घूस देकर आप अपना काम करवा सकते हैं।
- **Keep your cool:**
  Do not get angry.
  शांत रहो।
- You must **get your act together** and do this job properly:
  Improve your performance to get this work done properly.
  अपना काम अधिक बेहतर करने की कोशिश करो ताकि ये काम पूरा कर सको।
- It is high time you **wrap up** the whole game:
  It's time you finish the game.
  यह समय खेल समाप्त करने का है। / खेल समाप्त करने का समय आ गया है।
- Give a **pat on his back**:
  Praise him for his good performance.
  उसके अच्छे काम के लिए उसकी प्रशंसा करो।
- **Put the arm-lock on him:**
  Force him to do it.
  उसे ऐसा करने के लिए बाध्य करो।
- Don't **throw in the towel**:
  Don't give up or surrender.
  हार मत मानो।

- **Don't dabble around here:**
  Don't mess or fool around here.
  यहाँ बेवकूफियों में वक्त जाया न करो।
- It will help us to **look beneath the surface**:
  It will help us to study things in more detail.
  इससे चीजें हमें और भी गहराई से समझ में आएँगी।
- A **closer look** will reveal a **hidden pattern**:
  If you study things in detail you will uncover the real facts.
  यदि आप विस्तार से अध्ययन करेंगे तो आपको वास्तविक तथ्यों की जानकारी हो जाएगी।
- **You have to fit in the frame of politics**:
  You will have to learn how to adjust in politics.
  आपको राजनीति में तालमेल बैठाना सीखना होगा।
- You must **tear away your blinkers**, only then will you see the truth:
  Give up your bias and have an open mind and only after this will you realise the truth.
  अपने पूर्वाग्रहों से मुक्त हो जाओ तभी तुम्हें सच्चाई का पता चलेगा।
- You have to **start from scratch:**
  You must start from the very beginning.
  आपको प्रारम्भ से शुरुआत करनी होगी।
- Don't get **tied up** with old ideas:
  Forget the old way of thinking and adopt new ideas.
  पुराने तरीके भूलकर नए ढँग से काम करो।
- **You can't impose your will on children:**
  Children might think differently and you should accept it.
  आप अपनी बात बच्चों पर नहीं थोप सकते।
- It would not be fair to **put all the blame on him**:
  It will be unjustified to blame him for everything.
  उस पर सारा दोष मढ़ देना ठीक नहीं होगा।
- It will **stir up** new ideas:
  It will help new ideas come up.
  इससे नए विचार/उपाय मिलेंगे।

- **Let's carry the argument a little further:**
  Let's take the point a step ahead.
  चलो बहस को थोड़ा आगे बढ़ाते हैं।
- **I am prepared to meet you halfway:**
  I am willing to make concessions for you.
  मैं आपकी आधी माँगें मान लेता हूँ।
- **You are not worth your salt if you don't keep your word:**
  You are worthless if you cannot keep your promise.
  यदि आप अपने वादे पर कायम नहीं रह पाते तो आप किसी काम के नहीं हैं।
- **This is awfully out of date:**
  It is not relevant and is now out of fashion.
  ये पूरी तरह प्रचलन से बाहर हो गया है।
- It **speaks volumes** for his hard work:
  The results reveal that he has worked very hard.
  इससे साफ पता चलता है कि उन्होंने कितनी मेहनत की है।
- **I think it serves you right:**
  I think you deserve what you got.
  मुझे लगता है तुम्हारे लिए यही सही है। / मेरे ख़याल से तुम्हारी यही सज़ा है।
- **You will come to grief if you invest in the share market:**
  You will suffer losses if you put your money in shares.
  अगर आप शेयर बाज़ार में पैसा लगाएँगे तो घाटे में रहेंगे।
- Don't **pin your hopes** on her, she is unreliable:
  Don't depend on her since she is not reliable.
  उससे उम्मीद मत करो, उसका भरोसा नहीं है।
- If you put **two and two together** you will see a **clear picture**:
  Analyse it in more detail and you will find the truth.
  विस्तार से विश्लेषण करेंगे तो सच्चाई नज़र आ जाएगी।
- **It's all there, but you must have the vision to see it:**
  All the details are available, but you must be more perceptive to understand this.
  यहाँ सब कुछ है, आप ज़रा ध्यान से देखिए।

- All that was needed was to **push the ball into the goal**:
  it was so simple, yet he couldn't do it.
  सीधा-सा काम था, वह भी उससे नहीं हो सका।
- **It's a far cry:**
  It's a very distant/difficult goal.
  इसमें काफ़ी वक़्त लग जाएगा। / यह लक्ष्य पाना बहुत कठिन है।
- You should take her **under your wings** for proper grooming:
  You will have to protect and guide her personally to teach her the right things.
  उसे अपनी निगरानी में लेकर उसका मार्गदर्शन करना होगा तभी वह सही बातें सीख पाएगी।
- It's high time you **lay bare** the rules:
  The time has come for you to let the rules be known to all.
  वक्त आ गया है कि आप सबको नियम-कायदे बता दें।
- You can do so **at your own peril**:
  You can do it at your own risk.
  आप इस कार्य को जिम्मेदारी से निभाएँ। / इस कार्य के लिए आपको जोखि़म उठाना पड़ सकता है।
- Don't get **carried away**:
  Don't be overenthusiastic.
  बहको मत।
- **This will pave your way for success in life:**
  This will help you succeed in life.
  ये आपकी ज़िन्दगी में सफलता के नए अवसर पैदा करेगा। / यह आपको जीवन में सफलता दिलाएगा।
- **Various situations you encounter in war will make you a tough man:**
  Different situations in war will make you stronger.
  युद्ध में अलग आलग परिस्थितियों का सामना करने से आप मजबूत हो जाएँगे।
- You have to **arouse the interests** of the audience:
  You have to generate interest amongst the audience.
  आपको श्रोताओं में दिलचस्पी जगानी होगी।

- **There is virtue in speaking the truth:**
  Speaking the truth has many advantages.
  सच बोलने के बहुत लाभ हैं।
- **More ardent your practice, the more the reward:**
  More hard work will give you better results.
  जितनी मेहनत करोगे उतना फ़ायदा होगा।/परिश्रम का फल मीठा होता है।
- **It's a skill that you will have to master:**
  You will have to learn this art.
  आपको यह कला सीखनी चाहिए।
- He doesn't have time to **wade through** your long letter:
  Write a short letter since he doesn't have the time to read such a long one.
  उसे छोटा पत्र लिखना क्योंकि बड़े पत्र पढ़ने का उसके पास समय नहीं है।
- **Do you want to get him on your side or make him an enemy?**
  Do you want to make a friend or an enemy out of him?
  आप उसे दोस्त बनाना चाहते हैं या दुश्मन?
- **Cut down** your expenditure:
  Reduce your expenses.
  अपने खर्चों में कटौती करें।
- **He may be angling for your post, so be careful:**
  He may be trying for your post so be on your guard.
  वह शायद आपका पद पाने की कोशिश में है, उससे सावधान रहना।
- You might have to **eat your words**, so think before you speak:
  You may be proved wrong so think before you say anything.
  हो सकता है कि आप गलत साबित हो जाएँ, इसलिए बोलने से पहले सोचना जरूरी है।
- You have to learn how to **choose your words** before speaking:
  You must be very careful about what you say.
  बात करते समय आपको इस बात का ध्यान रखना होगा कि आप क्या बोलने जा रहे हैं।

- You must **recognise the malady before it becomes chronic**:
  You must act on this problem before it becomes a permanent or long-standing one.
  आपको समस्या का समाधान शुरू में ही कर लेना चाहिए इससे पहले कि वह ला-इलाज बीमारी बन जाए।
- You have to **assert your individuality**:
  You must learn to say or do what you think is right.
  आपको अपनी बात रखनी आनी चाहिए।
- **Don't sink into self-pity**:
  Don't have self-destructive thoughts and sentiments.
  अपने ऊपर दया करके दुःखी मत हों।
- **Don't bottle up your grief**:
  Don't keep things to yourself, but share your grief to lighten it.
  अपनी तकलीफ़ सबको बताओ तो दुःख कम हो जाएगा।
- **You have to bail her out of this situation:**
  You have to help her overcome this situation.
  आपको उसे इस समस्या से निजात दिलानी होगी।
- **Don't succumb to desperate gambits:**
  Don't take risky or hasty decisions but keep your cool.
  जल्दबाज़ी का शिकार मत बनो। / सोच-समझकर फ़ैसला लो।
- **If you are in the mood for a scrap, go ahead:**
  If you are looking for a fight, you are welcome to do so.
  अगर आपका लड़ाई का मन है तो ठीक है, लड़िए।
- **Don't besmirch her reputation:**
  Don't spoil or sully her reputation.
  उसकी प्रतिष्ठा को नुकसान मत पहुँचाओ।
- **You must be snappy as I have little time:**
  Please get to the point quickly since I am in a hurry.
  जल्दी कहिये, मेरे पास वक्त नहीं है।
- **Do keep in touch with me:**
  Continue writing to me or stay in contact.
  मुझसे मिलना-जुलना बनाए रखें। / मेरे साथ जुड़े रहें।

- All of you **put your heads together** and work out the problem:
  All of you work together to solve this problem.
  आप सब मिलकर इस समस्या का समाधान कर सकते हैं। / एकता में बल होता है।
- **Don't use too much slang:**
  Don't use local or impolite language too often.
  आप ज्यादा सड़कछाप / गँवारू भाषा में बात न करें।
- Please **get down to the basics:**
  Please work on the core principles.
  कृपया मूल तत्वों का ध्यान रखें।
- **Go for the jugular:**
  Go in for the kill by attacking a delicate spot.
  दुश्मन की कमज़ोरी समझकर उस पर हमला करो।
- Gentlemen, please **rise to the occasion**:
  Gentlemen, please act and do what is required under the circumstances by raising the level of your work.
  सज्जनो, समय की आवश्यकता के अनुसार कार्य करें।
- **Don't answer back or you will suffer:**
  Don't reply rudely or you will face the consequences.
  जवाब मत दो, नहीं तो पछताना पड़ेगा।
- I suggest you **cut down** on drinks:
  I suggest you reduce your alcohol consumption.
  मेरी सलाह है कि आप पीना कम कर दें।
- You shouldn't have **raked up** the issue in front of him:
  You shouldn't have asked this question in his presence.
  आपको उसके सामने ये बात नहीं उठानी चाहिए थी।
- **It will not be prudent on my part:**
  It will be incorrect on my part.
  मेरे लिए ऐसा करना उचित नहीं होगा।
- **The battle will be protracted:**
  The battle will continue for a long time.
  जंग लम्बी चलेगी।

- **Don't indulge in procrastination:**
  Don't keep postponing or delaying things.
  काम को आगे मत बढ़ाया करो।/काम को टाला मत करो।
- **Keep the lid on and it will show results:**
  Keep the pressure on and there will be results.
  दबाव बनाए रखो फिर देखो काम हो जाएगा।
- **Stop these silly pranks:**
  Stop being naughty.
  ये बेवक़ूफ़ी बंद करो।
- I suggest you **bury the hatchet with** him:
  I suggest you sort out your differences with him.
  मेरा खयाल है कि तुम उसके साथ समझौता कर लो।
- Put it **on hold** for a few days:
  Don't start work on it for a few days.
  कुछ दिन इसको मत करो।/कुछ दिन यह कार्य रोक लो।
- Don't **bite off** more than you can chew:
  Take only those responsibilities that you can handle.
  वही जिम्मेदारी लें, जिसे आप सँभाल सकें।
- **Don't be overawed by his personality:**
  Don't be afraid of his reputation.
  उसके व्यक्तित्व के दबाव में मत आओ।
- **You will be ostracised if you don't improve:**
  People will avoid you if you don't mend your ways.
  यदि आप नहीं सुधरे तो आप अलग-थलग पड़ जाएँगे।
- Although it's your first **big break**, don't be nervous:
  Even though this is your first big chance, relax.
  यद्यपि यह तुम्हारा पहला बड़ा काम है, घबराना मत।
- Don't keep your tongue **hanging out** always:
  Don't be so greedy.
  ज्यादा लालच मत करो।
- **Mull over** it for the next few days and come back to me:
  Study it in greater detail and then give me your feedback after a few days.
  अगले कुछ दिन इसका अध्ययन करो और फिर मुझे बताओ।

- **Tone up** your voice:
  Improve and modulate your voice.
  अपनी आवाज़ बेहतर करो।
- Please stop **horsing around**:
  Please stop fooling and come to the point.
  फ़ालतू बातें करना बंद करो।
- **Try to wangle out of this situation:**
  Try to come out of this situation by some way or the other.
  इस हालत से बाहर निकलने की कोशिश करो।
- **Don't allow it to linger on:**
  Finish it fast; don't delay it further.
  इसको अब ज्यादा मत लटकाओ, जल्दी से ख़त्म करो।
- Don't **rub him the wrong way**, as he is a useful fellow:
  Don't make an enemy out of him because he can be useful.
  उसको दुश्मन मत बनाओ, वो काम आ सकता है।
- Please keep your **nose out** of it:
  Please stay out of this issue.
  आप इसमें दख़लंदाज़ी न करें।
- **I suggest you send out a feeler to him:**
  I suggest you send him a tentative proposal to find out his opinion.
  मेरी राय है कि आप उसे प्रस्ताव भेजकर उसका विचार लें।
- **Don't try to piggyback on me:**
  Don't try to take advantage of me.
  मेरा फ़ायदा उठाने की कोशिश मत करो।
- Don't **pussyfoot**:
  Don't waste time or fool around.
  यहाँ अपना समय नष्ट न करें।
- **It was imprudent of him to say this:**
  It was unwise of him to say this.
  यह कहना उसके लिए समझदारी वाली बात नहीं थी।
- **Don't sit on your butt but do something:**
  Don't sit doing nothing but be active.
  खाली मत बैठो, कुछ काम करो।

- **Don't get under my skin or you will repent:**
  Don't annoy me or you will feel sorry for doing so.
  मुझे गुस्सा मत दिलाओ वरना पछताना पड़ेगा।
- Don't be **so impertinent** with me:
  Don't be so cheeky and rude with me.
  मेरे साथ चालाकी मत करो।
- **Get into the groove** fast:
  Get to know the system and put in your best quickly.
  हालत को समझकर उसके हिसाब से काम करना शुरू कर दो।
- **Down the road** you will remember my advice:
  You will remember my words later.
  आगे चलकर आपको मेरी सलाह याद आएगी।
- **What's all the fuss about?**
  Why make such an issue out of this?
  इतनी-सी बात का बतंगड़ क्यों बनाया जा रहा है?
- Don't get **into a brawl** with him:
  Don't get into a physical fight with him.
  उसके साथ मारपीट मत करना।
- You must get into the **nitty-gritty** of things:
  You must investigate the intricate details about things.
  आपको सारी बातें गहराई से समझनी होंगी।
- I suggest you **don't stick your neck out**:
  I suggest you don't get involved or take a risk.
  मैं तो यही सलाह दूँगा कि आप ये खतरा न उठाएँ।
- **Let's have a brainstorming session:**
  Let's discuss the issue in a group to come up with different solutions.
  आइए, इस पर चर्चा करें।
- Put **a damper** on him:
  Discourage him.
  उसे हतोत्साहित करो।
- Don't try to **run him down**:
  Don't criticise or find fault with him.
  दूसरों की निन्दा मत करो और उनमें गलती मत ढूँढ़ो।

- Don't **rush me** into any decisions:
Don't ask me to decide in a hurry.
मुझे जल्दी फ़ैसला करने को मजबूर मत करो।
- You can't **turn your back** on us:
You have to support us and must not let us down.
आपको हमारी मदद करनी होगी।
- He shouldn't break this **cardinal rule**:
He shouldn't break the basic principle.
उसे यह मूल सिद्धान्त नहीं तोड़ना चाहिए।
- **Your efforts will not be in vain:**
Your efforts will not be wasted.
आपकी मेहनत बेकार नहीं जाएगी।
- **You have to take the hard road to satisfy your desire:**
You will have to work hard to achieve your goals.
आपको अपने लक्ष्य की प्राप्ति के लिए परिश्रम करना पड़ेगा।
- **With that kind of drinking I wonder if you have any liver left:**
You have damaged your liver with excessive drinking.
अत्यधिक शराब पीने से आपका जिगर ख़राब हो जाएगा।
- **Don't be lulled by his smooth talk:**
Don't be taken off guard and fooled by his sweet talk.
उसकी मीठी बातों में मत फँस जाना।
- We have to **map out** some sort of policy:
We have to work out some specific policy.
हमें इस दिशा में कोई नीति निर्धारित करने की ज़रूरत है।
- **You had this coming because of your lifestyle:**
Your bad lifestyle ensured that you got into trouble sooner or later.
आपकी अनुचित जीवनशैली के कारण आपको ये तकलीफ़ आनी ही थी।
- **Mark my words**, he will come back:
Make no mistake about it, he will realise his mistake and return.
मेरी बात याद रखना, वह वापस आएगा।
- **Without your support it will languish:**
It will fail (or remain where it is) without your support.
आपकी मदद के बिना यह संभव नहीं होगा।

- **This is one way to get out of the muck:**
  This is one way to overcome the problem.
  इस परेशानी से बचने का यही एकमात्र रास्ता है।
- **Take it with a pinch of salt:**
  Don't consider all of it to be true.
  ये सारी बातें सही नहीं हैं।
- **You have to rough it out:**
  You will have to overcome all the hurdles and hardships.
  आपको इन परेशानियों से जीतना होगा।
- Keep him at **arm's length**:
  Don't let him come close to you.
  उसको अपने नज़दीक मत आने देना।
- **He is taking things easy and it will have repercussions:**
  He is not working seriously and will suffer the negative consequences.
  गंभीरता से कार्य न करने के कारण उसको इसका परिणाम भुगतना पड़ेगा।
- Take **a leaf out of his book** and improve:
  Learn from his example and improve.
  उससे सबक लेकर अपने आपको बेहतर बनाओ।
- **You have to work against time:**
  You are short of time and will have to make up for it.
  आपको कम समय में कार्य पूरा करना है।
- **Please take stock of the situation:**
  Please understand the situation fully.
  कृपया स्थिति को पूर्णरूप से समझ लीजिए।
- Try to **read between the lines**:
  Try to perceive things that are hidden and not stated clearly.
  छिपी हुई बातों को समझने का प्रयास करो।
- You have to **nip this evil in the bud**:
  You have to stop this problem in the very beginning, before it becomes too big to handle.
  इससे पहले कि परेशानी और बढ़े, इसे बढ़ने से रोकना होगा।

- Don't **give ear** to him, as he is not a reliable person:
  Don't listen to him since he is unreliable.
  उसकी बात मत सुनो, वह भरोसे के लायक नहीं है।
- **Don't show your hand** as yet, let them keep guessing:
  Don't disclose your plans so that they are unsure about your moves.
  अपनी योजना मत बताओ, उन्हें तुम्हारे अगले कदम के बारे में अनुमान लगाने दो।
- **The light touch works well rather than being angry:**
  Be cool and you will achieve more than by shouting and getting angry.
  अगर आप आराम से काम करेंगे तो सफलता मिलेगी, बजाय इसके कि आप क्रुद्ध हों।
- **This venture is not financially viable:**
  Commercially it's not possible.
  यह काम आर्थिक तौर पर फ़ायदेमंद नहीं है।
- **Pay him back in his own coin:**
  Use his own tactics to teach him a lesson.
  उसको सबक सिखाने के लिए उसके साथ उसके जैसे ही हथकंडे अपनाओ।
- Your performance is not **up to the mark**:
  Your performance is not good enough.
  आपका प्रदर्शन बहुत अच्छा नहीं है।
- **It's at your discretion:**
  The decision is totally yours.
  निर्णय पूरी तरह से आपको ही लेना है।
- In the **long run** it will help:
  It will be good for you over the years.
  आगे चलकर इसका फायदा मिलेगा।
- **More painstaking the effort, the more rewarding the result:**
  Hard and sincere work will ensure you better results.
  अथक परिश्रम से ही सफलता संभव है।
- **You can't leave me in the lurch:**
  You must not abandon me in this trouble.
  आप मुझे इस परेशानी में छोड़कर नहीं जा सकते।

- **It stands to reason to listen to him:**
  You must listen to him since it makes sense.
  आपको उसकी बात सुननी चाहिए क्योंकि यही उचित है।
- **Send the instructions in black and white:**
  Send these instructions in writing.
  निर्देशों को लिखकर भेजो।
- This argument does not **hold water**:
  This argument has no basis/logic.
  यह तर्क आधारहीन है।
- It's only a **pale hint of** things to come:
  This is just a minor clue about what will happen.
  ये घटित होने वाली घटनाओं का बस एक छोटा-सा संकेत है।
- **This belief will harden into dogma:**
  What you believe will turn into a principle that cannot be questioned.
  आपकी यह धारणा निःसंदेह हठधर्मिता बन सकती है।
- **You should cast your eyes onto the future:**
  Look ahead and don't turn back
  आपको भविष्य पर दृष्टि रखनी चाहिए।
- **This will help you extend your reach immensely:**
  This will allow you to increase your influence greatly.
  इससे आपके प्रभावक्षेत्र का बहुत विस्तार होगा।
- **This study is meaningless unless it helps people:**
  This study should be used for the benefit of people or it will not make any sense.
  जिस पढ़ाई से दूसरों का भला न हो, वह निरर्थक है।
- **No matter how seemingly unimportant he is, he will be needed:**
  He will still be useful to us although he does not seem very worthwhile.
  चाहे वह कितना ही बेकार क्यों न हो, उसकी ज़रूरत पड़ेगी।
- Does it **make sense**?
  It does not seem worth it.
  क्या यह बात समझ आती है?

- **You have to acclimatise yourself to the life of a married man:**
  You have to adjust to life as a married man.
  आपको एक शादीशुदा आदमी की तरह अपने को ढालना पड़ेगा।
- The **leading edge of technology** will decide the future:
  The best technology will decide what the future looks like.
  अच्छी तकनीक भविष्य की रूपरेखा तय करेगी।
- You are on **the right track**:
  You are doing a fine job.
  आप सही कह रहे हैं।
- **It should remain between you and me:**
  Keep it secret.
  इसे गोपनीय रखें।
- For the time being you **play ball with him**:
  For the moment, agree to his demands.
  कुछ समय के लिए उसकी बात मान लो।
- **You must stand up and be counted:**
  Make your views clear and take a stand.
  सबके सामने अपनी बात साफ़-साफ़ रखो।
- Don't worry but **give it your best shot**:
  Try your best without bothering about the results.
  परिणाम की चिन्ता किए बिना कठोर परिश्रम करें।
- **Relax, he is just a teenybopper:**
  Don't worry unduly about him since he is just a fashionable teenager.
  फिक्र मत करो, वह एक दिखावेबाज किशोर है।
- He **sticks like a leech**:
  He hangs on to anyone for personal gain.
  वह अपने फायदे के लिए किसी से भी चिपक जाता है।
- **Get your act together and** do it:
  Concentrate on the job at hand and get things done.
  अपने काम पर ध्यान दो और उसे पूरा करो।
- **Hang in there and you will get your dues:**
  Don't give up and you will get paid or rewarded.
  हार मत मानो, आपको अच्छा फल प्राप्त होगा।

- **Rattle his cage** and he will swing into action:
  Shake him up and he will act.
  उसको समझाओ, फिर देखो वह कितना अच्छा काम करता है।
- **Put the heat on him** to get the work done:
  Put pressure on him to complete the task.
  कार्य करने के लिए उस पर दबाव बनाये रखो।
- Take the **air out of his balloon**:
  Hurt his ego or discourage him.
  उसके अहम् को चोट पहुँचाओ।/उसको निरुत्साहित करो।
- **Take it or lump it:**
  You have no other choice but to accept it or leave it.
  इसे अपनाने या छोड़ने के अलावा आपके पास तीसरा रास्ता नहीं है।
- **Let off steam** and you will feel better:
  Express your feelings and you will feel unburdened.
  दिल की बात कहने से मन हलका होता है।
- **Lay off**!
  Stay out of it/don't bother me.
  दूर रहो।
- I suggest you **iron out the kinks**:
  You sort out the drawbacks or problems.
  समस्या की ख़ामियों को दूर करो।/समस्या का समाधान करो।
- Change into **high gear**:
  Raise your standards.
  अपना स्तर ऊँचा करो।
- Don't develop **cold feet** now:
  Don't be afraid when everything is ready.
  अब जब सब ठीक है, घबराओ मत।
- You will have to **go the extra mile**:
  You will have to put in the extra effort.
  आपको थोड़ी और मेहनत करनी होगी।
- **Just gatecrash**:
  Simply go uninvited.
  ऐसे ही बिन बुलाये चले जाओ।

- **Let's start from the top:**
  Let's begin with the seniors.
  चलिए बड़ों से/ऊपर से शुरू करते हैं।

- Give everybody **a little elbow room**:
  Give everybody some freedom.
  सबको कुछ आज़ादी दो।

- **Just elbow him out:**
  Get him out of the way through aggressive tactics.
  उसको जबरदस्ती रास्ते से हटा दो।

- You might have to **eat dirt**:
  You might lose and be humiliated.
  हो सकता है कि आपका अपमान हो जाए।

- **Don't be a doormat:**
  Don't allow others to take advantage of you and do as they please.
  लोगों को अपना फ़ायदा मत उठाने दो।

- Listen to the proposal and don't **knock it down** so early:
  Don't discard the proposal in the early stages without listening to it till the end.
  नकारने से पहले प्रस्ताव सुन लो।

- Don't think over it – **dish it out** to him:
  Don't hesitate to teach him a lesson.
  सोचो मत, उसको सबक सिखाओ।

- Don't act like a **dim bulb**:
  Don't act like a slow or foolish person.
  मूर्खों जैसी हरकतें मत करो।

- Don't become a **couch potato**:
  Don't spend all your time lying on the sofa, watching television.
  आरामतलब मत बनो।

- **Cool your heels:**
  Spend time waiting.
  थोड़ा इंतज़ार करो।

- You have to **come clean**:
  You have to make a confession or disclose the truth.
  अपनी गलती स्वीकार कीजिए।
- **Do chip in:**
  Please contribute.
  कृपया सहयोग कीजिए।
- **Please button your lips:**
  Please keep quiet.
  कृपया शांत रहें।
- **Buzz off**!
  Get lost!
  चले जाओ।
- Be careful, he **will bamboozle you**:
  He will confuse and trick you.
  सावधान रहना, वह आपको उलझा देगा।
- **Back off or** I will call the police:
  Leave me alone or I will call the police.
  वापस चले जाओ वरना मैं पुलिस को बुलाऊँगा।

2. Business/ Economics

- The experts point all the trends **leading to catastrophe**:
  The specialists give various reasons why it will fail disastrously.
  विशेषज्ञों ने नुकसान होने की सारी संभावनाएँ समझाईं।

- This is **the backdrop against which** you must study the paper:
  This is the background you must take into account while considering the paper or proposal.
  प्रस्ताव की सारी जानकारी इसमें है।

- The **cheating comes in various packages**:
  There are different ways to cheat.
  ठगने के कई तरीके हैं।

- The **crisis will come dressed as something else**:
  You won't recognise the crisis as a crisis when it appears.
  मुसीबत भेष बदलकर आएगी। / किस तरह की मुसीबत आएगी, आपको पता नहीं चल पाएगा।

- Huge slums **mushroomed** around Mumbai:
  Big hutments came up around Mumbai.
  मुम्बई में बहुत सारी झोंपड़पट्टियाँ बन गई हैं।

- A big project has been **set into motion**:
  A big project has begun.
  एक बड़ी परियोजना पर काम शुरू हो गया है।

- The **seesaw** of the share business **rocks on this fulcrum**:
  The share business revolves around this.
  शेयर का व्यवसाय इसी के चारों तरफ घूमता है। / शेयर मार्किट इसी के आधार पर चलता है।

- Although the **damage is done**, you have to get things **back into shape**:
  Although major damage has been done, you will have to put things back into order.
  यद्यपि नुकसान तो हो गया है पर अब आपको हालात ठीक करने हैं।

- The **fallout was dished out** to them also:
They were also made to face the negative impact.
नुकसान उन्हें भी उठाना पड़ा।

- He has **siphoned off** lots of money from the bank:
He has fraudulently withdrawn large amounts of money from the bank.
उसने बैंक से काफी पैसों का गबन किया।

- We need **no X-ray** to find out what actually happened:
It's clearly visible and requires no special instruments to reveal what occurred.
जो हुआ, वह साफ़ नजर आ रहा है।

- They live from **hand to mouth**:
They are barely able to meet all their monthly expenses.
वे मुश्किल से दो वक्त की रोटी जुटा पाते हैं।

- He **burnt his fingers** once and now he is out of it:
He suffered major losses once and is no longer involved in it.
एक बार उसने नुकसान उठा लिया है, अब वह ऐसा नहीं करेगा।

- I am quite **at sea** when it comes to shares:
I can hardly understand the share business.
शेयर की बात मुझे समझ में नहीं आती।

- She **made the most** of the opportunities:
She grabbed all the opportunities and succeeded.
उसने अधिकतर मौकों का फायदा उठाया और सफल हुई।

- It's **an irreversible** crisis and everything is lost:
It is not possible to repair the damage done, as things have been lost permanently.
इसमें अब कुछ भी नहीं किया जा सकता, सब कुछ ख़त्म हो गया है।

- This property **changed hands** recently:
This property was sold recently.
यह ज़मीन हाल ही में बिकी है।

- The **long and short** of it is that you are out of this project:
In short, you are not in this project any longer.
कुल मिलाकर बात ये है कि अब आप इस परियोजना से बाहर कर दिए गए हैं।

- My offer to you still **holds good**:
The offer that I made you is still valid.
मैंने आपको जो प्रस्ताव दिया है वह अभी भी काम का है।

- This will be **the framework** of our next project:
Our next project will be based on this blueprint.
हमारे अगले प्रोजेक्ट की यह रूपरेखा होगी।

- I am **done for**:
I am ruined.
मैं तो पूरी तरह से बर्बाद हो गया।

- The two brothers have **fallen out**:
The two brothers fought and are no longer torether.
दो भाईयों में मनमुटाव के कारण एक दरार पैदा हो गई।

- His bills have **run up** to a large amount:
He made major purchases and has big amounts to pay.
उसके खर्चों की देनदारी अब सीमा पार कर गई है।

- He has **run into large debts**:
He owes a lot of money.
उसका कर्ज़ा बहुत हो गया है।

- Sincerity is a major **rock of salvation** here:
Sincerity is the foundation of this place.
काम के प्रति निष्ठा यहाँ का नियम है।

- It's difficult to **make both ends meet**:
It's difficult to survive financially every month.
प्रत्येक माह वित्तीय रूप से जीवित रहना कठिन हो रहा है।

- I will get it by **hook or by crook**:
I will get it through any means, fair or unfair.
किसी भी तरह से मैं इसे पा के रहूँगा।

- His business has **fallen flat**:
His business is doing very badly.
उसका धंधा पूरी तरह चौपट हो गया है।

- **His stars are in the ascendant**:
He is having good luck and is doing well.
उसके सितारे उसके पक्ष में हैं।/उसका सितारा चमक रहा है।

- He very cleverly **turned the tables** on her:
  In a sudden move, he cleverly defeated her.
  उसने उसे एक झटके में हरा दिया।
- It is the **throbbing core of** our business:
  This is the central point in our business.
  यह हमारे धंधे का केन्द्रबिन्दु है।
- I would like to **settle the matter out of court**:
  I wish to have an out-of-court compromise.
  मैं चाहूंगा कि मामले को अदालत के बाहर ही सुलझा लिया जाए।
- He **plunged into the job with much fervour**:
  He started working extremely hard on the job from the very beginning.
  उसने बहुत मेहनत से काम शुरू कर दिया।
- This project will not **come into being** without a fight:
  You will have to work very hard and battle it out for this project.
  इस प्रोजेक्ट को पूरा करने के लिए आपको बहुत परेशानियों से जूझना होगा।
- He has developed an **aversion** to all kinds of **exorbitant labour**:
  He intensely dislikes making hefty payments on labour costs.
  वह कामगारों पर बहुत खर्चा करना पसंद नहीं करता।
- He will receive a **big booty** from his dad's properties:
  He will inherit lots of money from his father's properties.
  उसे अपने पिता की जायदाद से बहुत सारी दौलत मिली है।
- His **mediocrity** left him with debts and **alcoholic tantrums**:
  Not being a good worker he couldn't make money and took to throwing drunken fits of ill-temper.
  अच्छा काम न करने के कारण वह कर्जे और शराब का शिकार हो गया।
- Her **burdens were running ahead of her efficiency**:
  Her problems and burdens were too much for her capabilities.
  उस पर आई मुसीबतों और जिम्मेदारियों ने उसकी क्षमता को प्रभावित किया है।
- It was a **trick of the trade**:
  It was a strategy used regularly in the trade to boost output and profits.
  यह धंधे का एक गोपनीय फ़ायदेमंद तरीका है।

- He was **frantic to salvage** whatever he could:
  He desperately wanted to minimise the damage and recover whatever he could.
  जो भी बच सके वह बचाने के लिए आतुर था।
- The share market **nose-dived** in one session:
  The rates in the share market dropped drastically in one trading session.
  एक ही बार में शेयर मार्केट में गिरावट आ गई।
- He will sure make a **buck out of it**:
  He will make some money out of it.
  इससे वह पक्का कुछ पैसा कमा लेगा।
- **He has made a hash of the complete work**:
  He has spoiled the entire work.
  उसने सारा काम बिगाड़ दिया।
- He **embezzled a lot** from the bank where he was working:
  He siphoned money from the bank he was employed in.
  जिस बैंक में वह काम करता था उसने वहाँ काफ़ी हेराफेरी कर दी।
- Many **skeletons will tumble** out of the cupboard:
  Many scams will come to light.
  बहुत-से घोटाले सामने आएँगे।
- **He was empathetic towards her proposal**:
  He was favourably inclined towards her proposal.
  उसे उसका प्रस्ताव सहर्ष स्वीकार था।
- The boss gave the **go-ahead** to my project:
  The boss agreed to my project and gave it the green signal.
  बॉस ने मेरे प्रोजेक्ट को हरी झंडी दे दी। / बॉस ने मेरे प्रोजेक्ट को स्वीकार कर लिया।
- The price of land has been **jacked up**:
  The price of land has been raised deliberately.
  जमीन की कीमत बढ़ा दी गई है।
- **I got fleeced in Delhi:**
  I was cheated in Delhi.
  मैं दिल्ली में ठगा गया था।

- He worked **round the clock** for it:
  He worked very hard for it.
  इसके लिए उसने दिन-रात मेहनत की।

- **There are gremlins in our system:**
  There are some problems in our system.
  हमारे तंत्र में कुछ गड़बड़ियाँ हैं।

- I have paid **through the nose** for it:
  It was very expensive.
  मुझे इस कार्य की भारी कीमत चुकानी पड़ी।

- All my projects have **run into** the ground:
  All my project works have been stalled or have failed.
  मेरी सारी परियोजनाएँ असफल हो गई हैं।

- **He pilfered millions from the bank:**
  He stole millions from the bank.
  उसने बैंक से लाखों रुपये का गबन कर लिया।

- **It will have a profound effect on our sales:**
  It will have a major impact (usually negative) upon our sales.
  हमारे बिक्रय पर इसका बुरा प्रभाव पड़ेगा।

- The share market is in a **bull frenzy**:
  Share prices are booming with more buyers than sellers in the market.
  शेयर बाज़ार पूरी तरह से चढ़ाव पर है।

3. Comments and Observations

- She **half-jumped** out of her skin:
  She was startled and taken by surprise.
  वह बुरी तरह से हैरान रह गई।

- One sees things differently from **this end**:
  Things can be seen in a different way from the other side.
  यहाँ से तस्वीर का दूसरा रुख नज़र आता है।

- **He was good but for now he is dust:**
  He may have been big but he is no more a force to reckon with.
  उसमें बहुत क्षमताएँ थीं पर अब वह कहीं का नहीं रहा।

- It was a **moon trip** from the beginning and it never came down:
  I had a wonderful time all along.
  उस दौरान मुझे काफ़ी मज़ा आया।

- They are a **canny and clever lot**:
  They are very smart and shrewd people.
  वे बहुत चालाक लोग हैं।

- **He was in a funk**:
  He was in a state of panic and depression.
  वह बुरी तरह से डर गया था।

- You are **in it** only for money:
  You are only involved because of the money.
  आप केवल पैसों के लिए काम कर रहे हैं।

- The car **drew up** besides the steps:
  The car halted at the side of the steps.
  कार सीढ़ियों के पास रुक गई।

- He has **cracked up**:
  He is a completely broken man.
  वह पूरी तरह टूट चुका है।

- **He may not be all he seems:**
  He is a different man from what he appears to be.
  वह जैसा दिखता है, वैसा है नहीं।
- You are way **off line**:
  You are far away from the solution.
  आप समाधान से कोसों दूर हैं।
- **What an eventful day it was:**
  It was a good day for us.
  यह एक बहुत अच्छा दिन रहा।
- There are **few takers** for your product:
  Your product is difficult to sell.
  आपका उत्पाद बेचना मुश्किल है।
- **He is an improvement on his father:**
  He is better than his father.
  वह अपने पिता से कहीं बेहतर है।
- Don't be **penny wise and pound foolish**:
  In trying to save petty amounts do not end up losing large sums.
  थोड़ा बचाने के चक्कर में ज्यादा मत गँवा देना।
- We have given you **far too many** chances:
  No more chances for you.
  हमने आपको कई मौके दिए।
- **She is no fool either:**
  She may not be very intelligent but she is definitely not a fool.
  वह बहुत बुद्धिमान न भी हो, तो भी उसे कोई बेवक़ूफ़ नहीं बना सकता है।
- It's **worth its weight in gold**:
  It is very valuable.
  यह बहुत ही कीमती है।
- I don't see it **that way**:
  I don't look at the issue from this perspective.
  मैंने इस मसले पर उस तरह से नहीं सोचा।
- It **would be a lot better for you**:
  It will be in your interests.
  यह आपके लिए काफ़ी फ़ायदेमंद रहेगा।

- This **is arguable**:
  This issue is debatable.
  यह विवाद का विषय है।
- He did **no such thing**:
  He didn't do it.
  उसने यह सब नहीं किया।
- **What hope is there?**
  I don't think anything can be done now.
  मेरे ख्याल से अब कुछ नहीं हो सकता।
- I wouldn't trust him **out of my sight**:
  He is unreliable and should be kept on watch.
  उसका भरोसा नहीं किया जा सकता, उस पर नज़र रखनी चाहिए।
- **She had been lax at her job:**
  She was careless in her work.
  वह अपने कार्य के प्रति बहुत लापरवाह है।
- It is **so unnerving**:
  It's so scary.
  ये बहुत डरावना है।
- I really **cooked my goose** today:
  I got into serious trouble today.
  मैं आज बहुत मुश्किल हालत में फँस गया था।
- I **guess we could**:
  Perhaps we can do it.
  मुझे लगता है कि हम ये कर सकते हैं।
- **She was squirming:**
  She felt very uncomfortable.
  उसे बड़ी असहजता महसूस हो रही थी।
- He seemed **ill at ease**:
  He was not comfortable at all.
  वह बिलकुल भी सहज नहीं हो पा रहा था।
- **He is an iceberg:**
  He doesn't show any emotion.
  वह बिलकुल संवेदनाहीन है।

- **In the end it was a dampener:**
  It was an anti-climax.
  आखिर में आकर एकदम उलटा हो गया।
- He is a **pain in the neck**:
  He is a nuisance.
  वह बड़ी परेशानी पैदा करता है।
- **He loves his own voice:**
  He loves to talk non-stop.
  वह लगातार बातें करना पसंद करता है।
- **It suited him well to remain anonymous:**
  It was in his interests that people did not know his identity.
  अपनी पहचान छुपाए रखना उसके लिए फ़ायदेमंद था।
- He came up with **pure gold**:
  He came up with a money-spinning idea.
  वह बहुत ही कमाऊ तरकीब लेकर आया।
- **It was a fluke**:
  It was a chance occurrence.
  यह तुक्के से हो गया था।/संयोग से सफलता मिल गयी।
- Well, it seems a **long shot**:
  Well, it seems most unlikely.
  बिलकुल, ये तो हो ही नहीं सकता।
- **The results are nil:**
  The results are totally unsatisfactory.
  परिणाम कुछ भी नहीं निकला।/परिणाम पूर्णरूप से असंतोषजनक रहा।
- **He is a real whacko:**
  He is a crazy character.
  वह एक सनकी/पागल व्यक्ति है।
- **It all ended up in zilch**:
  Nothing came out of it.
  इससे कुछ भी हासिल नहीं हुआ।
- It was a **rocky road ahead**:
  The going ahead was very difficult.
  आगे बढ़ना बहुत मुश्किल था।

- He has **the hots** for that film star:
  That film star turns him on sexually.
  उस फिल्मी सितारे ने उसको यौन उत्तेजना से भर दिया।
- I am sure you will **pull it off**:
  I am sure you can do it.
  मुझे यकीन है, तुम ये कर लोगे।
- You have always lived on a **short fuse**:
  You have always been short-tempered.
  आपका हमेशा से ही गरम मिज़ाज हैं।
- You are an **absolute gem**!
  You are a great person.
  आप बहुत ही अच्छे आदमी हैं। / आप सचमुच हीरा हैं।
- **I think I look swell in this suit:**
  I feel I look great in this suit.
  मुझे लगता है यह सूट पहनकर मैं अच्छा लगता हूँ।
- **I can't gather what he sees in her:**
  I don't know why he likes her.
  मुझे नहीं समझ आता कि उसने उसमें ऐसा क्या देखा।
- It is simply **out of this world**:
  This is an excellent thing.
  यह एक अद्भुत वस्तु है।
- He is back **in the thick of things**:
  He is back in action.
  वह वापस अपनी लय में आ गया है।
- **I wonder if I have gone too far:**
  I hope I haven't crossed the limits.
  उम्मीद है कि मैंने अपनी सीमाओं का उल्लंघन नहीं किया होगा।
- **He has taken offence at it:**
  He did not like it and is angry.
  उसे ये बिलकुल अच्छा नहीं लगता।
- Things at business are a **little shaky** now:
  Business is not doing well.
  धंधा मंदा है।

- **I seemed to make things worse:**
  I cannot cope with the situation and only seem to have made it more bad.
  ऐसा लगा जैसे मैंने हालत और भी बिगाड़ दी।

- Don't go on a **guilt trip**:
  Don't feel guilty and hold yourself responsible.
  अपराधबोध अपने मन में मत लाओ।

- **Indians are so wrapped up in moral rigidity:**
  Indians place too much importance on moral values.
  भारतीय लोग नैतिकता पर बहुत विश्वास रखते हैं।

- **This information is worth a pound:**
  This information is very good.
  यह जानकारी बहुत काम की है।

- **You have chanced your luck once too often:**
  You have taken too many risks and are now paying the price.
  आपने अपनी तकदीर को कई बार आज़माकर कुछ ज्यादा ही खतरा उठाया है।

- The way things are **set up** now:
  The way things are at the moment.
  अभी जिस तरह की स्थिति है। / जैसे कि अभी हालात हैं।

- He is bent upon **hara-kiri**:
  He is bent upon self-destruction.
  वह आत्महत्या करने पर उतारू है।

- **The going since morning has been very sedate:**
  Things have been moving very slowly since morning.
  सुबह से ही काम कुछ धीरे चल रहा है।

- It's a **touch-and-go** situation:
  It's a situation in which the outcome desired is still possible but seems very unlikely.
  यह वह हालत है जहाँ उम्मीद तो है पर उसका भी कुछ ठिकाना नहीं।

- Pakistan has become **a rogue state**:
  Pakistan has become a nation that breaks international laws.
  पाकिस्तान एक धूर्त देश के रूप में कुख्यात हो चुका है।

- He has **thrown a wet blanket** on the celebrations:
  He has dampened or spoilt the celebrations.
  उसने सारा मज़ा किरकिरा कर दिया। / उसने उत्सव का सारा आनन्द भंग कर दिया।
- **He turned out to be a sagacious fellow:**
  He turned out to be a cool and discerning fellow.
  वह तो इसमें निष्णात निकला।
- **He has a sanctimonious attitude:**
  He puts on airs of moral superiority.
  वह पाखंडी प्रवृत्ति का है। / वह सदाचार का दिखावा करने वाला है।
- It's been a **hush-hush** affair from the beginning:
  It's been a secret affair from early on.
  ये शुरू से ही एक गुपचुप काम था।
- **The teacher reprimanded him:**
  His teacher scolded him.
  शिक्षक ने उसको फटकार लगाई।
- The enemy has **dug in its spurs**:
  The enemy has made preparations for a long battle.
  शत्रु ने एक लम्बे युद्ध की तैयारियाँ पूरी कर ली हैं।
- **He was rebuffed badly by the boss:**
  The boss took him to task strongly and turned down his idea.
  बॉस ने उसका विचार ठुकरा दिया।
- **He is still recuperating from his illness:**
  He is still recovering from the illness.
  वह अभी बीमारी से उबर रहा है।
- **The invaders ravaged the villages:**
  The invaders plundered the villages.
  आक्रमणकारियों ने गाँव लूट लिया।
- **It is simply drizzling**:
  It is only a light shower.
  ये बस जरा-सी रिमझिम है।

- My **entire house was ransacked**:
  My entire house was searched thoroughly, things thrown all around and the house looted.
  मेरा पूरा घर छान मारा गया।

- **The river had various degrees of rapids**:
  The river had various degrees of fast currents.
  नदी में कई प्रकार की तेज़ धाराएँ थीं।

- In a **queer twist of fate** he met with an accident:
  He met with an accident in a curious reversal of circumstances.
  बदले हुए हालात में वह दुर्घटना का शिकार भी हो गया।

- **He was stuck in the sustained fire of the enemy:**
  The heavy and non-stop enemy firing made it difficult for him to get out.
  दुश्मन की गोलियों की बौछार ने उसका रास्ता रोक दिया था।

- He **bled profusely**:
  He bled a lot.
  उसका बहुत खून बहा।

- Today we live in a **goldfish bowl**:
  Our life is not private any longer and people observe us at all times.
  आज के दौर में हमारा जीवन व्यक्तिगत नहीं रहा।

4. Instructions and Orders

- Will you **knock off your whiskers**?
  Will you shave your moustache?
  क्या आप अपनी मूँछें साफ़ करेंगे?

- **Please park yourself here:**
  Please sit-down here.
  कृपया यहाँ बैठिए।

- I **don't want any skulduggery**:
  I don't want any dirty tricks.
  मैं कोई घटिया चाल नहीं चाहता।

- Don't give the **sob story**, but just tell me your requirements:
  Don't tell me any story to elicit sympathy, but simply come to the point and tell me what you need.
  सहानुभूति अर्जित करने वाली बातें न करें, ये बताएँ कि आप क्या चाहते हैं।

- Throw it on **top of the heap**:
  Put it right on top of the other stuff.
  इसको दूसरी चीज़ों पर डाल दो।

- Give me a **rundown of events**:
  Give me a detailed account of the happenings.
  मुझे घटना की विस्तृत जानकारी दीजिये।

- **Will you recapitulate all that happened:**
  Please repeat all that has occurred.
  जो कुछ हुआ है, कृपया संक्षेप में कहिए।

- **I suggest you take a recess:**
  I suggest you take a break.
  मेरे ख्याल से तुम ज़रा आराम कर लो।

- **Don't get rattled by his rude behaviour:**
  Don't be disturbed by his bad behaviour.
  उसके दुर्व्यवहार से मत घबराइए।

- First **quench your thirst**:
  First drink some water.
  पहले अपनी प्यास बुझाइये।/पहले पानी पीजिये।
- **Put the squeeze on him**, only then will he work:
  Put some pressure on him if you want results.
  उसके ऊपर दबाव डालिए तभी वह काम करेगा।
- Have all the **pieces in place** before the boss arrives:
  Organise everything before the boss comes on the scene.
  बॉस के आने से पूर्व सब कुछ व्यवस्थित कर लो।
- **Stop and ponder over the issue:**
  Stop and think about it.
  रुको और इस पर विचार करो।
- Don't just think, but take **a shot** at it:
  Stop wasting time simply thinking, but take some action.
  सिर्फ सोचने से काम नहीं चलने वाला, कुछ करना पड़ेगा।
- You will have to **take the plunge**:
  You will have to take some action.
  आपको कुछ करना पड़ेगा।
- Don't push the **panic button as** yet:
  Don't be alarmed and overreact.
  अभी से मत घबराओ।
- Will you please do a **head count**?
  Will you please count every person here?
  कृपया सबकी गिनती कर लें।
- **Try to mollify him:**
  Try to pacify him.
  उसे शांत करने का प्रयास करें।
- Gentlemen, please **chill out**:
  Gentlemen, please relax and take it cool.
  सज्जनो, शांत हो जाइये।
- **Please stop your shenanigans:**
  Please stop your nonsense.
  कृपया अपनी बेवक़ूफ़ियाँ बन्द करें।

- Don't give such **lame excuses**:
  Do not make stupid excuses.
  ऐसे बेवक़ूफ़ी भरे बहाने मत बनाओ।
- Let's do the **boogie-woogie**:
  Let's dance.
  चलो नाचें।
- Don't take the **shine out** of his work:
  Don't discourage him and take the edge out of his work.
  उसके काम के लिए उसे हतोत्साहित मत करो।
- Don't **fritter away** your resources:
  Don't waste your resources.
  अपने संसाधनों को नष्ट मत करो।
- Be ready to **go on the mat**:
  Be ready to fight it out.
  सामना करने के लिए तैयार हो जाओ।
- **Don't spill the beans:**
  Don't let out the secret.
  यह राज़ किसी से कहना मत।/राज़ को राज़ ही रहने दो।
- **When will you bring it to daylight?**
  When will you produce it?
  आप इसे कब करेंगे?
- Please **shell out** some money:
  Please contribute some money.
  कृपया कुछ आर्थिक योगदान कीजिए।
- Try to **dig up** something from the old files:
  Try to find out something from the old files.
  पुरानी फाइलों से ज़रूरी जानकारियाँ जुटाइये।
- **You take the cake!**
  You are the most foolish person!
  आप सबसे बड़े बेवक़ूफ़ हैं।
- Will you tell me **what is eating you**?
  Will you tell me what is bothering or worrying you?
  क्या आप मुझे बताएँगे कि आपको कौन-सी चिन्ता खाए जा रही है?

- **Don't confide your secrets to her:**
  Don't let her know your plans, since she cannot be trusted.
  उसको अपनी योजना मत बताइये।

- You can't **wash off your hands** from this affair:
  You were also responsible for this affair and cannot escape blame.
  आप इस मामले से पल्ला नहीं झाड़ सकते।

- Do you wish to work **till the cows come home**?
  Do you plan to work very late?
  क्या आप शाम को देर तक काम करना चाहेंगे?

- Let's **set the ball rolling**:
  Let's begin work.
  चलो काम शुरू करें।

- **Chuck him out:**
  Throw him out/remove him from the job.
  उसे बाहर करो।/उसे काम से निकाल दो।

- Will you **lend a helping hand**?
  Will you help out?
  क्या आप मदद करेंगे?

- **You better believe it:**
  This is the truth and you have no option but to believe it.
  आपको सच मानना ही पड़ेगा।

- You will have to get into the **nuts and bolts** of things:
  You will have to go into intricate details to find out things.
  तुम्हें यह समझने के लिए काफ़ी गहराई में जाना पड़ेगा।/तुम्हें यह जानने के लिए काफ़ी मेहनत करनी पड़ेगी।

- Don't **cramp his style**:
  Give him some freedom.
  उसको कुछ आज़ादी दो।

- Don't open this **can of worms**:
  Don't try to investigate this dirty matter.
  इस समस्या से दूर ही रहो तो अच्छा है।

- Okay, please **pop your question**:
  Go ahead and ask your question.
  कृपया अपना प्रश्न पूछें।/ठीक है, पहले अपनी बात बताइए।
- He will have to take a **polygraph test**:
  He will have to take a lie detector test.
  उसको झूठ पकड़ने की मशीन से होकर गुज़रना पड़ेगा।
- **Let him off** this time:
  Don't punish him this time.
  इस बार उसको माफ़ कर दो।
- **Toss a few crumbs to him**:
  Give him some of the money.
  उसे कुछ पैसे दे दो।
- You must have a **look-see** before taking a decision:
  You must at least have a cursory look before you decide.
  फ़ैसला करने से पहले कम-से-कम एक बार ज़रा-सी नज़र तो डाल लो।
- Let him in, he is an **old buddy**:
  Let him come in, he is an old friend.
  उसे आने दो, वह पुराना दोस्त है।
- **Knock the bottom out of him:**
  Thrash him nice and proper.
  उसकी अच्छी तरह से कुटाई करो।
- Please stop, I have had **enough of this bullshit!**
  Please stop, since I have had enough of this nonsense!
  बस करो ये बेवकूफ़ी, मुझसे अब और बर्दाश्त नहीं होता।
- **Since you made this great proclamation:**
  Since you announced this.
  चूँकि तुमने ये घोषणा की है।
- You can't **close your eyes** to the fact that he was a thief:
  You have to accept the fact that he was a thief.
  आपको यह मानना होगा कि वह एक चोर था।
- **Stick to your guns:**
  Please stand firmly by what you have said.
  आप अपनी बात पर अडिग रहें।

5. Happenings and Events

- The price of oil went **through the roof**:
  The price of oil reached very high levels.
  तेल की कीमतें बहुत बढ़ गई हैं।/तेल की कीमतें आसमान छू रही हैं।
- **We haven't reached a decision and are still kicking it around:**
  We are yet to take a final decision and are still debating the issue.
  हम अभी तक बहस में उलझे हैं, फ़ैसला कब करेंगे।
- He stopped **dead in his tracks**:
  He stopped suddenly.
  वह अचानक रुक गया।
- The woman did not **take the bait**:
  The woman couldn't be fooled.
  उस औरत को बेवक़ूफ़ नहीं बनाया जा सकता।
- He parked the car and **killed the engine**:
  He parked his car and switched off the engine.
  उसने कार खड़ी करके इंजन बंद कर दिया।
- **His skimpy French was running out:**
  He had difficulty conversing in his limited French.
  टूटी-फूटी फ्रेंच के कारण वह बात नहीं कर पा रहा।
- **With an effort he shook off his paralysis:**
  He managed to recover from his immobility.
  वह बड़ी कोशिश के बाद चलने-फिरने लायक हो पाया।
- **To cut a long story short:**
  In brief.
  संक्षेप में।
- **He slapped her so hard that she saw stars:**
  He slapped her very hard and she felt giddy.
  उसने इतनी ज़ोर से उसको चाँटा मारा कि उसे तारे नज़र आने लगे।

- She researched into the **heart of the matter**:
  She researched the issue in depth.
  उसने मामले की गहराई में जाकर जाँच की।
- **All their efforts had been for naught:**
  All their efforts failed.
  उनके सारे प्रयास विफल हो गए।
- **I felt the madness coming over him:**
  He was getting very angry and losing his sense of reasoning.
  क्रोध में उसकी सोचने-समझने की शक्ति समाप्त हो गई थी।
- **Times have taken a turn:**
  Things are now different.
  अब हालात बदल गए हैं।
- Things are a **bit up** in the air but I will **coordinate** it:
  Things are still not settled but I will manage to organise it.
  हालात ठीक नहीं हैं लेकिन फिर भी मैं कोशिश करूँगा कि सब ठीक रहे।
- During her **on-again off-again affair**:
  During her affair that was on and off at repeated intervals.
  उसके रुक-रुककर चलने वाले प्रेम-संबंध के दौरान।
- They **hooked a few trout**:
  They caught some fish/they fooled some people.
  उन्होंने कुछ लोगों को बेवक़ूफ़ बनाया।
- He **cast magic** on the crowd:
  He hypnotised the audience/had them in a spell.
  उसने भीड़ पर जादू कर दिया।
- He **drifted into** the circle of bachelors:
  He got into a group of bachelors.
  वह कुँवारों के झुंड में शामिल हो गया।
- **I chill all over with fright** when I think of it:
  I get very scared thinking about it.
  मैं जब भी इस बारे में सोचता हूँ, डर जाता हूँ।
- She was at her **wits' end**:
  She simply did not know what to do.
  उसको बिलकुल नहीं समझ आया कि वह क्या करे।

- He **made a mark** on the little mind:
  He impressed the child.
  उसने बच्चे को प्रभावित कर दिया।
- The political scene here will never get its **face out of the muck**:
  The political scene here is very dirty and will not improve.
  यहाँ का राजनैतिक माहौल अपनी गंदगी से कभी नहीं उबर पाएगा।
- **The party pulsated on his arrival:**
  He brought life to the party when he came into it.
  उसके आने से पार्टी में जान आ गई।
- I knew he was **sizing me up**:
  I knew he was trying to judge my strength.
  मुझे पता था कि वह मेरी शक्ति का अनुमान लगा रहा था।
- He had **hit the mark** and the plans were approved:
  He had made the right decisions and the plans were given clearance.
  उसने सही फ़ैसला लिया और वह काम कर गया।
- **He was as welcome as a leper:**
  He was most unwelcome.
  उसका आना किसी को पसंद नहीं आया।
- **My offer did little to stir her:**
  I couldn't impress her at all.
  मैं उसे किसी भी प्रकार से प्रभावित नहीं कर सका।
- **He broke into laughter:**
  He began laughing.
  वह हँस पड़ा।
- **He knew his position was impossible from the beginning:**
  He was aware that he had no chance of winning.
  वह जानता था कि उसके जीतने के अवसर कम थे।/वह जानता था कि वह जीत नहीं सकता।
- **Yet the clashes were faint stuff:**
  The clashes were not violent.
  यद्यपि मुठभेड़ हिंसक नहीं थी।
- At the **bottom of things:**
  The real facts are.
  सही तथ्य अक्सर गहराई में ही मिलते हैं।

- **The doors that shunned him opened again:**
He was allowed entry once again at places that had barred him.
उसके लिए फिर से वहाँ के रास्ते खुल गए जहाँ पहले वह नहीं जा सकता था।

- He did not **rise to the challenge**:
He didn't make a sincere effort to win.
उसने गंभीरता से जीतने का प्रयास नहीं किया।

- He was **grabbed by the collar and hurled in**:
He was taken inside by force.
उसे जबरदस्ती अंदर ले जाया गया था।

- **The ladies placed themselves in evidence:**
The ladies ensured they were noticed at the party.
औरतों ने इस बात को सुनिश्चित किया कि जब वे पार्टी में आएँ तो सब उन्हें देखें।

- **I thought I would never live to grow a beard:**
I thought I would die as a young boy only.
मुझे लगा कि मैं जवान होने से पहले ही मर जाऊँगा।

- It is just a **storm in a teacup**:
It's a small matter and will soon pass.
ये तो चाय के प्याले में तूफान जैसी बात हो गई।

- The horror of it all **crashed on me**:
I had to suddenly face the harsh truth.
मुझे अचानक कटु सत्य का अनुभव हुआ।

- **He was the poet whose dreams faded:**
He was a creative man who failed to realise his dreams.
वह एक रचनाधर्मी व्यक्ति था जिसके सपने पूरे नहीं हुए।

- **A long silence of digestion followed:**
There was a long interval of silence in trying to accept the facts.
सहमति की स्तब्धता सुनी जा सकती थी।/ ख़ामोशी ने कह दिया कि बात मान ली गई है।

- **Three of us in accord turned to Jaswant for consensus:**
We three agreed and wanted Jaswant to do the same to ensure unanimity.
हम तीनों ने सहमत होकर चाहा कि जसवंत भी हमारे साथ हो जाए।

- He **stared at me blankly**:
  He stared at me without comprehending things.
  वह भावहीन होकर मेरी ओर देखने लगा।
- We were all **swept away** by her address:
  We were impressed by her speech.
  हम उसके भाषण से बहुत प्रभावित हुए।
- He **drummed his fingers** on the table:
  He tapped the table with his fingers.
  उसने अपनी उँगलियों से मेज़ को थपथपाया।
- **She wormed her way into the confidence of my family:**
  She gained the confidence of my family through her tricks.
  अपनी चालाकियों से उसने मेरे परिवार का भरोसा जीत लिया।
- They began to **cover their tracks** on **sensing defeat**:
  They tried to remove the evidence on realising they would lose.
  अपनी हार सामने नज़र आने लगी तो वे सबूतों को छिपाने लगे।
- Once the **word was out**:
  Once everyone knew about it.
  ज्यों ही सबको पता चला।
- He **hoped against hope** for a lifeline:
  Despite indications to the contrary, he hoped that someone could still save him.
  सारी आशाओं के टूट जाने के बाद भी वह उम्मीद कर रहा था कि उसकी ज़िंदगी बच जाएगी।
- **Her eyes settled on a familiar face:**
  She saw someone she knew.
  उसे लगा कि उसने उसे कहीं देखा है।
- He was more than ready to **take on the job**:
  He was very keen to do the job.
  वह काम करने के लिए बहुत उत्सुक था।
- An **idea began to form in his mind:**
  An idea took shape in his mind.
  उसके दिमाग में एक विचार उमड़ा।

- He gave **no signs** of caring for what others thought:
  He had no respect for others' feelings.
  उसे दूसरों की भावनाओं की कोई परवाह नहीं थी।
- It is a **sure thing**:
  It will surely happen.
  ये तो पक्का होगा।
- He quickly put his **problem on one side**:
  He disregarded his problem and got down to the task.
  उसने समस्या की परवाह न करते हुए काम पर ध्यान लगाया।
- **He set himself the task of learning:**
  He took the challenge of learning this.
  उसने सीखने का बीड़ा उठाया।
- **He held the audience spellbound:**
  He spoke very well and people heard him with rapt attention.
  उसने दर्शकों को मंत्रमुग्ध कर दिया।
- **He tried not to show his disappointment:**
  He tried to hide his disappointment.
  उसने अपनी निराशा छिपाने की कोशिश की।
- **Initially they both fenced gently:**
  Initially they tried to probe each other's defences gently.
  उन्होंने एक-दूसरे की सफ़ाई को ध्यानपूर्वक सुना।
- She **pulled some ranks** and secured the interview:
  She used influence to get an interview call.
  उसने अपने प्रभाव से अपने लिए इण्टरव्यू सुनिश्चित किया।
- **The warning signs were blazingly clear:**
  There were clear-cut indications that things were wrong.
  चेतावनी का संकेत स्पष्ट दिख रहा था।
- **His mind was racing:**
  He was thinking very fast.
  उसका दिमाग तेज़ी से चल रहा था।
- Time **hung heavily**:
  Time passed slowly.
  समय बहुत धीरे-धीरे बीता।

- The search **drew a blank**:
  Nothing was found during the search.
  खोज में कुछ भी नहीं मिला।
- There was a **pregnant pause**:
  There was a break in the conversation that held some meaning.
  यह एक सारगर्भित अन्तराल था।
- They have **tapped into a minefield** of gold:
  They have come upon a business that will make them a lot of money.
  उनको एक व्यवसाय मिल गया है जो उनके लिए सोने की चिड़िया साबित होगा।
- It turned into **quite a jolly** evening:
  The evening was full of fun and merrymaking.
  यह तो एक मज़ेदार शाम बन गयी।/वह शाम बहुत मज़ेदार थी।
- **The shadows grew longer in his mind:**
  He began having deep doubts and suspicion.
  उसके दिमाग में संदेह के बादल घुमड़ने लगे।
- He **turned up** at the door:
  He came to the place.
  वह घर वापस आया।
- He went on to make **a fortune out of it**:
  He became very rich from this thing.
  वह इसके सहारे बहुत अमीर बन गया।
- **The die was cast and there was no going back:**
  A final decision was taken and there was no way to go back.
  आख़िरी फ़ैसले के बाद अब वापसी का कोई रास्ता नहीं था।
- **His flowering career went bust:**
  His booming career suddenly went wrong.
  उसका सुनहरा भविष्य अचानक मिट्टी में मिल गया।
- The **ball now lies firmly in his court**:
  The next move now has to be made by him.
  अब तो अगला कदम उसको ही उठाना है।/अब तो उसके ही अगले कदम का इंतज़ार है।

- **His role was truncated:**
His role was cut short.
उसकी भूमिका काटकर छोटी कर दी गई।

- It **was like turning disaster into triumph**:
It was like a total defeat being turned into a victory.
ये एक बुरी पराजय थी जो अचानक जीत में बदल गयी।

- We **hung on** to the moment, never wanting to let go:
We enjoyed the moment and didn't want it to get over.
हमने उन लम्हों का मज़ा लिया और चाहा कि वक़्त वहीं रुक जाए।

6. Judgmental Statements

- **By any standard it was still uncommonly fast:**
  It was done very fast.
  किसी भी तरह से यह बहुत तेज़ी से हुआ।
- **It was abysmal work:**
  It was very bad work.
  ये बहुत ही बुरा काम था। / ये बहुत ही घटिया काम था।
- I think a problem is **in the making**:
  It will create a problem.
  मुझे लगता है, इससे समस्या होने वाली है।
- He **lost the will to combat life**:
  He no longer had the will to fight life's problems and live on.
  जीवन में दुख झेलते-झेलते उसकी जीने की इच्छा समाप्त हो गई।
- **One day the trickle will become a steady stream:**
  Gradually the results will keep getting better and yield big returns.
  धीरे-धीरे सफलता का सिलसिला बढ़ता जायेगा।
- There is a **missing link**:
  There is something required to complete the task/investigation.
  बेहतर कोशिश की ज़रूरत है।
- There is a very **thin line**:
  The margin of difference is very small.
  फ़र्क़ बहुत ही कम है।
- His **inefficiency** led to a **dead end**:
  Because of his inefficiency the work didn't progress.
  उसकी अयोग्यता के कारण काम आगे नहीं बढ़ पाया।
- Had he put his **theory into practice**:
  He didn't get down to actually trying out his ideas.
  अगर उसने अपने सिद्धांतों को अपने काम में भी अपनाया होता।

- **He should consign this antiquated system to the dustbin:**
He should stop following old methods of working.
उसको पुराने तरीके से काम करना बंद कर देना चाहिए।

- He could have **turned it around**:
He could have changed things for the better.
वे हालात को बिलकुल बदलकर अच्छा बना सकते थे।

- **Perhaps the time for action has come:**
It's time to act or it will be too late.
शायद अब कार्य को अमल करने का सही वक्त आ गया है।

- He is still **testing the waters**:
He hasn't taken a final decision and is still checking the advantages and disadvantages.
वह अभी भी नुकसान और फायदे के हिसाब में लगा है, इसलिए फ़ैसला नहीं ले पाया है।

- Her efforts **will end in tears:**
She will fail in her work.
अंततः उसका प्रयास असफल हो गया।

- **This was not the reason to lose the deal:**
The deal was not lost because of this.
सौदा खो देने का कारण यह नहीं है।

- **You would need to do some drastic surgery**:
You will have to make some major changes.
आपको आमूलचूल परिवर्तन करने होंगे।

- The whole process needs a little **fine-tuning**:
The entire process needs some restructuring.
पूरी प्रक्रिया में कुछ सुधार की आवश्यकता है।

- **I can't see the allies falling in line:**
The allies will not agree to this.
मित्रगण इसको स्वीकार नहीं करेंगे।

- It **wasn't turning out to be a glorious year for her:**
It was a bad year for her.
ये उसके लिए एक गौरवपूर्ण वर्ष सिद्ध नहीं हो रहा था।

- It **appears** as if he has got himself **a good deal**:
He seems to have struck a beneficial deal.
ऐसा लगता है कि उसे अच्छा व्यापार/सौदा मिल गया है।
- Your behaviour was **a pleasure** to watch:
You behaved very well.
आपका व्यवहार बहुत दर्शनीय था।
- **He did not fit into any of her plans**:
He did not receive any job/favour from her.
उसके कारण उसे कुछ (नौकरी या सहायता) प्राप्त नहीं हुआ।
- The company was facing difficulty in **breaking even**:
The company has not been able to overcome its losses and meet all expenses.
कंपनी अपने नुकसान से उबर नहीं पा रही है।
- **These people need no lesson in this kind of deceit**:
These people are very good at cheating.
ये लोग ठगने में बहुत माहिर हैं।
- **The struggles are ongoing but life's tests refine you:**
You learn from difficulties and become a better person.
आप ज़िंदगी की जंग से गुज़रकर बेहतर इंसान बनते हैं।
- He worked for it **only on the surface**:
He didn't put his heart and mind into it.
उसने दिल लगाकर ये काम नहीं किया।
- This **approach** is at the very **heart of the technique**:
This approach is crucial to the technique.
तकनीक के लिए ये विधि बहुत ज़रूरी है।
- Every job has challenges, its own **bag of rocks**:
There are problems of a kind in every job.
हर काम में चुनौतियाँ होती हैं।
- **There are powerful headwinds that will slow down your progress**:
You will face major problems that will reduce the pace of your work.
आपको कई बड़ी समस्याओं का सामना करना पड़ेगा जो कि आपकी प्रगति को प्रभावित करेंगी।

- To **go with the flow** is not always **advisable**:
  It is sometimes good to do things differently in order to succeed.
  सफलता पाने के लिए कभी-कभी रास्ता बदलना बेहतर होता है।
- It **proved to be his undoing**:
  It was a mistake that brought about his downfall.
  इस एक भूल ने उसके पतन की शुरुआत कर दी।
- **Do not break inviolate principles:**
  Do not disregard the basics that must be followed.
  आधारभूत नियम-कायदे मत भूलो।
- **He was no nearer to solving his problem:**
  Despite all efforts, he is still far away from solving his problem.
  तमाम कोशिशों के बावजूद वह अपने लक्ष्य से बहुत दूर था।
- So she finally **fell in** with your plans:
  Finally she agreed to your plans.
  आखिरकार वह तुम्हारी योजना से सहमत हो ही गई।
- For me, the **game is far from over yet**:
  I haven't given up yet and will continue my efforts.
  मैंने अभी हार नहीं मानी है।
- This is not the time to **sacrifice** the job on the **altar of principles**:
  Do not be rigid on principles and risk the job being lost.
  Be flexible.
  उसूलों पर नौकरी कुर्बान करना ठीक नहीं है।
- He realised quite late that he had **overplayed his cards**:
  He kept taking risks for too long and lost out.
  काफ़ी समय तक जोखिम उठाने के बाद उसे ज्ञात हुआ कि उसकी कोशिशें बेकार गईं।
- On this job we are not exactly on **home ground**:
  We are not in an advantageous position on this job.
  इस काम में निश्चित ही हमारे लिए बहुत-सी मुश्किलें आएँगी।
- It will do his **reputation no end of good**:
  It will help his reputation immensely.
  इससे उसकी प्रतिष्ठा में वृद्धि होगी।

- We will never **get to the bottom** of this:
  We will never come to know the real facts.
  इसकी सच्चाई हमें कभी पता नहीं चल पाएगी।
- I think it is just a **smoke-screen**:
  It is simply meant to deceive you.
  मेरे खयाल से ये एक धोखा है।
- It plugs the **breach in our defence perimeter**:
  It covers the loophole in our defence mechanism.
  हमारे सुरक्षातंत्र की ख़ामियों को ये छुपा लेता है।
- She will be **gobbled up by the system**:
  She will be finished by the system.
  इस पूरे तंत्र में फँसकर वह ख़त्म हो जायेगी।
- **This incident will chill the peace negotiations**:
  This occurrence will harm the peace negotiations.
  यह घटना शान्तिवार्ता को नुकसान पहुँचाएगी।
- It would be a **real scoop** for me:
  It will be a really big story for me.
  मेरे लिए ये एक बड़ी ख़बर साबित होगी।
- Newspapers definitely will get **wind of it** by tomorrow:
  Newspapers will come to know about it by tomorrow.
  कल तक समाचार-पत्रों को इसकी खबर हो जाएगी।
- Well, this seems a **long shot**:
  This seems very unlikely or improbable.
  इसकी संभावना बहुत ही कम है।
- **Despite the flowery language, I am sure nothing will be forthcoming**:
  Despite the sweet talk there will be no real gains.
  मुझे यकीन है, अत्यंत मधुर वार्तालाप के बावजूद कुछ प्राप्त नहीं होगा।
- The report was **without frills or exaggeration**:
  The report was to the point.
  रिपोर्ट प्रासंगिक / उपयुक्त थी।
- **These are unfounded rumours:**
  These are lies.
  ये सब झूठ है।

- **It is rudimentary** – I am surprised you don't know this:
  It's basic knowledge and something even you should know.
  यह सामान्य जानकारी है जो आपको भी होनी चाहिए।
- **It is ridiculous**.
  It is absurd.
  यह बेवक़ूफ़ी है।
- **How do you tolerate it?**
  How do you accept it?
  तुम यह कैसे बर्दाश्त करते हो?
- **It is unbelievable.**
  Why do you accept it?
  हैरानी की बात है, आप उसको कैसे सह लेते हैं?
- He has been **a revelation** of the tour:
  He has been the find of the tour.
  इस युद्ध में उसके जैसा एक जाँबाज मिला है।
- **He showed great resilience during the battle:**
  He displayed great calm and courage during the battle.
  उसने युद्ध में बहुत दृढ़ता दिखाई।
- There is no **quick-fix solution** for this problem:
  There is no readymade solution for this problem.
  इस समस्या के समाधान में समय लगेगा।
- He has made **a bloody mess**:
  He has spoilt everything thoroughly.
  उसने बहुत बड़ी गड़बड़ कर दी है।
- Oh, it's worth a **king's ransom**:
  Oh, it is extremely expensive.
  ये बहुत अधिक मूल्यवान वस्तु है।
- **It's invaluable:**
  It's very valuable and priceless.
  यह बहुत अधिक कीमती है।
- **His philandering behaviour will lead to tension:**
  His flirtatious behaviour will cause problems.
  उसका विलासी स्वभाव उसके लिए परेशानियाँ खड़ी करेगा।

- He has **gone to pieces**:
  He has totally lost his balance.
  उसका संतुलन बिगड़ गया है।
- **It's top flight** – so don't worry:
  It is of a very high quality, so don't worry about it.
  इसकी गुणवत्ता बहुचर्चित है, चिंता मत कीजिये।
- It will be an **eye-opener** for you:
  It will be a surprise for you.
  यह आपके लिए एक अप्रत्याशित घटना साबित होगी।
- This will serve as the **curtain-raiser**:
  This will serve as the preceding event.
  यह एक नए सिलसिले की शुरुआत करेगा।
- Don't worry, he will work **under your thumb**:
  Don't worry, he is a good subordinate and will follow your orders.
  आप चिंता न करें, वह आपके निर्देश के अनुसार काम करेगा।
- It's a **middle-of-the-road** response:
  It's a response that seeks to please both sides.
  यह एक ऐसा जवाब है जो दोनों तरफ पसंद किया जाएगा।
- It's **very heavy stuff** for me to understand:
  It is too difficult for me to understand this.
  मेरे लिए इसे समझ पाना बहुत मुश्किल है।
- I think you have got the **lion's share**:
  I think you have got a bigger share.
  मुझे लगता है कि आपको बड़ा हिस्सा मिला है।
- He committed a **faux pas**:
  He made a major error/blunder.
  उसने बहुत बड़ी गलती की है।
- It's at the **cutting edge of technology**:
  It's the latest technology.
  यह एक नवीनतम तकनीक है।
- It was a **morbid affair**:
  It was a terrible affair.
  यह एक बेमतलब का मामला था।

- You have **missed it by a mile**:
  You are grossly incorrect.
  आप पूरी तरह से गलत हैं।
- **He came a cropper:**
  He fared miserably/failed.
  वह बुरी तरह से असफल हो गया।
- **You will get mauled by him:**
  You will be badly beaten by him.
  वह आपको बुरी तरह से पीटेगा।
- He is still **going around in circles**:
  He is still groping around for the solution.
  वह अभी भी हाथ-पैर मार रहा है। / वह अभी भी कोशिश में लगा है।
- His **fate was sealed**:
  There was no escape for him.
  उसके पास अब बच निकलने का कोई रास्ता नहीं है।
- The **discussion is still wide open**:
  The debate is still on and has not been decided conclusively.
  अभी बहस ख़त्म नहीं हुई है।
- It's like an **albatross around his neck**:
  It is a heavy burden that's weighing him down.
  यह उसके लिए गले का फंदा है।
- It's a **white elephant**:
  It is something that requires costly maintenance and is difficult to dispose of.
  ये सफेद हाथी है। / ये बहुत ज्यादा खर्चीला मामला है।
- It is difficult to remain **level-headed** in this situation:
  It is difficult to retain one's balance and poise in this situation.
  इस हालत में इसको काबू में रखना मुश्किल है।
- It will soon **fizzle out**:
  It will soon die its own death.
  यह जल्दी ही अपने आप ख़त्म हो जाएगा।

- He has **gone bonkers**:
  He has gone mad.
  वह पागल हो गया है।
- He has **blown all his chances**:
  He has lost all his chances.
  उसकी सारी कोशिशें नाकाम रही हैं।
- It's the **in-thing**:
  It's the latest craze/fashion.
  ये आजकल का चलन है।
- The **whole thing still intrigues me**:
  The entire affair is still a mystery to me.
  ये सारा मामला मेरी समझ से बाहर है।
- I think it is **too little and too late**:
  I think the measures are insufficient and are also being implemented at a stage when it is too late.
  इतने कम समय में तो वैसे भी नहीं हो सकता और फिर वक़्त भी हाथ से निकल चुका है।
- **I haven't the foggiest idea**:
  I have no idea at all.
  मुझे बिलकुल पता नहीं है।
- **It failed to stir him:**
  It failed to motivate him.
  इससे उसको प्रेरणा नहीं मिल पाई।
- This is the **lull before the storm**:
  An extremely bad situation is building up/around the corner.
  यह तूफान के आने का संकेत है।
- **His atrocities made even Hitler pale by comparison:**
  He committed horrifying crimes that were worse than Hitler's.
  उसने इतने भयंकर अपराध किए कि हिटलर को भी पीछे छोड़ दिया।
- **The rich are more covetous of money than the poor:**
  The rich hanker for money more than the poor.
  अमीर लोग पैसे के ज्यादा लोभी होते हैं, बनिस्बत गरीब लोगों के।

- **But the facts point to the contrary:**
  But the facts reveal just the opposite.
  किन्तु सत्य तो बिलकुल इसके विपरीत है।

- **Long indulgence in alcohol impaired his health:**
  Excessive drinking ruined his health.
  अधिक मदिरापान से उसका स्वास्थ्य खराब हो गया है।

- It will make a **major dent** in our business:
  It will lead to a major loss for us.
  इससे हमें बहुत नुकसान होगा।

- He **rendered yeoman** service in the hospital:
  He did extremely good work in the hospital.
  उसने हॉस्पिटल में बहुत अच्छा कार्य किया।

- The facts are **self-explanatory**:
  The facts can be understood at face value and do not need to be explained.
  सत्य को समझाने की आवश्यकता नहीं होती, वह तो स्वयं ही समझ में आ जाता है।

- He definitely had **a hand in this plot**:
  He was also involved in this plot.
  वह भी इस षड्यंत्र में शामिल है।

- He was **hand-in-glove** with the thieves:
  He was supporting the thieves.
  वह चोरी में मदद कर रहा था।

- He knows the **ins and outs** of this office:
  He knows all the secret and basic facts about this office.
  वह इस ऑफिस की हर बात से परिचित है।

- He **made the most** of his opportunities:
  He fully utilised all his chances.
  उसने अपनी पूरी संभावनाएँ तलाश लीं।

- He is just **passing time** and his **heart is not in it**:
  He is not sincere and is only doing things for the sake of it.
  वह इसे गम्भीर होकर नहीं कर रहा है, बस यहां समय व्यतीत कर रहा है।

- The situation is now **well in hand**:
  The situation is totally under control.
  अब स्थिति पूरी तरह नियत्रंण में है।
- Most of it is a **sniff in the wind**:
  Most of it is in thin air and not concrete.
  ये आसानी से जाना जा सकता है।
- It is a **dying art** in India:
  The art is fast losing popularity in India and is on its way out.
  भारत में इस कला का अस्तित्व समाप्त हो रहा है, धीरे-धीरे यह विलुप्त हो जाएगी।
- **The stress is telling upon his health:**
  The stress is making him sick.
  तनाव का उसके स्वास्थ्य पर बुरा असर पड़ रहा है।
- Winter will **set in** by October:
  Winter will begin in October.
  सर्दियाँ अक्टूबर से शुरू होंगी।
- He will try to **run you** down:
  He will try to criticise you.
  वह आपकी निन्दा करने की कोशिश करेगा।
- This will create a crisis of **epidemic proportions**:
  This will create a major crisis that will be difficult to handle.
  यह एक भीषण समस्या को जन्म देगी।
- We have reached a **turning point** in history:
  It is a very important landmark that will change the course of history.
  यह इतिहास के पन्नों को बदल देने वाली कड़ी है।
- The Bermuda triangle is an **unfathomable mystery**:
  The Bermuda triangle is a mystery that cannot be solved.
  बर्मूडा ट्राइऐंगल का रहस्य समझ से परे है।
- It's like setting the **Thames on fire**:
  It's a very difficult act that will attract all-round attention.
  यह बहुत मुश्किल और बड़ा काम है।
- I **smell a rat**:
  There is something wrong.
  मुझे यहाँ कुछ गड़बड़ लग रही है।

- Things are **very fishy**:
  Things seem very suspicious.
  चीज़ें बहुत संदेहास्पद प्रतीत होती हैं।
- The situation has gone **out of hand**:
  The situation is no longer in control.
  हालात नियंत्रण से बाहर हो गये हैं।
- It **was an irresistible opportunity**:
  It was a chance that one couldn't let go.
  यह एक ऐसा अवसर था जिसे कोई भी हाथ से जाने नहीं देना चाहेगा।
- **This concept has overlooked a major fact:**
  This concept has forgotten an important truth.
  इस अवधारणा में एक महत्त्वपूर्ण तथ्य का ध्यान नहीं रखा गया है।
- **The troops-to-task ratio was often lopsided:**
  The number of troops allotted for a task was improper.
  काम के लिए दिये गए लोग पर्याप्त नहीं थे।
- Doing business in India is a **fine art**:
  It's not easy to do business in India.
  भारत में व्यापार करना कोई आसान काम नहीं है।
- **They were pulverised into inaction:**
  They were rendered immobile and were unable to act in any way.
  उन्हें बिलकुल जड़वत् कर दिया गया।
- It was a **red-letter day** in the history of Europe:
  It was an extremely memorable day in Europe's history.
  यूरोप के इतिहास में यह दिन कभी नहीं भुलाया जा सकेगा।
- **This study has proved extremely fruitful:**
  This study has been very helpful.
  यह अध्ययन बहुत उपयोगी सिद्ध हुआ है।
- **Herein lies the danger:**
  This is where the dangerous part is.
  यहाँ खतरा है।
- The days immediately ahead are likely to be stormy and **crisis-ridden**:
  The coming days will be very difficult and full of major problems.
  आने वाले दिनों में परेशानियों की बहुत आशंका है।

- There seems to be some **hanky-panky** going on:
  There is something wrong that's happening here.
  यहाँ ज़रूर कुछ गड़बड़ हो रही है।
- He is **bang on target**:
  He is absolutely correct.
  वह बिलकुल सही है।
- **Off the record**, he is guilty:
  Unofficially, he has been held guilty.
  अनधिकृत तौर पर वह दोषी है।
- **It will boost his morale:**
  It will increase his self-confidence.
  इससे उसका आत्मविश्वास बढ़ेगा।
- **He is an astute character:**
  He is a very sharp man.
  वह बहुत चतुर व्यक्ति है।
- He is **quick on the draw**:
  He is an alert man and quick to respond.
  वह बहुत ही चौकस है।/इस विषय पर वह बहुत सतर्कता दिखाएगा।
- **It is all poppycock**:
  It's all nonsense.
  ये सब बकवास है।
- **It is phoney**:
  It is not genuine.
  यह नकली है।
- There is an **outside chance** of victory:
  There is still some hope of winning, although slender.
  अभी भी जीत की थोड़ी उम्मीद बाकी है।
- It's a **no-win situation**:
  It is a situation in which there is no way of winning at all.
  यहाँ इस हालात में अब कोई कोशिश काम नहीं आएगी।
- It is a **no-go situation**:
  It is a hopeless situation.
  इस हालत में कुछ नहीं किया जा सकता।

- This will make **a big splash**:
  This will make big news.
  यह एक बड़ी ख़बर बनेगी।

- She is **in hot water**:
  She is in deep trouble.
  वह बड़ी मुसीबत में फँस गई है।

- The **honeymoon period** is over:
  The early days of goodwill are over and things are now on the routine track.
  आराम के दिन गए, अब काम करना होगा।

- It was like **having a tiger by the tail**:
  It was a nasty situation cne didn't know how to get out of.
  यह एक ख़तरनाक स्थिति थी, जिसमें बहुत ज़्यादा सावधानी की ज़रूरत है।

- **It is an eyewash**:
  It is false propaganda/pretence.
  यह एक छलावा है।

- **It will click**:
  It will work.
  इससे काम हो जाएगा।/ये काम करेगा।

- It's a **catch-22** situation:
  It's a situation from which there is no escape because it involves mutually conflicting conditions.
  ऐसे हालात जिनसे भागा नहीं जा सकता।

- Why are they so **tight-lipped** over it?
  Why are they so secretive about it?
  वे इस विषय पर इतने ख़ामोश क्यों हैं?

- **We are in a quandary**:
  We don't know what to do.
  हमें पता नहीं, अब क्या किया जाए?

- **He is prejudiced against me:**
  He is biased against me.
  मेरे लिए उसके मन में कड़वाहट है।

- **He is opinionated:**
He holds strongly prejudiced views.
उसके मन में काफ़ी दुराग्रह है।

- The **flip side** of the story is:
The other side of the story is.
कहानी का दूसरा पहलू यह है।

- **He dealt with the situation nonchalantly:**
He dealt with the situation coolly.
उसने परिस्थिति को बहुत आराम से सँभाला।

- It turned out to be **a cliffhanger**:
It was a very close and exciting match.
यह एक बहुत ही काँटे की टक्कर निकली।

- **With the passage of time he mellowed:**
Over the years he changed for the better.
कुछ सालों में वह बेहतर हो गया है।

- **This has spooky looks:**
This has ghostly/scary looks.
ये तो डरावना लगता है।

- It's a **white-collar** job:
It's an office job.
यह एक इज़्ज़तदार ऑफिस की नौकरी है।

- **It was a swanky party:**
It was an excellent party.
यह एक बहुत ही मज़ेदार पार्टी थी।

- **No problem is insurmountable:**
No problem is such that it cannot be resolved.
कोई भी समस्या ऐसी नहीं होती जिसे हल न किया जा सके।

- The doctor will **give him a shot**:
The doctor will give him an injection.
डॉक्टर उसको इंजेक्शन लगाएगा।

- He has got a **raw deal**:
He has been given a very bad deal.
उसका यह सौदा फ़ायदेमंद नहीं है।

- **This boy is incorrigible:**
  This boy is beyond hope and improvement.
  इस लड़के का कुछ नहीं हो सकता।/इस लड़के से कोई उम्मीद नहीं है।
- It's an **open-and-shut** case:
  It is an indisputable case where the facts are very clear.
  ये एक खुला हुआ मामला है जिसमें सब साफ़-साफ़ नज़र आ रहा है।
- He has taken a **shot in the dark**:
  He has taken a wild chance.
  उसने अँधेरे में एक तीर फेंका है, शायद निशाना लग जाए।
- It will never **see the light** of day:
  It will never be done.
  यह काम कभी पूरा नहीं हो पाएगा।
- I **feel someone has bugged my office:**
  I think someone is spying on me.
  मुझे लगता है कि कोई मेरी जासूसी कर रहा है।
- I think he is **two-timing** me:
  I think he is cheating on me and seeing someone else too.
  मुझे लगता है उसका किसी और से भी प्रेम संबंध है और वह मुझे धोखा दे रहा है।
- It is an **uphill task** for him:
  It's a very difficult task for him.
  यह उसके लिए बहुत कठिन कार्य है।
- The city will **grow on** you slowly:
  Slowly you will start liking the city.
  इससे हम सम्मान के साथ इस समस्या का समाधान कर सकेंगे।
- It will serve as a **face-saving** gesture:
  It will allow a respectable escape route from this problem.
  इस समस्या से मुक्ति पाने का यह एक सम्मानपूर्ण उपाय है।
- **This ruse will not last long:**
  This excuse will not work for too long.
  यह बहाना ज़्यादा नहीं चलने वाला।

- **That puts a different light on everything:**
  That changes everything.
  इससे दूसरी कई बातों का पता चलता है।
- **He is too wise to be felled like this:**
  He is not a fool to be defeated so easily.
  उसको इतना बेवक़ूफ़ मत समझो कि इतनी जल्दी हार मान लेगा।
- They required some time to put the **broken pieces** together:
  They needed some time to repair the damage done.
  हालत सँभालने के लिए उन्हें कुछ वक़्त की ज़रूरत है।
- His **success lay in casting his lot with the Americans:**
  He could only succeed if he sided with the Americans.
  वह अमेरिकन लोगों के साथ चलकर ही सफल हो सकता है।
- **Nothing is common between us and we might as well be living on different planets:**
  We are on totally different wavelengths and will not get along together.
  हम एक-दूसरे से नहीं मिलते और हमारा साथ भी मुमकिन नहीं।
- He **will not do anything detrimental to our interests:**
  He will not work against our interests.
  वह हमारे हित के विरुद्ध कुछ नहीं करेगा।
- He **will not do anything repugnant to his parents:**
  He will not do anything that his parents are totally against.
  वह अपने माता-पिता की इच्छा के विपरीत कुछ नहीं करेगा।
- **It's Greek to me:**
  I don't understand anything.
  मैं कुछ भी नहीं समझ पा रहा।
- He is **swollen-headed**:
  He is very proud.
  वह बहुत घमंडी है।
- I don't think he is in the **good books** of the boss:
  The boss does not like him.
  मुझे नहीं लगता कि बॉस उसे पसन्द करते हैं।

- He has **an axe to grind**:
  He has a vested interest.
  इसमें उसका भी स्वार्थ निहित है।

- This news will **spread like wildfire**:
  This news will spread very fast.
  यह ख़बर जंगल की आग की तरह तेज़ी से फैल जाएगी।

- It has **brought to light** some new issues:
  Some new issues have emerged.
  इसके कारण कुछ नए मामले सामने आये हैं।

- It has no **bearing on the subject** at hand:
  It is irrelevant to this subject.
  इसका इस मामले से कोई लेना-देना नहीं।

- Don't worry, I will get **the better of him**:
  There is nothing to worry, as I will defeat him.
  फ़िक्र न करें, मैं उसे हरा दूँगा।

- You have **hit the nail** on the head:
  You have found out the exact solution.
  आपको बिलकुल सही हल मिल गया है।

- **He was too cocky**:
  He was overconfident.
  उसे कुछ ज़्यादा ही आत्मविश्वास था।

- Indian cricket **picked up steam** on the arrival of Kapil Dev:
  Indian cricket improved vastly after Kapil Dev began playing.
  कपिल देव के आने के बाद भारतीय क्रिक्रेट प्रगति के पथ पर बढ़ने लगा।

- As an employer, he is **a bloodsucker**:
  He makes all his employees work extremely hard, exploiting them totally.
  एक नियोक्ता के रूप में वह अपने कर्मचारियों का बहुत शोषण कर रहा है।

- He knows how to **read between the lines**:
  He knows how to guess unstated things.
  उसे पता है कि असल बात कैसे जानी जाती है।

7. Moods and Emotions

- I am sorry to have **come down** so hard on your proposal:
  My apologies for being very harsh on your proposal.
  आपके प्रस्ताव पर इतना बिगड़ने के लिए मुझे अफ़सोस है।
- The boss **dismissed him** from service:
  The boss sacked him.
  बॉस ने उसे नौकरी से निकाल दिया।
- She was **white-faced** on getting caught:
  She was very embarrassed on being caught.
  पकड़े जाने पर वह बहुत शर्मिंदा थी।
- His **legs turned to jelly and his hands went clammy**:
  His legs felt weak and his hands were sweating.
  उसके पैर काँपने लगे और हाथों में पसीना आने लगा।
- **He was consumed with madness:**
  He seemed to have lost his mental balance.
  ऐसा लगता है कि उसने अपना मानसिक संतुलन खो दिया है।
- He is totally **gung-ho**:
  He is very eager.
  वह इसके लिए पूरी तरह उत्सुक था।
- I **can't stomach any more of this**:
  I can't take any more of this.
  अब मैं और नहीं खा सकता।
- If he **goes back** on his words, it is **war**:
  If he breaks his promise, there will be major trouble.
  अगर उसने अपना वादा तोड़ा तो बड़ी समस्या पैदा हो जाएगी।
- **He got red on being rebuffed:**
  He got very angry on being turned down.
  झिड़के जाने पर वह गुस्से से लाल हो गया।

- John **went pale with shock**:
  John's face lost colour and went white due to the shock.
  सदमा लगने के कारण जॉन का चेहरा पीला पड़ गया।
- Allow reality to **sink in**:
  Allow the situation to be accepted/understood.
  परिस्थितियों से समझौता करो।
- He seemed a shadow of his **former self**:
  He no longer looked like his old self and seemed out of touch.
  वह अब बिल्कुल भी पहले जैसा नहीं रहा।
- He seemed **lost in the woods**:
  He looked totally confused.
  वह पूरी तरह से उलझा हुआ-सा लगा।
- He knew how to **guard his flanks**:
  He knew how to guard himself from being attacked on the sly.
  वह अपने आपको बचाना जानता था।
- My dreams **came crashing to earth**:
  All my plans and hopes were dashed to the ground.
  मेरे सपने बुरी तरह टूट गए।
- **I suspect he took soiled money** to favour Rohan:
  I suspect he took a bribe to favour Rohan.
  मुझे शक है कि उसने रोहन का पक्ष लेने के लिए रिश्वत ली थी।
- Can you decide on the **spur of the moment**?
  Can you decide immediately?
  क्या आप अभी फ़ैसला कर सकते हैं।
- She **wept in happiness**:
  She was so happy that she cried.
  वह इतनी खुश थी कि उसे रोना आ गया।
- I know you **feel miffed**:
  I know you feel offended.
  मुझे पता है कि आप अपमानित महसूस कर रहे हैं।
- He was **raring to go**:
  He was very eager to begin.
  वह शुरू करने के लिए बेताब हो रहा था।

- He was **constantly on edge** in the presence of the boss:
  He was always uncomfortable and nervous in the presence of the boss.
  वह हमेशा बॉस की मौजूदगी में बेचैनी महसूस करता था।
- He managed to keep **a straight face**:
  He managed to hide his true feelings.
  वह अपने भाव छिपाने में कामयाब रहा।
- Dad **blew his top** at me:
  Father was very angry and upset with me.
  पिताजी मुझसे बहुत नाराज़ थे।
- I have **never felt better**:
  I am feeling absolutely fine.
  मैं बहुत अच्छा महसूस कर रहा हूँ।
- He was **pleased as punch** with the idea:
  He was extremely delighted with the idea.
  उस उपाय पर वह बहुत प्रसन्न हुआ।/उस विचार ने उसे खुश कर दिया।
- He felt he was **set up** by his friends:
  He felt his friends had deliberately got him into trouble.
  उसे लगा कि उसके दोस्तों ने उसे जानबूझकर फँसाया है।
- He felt as if his tongue was **on fire**:
  His tongue was burning.
  उसकी जुबान जल रही थी।
- He **felt zonked** after a **hard day's work**:
  He felt totally drained after working hard for the entire day.
  सारा दिन काम करके वह बुरी तरह से थक गया था।
- The police **play their own games**:
  The police are not to be trusted as they have their own vested interests.
  पुलिस पर भरोसा नहीं किया जा सकता क्योंकि उनका अपना स्वार्थ इसमें छिपा हुआ है।
- He was **beside himself with rage**:
  He was extremely angry and beyond control.
  वह गुस्से से पागल हो गया था।

- He wanted to **drive his guilt away**:
  He wanted to be freed of his guilt.
  वह अपने अपराधबोध से मुक्त होना चाहता था।
- He was **white with anger**:
  He got very angry.
  वह बहुत गुस्से में है।
- The Russians were **very frosty**:
  The Russians were most unfriendly and aloof.
  रूसी अजनबियों की तरह बहुत ही रूखा व्यवहार कर रहे थे।
- There was **an edge** to his voice:
  His voice was very sharp.
  उसकी आवाज़ बहुत तीखी थी।
- **The light of combat was in his eyes:**
  He wanted to fight it out.
  वह लड़ने के लिए पूरी तरह तैयार था।
- His **mood darkened** on seeing her:
  His mood turned bad when he saw her.
  उसको देखकर उसका मुँह बन गया।
- She wanted to catch him by the **scruff of his neck**:
  She wanted to grab him by the collar.
  वह उसे कॉलर से पकड़ लेना चाहती थी।
- **Her spirits zoomed again:**
  She felt much better again.
  वह फिर से बहुत अच्छा महसूस करने लगी।
- I was **awestruck**:
  I was very impressed.
  मैं बहुत प्रभावित हुआ।
- She was stung by the **false accusations** aimed at her:
  She was very angry and hurt by the false charges levelled at her.
  वह अपने ऊपर लगे आरोपों से बहुत दुःखी थी।
- **He was in knots:**
  He was totally confused and did not know what to do.
  वह पूरी तरह उलझ गया था और समझ नहीं पा रहा था कि क्या करे।

- It broke his heart to see **his dreams fading**:
  He felt dejected and heartbroken on realising his dreams would not be fulfilled.
  जब उसे पता चला कि उसके सपने पूरे नहीं हो पाएँगे उसका दिल बहुत दुःखी हो गया।
- It **was unnerving**:
  It was very scary.
  वह बहुत डरावना था।
- **He allowed no trace of recognition to cross his face:**
  He did not show that he knew her.
  उसने जाहिर नहीं किया कि वह उसे जानता था।
- He was **totally isolated** by everyone:
  Everyone avoided him totally.
  हर किसी ने उसकी उपेक्षा की।
- I am tired and want to **hit the sack**:
  I am tired and wish to sleep.
  मैं थका हुआ हूँ और सोना चाहता हूँ।
- He was **seething with anger**:
  He was bursting with anger.
  वह गुस्से से भरा हुआ था।
- He was **mad as a hornet**:
  He was as angry as a bee.
  वह बहुत क्रोधित था। / वह लाल-पीला हो रहा था।
- **He remained reticent during the crisis:**
  He spoke very little during the crisis.
  वह समस्या के समय ख़ामोश रहा।
- The crowd **went on a rampage**:
  The crowd became violent and broke everything in sight.
  भीड़ हंगामे पर उतारू हो गई।
- He **kept to himself** at the party:
  He was quiet at the party and avoided mixing with others.
  वह पार्टी में गुमसुम अकेला खड़ा था।

- She was **petrified and stood still**:
  She was very scared and didn't move.
  वह डर के कारण हिल न सकी।
- **Tension pervaded the room:**
  The entire room was very tense.
  सारा कमरा तनावग्रस्त था।
- **I was perplexed by his shocking behaviour:**
  I was surprised by his unexpected behaviour.
  उसके शर्मनाक व्यवहार से मैं हैरान था।
- His **behaviour was outrageous**:
  His behaviour was very shocking.
  उसका व्यवहार बहुत बीभत्स था।
- It brought back lots of **nostalgic memories**:
  It reminded us of the good old times.
  इसने न जाने कितनी पुरानी यादें ताज़ा कर दी।
- **His response flummoxed me:**
  His answer totally surprised me.
  उसके उत्तर से मुझे हैरानी हुई।
- He is always a little **wired up**:
  He is always a little edgy/nervous.
  वह हमेशा ही कुछ घबराया-सा रहता है।
- I will **give my right arm** for it:
  I am willing to do anything for it.
  मैं इसके लिए कुछ भी कर सकता हूँ।
- I **freak out** on good food:
  I love eating good food.
  मुझे अच्छा खाना बहुत पसंद है।
- He **got psyched out** and lost the battle:
  He was defeated because he lost courage.
  हिम्मत हारने के कारण जंग में उसकी हार हो गई।
- **Happy days are here again:**
  The good times are now back.
  अब अच्छे दिन वापस लौट आए।

- It's given me a **big jolt**:
  It has given me a big shock.
  इसने मुझे ज़ोर का झटका दिया है।
- After your **pep talk** he felt **pumped up**:
  After you motivated him he was fully charged up.
  आपसे प्रेरणा पाकर उसका हौसला बढ़ गया।
- **His mood was upbeat:**
  His mood was very good.
  वह बहुत ख़ुश था।
- He is on **cloud nine**:
  He is extremely excited and happy.
  उसकी ख़ुशी सातवें आसमान पर थी।
- **He was euphoric** on winning the game:
  He was overjoyed on winning the game.
  खेल जीतने के कारण वह फूला नहीं समा रहा था।
- He started **shaking in his boots**:
  He was shivering with fright.
  वह डर के मारे काँपने लगा।
- I have **butterflies in my stomach**:
  I am very nervous.
  मैं बहुत घबराया हुआ हूँ।
- **He was disdainful with her:**
  He showed her no respect.
  उसने उसके प्रति कोई सम्मान नहीं दिखाया।
- He **blinked in disbelief**:
  He couldn't believe his eyes.
  उसे अपनी आँखों पर भरोसा नहीं हुआ।/उसे बहुत आश्चर्य हुआ।
- You must **learn the ropes**:
  You must learn the way of doing things.
  आपको काम करने का तरीका सीखना ही होगा।
- I **don't deserve your scorn**:
  I don't deserve to be treated so badly by you.
  मुझसे आप इस तरह बर्ताव नहीं कर सकते।

- **Don't go overboard:**
  Don't overdo things.
  हद से बढ़कर मत करो।
- He **berated himself** for being such a bad father:
  He scolded himself for not being a good father.
  उसने एक बुरा पिता होने के कारण अपने आपको बहुत कोसा।
- A smile **crossed his face**:
  He began smiling.
  वह मुस्कुराने लगा।
- His **calm demeanour was a facade**:
  His calm exterior was just a pretence.
  उसका शांत व्यवहार एक धोखा था।
- He tried to **drown his grief** in every bar across town:
  He tried to forget his sorrow by drinking in different bars all over the city.
  अपने दुःख को भुलाने की कोशिश में उसने शहर के हर शराबघर में शराब पी।
- **Even in anguish there was pride:**
  Despite his grief, he was still proud.
  अत्यन्त दुःख झेलने के बाद भी उसके स्वाभिमान में कमी नहीं आई।
- He **made no bones about** his dislike for Americans:
  He did not hide his dislike for Americans and was not apologetic about it.
  उससे अमरीकी लोगों के प्रति अपनी घृणा छिपाई नहीं गई।
- He sank deeper into a **slough of despond**:
  He went further into despair and depression.
  वह दुःख की गहराइयों में डूब गया।
- **All the false messiahs fell:**
  All the false gurus failed.
  सभी गुरुघंटाल नाकाम रहे।
- **He wilted under pressure:**
  He couldn't stand the pressure.
  वह दबाव का सामना नहीं कर पाया।

- **Little by little she divorced herself from grief:**
  Slowly she forgot her grief.
  धीरे-धीरे वह अपना दुःख भूल गई।
- I can't **put on a front all** the time:
  I can't pretend all the time.
  मैं हमेशा बहाने नहीं बना सकता।
- His mouth **went dry**:
  He was nervous.
  वह घबरा गया।
- The words **rained down** on him like a blow:
  The news hit him very hard.
  खबर सुनकर उसे बहुत दुःख पहुँचा।
- You are in for a **rude awakening**:
  You will get a rude shock.
  आपको एक बुरा झटका लगेगा।/आपको ज़ोर का झटका लग सकता है।
- He is **absorbed in his own thoughts**:
  He is thinking about something.
  वह कुछ सोच रहा है।/उसके दिमाग में कुछ चल रहा है।
- She is too **sensitive to criticism**:
  She cannot take criticism.
  वह इतनी संवेदनशील है कि आलोचना नहीं सुन सकती।
- **He is devoid of emotional warmth:**
  He lacks feelings.
  वह भावनाशून्य व्यक्ति है।/वह संवेदनशील नहीं है।
- **He refuses to be vanquished:**
  He will not accept defeat.
  वह हार नहीं मान सकता।
- Old memories of this will always come **back to haunt you**:
  Old memories will come back and always trouble you.
  पुरानी यादें हमेशा वापस आ-आ के तुमको दुखी करेंगी।
- **It was a nightmarish situation:**
  It was a very bad situation.
  वह एक भयावह स्थिति थी।

- He puts on **an air of dignity**:
He tries to look very dignified.
उसने स्वयं को शानदार ढँग से प्रस्तुत करने का प्रयास किया।

- He **cried out against the injustice**:
He protested against the injustice.
उसने अन्याय के विरुद्ध आवाज़ उठाई।

- He **is undergoing great mental agony**:
He is under great mental stress.
वह गहरी मानसिक पीड़ा से गुज़र रहा है।

- **The convergence of different pressures will eventually break him:**
Simultaneous pressures from all sides will finally be too much for him to handle.
एक ही समय में अत्यधिक दबाव से एक वक़्त ऐसा आ जाएगा कि फिर उसे सँभाल पाना उसके लिए मुश्किल हो जाएगा।

- It came like a **shot of adrenalin** for him:
It boosted his courage and motivation like an injection.
इससे उसे हिम्मत और हौसला मिला।

- **She has been yearning for this freedom:**
She has wanted this freedom badly.
उसे इस आज़ादी की सख्त ज़रूरत थी।

- He **took this to heart and suffered a stroke:**
He was extremely upset by this and suffered a paralytic stroke.
उसे इस बात का इतना दुःख पहुँचा कि उसे पक्षाघात/पैरालिसिस हो गया।

- There is **no love lost between them**:
They are not on the best of terms with each other.
अब उनके संबंधों में मिठास नहीं रही।

- **Torn apart** by the pain of losing his son, he became a **recluse**:
He couldn't bear the pain of losing his son and avoided everyone, keeping to himself.
अपने पुत्र के शोक में उसने अपने आपको सबसे दूर कर लिया।

- It has **shaken my confidence** in him:
I no longer trust him due to this.
इस बात से मेरा उस पर से विश्वास उठ गया है।

- **He was groping for words:**
  He couldn't find words to express himself.
  वह अपनी बात व्यक्त नहीं कर पा रहा था।
- She **gave a cold shoulder to his advances:**
  She ignored his attempts to woo her.
  उसने अपने प्रति उसके बढ़ते कदमों पर ध्यान नहीं दिया।
- She has **fallen for him**:
  She is in love with him.
  उसे उससे प्यार हो गया है।
- This will **blow his fuse off**:
  This will make him very angry.
  इस बात से वह बहुत क्रोधित हो गया।
- **He is badly smitten by her:**
  He is totally infatuated with her.
  वह उसके प्यार में पागल हो गया है।
- He still **carries the torch** for her:
  He still loves her although she isn't interested.
  वह आज भी उसे प्यार करता है, यह जानते हुए भी कि वह उसे प्यार नहीं करती।
- **She felt a bit randy:**
  She was sexually aroused.
  वह यौन उत्तेजना से भर गई।
- **I got peeved**:
  I was irritated.
  मुझे चिढ़ होने लगी।/मैं चिड़चिड़ा हो उठा।
- **I got mushy with her:**
  I got sentimental with her.
  मैं उसके साथ भावनाओं में बह गया।
- She will **hit the ceiling**:
  She will get furious.
  वह गुस्सा हो जाएगी।

- **Don't get physical:**
  Don't touch me.
  मुझे न छुएँ।/शारीरिक रूप से मेरे करीब न आएँ।
- She was **floating on air**:
  She was ecstatic.
  उसकी ख़ुशी का ठिकाना नहीं रहा।
- She was in **seventh heaven**:
  She was excited and full of joy.
  उसकी ख़ुशी सातवें आसमान को पार कर गई।
- **She is always deadpan:**
  She has an expressionless face.
  उसके सपाट चेहरे पर कोई भाव नहीं आते।
- She will **cut no ice** with him:
  She won't be able to get any closer to him.
  वह उसके करीब नहीं जा सकेगी।
- I am **cut up** with him:
  I am angry with him.
  मैं उससे नाराज़ हूँ।
- I don't **share good vibes** with him:
  I don't get along well with him.
  मेरी उससे नहीं बनती।/मेरा उसके साथ चलना मुश्किल है।
- **You don't know my predicament:**
  You don't know what my problem is.
  आपको मेरी समस्या नहीं पता है।
- **I have a penchant** for movies:
  I am very fond of movies.
  मुझे फिल्में देखना बहुत पसंद है।
- I will **be mortified if** defeated by him:
  I will be horrified and die of shame if he defeats me.
  अगर उससे हार हुई तो ये मेरे लिए शर्मनाक बात होगी।
- His mood is **blow hot blow cold**:
  His mood keeps fluctuating from good to bad and vice-versa.
  उसका मूड बनता-बिगड़ता रहता है।

- **I loathe him:**
  I detest/hate him.
  मुझे उससे बहुत नफ़रत है।
- The **daily grind** is killing me:
  The tough daily routine is too much for me.
  इस व्यस्त दिनचर्या से मेरी जान निकली जा रही है।
- She was **jilted by** her lover:
  Her lover ditched her.
  उसके प्रेमी ने उसे धोखा दे दिया।
- If he comes to know of it he will **turn green with envy**:
  If he comes to know this he will be very jealous.
  अगर उसे इस बारे में पता चला तो उसे बहुत जलन होगी।
- I am still suffering from **last night's hangover**:
  I have a headache and am feeling uneasy because of last night's drinks.
  कल रात की शराब के कारण मुझे सरदर्द है और कुछ चक्कर-से आ रहे हैं।
- I am **feeling groggy**:
  I am feeling dazed and unsteady due to the effect of alcohol.
  शराब के नशे के कारण में बेहोश-सा हो रहा हूँ
- He was **in a murderous frenzy**:
  He was in a terrible and murderous mood.
  वह खून करने पर उतारू था।
- **He is the most complexed person:**
  He is very difficult to understand and get along with.
  वह बहुत ही पेचीदा किस्म का इंसान है।/उसको समझ पाना आसान नहीं।
- **I am allergic to her:**
  I don't like her at all and cannot get along with her.
  मैं उसे पसंद नहीं करता इसलिए उसके साथ नहीं निभा सकता।
- **He is a malicious character:**
  He is full of hatred and negative feelings.
  वह एक बुरा व्यक्ति है।/वह एक दुर्भावनाग्रस्त व्यक्ति है।

- There was some **flicker of hope**, despite the problem:
  In spite of the trouble, it seemed there were some chances.
  समस्या के बाद भी सफलता की आशा बची हुई थी।
- I am **dog-tired**:
  I am exhausted.
  मैं बुरी तरह से थका हुआ हूँ।
- His **face dropped** in his hands in **utter defeat**:
  He held his face in his hands, totally defeated.
  उसने हार मानकर अपना सिर पकड़ लिया।
- She **was agog** with excitement:
  She was very excited.
  वह ख़ुशी से पागल हो रही थी।
- She was suddenly **flooded** with emotions:
  She suddenly felt very emotional.
  अचानक ही वह बहुत भावुक हो उठी।
- For a **fleeting moment** he had a **twinge** of conscience:
  For a moment, he felt guilty.
  एक क्षण के लिए उसे लगा कि उसने गलत किया है।
- **She admired his candour:**
  She admired his frankness.
  उसकी साफ़गोई की उसने तारीफ़ की।
- **Livid with rage**, he cursed her **roundly**:
  He was filled with anger and cursed her in every way.
  गुस्से से भरकर उसने उसे बहुत गालियाँ दीं।
- She would match him **fury for fury and passion for passion**:
  She was an equal for him in every way.
  उसके लिए वह सब तरह से टक्कर की थी।
- He **blurted out** an **awkward apology**:
  He hurriedly said sorry, feeling very embarrassed.
  बहुत शर्मिंदा होकर उसने क्षमायाचना की।

- I can't **put my finger** on it:
  I know there is something wrong but cannot pinpoint it.
  मुझे समझ में आ रहा है कि कुछ गड़बड़ है, पर क्या गड़बड़ है, ये समझ में नहीं आ रहा।
- They are **at daggers drawn**:
  They are at war with each other.
  वे आपस में कट्टर दुश्मन हैं।
- The celebrations are **now in full swing**:
  The celebrations are currently on in a big way.
  उत्सव का रंग अपने शबाब पर था।
- He is always **building castles in the air**:
  He is always making fancy plans that have no chance of succeeding.
  वह हमेशा हवाई किले बनाता रहता है।/वह हमेशा बड़े-बड़े सपने देखता रहता है।
- The situation was one **of total chaos**:
  The situation was filled with absolute confusion.
  हालत ये थी कि सब गड़बड़झाला बन चुका था।/हालत ये थी कि सब कुछ उलझा हुआ लग रहा था।

8. Personality Traits

- It was her **carriage** that **turned heads**:
  It was her manner of walking that attracted attention.
  उसके चलने के अंदाज़ से लोग उसकी ओर देखने को मंजबूर हो जाते थे।

- She still **cuts an attractive figure** for her age:
  She is still beautiful despite her age.
  अपनी उम्र के बाद भी वह सुन्दर है।

- **He is a fox**:
  He is cunning and untrustworthy.
  वह बहुत ही चालाक और धूर्त है।

- He is **totally unscrupulous** and could trade his own mother:
  He has no principles whatsoever and could even sell his own mother.
  उसका कोई उसूल नहीं है, अपने मतलब के लिए वह कुछ भी कर सकता है।

- His word **carries weight**:
  He is very influential.
  वह बहुत प्रभावशाली है।

- She is cute **in her own way**:
  She has her own charm.
  उसका आकर्षण अलग किस्म का है।

- He can afford to **go by his whims**:
  He can do whatever he pleases.
  वह जो चाहे कर सकता है।

- He is a **pain in the neck**:
  He is a very annoying man.
  वह अपने आपमें एक सिरदर्द है/समस्या है।

- He still commands a **modicum of respect**:
  He is still respected to some extent.
  उसे अभी भी कुछ सम्मान मिलता है।

- He has **become a total wreck**:
  He is a totally broken man who has lost all hope.
  वह एक पूरी तरह से टूटा हुआ इंसान है।
- She **had no stomach** to run the business:
  She had no inclination or capability to run the business.
  उसके अन्दर व्यवसाय को चलाने की शक्ति/योग्यता नहीं है।
- **Be wary** of him:
  Be careful.
  उससे सावधान रहना।
- He is too **cocksure** and needs to be **pulled down a notch**:
  He is overconfident and must be knocked down a little.
  वह अति-आत्मविश्वासी है इसलिए उसे एक बार तो हार का मुँह देखना ही पड़ेगा।
- **He is a hideous man:**
  He is a hateful man.
  वह एक घृणित आदमी है।
- He is a **black sheep**:
  He is the one bad person in the group.
  वह इस समूह में इकलौता बुरा इंसान है।
- He turned out to **be the dark horse**:
  He turned out to be a winner against everyone's expectations.
  वह तो छुपारुस्तम निकला।/उसने सफलता हासिल करके सबको हैरान कर दिया।
- He **keeps abreast of the times**:
  He follows the latest trends.
  वह समय के साथ चलने वाला इंसान है।
- He has the **gift of the gab**:
  He has a quick tongue and can speak fluently on any topic.
  बोलने में तो उसे महारथ हासिल है।
- He is a **chip of the old block**:
  He is just like his father.
  वह बिलकुल अपने पिता जैसा है।

- She knows how to **wrap men around her little finger**:
  She has the ability to make use of men.
  उसे लोगों को अपनी उँगलियों पर नचाना आता है।

- She could **start a fight in an empty house**:
  She is a quarrelsome lady.
  वह बहुत झगड़ालू औरत है।

- He will **carve a tidy niche** for himself:
  He will become famous and successful.
  वह प्रसिद्ध और सफल होगा।

- She **calls for attention**:
  She is worthy of being looked at.
  वह इतनी सुन्दर है कि कोई उसे देखे बिना रह ही नहीं सकता।

- He has **gone heavily on** the bottle:
  He has started drinking heavily.
  उसने बहुत शराब पीनी शुरू कर दी है।

- **He is an incoherent speaker:**
  He doesn't speak clearly.
  वह साफ़-साफ़ नहीं बोलता।

- She is only **skin and bones**:
  She is very thin.
  वह बहुत पतली-दुबली है।

- He is **a born loser**:
  He has a totally negative attitude and always ends up losing.
  उसका नकारात्मक दृष्टिकोण उसके जीवन की हर असफलता में भी दिखाई देता है।

- He is **stiff as a board**:
  He is not flexible.
  वह बहुत कठोर है।

- He was **caught in a time warp**:
  He was old-fashioned and did not move with the times.
  वह एक पुरातनपंथी व्यक्ति है जो समय के साथ आगे बढ़ना पसंद नहीं करता।

- We are **a canny and clever lot**:
  We are smart people.
  हम चतुर लोग हैं।
- **He is like a zombie:**
  He is like a dead or drugged person.
  वह तो ज़िंदा लाश जैसा है।
- There is **not a drop** of Congress blood in his body:
  He is definitely not a Congressman.
  वह किसी तरह से कांग्रेसी नहीं है।
- He is a **publicity hound**:
  He **hankers** for publicity.
  वह लोकप्रिय होने के लिए मरता है।
- He never **lets** anyone **in on his secrets**:
  He doesn't reveal his plans to anybody.
  वह अपनी योजनाएँ किसी को नहीं बताता।
- Once he is **into full stride**, there is **no stopping him**:
  Once he is into the full flow of things, nobody can beat him.
  एक बार वह शुरू हो जाए तो फिर उसको पीछे कर पाना किसी के बस की बात नहीं।
- She **sticks out like a sore thumb**:
  She is a total misfit.
  वह बिलकुल ही अयोग्य है।
- He is an **early bird**:
  He gets up early/begins his tasks early.
  वह पहले आकर ही बाज़ी मार लेता है।
- He is not given to **overt display of emotion**:
  He does not reveal his true feelings.
  वह अपने मन की बात किसी को नहीं बताता।
- She is **a workaholic**:
  She has to work all the while and cannot do without work.
  उसे काम करना बहुत पंसद है, वह काम किए बिना रह ही नहीं सकती।

- She is **stationed in** the Middle East:
  She has been posted on duty in the Gulf.
  उसकी खाड़ी में नियुक्ति हुई है।

- She has **crow's feet**:
  She has dark circles under her eyes.
  उसके आँखों के नीचे कालापन है।

- He was **totally stoned**:
  He was not at all in his senses and under the influence of drugs/alcohol.
  वह नशे में पूरी तरह धुत था।

- He hasn't a **mean bone** in his body:
  He is not at all mean.
  वह घटिया किस्म का इन्सान नहीं है।

- The son was **cut out of another mould**:
  He was totally different from his father.
  वह अपने पिता के बिलकुल विपरीत था।

- He **plans like a surgeon**:
  He is a meticulous planner.
  वह बहुत अच्छी योजनाएँ बनाता है।

- He was a **scion of the royal family**:
  He is a son of the royal family.
  वह राजपरिवार से सम्बंधित था। / वह राजवंश का एक वारिस था।

- He was a **tactician of rare acumen**:
  He was a brilliant tactician.
  वह बहुत ही अच्छा रणनीतिज्ञ था।

- The **odds** were totally **stacked against him**:
  All the chances were totally against him.
  सभी संभावनाएँ उसके प्रतिकूल थीं। / परिस्थितियाँ उसके अनुकूल नहीं थीं।

- She will not **go back on her words**:
  She is a reliable person and will stick to her promise.
  वह भरोसेमंद है और अपने वादे पर कायम रहेगी। / वह अपने वादे से नहीं मुकरेगी।

- He was **made of sterner stuff**:
  He was a tough man.
  उसको आसानी से दबाना मुश्किल था।
- She will not **be my first choice** to do the business:
  She will not be the first person I choose to do business with.
  वह साथ में व्यवसाय करने के लिए मेरी पहली पसंद नहीं होगी।
- He has not **lost his touch**:
  He is still good/efficient.
  वह अभी भी अच्छा है।/वह अभी तक अच्छा है।
- She likes to **steer the ship**:
  She likes to be in control.
  वह नियंत्रण में रहना पसंद करती है।
- He likes **to call the shots**:
  He likes to do things his way and control the situation.
  वह चीज़ों को आज़ादी के साथ अपने हिसाब से करना पसंद करता है।
- He is **an art buff**:
  He loves things related to art.
  वह कलात्मक वस्तुओं को बहुत पसंद करता है।
- He **places infinite value on** education:
  He gives lots of importance to education.
  वह शिक्षा को काफ़ी महत्त्व देता है।
- You are the most beautiful thing I have **laid my eyes upon**:
  You are the most beautiful woman I have seen.
  अब तक मैंने अपने जीवन में जितनी भी महिलाएँ देखी हैं तुम उनमें सबसे सुन्दर हो।
- There is **no reasoning** with him now:
  He will not listen to any viewpoint now.
  वह अब किसी भी विचार को सुनना नहीं चाहता।
- He has gone **belly-up**:
  He has gone bankrupt.
  वह कंगाल हो चुका है।/वह दिवालिया हो गया है।

- He is **still a toddler**:
He is still a baby.
वह अभी भी बच्चा है।

- He is **numero uno**:
He is the best/number one.
वह सर्वोत्तम है। / वह सबसे आगे है।

- He is such **a blabbermouth**:
He speaks too much.
वह बड़बोला किस्म का आदमी है।

- **He is a smart alec:**
He is an oversmart fellow.
वह कुछ ज्यादा ही चतुर बनता है।

- He is **flat as a pancake**:
He is a boring man.
वह बहुत उबाऊ व्यक्ति है।

- He will **botch up** the operations:
He will mess up the venture.
वह काम ख़राब कर देगा।

- He is quite **a handsome dude**:
He is a handsome man.
वह बहुत सुन्दर आदमी है।

- He is **quite brazen**:
He is quite bold and shameless.
वह काफ़ी निर्लज्ज किस्म का है।

- He **knows his marbles**:
He is a capable man and knows the job.
उसे अपना काम आता है।

- She **does things by halves**:
She is careless in her work.
वह अपने काम में लापरवाह है।

- He is an **astute character**:
He is a sharp man.
वह एक चतुर व्यक्ति है।

- He has a **laid-back attitude**:
  He is very casual in his approach.
  वह लापरवाह किस्म का व्यक्ति है।
- She does not **have her head on her shoulders**:
  She is not in her proper senses and does not know what she is doing.
  वह अपने आपे में नहीं है इसलिए उसे सही-गलत की पहचान नहीं है।
- He is quite a **clumsy and uncouth** fellow:
  He is a foolish and vulgar person.
  वह एक बेवक़ूफ़ और घटिया किस्म का इंसान है।
- He is likely to **go along with the crowd**:
  He will comply with the majority decision.
  वह सर्वसम्मति का ही साथ देगा।/जो फ़ैसला सबका होगा वही उसे मान्य होगा।
- He is **a debauched** man:
  He is a man with wicked habits.
  वह आदमी बुरी आदतों का शिकार है।
- He is a **spent force**:
  He is finished.
  उसकी शक्ति ख़त्म हो चुकी है।
- **He is obsessed with making money:**
  He is only concerned with making money.
  उसे पैसा कमाने का जुनून है।
- He wants to **mint money:**
  He wants to earn lots of money.
  वह बहुत धन कमाना चाहता है।
- **He is generous to a fault:**
  He is too generous and will suffer for it.
  वह इतना शरीफ़ है कि उसको ये तकलीफ़ उठानी ही पड़ेगी।
- He **made his mark** at an early age:
  He was recognised for his talent when still young.
  वह कम उम्र में ही सफलता की सीढ़ी चढ़ने लगा है।

- He **has his heart in the right place**:
He is very sincere.
वह बहुत ही सच्चा है।
- He is **every inch** a gentleman:
He is a thorough gentleman.
वह बहुत शरीफ़ इंसान है।
- He is **head and shoulders above** his classmates:
He is far better than his classmates.
वह अपनी कक्षा में दूसरों से बेहतर है।
- He will have **to be led by the nose**:
He will not do things on his own and will have to be prodded into it.
वह अपने आप काम नहीं करता, उससे काम कराना पड़ता है।
- He is not quite **up to the mark**:
He is not good enough.
वह बहुत अच्छा नहीं है।
- He seems to be **well off**:
He is quite rich.
वह बहुत धनी है।
- **He learned by rote**:
He learned by mugging things up.
वह रटकर चीज़ों को सीखता था।
- It's hard **to get along with** such a **finicky** man:
It is difficult to adjust with such a fussy man.
ऐसे नखचढ़े इंसान के साथ निभाना बहुत मुश्किल है।
- **He always seems harried:**
He always looks worried.
वह हमेशा चिंतित दिखाई देता है।
- She is a **real doll**:
She is such a sweet person.
वह बहुत प्यारी बच्ची है।
- He is **bursting with** goodwill:
He is always thinking about the good of others.
वह हमेशा दूसरों के बारे में सोचता है।

- His self-control **is fragile**:
  He doesn't have any self-control.
  उसका स्वयं पर कोई नियंत्रण नहीं है।
- He is like **a cat on the prowl**:
  He is like a hungry person looking for something to grab.
  वह भूखे की तरह झपट्टा मारने को तैयार है।
- He is just **a glib talker**:
  He just talks nicely and makes empty promises.
  वह बस बड़ी-बड़ी बातें करता है।/वह बड़े बोल बोलता है।
- He is **a con man**:
  He specialises in cheating people.
  वह एक ठग है।/उसे दूसरों को ठगने में महारथ हासिल है।
- She has **turned a new leaf**:
  She has changed totally for the better.
  वह पूरी तरह से बदल गई है।
- He is **sitting on the fence**:
  He is undecided.
  वह फ़ैसला नहीं ले पा रहा है।/वह नहीं समझ पा रहा कि उसके लिए क्या अच्छा है और क्या बुरा।
- He is **in high spirits**:
  He is in a good, happy mood.
  वह बहुत अच्छे मूड में है।/वह बहुत ख़ुश है।
- Politics **runs in his blood**:
  He is a very political man.
  राजनीति तो उसके खून में है।/वह एक कुशल राजनीतिज्ञ है।
- She was **born with a silver spoon** in her mouth:
  She was born to rich parents.
  वह एक अमीर घर में पैदा हुई थी।
- He is a **man of substance**:
  He is a man of strong character.
  वह एक चरित्रवान व्यक्ति है।

- He is **a wolf in sheep's clothing**:
  He is a deceptive chap and not what he seems to be.
  वह भेड़ की खाल में भेड़िया है।/वह बिलकुल भरोसे के लायक नहीं है।
- He is **under the thumb** of his wife:
  His wife controls him.
  वह अपनी पत्नी के इशारों पर नाचता है।
- **He is henpecked**:
  He is afraid of his wife and is dominated by her.
  वह जोरू का गुलाम है।
- She **excels in** dancing:
  She is a very good dancer.
  वह एक बहुत अच्छी नर्तकी/डांसर है।
- He always **sits on his high horse**:
  He is very snobbish and proud.
  वह हमेशा अपनी अकड़ में रहता है।
- He is **a dunce** in maths:
  He is totally useless in maths.
  वह गणित में एकदम फिसड्डी है।
- He is **too miserly to part with** his money:
  He will never spend money, as he is a miser.
  वह पैसे के मामले में बहुत ज़्यादा कंजूस है।
- He would get **roaring drunk**:
  He would get totally drunk.
  वह पूरी तरह से नशे में धुत हो जाएगा।
- He is **always loaded**:
  He always has money with him.
  उसके पास हमेशा पैसे रहते हैं।
- He is **a man with a mission**:
  He is totally focused on what he wants to do.
  उसका ध्यान हमेशा अपने काम पर रहता है।
- He **seemed normal on the surface**:
  Nothing looked abnormal about him.
  वैसे तो वह सामान्य लग रहा था।

- He can **sell a refrigerator to an Eskimo**:
  He is an excellent salesman.
  वह बहुत अच्छा विक्रेता है।
- He is a **devious fellow**:
  He is a cunning and untrustworthy person.
  वह एक धूर्त व्यक्ति है।
- He was **a nonentity**:
  He had no importance whatsoever.
  उसका होना न होना बराबर है।/उसका कोई महत्त्व नहीं है।
- She **plays by the rules**:
  She is disciplined and sticks to the rules.
  वह बहुत नियम-कायदे वाली है।
- He **lived by his wits**:
  He used common sense to survive.
  उसने अपने विवेक से अपने को बचा लिया।
- **He is cockeyed**:
  He is squint-eyed.
  उसकी आँखें भेंगी हैं।
- He cannot **hold his drinks**:
  He gets drunk very fast.
  वह बहुत जल्दी नशे में आ जाता है।
- He **keeps off the beaten** track:
  He doesn't like to do what everyone else is doing.
  वह लकीर का फ़क़ीर नहीं है।
- **He is a wizard**:
  He is exceptional.
  वह बहुत ही प्रतिभाशाली है।/वह तो जादूगर है।
- **He is an eyesore:**
  He is difficult to put up with.
  उसके साथ रहना तो बड़ा मुश्किल है।
- He has **run out of steam**:
  He doesn't have any enthusiasm/energy.
  उसके पास अब ताकत नहीं बची।

- **He is a glutton:**
  He eats a lot/is very greedy.
  वह तो बहुत ही भुक्खड़ है।/वह बहुत लालची है।
- She is **drop-dead gorgeous**:
  She is extremely beautiful.
  वह बहुत ज़्यादा सुन्दर है।
- She has **irresistible charm**:
  It is difficult to resist her charms.
  उसके सौन्दर्य को देखकर तो मुग्ध हुए बिना रहा ही नहीं जा सकता।
- **He is a headstrong fellow:**
  He does what he wants and does not listen to anyone.
  वह बहुत ही ज़िद्दी इंसान है।
- He is **on his last legs**:
  He is nearing his end.
  वह अपने अंत के समीप है।
- He was a **henchman of the don**:
  He was one of the followers of the gang leader.
  वह उस अपराधी सरदार का वफ़ादार है।
- **He is quite an inane fellow:**
  He is a senseless man.
  वह काफ़ी बेहूदा किस्म का आदमी है।
- **He daydreams the whole day long:**
  He keeps dreaming or building castles in the air throughout the day.
  वह सारे दिन आसमानी ख़्वाब देखता रहता है।/वह दिनभर हवाई किले बनाता रहता है।
- She is **no great shakes**:
  She is just an ordinary person.
  वह बस एक साधारण-सी औरत है।
- **This boy is gauche:**
  This boy is clumsy/tactless.
  वह एक अशिष्ट लड़का है।
- He is such a **raunchy fellow:**
  He is a man who uses sexually explicit language.
  वह बहुत विलासी व्यक्ति है।

- He is **a maverick**:
  He is a rebel.
  वह एक विद्रोही/बाग़ी है।
- He is a **total greenhorn**:
  He is very inexperienced.
  वह बिलकुल नौसिखिया है।
- He has **gone off his rocker**:
  He has gone mad.
  वह पागल हो गया है।
- Be careful, he is an **insidious fellow**:
  Be careful since he is not a reliable man and could play dirty tricks.
  इस धोखेबाज़ व्यक्ति से सावधान रहो।
- He is such **an insipid chap:**
  He is an uninspiring and boring man.
  वह बहुत उबाऊ आदमी है।
- She is **a traffic stopper**:
  She has stunning looks.
  वह बहुत अधिक सुंदर है।
- She is **quick on the uptake**:
  She is sharp and quick to grasp the point.
  वह बहुत जल्दी समझ/सीख लेती है।
- **He is lacklustre**:
  He has no enthusiasm at all.
  वह बहुत ही थका हुआ है।
- He is a **ladies' man**:
  The ladies like him and he is always in their company.
  वह औरतों में बहुत ही लोकप्रिय है।
- He is a **bloody crook**:
  He is a cheat.
  वह बहुत बड़ा ठग है।
- He loves to remain on **centre-stage**:
  He loves to be at the centre of attention.
  वह हर जगह केन्द्रबिन्दु बनकर रहना चाहता है।

- **He is a business tycoon/magnate:**
  He is a big businessman.
  वह एक बड़ा उद्योगपति है।
- He died **in the prime of life**:
  He died when young/at the peak of his career.
  उसकी मृत्यु युवावस्था में ही हो गई।
- **He is a big malingerer:**
  He fakes injury or illness to escape work.
  वह तो कामचोर है।
- He **has a bleeding heart**:
  He is a soft person who gets fooled by others.
  वह एक सीधा आदमी है जो दूसरों से बेवक़ूफ़ बनता रहता है।
- He has **fire in his belly**:
  He is a passionate and ambitious person.
  वह बहुत ही महत्त्वाकांक्षी व्यक्ति है।
- He is a **handsome hunk**:
  He is a handsome man.
  वह एक बांका छैला है।
- He **has reached his nadir**:
  He has reached his lowest point.
  वह अपने सबसे निचले स्तर पर आ गया।
- He is the **new kid on the block**:
  He is the latest sensation.
  वह एक नई सनसनी के तौर पर यहाँ आया है।
- He is a **bloody nincompoop**:
  He is absolutely stupid.
  वह एकदम बेवक़ूफ़ है।
- He is an **obnoxious fellow**:
  He is a repulsive/dislikeable person.
  वह एक घृणित व्यक्ति है।
- **His demeanour was ostentatious:**
  His attitude was flashy.
  उसका रंग-ढंग एक दिखावा था।

- He never knows whether he is **coming or going**:
  He is always confused.
  वह हमेशा भ्रांतिमान-सा रहता है।
- His behaviour **is peevish**:
  His behaviour is irritating.
  उसका व्यवहार चिड़चिड़ा है।
- **He is a perfidious fellow:**
  He is not to be trusted.
  वह एक संदेहास्पद व्यक्ति है।
- The staff were running like **headless chickens**:
  The staff were running around confused, not knowing what to do.
  विभाग के कर्मचारी किंकर्तव्यविमूढ़ होकर इधर-उधर घूम रहे हैं।
- She **spoke in a plaintive voice**:
  She spoke in a sad and mournful voice.
  वह बहुत दुखी आवाज़ में बोली।
- She was **out of sorts**:
  She was not in the best touch/mood.
  वह अच्छे मिजाज़ में नहीं लग रही थी।
- He **keeps ogling** girls:
  He keeps staring lustily at girls.
  वह लड़कियों को ललचाई निगाहों से देखता रहता है।
- She is very **roly-poly**:
  She is obese.
  वह बिलकुल गोलमटोल है।
- He is such a **pretentious fellow**:
  He pretends to be more important than he actually is.
  वह बहुत आडंबरी व्यक्ति है।
- He is a **proclaimed offender**:
  He has been declared a habitual criminal.
  वह एक कुख्यात अपराधी है।
- He is a **child prodigy**:
  He is a child genius.
  वह एक बाल प्रतिभा है।

- **She is precocious:**
  She is very talented for her age.
  वह अपनी उम्र से ज़्यादा प्रतिभाशाली है।

- **He uses profane language:**
  He uses foul language.
  वह अशोभनीय भाषा का प्रयोग करता है।

- **She is very promiscuous:**
  She has many sexual flings.
  उसके कई लोगों के साथ नाजायज़ संबंध हैं।

- **He believes in prophecies:**
  He believes in future predictions.
  वह भविष्यवाणी में विश्वास करता है।

- He was **a psychopath**:
  He was mentally unstable and violent.
  वह एक मनोरोगी है।

- He is a **quintessential fighter**:
  He is a typical/classic fighter.
  वह एक उत्कृष्ट योद्धा है।

- They were so **aroused, they felt like ravishing** each other there and then:
  They were so sexually excited that they felt like making love there itself.
  वे इतने उत्तेजित थे कि उसी समय उनका रति-क्रिया करने का मन हो गया।

- He will **swear at the drop of a hat**:
  He uses swear/abusive words at the slightest provocation/pretext.
  वह ज़रा-ज़रा सी बात पर कसम खाने लगता है।

- He is a **renegade**:
  He is a rebel.
  वह एक विद्रोही है।

- He is very **self-righteous**:
  He feels he is always right or morally superior.
  वह हमेशा अपने को सही समझता है।

- **They are ruffians**:
  They are goondas.
  वे गुंडे हैं।
- He will not fail since he is a **seasoned fellow**:
  He is an experienced person and will not fail.
  अनुभवी होने के कारण वह असफल नहीं होगा।
- He is **very upfront**:
  He is very honest.
  वह बहुत ईमानदार है।
- He is **a sissy**:
  He is a weak, cowardly person.
  वह एक डरपोक इंसान है।/वह मेहरा/जनख़ा है।
- He is a **rugged** fellow and can **take a lot**:
  He is a tough fellow and can cope with a lot of things.
  वह बहुत कठोर व्यक्ति है और बहुत कुछ सह सकता है।
- He can take things **square on the chin**:
  He can face problems boldly.
  वह बहादुरी के साथ समस्याओं का सामना कर सकता है।
- He is a **resolute fellow**:
  He is a firm person.
  वह बहुत ही मज़बूत व्यक्ति है।
- He has got **radical thoughts**:
  He holds extreme views.
  वह बहुत अतिवादी विचारों का व्यक्ति है।
- He led a very **pompous lifestyle**:
  He led a very rich and showy life.
  वह बहुत ऐशो-आराम की ज़िन्दगी जीने वाला है।
- He has a **nonconformist attitude**:
  He does not believe in following traditions and the norm.
  वह अपरम्परावादी व्यक्ति है।
- She has the **habit of nagging** her husband:
  She has the habit of picking faults in her husband and criticising him continuously.
  उसकी अपने पति की गलतियाँ निकालकर शिकायत करने की आदत है।

- He is **the mainstay** of our office:
  He is our most efficient employee and many things depend on him.
  वह हमारे दफ़्तर का केन्द्रबिन्दु है।

- You have to always **egg him on**:
  You have to constantly motivate him.
  आपको उसे हमेशा प्रेरित करते रहना होगा।

- He **has butter fingers**:
  He has slippery hands.
  इस काम के लिए वह योग्य व्यक्ति नहीं है।

- He behaves as if he has **ants in his pants**:
  He is very fidgety and can never sit quietly.
  वह बहुत चंचल मन का है।

- He is **completely down and out**:
  He is totally defeated and de-motivated.
  वह पूरी तरह परास्त हो गया है।

- He worked in **plush surroundings**:
  He worked in very good surroundings.
  वह बहुत अच्छी जगह काम करता है।

- He will **create a ruckus**:
  He will create a very noisy scene.
  वह हंगामा मचा देगा।

- She is **on the comeback trail**:
  She is staging a return.
  वह अब वापसी कर रही है।

- He seems **to be out of the race**:
  He is no longer in contention.
  लगता है वह दौड़ से बाहर हो गया है।

- She **looked out of shape**:
  She was not physically fit.
  वह शारीरिक तौर पर अस्वस्थ लगती है।

- He tried to **put up a façade**:
  He tried to pretend and put up a false front.
  उसने नकली दिखावा करना चाहा।

- **She wears trendy dresses:**
  She wears modern/fashionable dresses.
  वह आधुनिक कपड़े पहनती है।
- He has got **one leg in the grave**:
  He is half finished/nearing his end.
  वह अपने ख़ात्मे की तरफ बढ़ रहा है।
- He has not changed **an iota** from his younger days:
  He has not changed at all since his youth.
  वह अपनी जवानी के दिनों जैसा दिख रहा है, बिलकुल नहीं बदला।
- **His forte was to keep people in high spirits:**
  He specialised in keeping people in a good mood.
  वह लोगों को प्रसन्न रखने में कुशल है।
- He always **puts a spoke in the wheel**:
  He always tries to create hurdles/obstructions.
  वह हमेशा कुछ-न-कुछ समस्या पैदा करता है।
- Recently he has **taken to drugs**:
  Recently he has started taking drugs.
  हाल ही में उसने नशे की आदत डाल ली है।
- He will always **stand up for** the weak and the **oppressed**:
  He will fight for the weak/the harassed.
  वह हमेशा पीड़ित लोगों की सहायता के लिए खड़ा रहेगा।
- I told you he is **hard of hearing**:
  I told you he couldn't hear well.
  मैंने आपको बोला था, वह अच्छी तरह नहीं सुन पाता।
- He keeps **changing colours**:
  He is unreliable and keeps changing his stand.
  वह अविश्वसनीय व्यक्ति है।
- Your bad behaviour **reflects your upbringing**:
  Your bad behaviour indicates you were brought up badly.
  तुम्हारा दुर्व्यवहार यह बताता है कि तुम्हें अच्छे संस्कार नहीं मिले हैं।

9. History, Politics and Society

- A powerful tide is **surging across** India today:
  India is experiencing a wave of new thinking.
  भारत में एक नई विचारधारा जन्म ले रही है।

- **The new civilisation is profoundly revolutionary:**
  The new civilisation thinks in a different, radical and advanced manner.
  नई सभ्यता बिलकुल विद्रोही किस्म की है।

- Indians need to take a **quantum leap forward**:
  Indians need to take giant steps to progress fast.
  भारतीयों को प्रगति की एक बड़ी छलांग की आवश्यकता है।

- A new lifestyle is **emerging on the horizon**:
  A different kind of lifestyle is coming about.
  एक नई जीवन-शैली की शुरुआत होने जा रही है।

- **Societal uncertainty** is **battering our lives** today:
  The uncertain times in modern society are making our lives difficult.
  आधुनिक समाज की अनिश्चितता हमारे लिए समस्याएँ खड़ी रह रही है।

- The **momentum of the mutiny** is still being felt:
  Even after the mutiny is over its impact is still visible.
  विद्रोह के समाप्त हो जाने के बाद आज भी विद्रोह की गूँज सुनाई पड़ रही है।

- They **grappled for control** of the municipal corporation:
  They fought to control the municipal corporation.
  उन्होंने नगर निगम को नियंत्रण में लेने के लिए लड़ाई लड़ी।

- Hindus as a society are **a fractured lot**:
  Hindu society is not united.
  हिन्दू समाज बँटा हुआ है।

- Five hundred years ago, **give or take** fifty:
  Five hundred years ago, plus or minus 50 years.
  लगभग पाँच सौ साल पहले।

- **Hard on the heels** of the Portuguese came the British:
  The British followed the Portuguese into India.
  पुर्तगालियों के बाद ब्रिटिश लोग भारत आये।
- This war is **unparalleled in the history** of India:
  This is the most important war in Indian history.
  भारतीय इतिहास की यह सबसे महत्त्वपूर्ण लड़ाई थी।
- Education is the **greatest blessing bestowed on** humankind:
  Education has helped mankind the most.
  मानवता के लिए शिक्षा सबसे बड़ा वरदान सिद्ध हुई।
- This change in law **opened the floodgates** for migrants:
  This change in law helped migrants to enter in large numbers.
  कानून में इस परिवर्तन ने प्रवासी लोगों के लिए भारत में बड़ा दरवाज़ा खोल दिया।
- The world is still **reeling from** the events of 11 September:
  The world has still to recover from the events of 11 September.
  दुनिया अभी भी 11 सितम्बर की घटना से पूरी तरह उबर नहीं पाई है।
- **India is a software superpower:**
  India is the biggest power in computer software.
  कंप्यूटर सॉफ्टवेयर की दुनिया में भारत एक महाशक्ति है।
- America **opened its door** to Indian software specialists:
  Indians were allowed to enter the American software industry.
  अमेरिका ने भारतीय सॉफ्टवेयर उद्योग के लोगों के लिए अपने दरवाज़े खोल दिए।
- Small industries **sprang up** everywhere:
  Small industries opened everywhere.
  लघु-उद्योग सर्वत्र खुल गए।
- It was a **gigantic wedge** that **tore the world asunder**:
  A big division split the world into two parts.
  एक बड़े विभाजन ने दुनिया को दो भागों में विभक्त कर दिया।
- This represents only a **trace element** in Indian history:
  This is a very small incident in Indian history.
  यह भारतीय इतिहास की एक छोटी-सी घटना मात्र है।

- This cannot be **attributed** to a politician's **way of thinking**:
  It's not because of the way a politician thinks.
  यह विचार किसी राजनेता को शोभा नहीं देता।

- It will **keep the wheels** of development **turning**:
  Thanks to this, now the development won't stop.
  इसके कारण अब विकास की गति नहीं रुकेगी।

- The hidden **dynamics** of war are **laid bare** in this battle:
  The hidden forces of war are displayed very clearly in this confrontation.
  इस मुठभेड़ में छिपी हुई शक्तियाँ सामने आ गईं।

- **Armed with** a degree, **every second** Indian ran abroad:
  Almost half the Indians with a degree went abroad.
  लगभग हर दूसरा भारतीय जिसके पास डिग्री है, विदेश चला गया।

- The Second World War **had its genesis** in the First World War:
  The real reasons of the Second World War lay in the First World War.
  द्वितीय विश्वयुद्ध के बीज प्रथम विश्वयुद्ध में ही बो दिए गए थे।

- By 1930, almost all Indians had begun **clamouring for** independence:
  By 1930, the majority of Indians had started seeking independence vigorously.
  1930 के आते-आते हर भारतीय स्वतंत्रता की माँग करने लगा था।

- Politics and war go **hand in hand**:
  War and politics are interlinked.
  राजनीति और युद्ध एक-दूसरे के पूरक हैं।

- The management has to **work in unison** with workers:
  The management and workers have to work together.
  मैनेजमेंट और कर्मचारियों को साथ-साथ चलना होगा।

- **Industrialisation spawned capitalism:**
  Capitalism arose because of industrialisation.
  औद्योगीकरण के कारण पूँजीवाद का जन्म हुआ।

- The **schism** between Hindus and Muslims ran deep and resulted in Partition:
  Hindus and Muslims were deeply divided, which led to division of the country.
  हिन्दू और मुसलमानों के बीच पड़ी फूट ने भारत के विभाजन को जन्म दिया।

- **Communist governments had many failings:**
  Communist governments had many weaknesses.
  साम्यवादी सरकारों में कई ख़ामियाँ थीं।
- The business was **relegated into insignificance**:
  The business was not given any importance.
  व्यापार को महत्त्व नहीं दिया गया।
- There were **major upheavals** after Partition:
  The country saw many ups and downs after Partition.
  विभाजन के बाद देश में काफ़ी खलबली मच गई।
- Slums have **sprung up** at an alarming rate:
  Slums have grown at a worrisome pace.
  झुग्गी-बस्तियाँ बहुत बड़े पैमाने पर विकसित हो गईं।
- The British followed the **Divide and Rule policy**:
  The British were experts at pitting one community against the other to keep them divided.
  अंग्रेज़ों ने फूट डालो और राज करो की चाल चली।
- He **felt a driving need** to be in power:
  He badly wanted to be in power.
  वह पूरी तरह सत्ता का भूखा हो गया।
- The Indian system is corrupt **across the board**:
  The Indian system is totally corrupt from top to bottom.
  भारतीय तंत्र ऊपर से लेकर नीचे तक भ्रष्ट है।
- Religion is **deep-rooted** in every Indian:
  Religion is part and parcel of every Indian's life.
  धर्म हर भारतीय की ज़िंदगी से जुड़ा हुआ है।
- Communism always **fell short** of its promises:
  Communism couldn't fulfil any of the promises it made.
  साम्यवाद अपने वायदे पूरे नहीं कर पाया।
- In a democracy, elections **foster the illusion** of equality:
  In democracy, elections give an impression of equality.
  प्रजातंत्र में चुनावों ने समानता के नकली चेहरे को प्रश्रय दिया।

Unless we cut through the **foggy rhetoric** that surrounds the talks we will get nowhere:
We will make no progress until we are able to overcome meaningless words during negotiations.
समझौते के दौरान की गई कई अनावश्यक बातों से जब तक हम परहेज़ नहीं करेंगे तब तक हम प्रगति नहीं कर पाएँगे।

- Politicians always **paint themselves into** a corner:
Politicians always say or do things that leave them with no escape route.
राजनेता अधिकतर अपने को फँसा लेते हैं, और उससे उबर नहीं पाते।

- India was **willy-nilly sucked into a debt trap**:
India unknowingly and without planning borrowed money that she couldn't return.
भारत ने अनजाने में अपने को कर्ज के भँवर जाल में फँसा लिया।

- At the end of the Second World War Europe **lay in shambles**:
Europe was in total ruins when the Second World War ended.
द्वितीय विश्वयुद्ध के बाद यूरोप पूरी तरह से बिखर गया था।

- The Indian political system **was in disarray**:
The Indian political system was totally disorganised and chaotic.
भारतीय राजनीतिक व्यवस्था पूरी तरह से बिखरी हुई है।

- The three nations were **wired together** by a common religion:
A common religion held the three countries together.
एक समान धर्म होने के कारण तीन देश साथ आ गए।

- India was **inclined towards** socialism after Independence:
After gaining Independence, India was more interested in adopting socialism.
भारत स्वतंत्रता के बाद समाजवाद की तरफ उन्मुख हुआ।

- Terrorist elements have **spread their tentacles** around the world:
Terrorists have now spread their influence throughout the world.
आतंकवाद ने पूरी दुनिया में अपना जाल बिछा लिया है।

- The Marathas were **pastmasters in guerrilla** warfare:
The Marathas were experts at hit-and-run war tactics.
मराठा सैनिक गुरिल्ला युद्ध में बहुत कुशल थे।

- Long before the **dawn of the** Indus civilisation:
  Before the arrival of the Indus civilisation.
  सिन्धु सभ्यता के उदय से काफी पहले।
- It is now **disintegrating** under an **avalanche of change**:
  It is breaking up because of so many changes.
  कई परिवर्तनों के कारण अब ये छिन्न-भिन्न हो गया है।
- Today man sees a **blurry future**:
  Today man is not very clear about the future.
  वर्तमान में मनुष्य अपने भविष्य के बारे में निश्चिंत नहीं है।
- The question was **put up** in Parliament:
  The question was asked in Parliament.
  यह सवाल संसद में गूँजा।
- The project has **fallen through** for want of money:
  The project is off due to lack of funds/money.
  पैसे की कमी के कारण प्रोजेक्ट बंद करना पड़ा।
- He is **one of the select** officers:
  He is counted amongst the best officers.
  वह सर्वोत्तम अधिकारियों में से एक माना गया।
- He is in **contention** for the Governor's post:
  He is in the race for the Governor's post.
  वह राज्यपाल पद की दौड़ में शामिल है।
- Politics is indeed the last **refuge of scoundrels**:
  Rogues ultimately end up joining politics when they have no other option.
  कोई शक नहीं कि राजनीति गुंडे-बदमाशों का आखिरी विकल्प होती है।
- There is no **magic wand** for these complex problems:
  These complex problems cannot be sorted out so easily.
  ये मुश्किल समस्याएँ इतनी आसानी से हल होने वाली नहीं हैं।
- Bush's decision **struck** the Middle East countries **like a thunderbolt**:
  Bush's decision was a harsh one for the Gulf countries.
  बुश का फ़ैसला खाड़ी देशों के लिए कठोर साबित हुआ।
- TV news is full of **blood and gore**:
  The news on television always covers bloody and violent activities.
  टेलीविज़न के समाचार खून और हिंसा से भरे होते हैं।

- The auto industry is undergoing a **deep recession**:
  The car industry is going through a deep slump in business.
  कार उद्योग घाटे में चल रहा है।

- The king **scoffed at** rumours of a revolution:
  The king dismissed speculative talk about a revolution.
  राजा ने विद्रोह की अफ़वाह को ख़ारिज कर दिया।

- Rumours are **rife** that the **don has surrendered**:
  There are strong rumours that the gang leader has given up.
  अफ़वाह है कि बदमाशों के सरदार ने आत्मसमर्पण कर दिया।

- He made a **noble contribution** to the **cause of the poor**:
  He worked selflessly for the poor.
  उसने गरीबों के हित में निःस्वार्थ योगदान दिया।

- They **took their cue** from history:
  They learned their lessons from history.
  उन्होंने इतिहास से सबक सीखा।

- He was the **frontman who shielded the inner circle**:
  He was the man who appeared publicly so that the main group could avoid bad publicity.
  उसने सामने आकर अंदर के बाकी लोगों की छवि बिगड़ने से बचा ली।

- The brief **marriage of convenience** between the Americans and Russians was **annulled**:
  The brief period of motivated peace between the Americans and Russians was ended.
  अमेरिका और रूस के बीच कम समय वाला शान्ति समझौता टूट गया।

- In the stock market, avoid the **herd mentality**:
  In the stock market, avoid following the majority blindly.
  शेयर बाज़ार में आँख मींचकर भीड़ के पीछे नहीं चलना चाहिए।

- Hitler carried out **a pogrom** against the Jews:
  Hitler deliberately killed Jews in large numbers.
  हिटलर ने बड़ी संख्या में यहूदियों को मार दिया।

- It will continue **to plague** Indian society:
  It will continue to harm Indian society.
  यह भारतीय समाज को नुकसान पहुँचाता रहेगा।

- I am **appalled** at the **state of affairs** here:
  I am shocked at the bad state of affairs.
  मैं यहाँ के बुरे हालात देखकर दहल गया।
- As the first American tanks **rolled into** Baghdad:
  As the first American tanks entered the streets of Baghdad.
  जैसे ही पहला अमेरिकन टैंक बगदाद में घुसा।
- Enemy troops **went on the rampage**:
  Enemy soldiers caused destruction all around.
  दुश्मन की फ़ौज ने चारों ओर तबाही मचा दी।
- They all **looked famished**:
  They all looked as if they hadn't eaten for a long time.
  वे सभी बुरी तरह से भूखे नज़र आये।
- He displayed **great fortitude** in battle:
  He showed great courage during the battle.
  युद्ध के दौरान उसने बहुत बहादुरी दिखाई।
- The **grapevine is that she will be the next President**:
  Rumours/unofficial talks indicate that she will be the next President.
  ख़बर यह है कि वह अगली राष्ट्रपति बनेगी।
- **Big brother** is watching:
  The government is keeping track.
  सरकार की नज़रें लगी हैं।
- He was a **stool pigeon** planted amongst the terrorists:
  He was a police informer who had entered the terrorist ranks.
  वह आतंकवादियों के ख़िलाफ़ तैयार किया गया एक मुख़बिर था।
- **He has gained entry into the inner circle:**
  He has become a member of the circle that wields power and influence.
  उसने अंदर तक अपनी पहुँच बना ली है।
- The company is planning a **big layoff**:
  The company will sack many people.
  कंपनी कई लोगों को निकालेगी।
- The company will distribute a lot of **pink slips**:
  The company will issue many letters/notices of dismissal.
  कंपनी बहुत लोगों को निकालने के आदेश-पत्र जारी करेगी।

10. Verbal Expressions

- I have been **toying with a couple** of ideas:
  I have been considering two ideas.
  मैं कुछ विचारों पर ग़ौर करता रहा हूँ।

- It **brings back fond memories**:
  It fills one with pleasant remembrances.
  इससे अच्छी यादें दिमाग में उभर आती हैं।

- Of course, it **goes without saying**:
  Yes, there is no doubt about it.
  जी हाँ, बिलकुल, यह तो ज़ाहिर-सी बात है।

- **Pleased as punch** to meet you:
  Extremely glad to meet you.
  आपसे मिलकर बहुत ख़ुशी हुई।

- He **rummaged through his pocket** for the diary:
  He searched his pocket for the diary.
  डायरी ढूँढ़ने के लिए उसने अपनी जेब खँगाली।

- I want to **get** my project **off the ground**:
  I want to start my project work.
  मैं अपने प्रोजेक्ट का कार्य शुरू करना चाहता हूँ।

- Her money was **running low**:
  She had very little cash.
  उसके पास बहुत कम पैसे बचे थे।

- You should have **sounded me out** earlier:
  You should have informed me before.
  आपको मुझे पहले बताना चाहिए था।

- I won't keep you **very long**:
  I will not take too much of your time.
  मैं आपका अधिक समय नहीं लूँगा।

- Go on, have a drink! I will not **spill the beans**:
  Do have a drink. I will not tell others that you drink!
  चलो पी लो, मैं किसी को नहीं बताऊँगा।
- He **wound up** his car window:
  He closed his car window.
  उसने अपनी कार की खिड़की बंद कर ली।
- **Folks**, the drinks are **on the house**:
  The drinks are complimentary/I am paying for the drinks.
  दोस्तो, शराब मेरी तरफ़ से आपके लिए आ चुकी है।
- If it is not **too much of a bother**:
  If it is not much trouble.
  अगर ज़्यादा परेशानी न हो तो.....।
- He answered **as best as he could**:
  He tried his best to answer.
  उसने जवाब देने की पूरी कोशिश की।
- You **take one's breath away**:
  You are amazing.
  आपका जवाब नहीं।/आप तो कमाल के हैं।
- I **don't see much of her**:
  I don't see her too often.
  वह मुझे ज़्यादा नहीं दिखती।/वह मुझे कम दिखती है।
- He asked for 100 **bucks** but I **knocked him down** to 80:
  I bargained and brought the price down to 80 bucks from 100.
  मैंने 100 से 80 रु. में बात पक्की कर ली।
- I **will escort** you to your car:
  I will accompany you to where your car is parked.
  मैं आपको कार तक छोड़ने चलता हूँ।
- I have been **partying so hard**:
  I have been attending one party after another.
  मैं लगातार पार्टी कर रहा हूँ।
- **You aggravate me, man:**
  You irritate and upset me, man.
  जनाब, आप मुझे गुस्सा दिला रहे हैं।

- So **that settles the issue**:
  This clears the issue.
  तो अब समस्या का समाधान हो गया है।
- Don't **try to get fresh** with her:
  Don't try to take physical liberties with her.
  उसके साथ शारीरिक सम्बन्ध बनाने का प्रयास मत करो।
- You **come on too strongly** with the girls:
  You try too hard to befriend/seduce the girls.
  आप ज़बरदस्ती करके लड़कियों के करीब आने की कोशिश करते हैं।
- He **cracked up with laughter**:
  He couldn't control his laughter
  वह अपनी हँसी नहीं रोक सका।
- Have you **lost your mind**?
  Are you in your senses?
  क्या आपका दिमाग़ ख़राब हो गया है?
- No, you have done nothing **out of turn**:
  No, you have not done anything wrong.
  नहीं, आपने कुछ भी ग़लत नहीं किया।
- I will talk to you later when you are **in a civil mood**:
  I will speak to you afterwards when you are in a decent/proper frame of mind.
  जब आप शांत होंगे, मैं आपसे तभी बात करूँगा।
- Beyond a **shadow of doubt**:
  There is no doubt at all.
  इसमें कोई संदेह नहीं है।
- It's **raining cats and dogs**:
  It's raining very heavily.
  मूसलाधार बारिश हो रही है।
- Things were **at sixes and sevens**:
  The situation was very bad/chaotic.
  हालात बहुत ख़राब थे। / हालत बड़ी ख़राब थी।

- He had no idea what was **in store for** him:
  He had no clue of the trouble he was to face.
  उसे नहीं पता था कि कौन-सी मुसीबत उसका इंतज़ार कर रही है।
- He **saw through me**:
  He uncovered my game.
  उसने मेरी चालाकी पकड़ ली।
- Was I ever **in luck**?
  My luck is always bad.
  मेरा भाग्य कभी मेरा साथ नहीं देता।
- **Are you daft?**
  Don't act like a fool.
  बेवक़ूफ़ों की तरह हरकतें मत करो।
- This money will **see me through** college:
  This money will suffice me to complete college education.
  यह पैसा मेरी कॉलेज की शिक्षा के लिए पर्याप्त है।
- I will **make him see sense**:
  I will explain things to him so that he is reasonable.
  मैं सही बात उसके सामने लाऊँगा।
- What is **holding you back**?
  What is preventing you from doing this?
  आप किस बात का इंतज़ार कर रहे हैं?
- You have to **place more value on** our friendship:
  You must give our friendship due importance.
  आपको हमारी मित्रता को पूरा महत्त्व देना होगा।
- How will you **earn a living**?
  What will you do to survive?
  आप अपनी आजीविका कैसे चलाएँगे?
- He **talks through his hat**:
  He speaks rubbish/he speaks without thinking.
  वह बिना कुछ सोचे-समझे बात करता है।
- **To top it all**:
  Over and above everything else/to make matters worse.
  मुसीबत को और बढ़ाने के लिए।

- I will do this in **double-quick** time:
  I will do this quickly.
  मैं इसे जल्दी करूँगा।
- He knew his position **was impossible**:
  He knew he had no chance of succeeding/winning.
  उसे पता था कि सफलता की संभावना नगण्य है।
- He **shot his bolt**:
  He did everything possible but still failed.
  उसने अपनी कोशिश पूरी कर ली थी, लेकिन फ़ायदा नहीं हुआ।
- He was **smarting from the humiliation**:
  He was in a very bad mood because of the insult.
  अपमान के कारण उसकी मानसिक स्थिति ठीक नहीं थी।
- The boss **ticked him off roundly**:
  The boss spoke to him very sternly.
  बॉस ने उससे बड़ी ही कठोरता से बात की।
- Can I **have a civil word with** you?
  Can I have a polite chat with you?
  क्या मैं आराम से आपसे कुछ बात कर सकता हूँ?
- Have faith, I won't **rat on** you:
  Believe me, I won't disclose your secrets.
  यकीन करो, मैं तुम्हारा राज़ किसी से नहीं कहूँगा।
- You sing **grossly off** key:
  You sing badly and out of tune.
  आप बहुत बेसुरा गाते हैं।
- Stop **braying like an ass**:
  Stop shouting/talking loudly.
  बकवास बंद कीजिए।
- It seems the **work of a lunatic**:
  It looks as if a madman has done it.
  ऐसा प्रतीत हो रहा है, यह किसी पागल का काम है।
- He removed all the **bulky wads** of cash:
  He removed large bundles of cash.
  उसने रुपयों की एक बड़ी गड्डी हटा दी।

- Once the **word was out**:
When people came to know about it.
जब लोगों को इसका पता चला।

- I don't know him a **great deal**:
I don't know him very well.
मैं उसे अच्छी तरह नहीं जानता।

- Get her **out of your system**:
You will have to forget her totally.
तुम्हें उसे पूरी तरह भूलना होगा।

- A **promotion** seems to be **on the cards**:
A promotion seems likely.
आपकी पदोन्नति के आसार हैं।

- Can I **count on** your support?
Will you support me?
क्या मैं आपसे समर्थन की उम्मीद कर सकता हूँ?

- My contacts **have all gone cold**:
I am no longer actively in touch with the people I once knew.
जिन लोगों को मैं जानता था उनसे अब मैं संपर्क में नहीं हूँ।

- **Scotch flowed freely** like water:
Scotch was served very liberally.
स्कॉच जमकर बाँटी गई।

- Here relaxing is usually not **on the menu**:
You have to work very hard here and cannot take it easy.
आपको परिश्रमपूर्वक अपना काम करना है।

- This **bugs me no end**:
This irritates me intensely.
मुझे इस बात से बहुत चिढ़ है।

- He may not **be all he seems**:
He is not what he appears/pretends to be.
वह वैसा नहीं है जैसा नज़र आता है।

- Let's **start afresh**:
Forget about what has happened earlier and let's make a new beginning.
चलिए पुरानी बातें भूलकर नई शुरुआत करें।

- He **gets my vote**:
He will have my support.
आपको मेरा समर्थन है।

- It was one **hell of a day**:
It was an exciting and eventful day.
आज बहुत गहमागहमी वाला दिन रहा।

- Your product is **barely moving off the shelf**:
Your product is not selling very well.
आपका उत्पाद अच्छी तरह नहीं बिक पा रहा है।

- There were **streaks of grey** in her temple:
Her hair was turning white at the temple.
उसके बाल माथे पर सफ़ेद हो रहे हैं।

- The file **landed on** my desk:
The case was handed over to me.
यह मामला मुझे सौंपा गया है।

- It **goes over my** head:
I don't understand this.
मुझे यह बिलकुल समझ नहीं आया।

- I wish I could **turn it around**:
I wish I could change things for the better.
काश कि मैं हालात में सुधार ला सकता।

- He is taking an **outstation break**:
He has gone out of town on holiday.
वह शहर से बाहर छुट्टी मनाने गया है।

- He **pushed** his staff **day and night**:
He made his staff work hard.
वह अपने कर्मचारियों से दबाव देकर मेहनत करवाता है।

- He is an absolute **slave-driver**:
He overworks his employees.
वह अपने कर्मचारियों से बहुत अधिक काम करवाता है।
- We will **bump into each other** more often:
We will meet more often.
एक-दूसरे से हम अकसर मिलेंगे।
- I don't see **eye to eye** with him:
I don't agree with him/don't get along well with him.
मैं उससे सममत नहीं हूँ। / मेरी उससे नहीं बनती।
- I will **play my part** as per your wishes:
I will conduct myself as you want.
मैं आपकी इच्छानुसार कार्य करूँगा।
- If your **hunch turns out to be right**:
If your intuition turns out to be correct.
अगर आपका पूर्वाभास सही निकला।
- We must **catch up** on old times:
Let us remember the old times spent together.
हमें एक-दूसरे के साथ गुज़ारा हुआ वक़्त याद करना होगा।
- If I **pull off** this one:
If I can accomplish this task.
यदि मैंने यह कार्य सम्पन्न कर लिया।
- With this, he's **home and dry**:
With this, he has accomplished his goal.
उसके साथ ही उसने अपना लक्ष्य पा लिया।
- Do **you get me**?
Do you understand what I am saying?
क्या आप समझ रहे हैं जो मैं कह रहा हूँ?
- It will be over **within a matter of months**:
It will take only a few months to get done.
कुछ महीने के भीतर यह समाप्त हो जाएगा।
- A **real shouting match** followed between the two:
They kept shouting at each other.
उन्होंने एक-दूसरे पर चिल्लाना शुरू कर दिया।

- Rita and her husband had a **slanging match**:
  Rita and her husband kept insulting each other for some time.
  काफ़ी समय तक रीता का अपने पति से टकराव होता रहा।
- **Don't digress from the issue:**
  Keep the talks focused on the issue and don't bring up other things.
  बातचीत के दौरान विषय से न हटें।
- He **goofed up**:
  He committed a blunder.
  उसने भारी गड़बड़ कर दी।
- **Do be serious for once:**
  Get serious at least this time.
  कम-से-कम इस बार तो गंभीर हो जाइये।
- It would be hard for you **to comprehend**:
  It will be difficult for you to understand.
  आपके लिए यह समझना मुश्किल होगा।
- Are you **up to it**?
  Can you do it?
  क्या आप यह कर सकते हैं?
- Is she **cut out for** this task?
  Is she the right person for this job?
  क्या वह इस काम के लिए उपयुक्त है?
- I am **at your service, Sir**:
  I am here to do your work, Sir.
  श्रीमान, मैं आपकी सेवा में प्रस्तुत हूँ।
- It is **about time** we leave:
  It is time for us to go.
  अब प्रस्थान करने का समय आ गया है।
- We will give **it a go**:
  We will work on it and try our best.
  हम इस पर कार्य करने का प्रयास करेंगे।
- Don't **pull a fast one** on me:
  Don't try to fool me.
  मुझे बेवक़ूफ़ बनाने की कोशिश मत करो।

- I am **deluged with work**:
  I have too much work.
  मेरे पास काम की बाढ़-सी आ गई है।
- I **grew on** it:
  I grew up having this.
  मैं यही सब देखते हुए बड़ा हुआ हूँ।
- Will you stop being **a spoilsport**?
  Will you stop spoiling the fun?
  क्या आप मज़ा किरकिरा करने से बाज़ आएँगे?
- **Let's face it:**
  We have to accept it.
  हमें इस सच को स्वीकार करना होगा। / हमें इसका सामना करना होगा।
- Don't **drive me up** the wall:
  Don't irritate/anger me.
  मुझे चिढ़ाने की कोशिश मत करो।
- I would **rather not talk about** it:
  It was so bad that I don't feel like discussing it.
  मैं तो इसके बारे में बात नहीं करना चाहता।
- He is the boss's **blue-eyed** boy:
  The boss favours him heavily and is partial to him.
  वह बॉस का ख़ास है।
- She gave me the **brush off**:
  She rebuffed me and did not let me get close to her.
  उसने मुझे बुरी तरह झिड़क दिया।
- Marketing is not my **cup of tea**:
  Marketing is not my strong point and I am not fond of it.
  मार्केटिंग मेरे कार्यक्षेत्र का विषय नहीं है।
- You are **a weirdo**:
  You are a strange person.
  तुम अजीब आदमी हो।
- You are **a tubelight**:
  You fail to understand things quickly.
  आपको जल्दी से बात समझ नहीं आती।

- Should I read out the **riot act to them**?
Should I give them a severe warning?
क्या मैं उन्हें कड़ी चेतावनी दूँ?

- You are slow to **catch on**:
It takes you time to understand things.
तुम्हें समझने में देर लगती है।

- I am **through for the day**:
I have finished my work for the day and am now free.
मेरा आज का काम ख़त्म हो गया।

- **Let's call it quits:**
Let us stop now.
चलो आज से ये बंद!

- **Mum's the word:**
Keep quiet.
चुप रहो!

- **I've had my fill:**
I have eaten/drunk enough.
मैंने पर्याप्त रूप से खा/पी लिया है।

- I **can't thank you enough**:
Thanks a lot for this.
आपको धन्यवाद देने के लिए मेरे पास शब्द नहीं हैं।

- The boss gave him some **seed money**:
The boss gave him some money to start the project.
बॉस ने काम की शुरुआत के लिए उसे पैसे दिए।

- He is now **off the hook**:
He is no longer in difficulty/trouble.
अब वह परेशानी से उबर चुका है।

- If anything goes wrong **you have had it**:
If things go wrong you will be in serious trouble.
अगर कोई गलती हुई तो समझ लेना तुम्हारी ख़ैर नहीं।

- If you don't **watch your step** you will get **what's coming**:
If you don't be careful, you will surely get into trouble.
अगर तुमने सावधानी नहीं बरती तो मुश्किल में पड़ोगे।

- I am glad I **ran into you**:
  I am glad I met you.
  मुझे ख़ुशी है कि आपसे मुलाकात हुई।
- We will be in **double trouble**:
  We will be in deep trouble.
  हम बड़ी परेशानी में पड़ जाएँगे।
- This **is arguable**:
  This is debatable/doubtful.
  यह विवाद का विषय है।
- You have **no hope** in hell:
  You have no chances whatsoever.
  आपके लिए कोई संभावना नहीं है।
- He can **be trusted as much as a rattlesnake**:
  He is totally untrustworthy, just like a rattlesnake.
  उस पर तो बिलकुल भी भरोसा नहीं किया जा सकता।
- Good luck! I will be **rooting for** you:
  Good luck! I will be backing you.
  सौभाग्यवान भव! मैं आपके साथ हूँ।
- She was **lax in her job**:
  She was careless in her job.
  वह अपने काम में लापरवाह है।
- She decided to **quit for the day**:
  She was tired and went home.
  उसने आज का काम ख़त्म करके अब घर जाने का फ़ैसला किया है।
- I need a **shoulder to cry on**:
  I need somebody to share my problems with and confide in.
  मुझे किसी का सहारा चाहिए।
- Your **guess** is **as good as mine**:
  I am as clueless as you are.
  मैं भी आपकी तरह समझ नहीं पा रही हूँ।
- You could not have come **a day too soon**:
  You are right in time and would have lost out had you come a day late.
  आप बिलकुल सही समय पर आ गए वरना चूक जाते।

- The day began **on the wrong foot**:
The day began badly.
दिन की शुरुआत ख़राब हुई।

- Don't be **so snooty**:
Don't be haughty and treat us with contempt.
ज़्यादा घमंड मत करो।

- Time is fast **running out**:
There is very little time left.
बहुत कम समय बचा है।

- I decided to **snoop around** a bit:
I decided to spy a little.
मैंने थोड़ी जासूसी करने का फ़ैसला किया।

- Don't **lose your nerve** at any cost:
Don't panic despite anything that happens.
चाहे जो हो, घबराना मत।

- The two boxers **squared up** against each other:
The two boxers got into position against each other, ready to fight.
दोनों मुक्केबाज़ लड़ने के लिए तैयार हो गए।

- She will **keep the press off** your back for some time:
She will manage to save you from the press for some time.
काम के दौरान वह आप पर नज़र नहीं रखेगी। / वह आप पर नज़र नहीं रखेगी।

- I don't **swing much clout** here:
I don't have much influence over here.
मेरा यहाँ अधिक प्रभाव नहीं है।

- Don't be **such a sucker**:
Don't be such a fool.
बेवक़ूफ़ी मत करो।

- I will **make coffee in a jiffy**:
I will prepare coffee quickly.
मैं तुरंत कॉफ़ी बनाता हूँ।

- Can I **take you on your word**?
  Can I trust you on this?
  क्या मैं इस मामले में आप पर भरोसा कर सकता हूँ।
- He will **pull the plug on you**:
  He will let you down.
  वह आपको निष्क्रिय कर देगा ताकि आप कुछ न कर सकें।
- My mom **spoiled me rotten**:
  My mother pampered and spoilt me.
  मेरी माँ ने मुझे बिगाड़ दिया।
- **Cut the crap** out and come to the point:
  Stop talking rubbish and discuss business straightaway.
  फ़ालतू की बातें बंद करके मुद्दे की बात पर आओ।
- We **went our own ways** in the business:
  We parted ways in the business.
  हमने एक-दूसरे के साथ व्यावसायिक संबंध समाप्त कर लिए।
- You have **Yankee written** all over you:
  You can be recognised as an American by anybody.
  कोई भी बता सकता है कि आप अमेरिकन हैं।
- A top minister **on the take**! What a shame!
  A top minister in the pay of somebody. It is a real shame.
  एक चोटी के मंत्री की चोरी पकड़ी गई, कितनी शर्म की बात है।
- What **brings you** here?
  What is the purpose of your visit?
  यहाँ आपके पधारने का प्रयोजन क्या है?
- The day was **at its fag end**:
  The day was coming to an end.
  दिन बस ख़त्म ही होने वाला था।
- I have **made a new life** here:
  I have begun a new life over here.
  मैंने यहाँ एक नई ज़िंदगी की शुरुआत की है।
- He **snatched a few hours of sleep**:
  He managed to sleep for a few hours.
  वह कुछ घंटों की नींद ले पाया।

- He **dropped off in sheer exhaustion**:
He fell asleep since he was absolutely tired.
बुरी तरह थके होने के कारण वह बिस्तर पर लेटते ही सो गया।

- He **grew in confidence** with every word he spoke:
As he spoke, his confidence kept increasing with each word.
अपने हर शब्द के साथ उसका आत्मविश्वास भी बढ़ता गया।

- Don't **beat about the bush**:
Don't waste time. Come to the point.
साफ़-साफ़ बात करो।/मुद्दे की बात करो।

- He **slept like a baby**:
He had very sound sleep.
वह बहुत ही गहरी नींद सोया।

- You will **get bored stiff**:
You will be totally bored.
तुम बुरी तरह से ऊब जाओगे।

- **Thanks, but no thanks!**
Thanks, but I am not interested/don't want it.
धन्यवाद! मुझे इसकी ज़रूरत नहीं।

- Your contribution **has been zilch**:
You have done nothing.
आपने कुछ भी योगदान नहीं दिया।

- He gave her **short shrift**:
He was unsympathetic with her.
उसने उसके साथ जरा भी सहानुभूति नहीं दिखाई।

- **His heart tripped**:
It came as a mild shock.
उसका दिल टूट गया।/उसे ज़ोर का झटका लगा।

- She has a **short fuse**:
She is short-tempered.
वह बहुत ही जल्दी भड़क जाती है।

- **Keep things to yourself:**
Do not disclose this to anybody:
यह बात आप अपने आप तक ही रखें।

- Would you like a **peg or two**?
  Would you like to drink a little?
  क्या आप एक-आध जाम पीना पसंद करेंगे?
- **He was all ears:**
  He was listening keenly.
  वह कान लगाकर सुन रहा था।
- The house looked a little **run down**:
  The house looked improperly maintained.
  घर अस्त-व्यस्त था।
- He gave it **straight from the shoulder**:
  He revealed the real facts as they were.
  उसे तथ्यों की बिलकुल सही जानकारी मिली।
- I **curbed my tongue**:
  I managed to keep quiet.
  मैंने चुप्पी साध ली।
- He **dotes on** her:
  He is very fond of her.
  वह उसे बहुत पसंद करता है।
- **Take your pick** and **have anything you fancy**:
  Make your choice and take anything you want.
  जो चाहो वह ले सकते हो।
- **Count me out**:
  Don't include me in this.
  कृपया मुझे इसमें सम्मिलित न करें।
- **The cheek of you!**
  How dare you do such a thing!
  आपकी ऐसा करने की हिम्मत कैसे हुई!
- **You are a wonder:**
  You are remarkable.
  आपका जवाब नहीं।
- I **drank myself silly at the party**:
  I got totally drunk at the party.
  मैंने पार्टी में बहुत ज़्यादा शराब पी ली।

- May I **have a word with** you?
  May I speak to you?
  क्या मैं आपसे बात कर सकता हूँ?
- He was **harried round the clock**:
  He was troubled throughout the day.
  वह पूरे दिन परेशान रहा।
- Let's **make up for lost time**:
  We must recover lost time.
  चलिए खोया हुआ वक़्त दुबारा हासिल करें।
- I have been **working flat out** since last night:
  I have been working very hard since last night.
  मैं इस काम पर कल रात से जुटा हुआ हूँ।
- This **calls for** some celebration:
  This is an occasion for a celebration/party.
  ये तो जश्न का मौका है।
- He has **crossed all norms of propriety**:
  He has crossed all the limits of decency.
  उसने शराफ़त की सारी हदें पार कर लीं।
- As soon as he was **out of earshot**:
  As soon as he was not within hearing distance.
  ज्योंही वह सुनने की सीमा से बाहर हुआ....।
- I **got caught** in my own agenda:
  I couldn't come out of my own work problems.
  मैं अपनी ही परेशानियों में फँसकर रह गया।
- To **cut a long story short**:
  To come to the point.
  सीधे-सीधे काम की बात पर आ जाओ।
- Don't hit a **raw nerve**:
  Don't provoke me by touching a sensitive spot.
  मेरी दुखती रग पर हाथ मत रखो।
- He cares **two hoots** for her:
  He does not care for her at all.
  उसे उसकी कोई फ़िक्र नहीं।

- His business **is in the red**:
  His business is making a loss.
  उसका धंधा घाटे में चल रहा है।
- It really took a **load off**:
  It took the burden/pressure off me.
  इसके कारण मेरा भार कम हो गया।
- That question really **hit him hard**:
  That question unsettled him.
  उस सवाल ने उसे बुरी तरह परेशान कर दिया।
- You must **do whatever it takes**:
  You must do whatever is required.
  आपको अपनी हर कोशिश करनी होगी।
- **Let your** creative **juices flow**:
  Think creatively.
  अपनी रचनात्मक बुद्धि का प्रयोग कीजिए।
- Don't **go off track**:
  Remain focused and don't be diverted.
  अपनी निगाहें काम पर जमाये रखो।
- If I **pull this one off** I will be a millionaire:
  If I can do this I will be a millionaire.
  यदि मैं यह सब कर सका तो मैं लखपति बन जाऊँगा।
- The **cuffs in** his shirt were **beginning to fray**:
  The cuffs were old and shredded.
  उसकी शर्ट की बाहें काफ़ी पुरानी और कटी-फटी थीं।
- **How are things?**
  How are you doing?
  कैसे हैं आप?
- They failed to see the **writing on the wall**:
  They failed to realise that they could no longer get away with things.
  वे नहीं देख पाए कि उनके नसीब में क्या लिखा हुआ है।
- He has **loads of patience**:
  He is a very patient man.
  वह बहुत धैर्यवान है।

- Don't **pull your punches**:
  Don't do things half-heartedly but follow through with the work.
  अपने आपको रोको मत, अपनी पूरी क्षमता का इस्तेमाल करो।

- I am **one with you** on this:
  I fully agree with you on this.
  इस बात पर मैं आपसे पूरी तरह सहमत हूँ।

- Don't **spring a surprise**:
  Don't do anything unexpected.
  कुछ भी अलग-सा/अजूबा मत करना।

- He caught me **stifling a yawn**:
  He caught me in the act of suppressing a yawn.
  उसने मुझे उबास छुपाते हुए देख लिया।

- His **venture failed to take off**:
  His venture did not even begin.
  उसका काम तो शुरू भी नहीं हो सका।

- **He is incommunicado**:
  He is not communicating with anybody.
  वह किसी से भी संपर्क नहीं कर रहा।

- I want to **catch up** on the latest:
  Brief me on the latest happenings.
  मुझे हालिया घटनाओं की कुछ जानकारी दीजिए।

- **Don't give me all that jazz**:
  Don't tell me all this rubbish.
  मुझे ये सड़ी बकवास नहीं सुननी।

- Let's go **back to the drawing board**:
  Let us analyse things.
  चलिए हालात का जायज़ा लेते हैं।

- He is an **armchair traveller**:
  He is fond of reading travel writings.
  उसे यात्रा-संबंधी लेख पढ़ने का शौक है।

- He went **around the bend**:
  He lost his mental balance.
  वह अपना मानसिक संतुलन खो बैठा।

- It was **a backbreaking job**:
  It was a very tough job.
  यह तो बड़ा मुश्किल काम था।
- Keep this project on the **back burner**:
  Don't begin this project now but put it on hold.
  इस प्रोजेक्ट पर काम शुरू न करें, इसे यहीं रोक दें।
- It was a **different ballgame** altogether:
  It was a totally different thing.
  ये बिलकुल ही दूसरी चीज़ है।
- I **won't take this baloney:**
  I will not tolerate this nonsense.
  मैं यह मूर्खता बर्दाश्त नहीं करूँगा।
- I developed a **beer belly**:
  I have developed a pot belly/paunch.
  मेरी तोंद निकल गई है।
- He has got **a bee in his bonnet**:
  He is totally preoccupied with something.
  वह पहले से ही काम में व्यस्त है।
- He will **bend over backwards** to please you:
  He will do anything to please you.
  वह तुम्हें खुश करने के लिए सब कुछ करेगा।
- He will be a **bench warmer**:
  He is a reserve player and will not play.
  वह एक आपातकालीन खिलाड़ी है।
- **We have no benchmarks**:
  We do not have proper standards/targets.
  हम सही मानदण्ड लेकर नहीं चल रहे।
- He is a **big fish**:
  He is an important person.
  वह एक महत्त्वपूर्ण व्यक्ति है।
- He is a **bad apple** in the basket:
  He is one bad person amongst all the others.
  वहाँ सभी लोगों में वह इकलौता बुरा आदमी है।

- **When the chips are down**:
  When the going is not smooth.
  जब मुश्किल पेश आ रही हो।
- She is **quite chirpy**:
  She is full of energy and keeps on talking.
  वह बहुत प्रसन्नचित्त लड़की है।
- He kept talking **nineteen to the dozen**:
  He spoke fast and non-stop.
  वह लगातार बोलता रहा।
- He was completely **cleaned out at the casino**:
  He lost all his money gambling at the casino.
  वह जुए में अपने सारे पैसे हार गया।
- I had a **close shave**:
  I had a narrow escape.
  मैं बाल-बाल बच गया।
- They **took him to the cleaners**:
  They cheated him out of a large portion of his money/wealth.
  उन्होंने उसके सारे पैसे उड़ा लिए।
- **Come hell or high water**, I will do it:
  Whatever the obstacles, I will still do it.
  चाहे जो हो मैं यह करके रहूँगा।
- The project came to a **screeching halt**:
  Work on the project was halted suddenly.
  अचानक प्रोजेक्ट का काम रुक गया।
- We completed the project **under the wire**:
  The project was finished just in time.
  हमने प्रोजेक्ट बिलकुल सही समय पर समाप्त कर लिया।
- It is a **cooked-up** story:
  It is a false story.
  ये मनगढ़ंत कहानी है।
- **His goose is cooked**:
  He is finished/he will be in trouble.
  वह बुरी तरह परेशानी में फँस गया है।

- He will **crack under pressure**:
  If he is put under sustained pressure, he will reveal things.
  अगर उस पर दबाव बना रहेगा, तो वह सच उगल सकता है।

- There has been a **mix-up**:
  There has been some unintentional error.
  वहाँ कुछ अनजानी भूल हो गई है।

- It's not **a cushy job**:
  It's a tough job.
  यह आसान काम नहीं है।

- I suggest you **cut a deal** with him:
  I suggest you come to some understanding with him.
  मेरा तो यही कहना है कि किसी तरह आप उससे मामला जमा लो।

- There is no **cut-and-dried** solution:
  There is no readymade solution.
  इसके लिए कोई बना बनाया हल नहीं है।/इसका हल सोचना पड़ेगा।

- It is a **dandy joint**:
  It is a posh place.
  यह एक आलीशान जगह है।

- He will be as **dead as a dodo**:
  He will be dead.
  वह तो अब मरेगा।

- This is a **dead giveaway**:
  This will reveal everything.
  यह एक साफ़ संकेत है।

- Don't worry, he has got **deep pockets** and will see the project through:
  He has a lot of money and will be able to complete the project.
  उसके पास यह प्रोजेक्ट पूरा करने के लिए काफ़ी पैसा है।

- These are available **dime a dozen**:
  These are available very cheap.
  ये काफ़ी सस्ते हैं।

- For **donkey's years** I have been doing **donkey's work**:
  For so many years I have been doing all the hard work.
  काफ़ी सालों से मैं इतनी मेहनत कर रहा हूँ।

- We will **go Dutch**:
  We will share the expenditure.
  खर्चा हम बराबर बाँट लेंगे।
- He **dropped her like a hot potato**:
  He dropped her immediately.
  उसने उसको तुरंत छोड़ दिया।
- If she is not good, **ease her out**:
  If her work is not good, dismiss her over a period of time.
  अगर उसका काम ठीक नहीं है तो उसको कुछ दिनों बाद रफ़ा-दफ़ा कर देना।
- **Delighted to make your acquaintance**:
  Glad to meet you.
  आपसे मिलकर ख़ुशी हुई।
- We share a **good rapport**:
  We understand each other very well and have a good relationship.
  हमारी आपस में अच्छी बनती है।
- **I quite understand:**
  I am sympathetic towards your problem.
  मैं आपकी समस्या को समझ सकता हूँ।
- He is **an egghead**:
  He is a very academic/studious person.
  वह एक बुद्धिजीवी व्यक्ति है।
- It is enough to **choke a horse**:
  It's a very large quantity.
  यह तो काफ़ी मात्रा में है।
- In the end things will **even out**:
  Finally, things will work out fine.
  आख़िर में सब कुछ ठीक हो जाएगा।
- Your eyes will **pop out**:
  You will be surprised.
  तुम्हें हैरानी होगी।

- He will **fall flat**:
He will fail miserably.
वह बुरी तरह से असफल होगा।

- It was just a **fender-bender** car accident:
It was a minor car accident.
ये एक मामूली–सी कार दुर्घटना थी।

- **Fill me in** with the details:
Tell me everything in detail.
मुझे सब कुछ समझा दीजिए।/मुझे पूरा ब्योरा देना।

- He **flexed** his muscles and **that was that**:
He showed his power and that made things work.
उसने गुस्सा दिखाया और काम हो गया।

- The **flip side** of the story is:
The other side of the story is.
कहांनी का दूसरा पहलू है......।

- **He kept gawking at her:**
He kept staring foolishly at her.
वह उसे घूरता रहा।

- **Have you got his nod?**
Have you received his approval/consent?
आपको उसकी स्वीकृति मिल गई?

- All his plans **went up in smoke**:
All his plans failed.
उसकी सारी योजनाएँ धरी की धरी रह गईं।

- She was **caught in the act**:
She was discovered while committing the act.
वह रँगेहाथों धर ली गई।

- They were caught **in a compromising position**:
They were discovered making love/in a state of undress.
वे रतिक्रिया करते हुए पकड़े गए।

- He thinks he is a **big shot**:
He thinks he is a rich man.
उसे लगता है कि वह एक महत्त्वपूर्ण व्यक्ति है।

- He had **egg on his face**:
  He was in an embarrassing situation.
  वह बड़ी ही शर्मिंदगी की हालत में था।

- He has **hot pants**:
  He is full of lust.
  वह बड़ा कामुक व्यक्ति है।

- I ran **hell for leather**:
  I ran very fast.
  मैं बहुत तेज़ दौड़ा।

- Now there will be **hell to pay** for him:
  The outcome will be disastrous for him.
  इसका अंजाम उसके लिए ख़तरनाक होगा।

- You must **face the music**:
  You have to face the consequences.
  तुमको इसका अंजाम भुगतना पड़ेगा।

- He has **hit the bottle**:
  He has started drinking heavily.
  उसने बुरी तरह से पीना शुरू कर दिया।

- He seems to have **hit the jackpot**:
  He seems to have received a lot of money.
  ऐसा लगता है, उसे काफी धन-दौलत मिल गई।

- **It is all hogwash**:
  It is all rubbish/false.
  ये सब बकवास/गलत है।

- His work is just **ho-hum**:
  His work is mediocre/of very poor quality.
  उसका काम बहुत बेकार है।

- His book sold only because of **all the hype** created before the launch:
  His book only sold well because they generated a lot of intense publicity and made many claims before the book's release.
  पुस्तक के प्रकाशन से पहले किए गए अतिशय प्रचार ने पुस्तक की बिक्री में मदद की।

- It is all **hoopla and** nothing else:
  It is all unnecessary fuss.
  ये बेमतलब की गहमागहमी है।
- I just **horsed around a bit**:
  I simply fooled around.
  मैं तो बस बेवक़ूफ़ बनता रहा।
- Relax, don't **get hyper**:
  Don't get overexcited.
  आराम से, आपे से बाहर मत हो!
- I **kid you not**, this is the truth:
  I am not joking, believe me – this is the truth.
  मैं मज़ाक़ नहीं कर रहा, ये सच है।
- **I will be damned** if I go back to her:
  I will never return to her under any circumstances.
  मैं किसी भी सूरत में उसके पास वापस नहीं जाऊँगा।
- The project is **in cold storage**:
  No work is being done on the project.
  यह प्रोजेक्ट ठंडे बस्ते में चला गया।
- The **venture** has been **shelved for the time being**:
  The venture has been dropped for now.
  यह काम कुछ दिनों के लिए रुक गया है।
- **As things now stand:**
  The situation now is......
  जो अब हालत है वो ऐसी है ....।
- He is **in the doghouse**:
  He is totally out of favour.
  उसकी कोई मदद नहीं कर रहा।
- He is **in the driver's seat**:
  He is in full control of things.
  स्थिति पूरी तरह उसके नियंत्रण में है।
- It takes **two to tango**:
  You were equally involved.
  ताली एक हाथ से नहीं बजती।

- She thinks she is the **Queen of Sheba**:
  She thinks too highly of/overrates herself.
  उसे लगता है कि वह कहीं की महारानी है।

- **Don't jive me:**
  Don't tease/taunt me.
  मुझे चिढ़ाओ मत।

- She acted **a bit jumpy**:
  She was somewhat nervous.
  वह थोड़ी-सी घबराई हुई है।

- She is **just another pretty face**:
  She is just pretty to look at but has no other qualities or qualifications.
  सुंदर होकर भी वह बस एक सामान्य लड़की है।

- He is trying to **keep up with the Joneses**:
  He is living beyond his means in trying to copy his neighbours.
  वह अपनी सीमाओं से बाहर जाकर अपने पड़ौसियों से मुक़ाबला करने की कोशिश कर रहा है।

- He will soon **kick the bucket**:
  He will die soon.
  उसका जल्दी ही राम नाम सत्य हो जाएगा।

- You think this is **kid stuff**?
  You think this is very easy and everybody could do it?
  तुम्हें लगता है कि ये बहुत आसान काम है?

- It was **kinky stuff**:
  It was strange/bizarre stuff.
  ये एक विकट घटना/बात थी।

- The government reacted in a **knee-jerk** manner:
  The government responded hastily without thinking things through.
  सरकार ने बिना सोचे-समझे जल्दबाज़ी में प्रतिक्रिया व्यक्त कर दी।

- He runs a very **lean organisation**:
  He runs an organisation with limited staff.
  वह इस संस्था को काफ़ी सीमित कर्मचारियों की दम पर चला रहा है।

- His company **is obese**:
His company is overstaffed.
उसकी कंपनी में आवश्यकता से अधिक कर्मचारी हैं।

- I will **give him no margin for error**:
I will not allow him to get away with any mistake.
हम उसे उसकी किसी भी गलती की सज़ा से बचकर नहीं जाने देंगे।

- She is such a **lovey-dovey** person:
She is such a lovable person.
वह बहुत ही प्यारी है।

- He **made a pass at** her:
He passed a remark with sexual overtones.
उसने उसे अश्लील इशारे किए।

- **He made overtures to her:**
He made the initial moves to begin a relationship with her.
उसने उसके साथ संबंध जोड़ने की कोशिश की।

- **Don't speak with innuendoes:**
Don't speak in riddles but come to the point.
पहेलियाँ मत बुझाओ, सीधे-सीधे कहो।

- I **hold all the aces**:
I have the upper hand.
यहाँ मेरा प्रभुत्व है।

- She will **make mincemeat** of him:
She will take full advantage of him.
वह उसका पूरा फ़ायदा उठाएगी।

- **You must make things snappy:**
You must do things quickly.
तुम्हें इस काम में जल्दी करनी होगी।

- It will **make my day**:
It will make me very happy/accomplish what I want.
ये मेरे लिए बड़ी ख़ुशी की बात होगी।

- He **made no bones** about it that he **detested** her:
He did not hide the fact that he disliked her intensely.
उसने उसके प्रति अपनी नफ़रत नहीं छुपायी।

- Will he be able to **make the grade**?
  Will he be able to meet the criteria?
  क्या वह उस मानदण्ड को छू सकेगा।

- She is already **making waves** in music circles:
  She is already doing well and getting noticed in the music industry.
  वह पहले से ही संगीत की दुनिया में छायी हुई है।

- **He is a maven:**
  He is an expert.
  वह तो इस काम में उस्ताद है।

- He is **an all-rounder**:
  He is capable of doing many tasks.
  वह बहुत-से काम कर सकता है।

- He gave us **merry hell**:
  He gave us a very difficult time.
  उसने हमें बहुत तकलीफ़ दी है।

- I got a **Mexican promotion**:
  I got promoted with no hike in salary.
  मुझे पदोन्नति तो मिली पर वेतन नहीं बढ़ा।

- I have been **kicked upstairs**:
  I got promoted to a post that has no importance.
  मुझे ऐसी पदोन्नति मिली जो अर्थहीन है।

- You have **missed the boat**, sorry:
  You are too late and will not be given a chance.
  आप देर से आए अब कुछ नहीं हो सकता।

- He is **a mutt**:
  He is a stupid/incompetent person.
  वह एक बेवकूफ़ इंसान है।

- She started **calling me names**:
  She began abusing me/saying uncomplimentary things.
  उसने मुझे गालियाँ देनी शुरू कर दीं।

- The **name of the game** is:
  The thing to do is...
  जो काम करना है वह यह है...।

- It is a **nine days'** wonder:
  This is not something that will last very long.
  यह ज़्यादा दिन नहीं चलने वाला।
- It is a **9 to 5 job**:
  It's a regular/routine job with little excitement/it is an office job.
  यह एक सीधी-साधी ऑफिस की नौकरी है।
- It's no **great shakes**:
  It is average stuff.
  यह एक सामान्य-सी बात/घटना/वस्तु है।
- They **fought no-holds barred**:
  They fought without any rules and used all tactics.
  उन्होंने लड़ाई में हर हथकंडा अपनाया।
- **I don't give a damn**:
  I don't care/I am not bothered.
  मुझे कोई परवाह नहीं है।
- I **have no clue**:
  I know nothing.
  मुझे बिलकुल नहीं पता।
- **Not tonight, darling:**
  Sorry, I'm not interested in having sex tonight.
  आज की रात मैं रतिक्रिया के लिए इच्छुक नहीं हूँ।
- **He yaps a little too much:**
  He talks too much.
  वह बहुत बातूनी है।
- He was **out of his depth**:
  He could not cope with the situation/he was not able to take part in the conversation since he lacked knowledge.
  उसमें ज्ञान की गहराई कम है।
- He is **out of sync** with his boss:
  He does not get along well with his boss.
  उसकी अपने बॉस से नहीं बनती।

- She is **in the zone**:
  She is in perfect touch.
  वह बहुत कर्मनिष्ठ है।
- **Keep me in the loop**:
  Keep me informed of developments.
  मुझे बताते रहिए।
- He is **out on a limb**:
  He is in deep trouble.
  वह गहरे संकट में है।
- He is **over a barrel**:
  He is in a very bad situation.
  वह बहुत बुरी हालत में है।
- He is **over the hill** now:
  He is no longer effective/has grown old.
  वह अब बूढ़ा हो चला है।
- Will you **stop sitting** on the fence?
  Will you please take a decision one way or the other?
  क्या आप कोई-न-कोई निर्णय लेना चाहेंगे।
- **He is a pansy**:
  He is weak/feminine.
  वह बहुत नाजुक/स्त्रैण है।
- He was **pissed out** at the party:
  He was heavily drunk at the party.
  वह पार्टी में बहुत पिए हुए था।
- He gave her **a light peck**:
  He kissed her gently on the cheeks.
  उसने उसके गालों पर धीरे-से चुम्बन लिया।
- She is **a peppy girl**:
  She is a chirpy and energetic girl.
  वह एक जोशीली लड़की है।
- I will give **a piece of my mind to** her:
  I will scold her.
  मैं उसे डाँट लगाऊँगा।

- He did a bit of **pillow talk** with her:
  He spoke intimately with her.
  उसने उससे काफ़ी अंतरंगतापूर्वक बात की।
- I was **pissed off** at her presence:
  Her presence made me very angry.
  उसकी उपस्थिति ने उसे गुस्सा दिलाया।
- He **keeps things close to his chest**:
  He is very secretive and does not reveal his plans.
  वह अपनी योजनाएँ किसी को नहीं बताता।
- I don't like to **play second fiddle**:
  I would like to be in control of things/don't like to take orders from someone else.
  मैं किसी के द्वारा नियंत्रित होकर काम नहीं कर सकता।
- He is **poker-faced**:
  He is expressionless.
  उसके चेहरे पर कोई भाव नहीं है।
- He is a **wooden actor**:
  He cannot act and does not have any expressions.
  वह एक सपाट चेहरे वाला / भावहीन अभिनेता है।
- He is **randy as hell**:
  He is a very lusty man.
  वह बहुत लोभी प्रवृत्ति का है।
- He behaved **out of line**:
  He behaved badly.
  उसने बहुत दुर्व्यहार किया।
- She **called it quits**:
  She stopped the work.
  उसने काम बंद कर दिया।
- Don't have **pipe dreams**:
  Don't make grand plans that you cannot realise.
  ऐसे वादे मत कीजिए जिनको पूरा करना आपके बस की बात नहीं।

- **Come hell or high water** I will do it:
  I will do it despite obstacles and will not give up.
  चाहे जो हो जाए, मैं इसे करके ही रहूँगा।

- The **door is always open** for you:
  You can always approach me.
  मेरा दरवाज़ा आपके लिए हमेशा खुला है।

- I am not at your **beck and call**:
  You cannot take me for granted/cannot expect me to do whatever you want.
  मैं आपके लिए आपका मनचाहा कार्य नहीं कर सकता।

- At least I have a **roof over** my head:
  I am thankful that I have shelter/accommodation.
  कम-से-कम मेरे पास रहने के लिए जगह है।

- **He has won many laurels**:
  He has received much recognition and accomplished a lot.
  उसने अपने कर्मों से बहुत तकलीफ़ें हासिल की हैं।

- He has **made his mark** and won the boss over:
  He has impressed the boss with his work.
  उसने अपने कार्य से अपने बॉस के दिल में जगह बनाई है।

- He will be **where the action** is:
  He is always in the centre of action.
  वह काम के लिए हमेशा तैयार रहता है।

- I thought you were **a man of action**:
  I thought you were a person who could get things done.
  मेरा ख़याल था कि आप ही काम के आदमी हैं।

- He is a bit **hard-nosed**:
  He is adamant.
  वह थोड़ा अड़ियल किस्म का है।

- He is **just like a mule**:
  He is very stubborn by nature.
  वह बहुत ज़िद्दी है।

- He has become **a junkie**:
  He has become addicted to drugs.
  वह नशे का आदी हो चुका है।
- Presently he is **top of the line**:
  Currently he is the best in the business.
  इस समय वह व्यापार में सबसे आगे है।/इस समय उसका व्यापार बढ़िया चल रहा है।
- He will not **spill his guts** with her:
  He will not let her know his secrets.
  वह उसे अपने राज़ नहीं जानने देगा।
- He **is nuts** about her:
  He admires her greatly.
  वह उसे बहुत पसंद करता है।
- I think he is **having a fling** with her:
  I think he is having an affair with her.
  मेरा ख्याल है कि उसका उसके साथ प्रेम संबंध है।
- They are **seeing each other**:
  They are having an affair.
  उनमें प्रेम संबंध है।
- Don't **get onto the bandwagon**:
  Don't do something simply because others are doing it.
  दूसरों का बिना सोचे अनुसरण मत करो।
- He is a **big boozer**:
  He drinks heavily.
  वह बहुत शराब पीता है।/वह पियक्कड़ है।
- He is **quick on the uptake**:
  He is quick to understand things.
  वह जल्दी ही काम समझ/सीख लेता है।
- She is a **man-eater**:
  She is fond of having affairs with men.
  वह मर्दों के साथ प्रेम-सम्बन्ध बनाने की शौकीन है।

- It was **mind-blowing** action:
  It was amazing action.
  यह कमाल का काम था।
- **She took things to heart:**
  She was very hurt by what happened.
  वह इस घटना से बहुत दुःखी थी।
- **This is just what the doctor ordered:**
  This is the right thing to do.
  यह काम करना सही होगा।
- You have got a habit of **locking horns** with me:
  You have the habit of arguing with me.
  तुम्हें मुझसे विवाद करने की आदत पड़ चुकी है।
- He will **get stumped** when he sees it:
  He will be astonished when he sees it.
  वह यह देखकर हैरान रह जाएगा।
- He is **an astute character**:
  He is a very sharp man.
  वह बहुत चतुर व्यक्ति है।
- **No sweat**, this job will **fall into my lap**:
  No problem, this job will come to me easily.
  कोई चिन्ता की बात नहीं, यह काम मेरे ही हिस्से आएगा।
- It's straight from the **horse's mouth**:
  This news comes straight from the person in authority.
  यह जानकारी हमें सीधा अधिकारी से प्राप्त हुई है।
- He is a **pseudo-intellectual**:
  He pretends to be an intellectual.
  वह बुद्धिजीवी होने का ढोंग करता है।
- **He got badly roughed up:**
  He was beaten up badly.
  उसे बुरी तरह पीटा गया।
- All **hell broke loose** when India lost the match:
  When India lost the match, people reacted violently.
  भारत की हार से निराश लोग हंगामे पर उतारू हो गए।

- I will **eat crow if** you can do this:
  I will accept defeat if you do it.
  मैं हार मान लूँगा यदि आप इसे करके दिखा सकें।
- All the **fingers point** towards his involvement in the crime:
  All the evidence indicates that he is involved in the crime.
  अपराध में उसके शामिल होने के सभी संकेत मिल रहे हैं।
- All that **baloney will not impress** me:
  All that big talk/boasting will not fool me.
  ये सारी मूर्खताएँ मुझे प्रभावित नहीं कर सकेंगी।
- He is **sold on** her:
  He is totally overcome by her charm.
  वह उसके आकर्षण पाश में बँध गया।
- It's **easy on** the pocket:
  It's cheap.
  ये काफ़ी सस्ता है।
- I bought it **for a song**:
  I bought it at a very low rate.
  मैंने इसे सस्ते में ख़रीदा है।
- You have been **taken for a ride**:
  You have been cheated.
  आपको धोखा दिया गया है।
- We should be on the **same wavelength**:
  We should be thinking similarly.
  हमें समान विचारों का होना चाहिए।
- We must **act in concert**:
  We must do things in cooperation.
  हमें मिलजुलकर काम करना होगा।
- He is **living on the edge**:
  He is leading a very uncertain/risky life.
  वह बहुत मुसीबत में है।
- He is **driving in the fast lane**:
  He is leading a risky life.
  वह एक ख़तरनाक रास्ते की ओर बढ़ रहा है।

- He began **to fire questions** at her:
He asked her quick questions without giving her too much time to think.
उसने उस पर सवालों की झड़ी लगा दी।

- **Every drop in the ocean counts:**
Every single effort will help.
हर छोटा योगदान भी महत्त्वपूर्ण होता है।

- **Let's quit when the going is still good**:
Let's stop when things are still in our favour.
जब सब ठीक होकर हमारे हिसाब से चल रहा है तो हमें अब इस काम को यहीं रोक देना चाहिए।

- There is **light at the end of the tunnel**:
There is hope that things will turn out better in the end.
उम्मीद है कि अंत में सब ठीक हो जाएगा।

11. Queries and Questions

- Do you share a **good rapport** with him?
  Do you share good relations with him?
  क्या आपकी उससे अच्छी बनती है?

- Are there any **hard-and-fast** rules?
  Are there any specific rules to be followed?
  क्या यहाँ कोई विशेष नियम-कानून हैं?

- Is it in the **realm of reality**?
  Is this possible and for real?
  क्या ये वास्तविकता से जुड़ी बात है?

- Is she a **cut above** the rest?
  Is she better than the others?
  क्या वह औरों से बेहतर है?

- Is he likely to **make the grade**?
  Is he likely to be selected?
  क्या उसके चयन की संभावना है?

- But who will **do the honours**?
  But who is going to do it?
  पर ये करेगा कौन?

- **What politicking is going on here?**
  Who is playing politics here?
  यहाँ पर कौन राजनीति खेल रहा है?

- **Is it pertinent** to do this?
  Is it necessary to do this?
  क्या यह करना ठीक है?

- **Why this hullabaloo?**
  Why all this fuss and noise?
  इस बात पर इतनी हायतौबा क्यों?

- Is there any place where we can **hang out**?
  Is there a place where we can relax and enjoy?
  क्या यहाँ कोई स्थान है जहाँ हम मज़े कर सकें।
- Why does he still **loiter around here**?
  Why is he still roaming around here?
  वह अब भी यहाँ क्यों घूम रहा है?
- **So what's your alibi?**
  So what excuse do you have to offer?
  तो क्या सफ़ाई है आपकी?
- So what's your **game plan**?
  So what is your plan of action?
  तो आपकी कार्ययोजना क्या है?
- **How do we break this impasse?**
  How do we break this deadlock?
  हम इस गतिरोध को कैसे तोड़ेंगे?
- Do you **have designs** on me?
  Are you playing games with me?
  क्या आप मेरे प्रति गलत इरादे रखते हैं?
- Is he still **in the reckoning**?
  Is he still in the race/does he still hold any importance?
  क्या वह अभी भी दौड़ से बाहर नहीं हुआ है?
- Who is going to **foot the bill**?
  Who will pay the bill?
  बिल कौन भरेगा?
- Is there **a kernel of truth** here?
  Is there any truth in this?
  क्या इसमें कोई सच्चाई है?
- Is there even **an iota** of evidence?
  Is there any proof at all?
  क्या इस सिलसिले में कोई छोटा-मोटा साक्ष्य भी है?

- **How much is the damage?**
  How much will the total expenses work out to?
  कुल कितने पैसे भरने हैं?
- Who is responsible for **this snafu**?
  Who is responsible for this mistake?
  इस गलती का ज़िम्मेदार कौन है?
- Who is **calling the shots** here?
  Who is the boss here/who decides things here?
  यहाँ फ़ैसला किसके हाथ में है?
- How was **the binge**?
  How was the drunken spree?
  पीने-पिलाने का सिलसिला कैसा रहा?
- Will **you keep bingeing all day long**?
  Will you keep eating the whole day?
  क्या आप सारे दिन खाना-पीना करते रहेंगे?
- Who will **bell the cat**?
  Who will accept responsibility to get this done?
  बिल्ली के गले में घंटी कौन बाँधेगा?/ इस मुश्किल काम को करने का ज़िम्मा कौन लेगा?

12. Miscellaneous

- This **is in fact part of a larger phenomenon**:
This is not a single isolated incident but part of something larger.
दरअसल यह बात इतनी छोटी नहीं जितनी नज़र आ रही है, क्योंकि ये एक बड़े तथ्य की तरफ़ इशारा करती है।

- Let's **call a spade a spade**:
Let's speak plainly and frankly.
जो सच है वह तो कहना ही पड़ेगा।

- Their differences **were mirrored** in the different lifestyles they led:
Their differences were clear in the different lives they led.
उनका वैचारिक विरोध उनकी जीवनशैली से ही ज़ाहिर हो जाता है।

- There were **occasional hints of things to come**:
We had some idea about the things that could happen.
अक्सर समय से पहले ही होने वाली घटनाओं का पूर्वानुमान हो जाता है।

- The less competent colleges **faded soon**:
The colleges that were not good enough had to close down.
कमतर गुणवत्ता वाले महाविद्यालय अधिक नहीं चल सके।

- **Regardless of the tune** he is singing now he knew things beforehand:
Although he does not accept it now, he knew what was happening much before.
अब वह इसके लिए जो भी बहाने बनाए पर यह सच है कि उसे पता था कि आगे क्या होने वाला है।

- **Absurd as it may sound**:
It may sound foolish but it is a fact.
सुनने में यह चाहे कितना भी अप्रिय लगे, लेकिन यह सच है।

- When they started to expand, they **came up to the outer limits**:
Once they had expanded up to a certain point, there was no scope to expand any more.
एक सीमा पर पहुँचकर उनके विस्तार को विराम लगना ही था।

- They are **in tacit agreement** over this:
There is a secret/silent agreement over this between them.
इस विषय पर उनके बीच एक अनकही स्वीकृति पहले से है।

- This concept was based **on the fantasy** of the boss:
The boss planned this without taking the real facts into consideration.
चाहे यह कितनी भी अव्यावहारिक क्यों न हो यह अवधारणा बॉस की कल्पना से उपजी है।

- A **web of intrigue was woven around** her:
Mystery and deception surrounded her.
उसके आस-पास साज़िशों का जाल रचा गया था।

- This is **a case in point**:
This is a clear example.
इस बात का यह एक प्रत्यक्ष उदाहरण है।

- We are not concerned with the **side current but the mainstream**:
We are worried about the main problem and not about side issues.
हमारा संबंध मूल समस्या से है, आपस के मुद्दों से नहीं।

- There was **an undercurrent of** tension in the room:
There was heavy tension in the room.
कक्ष में सर्वत्र तनाव व्याप्त था।

- The fear amongst the people **was palpable**:
The fear that the people felt could be sensed heavily.
लोगों में व्याप्त भय आसानी से समझा जा सकता था।

- In the heat of the discussion the **main theme was lost**:
In the heated discussion the main problem was lost track of.
चर्चा की उत्तेजना के दौरान मुख्य विषय तो पीछे ही छूट गया था।

- He will be **taken to task**:
He will be punished.
उसको सज़ा दी जाएगी।

- I **take exception to your remarks**:
I don't like your remarks and object to it.
आपकी टिप्पणी से मुझे एतराज़ है।

- He visits me **on and off**:
He does visit me sometimes.
वह कभी-कभी मुझसे मिलने आता है।

- She stood by him **through thick and thin**:
She supported him during good and bad times.
उसने अच्छे-बुरे दिनों में उसका साथ दिया।

- The police are **hand in glove** with criminals:
The police are helping criminals.
पुलिस अपराधियों के साथ है।

- We shall fight **tooth and nail** for our rights:
We will fight vigorously for our rights.
हम अपने अधिकारों के लिए जमकर संघर्ष करेंगे।

- **He stood his ground against all adversaries:**
He fought against all his enemies without backing out.
उसने अपने विरोधियों से लड़ने में कोई कसर नहीं छोड़ी।

- He was **kept in the dark** about her affairs:
He wasn't told about her affairs.
उसके प्रेम संबंध की उसे कोई जानकारी नहीं थी।

- **That's where the shoe pinches:**
This is where it hurts me.
समस्या यहाँ पर है।

- This might create **bad blood** between the two brothers:
The two brothers may fight because of this.
इससे दोनों भाईयों में झगड़े का ख़तरा है।

- Presently my **hands are full**:
Presently I am extremely busy.
इस समय मैं पूरी तरह व्यस्त हूँ।

- He **kicked up a row** with her:
He began to fight with her.
उसने उसके साथ झगड़ा शुरू कर दिया।

- I can make **neither head nor tail** of it:
I don't understand anything of this at all.
मैं इससे अधिक कुछ नहीं जानता।

- His fate **hangs in the balance:**
His fate is stiil undecided/uncertain.
उसका भविष्य पूर्णतया अनिश्चित है।
- I understand he **knows a thing or two:**
I know he is aware of some things.
मैं जानता हूँ कि कुछ चीज़ों की उसे जानकारी है।
- I think **another party is on the cards:**
I think we will have another party soon.
मेरा ख़याल है कि हम जल्दी ही दूसरी पार्टी/महफ़िल भी आयोजित करने वाले हैं।
- He moved **heaven and earth** to get his book published:
He worked very hard and did everything to get his book published.
अपनी पुस्तक प्रकाशित कराने में उसने ज़मीन-आसमान एक कर दिया।
- His book will never see the **light of day:**
His book will never be printed.
उसकी पुस्तक कभी प्रकाशित नहीं हो पाएगी।
- His writing **is atrocious:**
He writes very badly.
उसके लेखन का स्तर गिरा हुआ है।
- **So important did they deem these problems:**
They gave a lot of importance to these problems.
इन समस्याओं को उन्होंने बहुत गम्भीरता से लिया।
- This new method brought **startling discoveries:**
This method uncovered new facts.
इस नए तरीके से कई चौंका देने वाली खोजें हुईं।
- The new boss liked to **throw his weight around:**
The new boss was unpleasantly self-assertive.
नए बॉस ने अपने को अधिक महत्त्वपूर्ण और शक्तिशाली जाहिर करने की अनुचित शैली अपनायी।
- **Much that hitherto was difficult seemed simple:**
Earlier whatever was difficult became easy.
जो पहले मुश्किल लग रहा था अब आसान हो गया।

- Many **streams of thought flowed** together to impact the concept:
  Many different thoughts changed the overall concept.
  अलग-अलग विचारों ने पूरी अवधारणा को ही बदल दिया।
- What is the **driving force** of this man's energy?
  What is the secret of this man's tremendous energy?
  इस व्यक्ति की ऊर्जा के पीछे क्या रहस्य है?
- Women are always **at loggerheads** with him:
  Women are always unable to get along with him.
  स्त्रियों की उससे बिलकुल नहीं बनती।
- Teacher **called for an explanation** from the students:
  Teacher asked for an explanation from the students.
  शिक्षक ने छात्रों से स्पष्टीकरण माँगा।
- The professor gave the students a **dressing down**:
  The professor scolded his students sternly.
  प्राध्यापक ने छात्रों को काफ़ी फटकार लगायी।
- He **called on me** this Tuesday:
  He came to my house on Tuesday.
  उसने मुझे इस मंगलवार को मिलने के लिए आमंत्रित किया।
- **At last the truth has come out**:
  The truth was finally revealed.
  आख़िरकार सच सामने आ ही गया।
- I was **let into** her secrets:
  I was told about her secrets.
  मुझे उसके राज़ बताए गए थे।
- I am sorry **to put** you to so much trouble:
  I am sorry to have caused you all this trouble.
  आपको इतना कष्ट देने का मुझे दुःख है।
- This large cupboard **takes up** so much room:
  This cupboard is very large and occupies more space.
  यह बड़ी अलमारी काफ़ी जगह घेरती है।
- He **threw up** whatever he ate:
  He vomited whatever he ate.
  उसने जो भी खाया सब उल्टी करके निकाल दिया।

- **He puked** repeatedly:
He vomited repeatedly.
उसने बार-बार उल्टी की।

- **He turned out to be bogus:**
He turned out to be a fake person.
वह तो जालसाज निकला।

- All his earlier friends **turned against him**:
All his old friends went against him.
उसके सभी पुराने मित्र उसके शत्रु हो गए।

- He worked **for nothing**:
He did the work free.
उसने मुफ़्त में काम किया।

- Will you do **this gratis**?
Will you do this free?
क्या आप यह मुफ़्त में करेंगे?

- Is this **pro bono** work?
Does this work have to be done free/without a fee?
क्या यह मुफ़्त का काम है?

- I feel like **tearing my hair out**:
I feel very frustrated.
मैं बुरी तरह हताश महसूस कर रहा हूँ।

- You will have to **speak on the record**:
You will have to speak officially.
आपको आधिकारिक तौर पर बात करनी होगी।

- His son has a fine **scholastic record**:
His son is good in studies.
उसका बेटा पढ़ाई में बहुत अच्छा है।

- I will **drop you a line**:
I will write to you.
मैं आपको पत्र लिख दूँगा।

- **E-mail has spelt finish to the art of letter writing:**
E-mail has killed the practice of writing letters.
ई-मेल के कारण पत्र लेखन की आदत जैसे ख़त्म ही हो गई है।

- Let's not read **too much into this**:
  Let us not give undue importance to this.
  बेहतर होगा कि हम इस पर अधिक ध्यान न दें।
- Once all systems are **on board**:
  Once everything is operational.
  एक बार बस सब कुछ शुरू हो जाए।
- She **won't budge**, so forget it:
  She will not change her stand/mind, so forget it.
  वह अपनी बात पर अड़ी रहेगी, इसलिए अब इस बात को छोड़िये।
- She made **a bitchy comment** about you and I lost my **temper**:
  She made a dirty remark about you and I became angry.
  उसने तुम्हारे बारे में एक घटिया टिप्पणी की जिसे सुनकर मैं आपे से बाहर हो गई।
- He beat a **hasty retreat**:
  He quickly went back.
  वह तुरंत वापस चला गया।
- He was received with **open arms**:
  He was welcomed with warmth.
  उसका गर्मजोशी से स्वागत हुआ था।
- He turned a **deaf ear** to my advice:
  He didn't listen to my advice.
  उसने मेरी सलाह पर कोई ध्यान नहीं दिया।
- I **take exception** to your remark:
  I object to your remark.
  मुझे आपकी टिप्पणी पसंद नहीं है।
- It's **at my fingertips**:
  I know it by heart.
  ये तो मुझे पूरा याद है।
- He was saved in the **nick of time**:
  He was saved just in time.
  उसे एकदम सही समय पर बचा लिया गया।

- The entire city was **thrown out of gear**:
  The entire city was badly affected.
  पूरा शहर बुरी तरह प्रभावित हुआ।
- My house is within a **stone's throw** from the bank:
  My house is very close to the bank.
  मेरा घर बैंक के बहुत नज़दीक है।
- The police **left no stone unturned** to catch the **culprits**:
  The police did everything possible to catch the persons responsible.
  पुलिस ने अभियुक्त को पकड़ने में कोई कसर नहीं छोड़ी।
- He is leaving India **for good**:
  He is leaving India and settling abroad permanently.
  वह हमेशा के लिए भारत छोड़कर जा रहा है।
- We **have our differences**:
  We do not agree on some issues.
  हमारे बीच कुछ बातों को लेकर सहमति नहीं है।
- We have **announced a ceasefire**:
  We have suspended our hostilities/fights.
  हमने अपनी लड़ाई को रोक दिया।
- I don't like **to mince words**:
  I am very straightforward.
  मैं सीधी बात करना पसंद करता हूँ।
- We are **having a close look** at many possibilities:
  We are working hard on various fronts and considering things.
  हम कई संभावनाएँ तलाश कर रहे हैं।
- It's only **a pale hint** of what lies **in store** for you:
  It is only a minor indication of things awaiting you.
  यह तो आगे आने वाली परिस्थितियों का एक छोटा-सा संकेत है।
- **There is no exception to this rule:**
  Everybody has to follow this rule.
  इस नियम के साथ कोई समझौता नहीं किया जा सकता है।
- Her path **was beset** with difficulties:
  She had to face lots of difficulties.
  उसके रास्ते में बहुत परेशानियाँ आईं।

- He **will concede** some of our demands only:
  He will only agree to some of our demands.
  वह हमारी कुछ ही माँगों पर सहमति देगा।
- This is **now passé**:
  This is no longer in fashion.
  अब तो यह प्रचलन में नहीं है।
- **If past lessons are any barometer:**
  If earlier lessons are any indication...
  अगर पुरानी सीख को मापदण्ड बनाकर देखा जाए...।
- If **past history is anything to go by:**
  If the events of the past are any guide/indication...
  अगर पुराने इतिहास पर विश्वास करके देखें...।
- **As a model, her calendar never lacked dates:**
  She was an extremely busy model.
  वह एक बहुत ही व्यस्त मॉडल थी।
- Once on the **scent** of the criminal the dog **quickened the chase**:
  After the dog picked up the scent, he began chasing the criminal quickly.
  जैसे ही कुत्ते ने गंध पकड़ी उसने अपराधी का पीछा शुरू कर दिया।
- It was a **stag party**:
  It was a party meant for men only.
  वह पार्टी सिर्फ पुरुषों के लिए ही थी।
- Everyone commented on **his masterstroke**:
  Everyone praised his smart move.
  सबने उसकी चतुराई को सराहा।
- **Don't covet your neighbour's wife:**
  Don't be interested in your neighbour's wife.
  अपने पड़ोसी की पत्नी पर नज़र न डालें।
- You have been **running the show** all your life:
  You have been handling things yourself throughout your life.
  आपने जीवनभर सारा काम खुद ही सँभाला।

- She **knew without a shadow of doubt** that he was her man:
  She knew clearly that he was the kind of man she would like to marry/be with.
  उसको कोई संदेह नहीं था कि यही वह व्यक्ति है, जो उसके लिए उपयुक्त है।

- He was **a symbol of strength** for his family:
  He supported his family very well and gave them courage.
  वह अपने परिवार के लिए शक्ति-स्तम्भ की तरह था।

- She cannot **keep things moving** without him:
  Without his support she will not be able to manage things.
  वह उसके बिना जीवन की कल्पना भी नहीं कर सकती थी।

- He knew he was **up against a wild mare**:
  He knew that he would now have to handle this strong, difficult-to-control lady.
  उसे पता था कि इस ज़िद्दी महिला से पार पाना मुश्किल है।

- He knew how to back down from a **hopeless conflict**:
  He knew how to avoid a conflict that he couldn't win.
  उसको पता था कि इस बेमतलब की लड़ाई को वापस कैसे किया जाए।

- She **went out of her way** to make friends in the new colony:
  She made special efforts to befriend people in the new colony.
  इस नई बस्ती में दोस्त बनाने के लिए उसने हर कोशिश कर डाली।

- He **dug deep and threw a knockout punch**:
  He used all his remaining energy and threw a blow that knocked out his opponent.
  उसने अपनी सारी शक्ति लगाकर एक प्रहार से ही अपने शत्रुओं को धूल चटा दी।

- He came **inching back** from the jaws of defeat:
  He pulled his way back slowly from what would have been a certain defeat.
  अपनी पराजय के करीब पहुँचकर भी उसने अपनी जीत सुनिश्चित कर ली।

- He **received a standing ovation**:
  People stood up and clapped/cheered for him.
  लोगों ने खड़े होकर उसके लिए तालियाँ बजाईं।

- He got up to receive **well-deserved accolades**:
  He stood up to receive the praise/cheers that he fully deserved.
  उसने खड़े होकर अपनी प्रशंसा को स्वीकार किया जो कि उसकी योग्यता के अनुरूप थी।

- **His mind went numb:**
  He was unable to think due to fear/confusion.
  उसका दिमाग कुछ भी सोच नहीं पा रहा था।

- She is **mad as a hatter**:
  She is a crazy person.
  वह एक पागल औरत है।

- Angry young men **threw off the shackles** of the past:
  Angry young men forgot about the limitations of the past and wanted to make a new beginning.
  वे क्रुद्ध नवयुवक अपने पुराने संबंधों को भूलकर एक नई शुरुआत के लिए संकल्पित थे।

- What he **craved the most eluded him**:
  He never got what he wanted the most.
  जो भी उसकी दिली तमन्ना थी उसे कभी हासिल नहीं हुआ।

- The boxer took a **standing count**:
  The boxer managed to stand while he was being counted out.
  उस मुक्केबाज ने अपनी पराजय की गिनती के बावजूद खड़े होकर लड़ाई के लिए अपने को फिर से तैयार कर लिया।

- I will **fix you** a good warm meal:
  I will make a good warm meal for you.
  मैं तुम्हारे लिए गर्मागर्म गोश्त पकाऊंगा।

- It was **an awesome display** of power:
  It was a show of power that was impressive/frightening.
  यह एक अद्भुत शक्ति-प्रदर्शन था।

- The streets were **choc-a-bloc** with people:
  The roads were filled with people.
  सड़क लोगों से ठसाठस भरी हुई थी।

- She looked like **an overdecorated Christmas tree**:
  She had used too much makeup and ornaments, making her look silly.
  ज़रूरत से ज़्यादा सजे-धजे होने के कारण वह बहुत भोंडी लग रही थी।
- He **had no qualms** about the murder:
  He had no regrets whatsoever about committing the murder.
  उसे अपने अपराध पर कोई पछतावा नहीं था।
- He reached **a point of no return**:
  He couldn't come back/rise up from that point onwards.
  अब वह उस बिन्दु पर पहुँच गया था जहाँ से वापस जाना नामुमकिन था।
- The **argument** reached **a dead end**:
  The argument reached a stage where no decision was possible.
  बहस उस बिन्दु पर पहुँच गई थी जहाँ कोई भी निर्णय संभव नहीं था।
- He was **branded a harbinger of doom**:
  He was known as a person who brought trouble/disaster.
  उसे आफ़त का परकाला कहा जाता था।
- He simply **floated with the tide**:
  He simply did what all the others did/what circumstances dictated.
  परिस्थितियों से समझौता कर उसने भी वही किया जो सबने किया।
- He could **still troubled waters**:
  He could bring peace/calm to a difficult situation.
  बुरी परिस्थितियों से निपटना उसे आता है।
- I shall **get right to the point**:
  I shall not waste any time.
  मैं समय बर्बाद नहीं करना चाहता।
- Let's get down to **brass tacks**:
  Let us get to the main business.
  चलिए सीधे काम की बात करें।
- She **held her tongue** and went with him:
  She kept quiet and did what he wanted.
  उसने चुपचाप उसकी बात मान ली।
- There has to be a certain amount of **give and take**:
  There has to be some concessions on both sides.
  दोनों तरफ समझौते की गुंजाइश होनी चाहिए।

- It was a **second religion** for him:
It was very important for him.
ये उसके लिए अत्यंत महत्त्वपूर्ण था।
- He somehow managed **to get around her**:
He was somehow able to convince/seduce her.
किसी तरह वह उससे अपनी बात मनवाने में कामयाब हो गया।
- How long he could **evade** arrest, was a **moot point**:
How long he could avoid being arrested was debatable/uncertain.
वह कितने दिन अपनी गिरफ़्तारी से बच सकेगा, कहा नहीं जा सकता।
- He left in a **huff**:
He left angrily and hurriedly.
वह गुस्से में वहाँ से तेजी से निकल गया।
- He **set out to cultivate** her:
He began moves to woo her.
उसने उसे अपना बनाने की कोशिश शुरू कर दी।
- The newspapers **stepped up their tirade** against him:
The newspapers increased the degree of their opposition to him.
अख़बारों ने उसका विरोध तीव्र कर दिया।
- He **let her play** her role in this business:
He allowed her to have a role in the business.
उसने अपने व्यवसाय में उसे सक्रिय भूमिका निभाने की सहमति दे दी।
- He is **a restless soul**:
He cannot stay still/without doing something.
वह कुछ किए बिना नहीं रह सकता।
- He sat **fidgeting** in the chair:
He sat shifting around uncomfortably in the chair.
वह अपनी कुर्सी पर पहलू बदलता रहा।
- He is a **shifty character**:
He is an evasive/untrustworthy person.
वह एक धूर्त व्यक्ति है।
- She **picked up the threads** of her life once again:
She started a new life once more.
उसने फिर एक नया जीवन शुरू किया।

- All his **arguments came to naught**:
  His arguments did not have any impact.
  उसके तर्क असफल रहे।
- The situation **plumbed new depths**:
  The situation became much worse than ever before.
  परिस्थिति और भी गंभीर हो गई।
- They kept themselves **going on liquor and hope**:
  They survived and lived because of drinks and hope.
  वे शराब और उम्मीदों के सहारे आगे बढ़ते रहे।
- Let's **switch the topic**:
  Let's stop discussing this and speak about something else.
  चलिए कोई और बात करें।
- The situation went **from bad to worse**:
  The situation turned very bad.
  स्थिति पहले से ख़राब हो गई।
- I have **come a long way** since the old days:
  I have improved a lot since the early years.
  पहले के मुकाबले मैंने काफ़ी प्रगति की है।
- This is a **blatant betrayal** of your boss:
  You have cheated your boss openly.
  आपने अपने बॉस को खुलेआम धोखा दिया है।
- He was **adept at aping** his teacher:
  He was very good at imitating his teacher.
  वह अपने शिक्षक की नकल उतारने में निपुण था।
- He **sank** to new **depths of decadence**:
  He became more depraved than before.
  वह पतन की गहराइयों में गिरता चला गया।
- A **stroke of fate** destroyed him:
  He was destroyed by his bad luck/destiny.
  भाग्य ने उसे बर्बाद कर दिया।
- This is just a **nominal salary** for this job:
  This is just a token pay for this job.
  इस कार्य के लिए यह तो नाममात्र का वेतन है।

- He **downed a shot of whisky quickly**:
He quickly gulped a peg of whisky.
उसने जल्दी से शराब का एक घूँट गले से उतार लिया।
- I **have my drinks neat**:
I have my drinks without any soda or water.
मेरी शराब ख़ालिस है।
- He **scoffed at** her fears:
He dismissed/laughed at her fears.
उसने उसके डर का मज़ाक बना दिया।
- The house was in a **dilapidated/ramshackle** state:
The house was old and in a very bad state.
वह मकान जीर्ण-शीर्ण हालत में था।
- She did the **vanishing act**:
She disappeared/went away quietly.
वह तुरंत गायब हो गई।
- I **have no truck with** him since March:
I have no contact/involvement with him since March.
मेरी मार्च से उससे कोई मुलाकात नहीं हुई।
- **So much mudslinging has been going on:**
People have been talking badly/hurling allegations against each other.
एक-दूसरे पर बहुत कीचड़ उछाला जा रहा है।
- She came running in a **dishevelled state** to the police:
She came running to the police in a bad state/with her hair and clothes in disarray.
वह बदहवास हाल में दौड़ती हुई पुलिस के पास पहुँची।
- He decided to **look the other way**:
He didn't want to interfere.
उसने बीच में पड़ना बेहतर नहीं समझा।
- On this subject I am **on slippery ground**:
On this subject my knowledge is limited.
इस विषय का मुझे अधिक ज्ञान नहीं है।

- She **drew a lot of mileage** out of it:
She gained much publicity out of it.
उसे इससे काफ़ी फ़ायदा पहुँचा।
- She **gave** the police **the slip**:
She dodged/ran away from the police.
उसने पुलिस को चकमा दे दिया।
- He is **an absolute enigma**:
Very little is known about him.
उसके लिए वह एक गूढ़ पहेली बनकर रह गया।
- It was such **a groovy party**:
It was such an excellent party.
पार्टी काफ़ी शानदार थी।
- People must **eschew violence**:
People must totally avoid violence.
लोगों को हिंसा से दूर रहना चाहिए।
- Let's **launch a test balloon**:
Let us first check the situation out.
पहले स्थिति का जायज़ा लेना बेहतर होगा।
- I will carry on **till hell freezes over**:
I will carry on forever.
मैं लगातार आगे बढ़ता रहूँगा।
- Despite sustained questioning the police **drew a blank with him**:
In spite of prolonged interrogation, the police couldn't ascertain anything incriminating against him.
काफ़ी पूछताछ के बाद भी पुलिस को उससे कोई जानकारी नहीं मिली।
- **What a godforsaken place this is:**
What a lonely/out-of-the-way place this is.
यह कैसी एकांत/सुनसान जगह है?
- The picnic was filled with **fun and frolic**:
The picnic was full of fun and enjoyment.
पिकनिक काफ़ी मज़ेदार रही।

- This is an excellent **gizmo**:
  This is an excellent gadget.
  यह एक बढ़िया युक्ति है।
- It was such a **garish affair**:
  It was a bad and noisy affair.
  यह एक तड़क-भड़क वाला काम है।
- It was a **grandiose affair**:
  It was a very pomp/lavish affair.
  वह एक भव्य कार्य था।
- The police had to **grill him for hours** to **extract the truth**:
  The police had to question/interrogate him for hours to discover the real facts.
  सच उगलवाने के लिए पुलिस को उससे घंटों पूछताछ करनी पड़ी।
- **In hindsight** I feel he was correct:
  Looking back on the event I feel he was right.
  पीछे मुड़कर देखने पर मुझे लगा कि वह सही था।
- It's a **total hotchpotch**:
  It's a totally confused/disorganised situation.
  यह पूरी तरह किसी गड़बड़झाले से कम नहीं था।
- She **will hoodwink** all of you and you won't even know it:
  She will cheat all of you and you will not even realise it.
  वह आप सभी को धोखा दे देगी और आपको पता भी नहीं चलेगा।
- It's just **a guesstimate**:
  It is just an estimate that has been guessed.
  यह सिर्फ़ एक अनुमान था।
- **Whose brainchild is this?**
  Who thought of this?
  यह किसके दिमाग़ की उपज है?
- I **have a brainwave**:
  I have an excellent idea.
  मुझे एक उपाय सूझा है।

- He was involved in a **bloody imbroglio**:
  He got involved in a bloody fight.
  वह एक हिंसक झड़प में शामिल था।
- I can't answer it **off the cuff**:
  I don't know the answer immediately and will have to think about it.
  इस समय मेरे पास इसका जवाब नहीं है।
- Do **give it a thought** and get back to me:
  Do think about it and let me know.
  आप इस पर सोचकर मुझे बताना।
- She **gave me such a bad time**:
  She created so many problems for me.
  उसने मुझे काफ़ी तकलीफ़ें दी।
- He **gave me a rough time**:
  He created problems for me.
  उसने मेरे लिए काफ़ी कठिनाइयाँ पैदा कीं।
- He was found in an **inebriated state**:
  He was found drunk.
  वह नशे में धुत मिला।
- **Don't get tipsy**:
  Don't get drunk.
  नशे में मत पड़ो।
- He seems to be **tanked up**:
  He seems to be drunk.
  ऐसा लगता है कि वह पूरी तरह से नशे में है।
- Let's **tank up** the vehicle:
  Let's fill fuel in the car.
  चलिए गाड़ी में पेट्रोल डाल लेते हैं।
- I had **no inkling** of it:
  I had no knowledge of it.
  मुझे इस बारे में कोई जानकारी नहीं थी।

- He just **hung in there by a thread**:
He kept at the task despite all odds and avoided failure by a very narrow margin.
वह तमाम परेशानियों के बाद भी जुटा रहा।

- It was a **slap in his face**:
He was badly insulted.
यह उसके लिए काफ़ी अपमानजनक था।

- You **are part and parcel of** this project:
You are involved in this project in every way.
आप इस प्रोजेक्ट का एक अनिवार्य अंग हैं।

- I believe in a **tit-for-tat** policy:
I believe in hitting back in the same manner.
मैं जैसे को तैसा वाली नीति पसंद करता हूँ।

- I will **pay you back in the same coin**:
I will do the same thing that you do to me.
मैं आपके साथ आपकी तरह ही पेश आऊँगा।

- They were **caught smooching** in the park:
They were discovered kissing in the garden.
वे पार्क में चुम्बन लेते पकड़े गए।

- **He received kudos for his win:**
He was praised and honoured for his win.
जीतने पर उसकी भूरि-भूरि प्रशंसा हुई।

- He has **rung the death knell** of the project:
He has ensured the project will fail.
उसने प्रोजेक्ट की सफलता को सुनिश्चित कर दिया।

- He **made a lewd remark** to her:
He passed a sexual remark at her.
उसनें उस पर एक अश्लील टिप्पणी की।

- He has a **king-size appetite**:
He has a huge appetite.
उसकी भूख बड़ी मुश्किल से शांत होती है।

- We must **bury the hatchet**:
  We must end our conflict.
  हमें आपसी विरोध को भूलना होगा।
- I **dig ice-cream**:
  I am very fond of ice-cream.
  मुझे आइसक्रीम पसंद है।
- The river **takes a meandering** course:
  The river flows in a zigzag manner.
  यह नदी घुमावदार रास्ते से होकर बह रही है।
- They tried **to muzzle** his voice:
  They tried to stop him from speaking.
  उन्होंने उसका मुँह बंद करने की कोशिश की।
- It's **a murky affair**:
  It's a secret/immoral affair.
  यह एक असामाजिक/अनैतिक मामला है।
- He finally **met his nemesis**:
  He finally met somebody who defeated him.
  आज वह उस व्यक्ति से मिला जिसने उसे हराया था।
- Sachin Tendulkar was **more than a match** for M.S. Dhoni:
  Sachin Tendulkar was better than M.S. Dhoni.
  खेल में एम.एस धोनी, सचिन तेंदुलकर की टक्कर का नहीं है।
- The responsibility of this **onerous task** rests on you:
  This difficult task is being given to you.
  यह कठिन कार्य आपको दिया जाता है।
- In the **pandemonium** he gave the police the slip:
  In the confusion he managed to run away from the police.
  शोर-शराबे में चोर पुलिस को चकमा देकर भाग गया।
- I had **a premonition** about it:
  I had a hunch/intuition about it.
  मुझे इसका पूर्वाभास हो गया था।

- This order was never **promulgated**:
  This order was never passed.
  यह आदेश कभी लागू नहीं किया गया।
- He **broke out** into cold sweat when I questioned him:
  He was confused, nervous and sweating when I questioned him.
  मेरे सवालों के सामने उसके पसीने छूट गए।
- The boss has to **ratify it**:
  The boss has to okay it.
  बॉस को इसके लिए स्वीकृति देनी पड़ी।
- I **will reiterate** my point of view:
  I will repeat my point of view.
  मैं अपनी बात फिर से रखूँगा।
- He was **relentless in pursuing** the criminal:
  He kept chasing the criminal without pause.
  उसने अपराधी का पीछा करना जारी रखा।
- He is a **rebel without cause**:
  He goes against everything without any proper reason.
  कारण हो या न हो वह तो हर बात का विरोधी है।
- He tried to **cover up**:
  He tried to hide the truth.
  उसने सच छुपाने की कोशिश की।
- She **played dirty** with him:
  She tricked/cheated him.
  उसने उसके साथ चालबाज़ी की।
- She was **two-timing** her husband:
  She was cheating her husband and having an affair with somebody.
  अपने छिपे प्रेम-संबंधों के द्वारा वह पति को धोखा दे रही थी।
- They tried **to patch up their differences**:
  They tried to come to an understanding and sort out their differences.
  उन्होंने अपने बीच की अनबन को ख़त्म करने की कोशिश की।

- You must **go the distance**:
  You must complete the job you have begun/You must fight till the end of the bout (used specifically for boxers).
  आपने जो काम शुरू किया है उसे अवश्य पूरा करें।
- Don't act **like a cry-baby**:
  Don't cry like a child.
  बच्चों की तरह रोना-धोना बंद कीजिए।
- He is **very childish**:
  He behaves badly like a child.
  उसके अंदर बहुत बचपना है।
- She **is childlike**:
  She is as innocent as a child.
  वह तो बच्चों की तरह मासूम है।
- Don't be **so uptight**:
  Don't be so rigidly conventional/orthodox.
  इतने अड़ियल मत बनिए।
- He is very **high-handed**:
  He has the habit of bossing over people.
  वह बहुत स्वच्छंद है।
- She is **very pushy**:
  She is very aggressive and self-assertive.
  वह अति महत्त्वाकांक्षी है।
- He has a **domineering personality**:
  He likes to dominate and boss over other people.
  वह बहुत निरंकुश व्यक्ति है।
- His death **cast** a **pall of gloom** all around:
  His death left everybody feeling very sad and depressed.
  उसकी मृत्यु पर सभी शोकाकुल थे।
- He was **roundly rebuked**:
  He received a thorough scolding.
  उसे बुरी तरह से डाँट पड़ी।

- He was **fired left, right and centre** by the boss:
  The boss scolded him severely.
  बॉस ने उसे बुरी तरह से लताड़ लगाई।
- He was on the **horns of a dilemma**:
  He was confused and in two minds/unable to decide what to do.
  वह दुविधा में था।
- Your argument **is untenable**:
  Your point is without basis/justification.
  आपका तर्क आधारहीन है।
- She loves **gaudy** costumes:
  She loves clothes that are too bright.
  उसे भड़कीले कपड़े बहुत पसंद हैं।
- She has **a garish** dress sense:
  Her choice of dresses is very bright, glaring and showy.
  उसे भड़कीले कपड़े पसन्द हैं।
- He is very fond of the **fair sex**:
  He likes women very much.
  उसे औरतें बहुत पसंद हैं।
- He was with his **better half**:
  He was with his wife.
  वह अपनी पत्नी के साथ था।
- He is at the **fag end** of his career:
  He is in the last years of his professional life.
  वह अपने व्यवसायिक जीवन के अंतिम दौर में था।
- He loves to **sow his wild oats**:
  He loves to have sexual affairs.
  उसे यौन-संबंध रखना बहुत पसंद है।
- He **played the field** in college:
  He had many girlfriends/affairs in college.
  कॉलेज के दिनों में उसके बहुतों से प्रेम-संबंध थे।
- I don't want a **face-off** with them:
  I don't want any confrontation with them.
  मैं उनसे टकराना नहीं चाहता।

- He is **on French leave**:
  He is absent without permission.
  वह बिना किसी पूर्व सूचना के अनुपस्थित है।
- He is an absolute **go-getter**:
  He is an ambitious person who loves to take the initiative and get things done.
  वह हमेशा अपने लक्ष्य को हासिल करने में लगा रहता है।
- Many employees were given a **golden handshake**:
  Many employees were removed from service after being given a generous settlement amount.
  कई कर्मचारियों का पूरा हिसाब-किताब करके नौकरी से निकाल दिया गया।
- The **grapevine has it** that she sleeps around:
  The rumour is that she has sexual relationships with many men.
  ख़बर यह है कि उसके कई लोगों के साथ यौन-संबंध हैं।
- I don't want any **half-baked ideas**:
  I don't want ideas or suggestions that are foolish or not properly thought out.
  मुझे बेवकूफ़ी भरा मशविरा नहीं चाहिए।
- I have absolutely no **hang-ups** about working with her:
  I have no problems or inhibitions in working with her.
  मुझे उसके साथ काम करने में कोई हिचक नहीं है।
- He is an **incorrigible flirt**:
  He flirts with all girls and simply cannot stay without flirting.
  यह एक ऐसा इश्कबाज़ है जो कभी नहीं सुधर सकता।
- The **company's USP** is excellent after-sales service:
  The company's strong point or Unique Selling Proposition is very good after-sales service.
  कम्पनी का उत्पाद का इस्तेमाल करने का तरीका ही उसका अद्वितीय विक्रय प्रस्ताव है।
- He is **a hardboiled** criminal:
  He is a thorough criminal without any feelings.
  वह एक हृदयहीन अपराधी है।
- He is **a hardnosed** businessman:
  He is an uncompromising and professional businessman.
  वह एक सयाना व्यापारी है।

- Their family is very **hard up**:
  Their family is in very bad circumstances.
  उसका परिवार बड़ी कठिनाइयों से गुज़र रहा है।

- There has to be **hard sell** to succeed:
  To succeed one has to promote things aggressively and persistently.
  सफलता के लिए निष्ठुरता से आगे बढ़ना पड़ता है।

- He has **gone totally haywire**:
  He has gone completely out of control.
  वह पूरी तरह से नियंत्रण से बाहर हो गया।

- It is **high time** you submitted your assignment:
  It is well past the deadline and you must submit your assignment.
  समय आ चुका है जब आपको अपना काम पूरा कर लेना है।

- The criminal gave him **hush money**:
  The criminal bribed him to cover up the crime.
  अपराधी ने उसको रिश्वत दी।

- She is very **fond** of the **idiot box**:
  She is very fond of watching television.
  उसे टेलीविज़न देखने का बहुत शौक है।

- This style is the **in-thing**:
  This style is now in fashion.
  यह शैली आजकल चलन में है।

- Why the **long face**?
  Why are you looking so gloomy and depressed?
  आप इतने दुःखी क्यों नज़र आ रहे हैं।

- *Stardust* is the **cash cow** of the Magna Group:
  Stardust is the leading magazine of the Magna Group that is making the most money.
  स्टारडस्ट, मैगना समूह की कमाऊ पत्रिका है।

- It is their **flagship** magazine:
  It is their most important magazine.
  यह उसकी प्रमुख पत्रिका है।

- This situation is **a no go**:
  This situation is hopeless.
  यह स्थिति निराशाजनक है।
- Many leaders are **paper tigers**:
  Many leaders simply make empty threats and cannot actually carry them out.
  बहुत से राजनेता सिर्फ बड़ी-बड़ी बातें करते हैं पर जब करके दिखाने का समय आता है तो वे बिल्कुल निकम्मे साबित होते हैं।
- He is **no pushover**:
  He is not easy to handle/overcome.
  उसको साधना बड़ा मुश्किल है।
- **Save something for a rainy day:**
  Save some money for bad times.
  कुछ पैसे बुरे दिनों के लिए भी बचाओ।
- There was a **torrential downpour**:
  It was raining non-stop and heavily.
  वहाँ मूसलाधार बारिश हुई थी।
- Due to **inclement** weather we had to postpone our trip:
  Due to bad weather we had to postpone our journey.
  ख़राब मौसम के कारण हमें अपनी यात्रा स्थगित करनी पड़ी।
- **Stop being an ass:**
  Stop behaving like a fool.
  मुर्खों की तरह बर्ताव मत करो।
- He **never misses his siesta**:
  He never misses his afternoon nap.
  वह अपनी दोपहर की नींद लेना कभी नहीं भूलता।
- No **underhand dealings** will be allowed:
  No secret/wrong dealings will be permitted.
  कोई भी गलत किस्म का लेन-देन स्वीकार नहीं किया जाएगा।
- We made an **under-the-table deal**:
  We made a secret deal.
  हम लोगों ने गुपचुप साँठगाँठ कर ली।

- He is **always upbeat**:
  He is always in a cheerful and optimistic mood.
  वह हमेशा प्रसन्न रहता है।
- **He will brook no nonsense:**
  He will not tolerate any nonsense.
  वह किसी भी तरह की बेवक़ूफ़ी पसंद नहीं करता।
- His **attitude was very noncommittal**:
  He was unwilling to make any kind of commitment.
  वह किसी तरह का वादा नहीं करना चाहता।
- The boss **holds the veto power**:
  The boss holds the ultimate power to say 'yes' or 'no'.
  बॉस के पास आख़िरी फ़ैसले का अधिकार है।
- She has **no scruples** whatsoever:
  She is a most unprincipled woman.
  वह एक सिद्धांतहीन स्त्री है।
- The police **watered down** the allegations against the politician:
  The police reduced/toned down the charges against the politician.
  पुलिस ने राजनेताओं के ख़िलाफ़ लगाए गए आरापों को कमज़ोर कर दिया।
- He **loves the good life**:
  He loves to party and have fun.
  उसे अच्छी ज़िंदगी जीना पसंद है।
- The **allegations are scurrilous**:
  The charges are false and without basis.
  उसके आरोप अपमानजनक हैं।
- He was **a bundle of nerves**:
  He was overcome by nervousness.
  वह बुरी तरह से घबराया हुआ था।
- He was **head over heels** in love with her:
  He was madly in love with her.
  वह उसे जी-जान से चाहता है।
- She simply **breezed through** the party:
  She came to the party for an extremely short while.
  वह पार्टी में ज़रा-सी देर के लिए आई थी।

- She is very fond **of bunking college**:
  She is in the habit of not attending her classes at college.
  उसे अपनी कक्षा से ग़ायब होने की आदत है।
- The **buck stops** at my table:
  I will take the blame/responsibility for all tasks.
  यह ज़िम्मेदारी मैं लेता हूँ।
- He won twenty **grand** in the contest:
  He won 20,000 rupees in the contest.
  उसने प्रतियोगिता में बीस हज़ार रुपये जीते।
- His victory was **a cinch**:
  His victory was easy and certain.
  उसकी जीत बहुत आसान थी।
- **Let's have a dekko:**
  Let's have a look/glance.
  चलो एक नज़र डालते हैं।
- You must **give me all the dope**:
  You must give me all the information.
  आपको मुझे सारी ख़बर देनी होगी।
- Do you have **any dough** on you?
  Do you have any money?
  तुम्हारे पास कुछ पैसे होंगे?
- He will be **a sitting duck**:
  He will be an easy target.
  वह एक आसान शिकार साबित होगा।
- He was **dead set** against the idea:
  He was absolutely opposed to the idea.
  उसे यह विचार बिलकुल पसंद नहीं आया।
- He was **dead to the world**:
  He was sleeping very soundly.
  वह बहुत गहरी नींद में सोया हुआ था।
- This is a **dead spit**:
  This is an exact image/carbon copy.
  यह तो हूबहू वही है।

- He is a **natural mimic**:
  He is very good at imitating others.
  वह दूसरों की नकल उतारने में माहिर है।
- It was **a charade**:
  It was a ridiculous pretence.
  वह सिर्फ़ एक दिखावा था।
- There is no **easy money** in life:
  Money cannot be acquired easily or without hard work in life.
  बिना परिश्रम के दौलत नहीं कमाई जा सकती है।
- Thanks to your foolishness, I'm **in a fix**:
  Due to your stupidity, I am in a difficult situation.
  तुम्हारी बेवक़ूफ़ी के कारण मैं परेशानी में पड़ गया हूँ।
- You must **figure this out** yourself:
  You must understand this through your own efforts.
  इसे तुम अपने आप ही समझो।
- Don't **fish in troubled waters**:
  Don't try to take advantage of the bad situation to promote your own vested interests.
  बुरी परिस्थितियों का फ़ायदा उठाने की कोशिश मत करो।
- He **drinks like a fish**:
  He drinks excessively.
  वह बहुत पियक्कड़ है।
- He is an **odd fish**:
  He has strange/queer habits.
  उसकी हरकतें बड़ी अजीब हैं।
- Don't you have other **fish to fry**?
  Don't you have anything else to do?
  क्या तुम्हारे पास कुछ और करने को नहीं है?
- He was like a **fish out of water**:
  He was in an unfamiliar situation/surroundings and felt most uncomfortable.
  वह बिनबुलाई मुसीबत में फँस गया था।

- They **indulged in fisticuffs**:
  They assaulted each other.
  उन्होंने एक-दूसरे पर घूँसेबाज़ी शुरू कर दी।

- They **came to blows**:
  They came to beating each other.
  वह एक-दूसरे से हाथापाई करने लगे।

- They **are incompatible**:
  They are not suitable for each other.
  वह दोनों एक-दूसरे के लिये नहीं बने हैं।

- They **can't stand the sight** of each other:
  They do not get along well at all.
  वे एक-दूसरे की शक्ल भी देखना पसंद नहीं करते।

- This money **is chickenfeed** for him:
  This money is like small change/of little value to him.
  ये पैसे उसके लिए ऊँट के मुँह में जीरे की तरह हैं।

- **Their match was fixed:**
  Their match was rigged/had a predetermined result.
  यह प्रतियोगिता पहले ही तय थी।

- He went **into a flap**:
  He panicked.
  वह घबरा गया।

- The politicians went abroad **on a junket**:
  The politicians went out of India on a free/sponsored trip.
  राजनेता जनता के खर्च पर विदेश भ्रमण के लिए गये।

- He is a **Mama's boy**:
  He listens to/does whatever his mother tells him and will not go against her wishes.
  वह अपनी मां के इशारों पर चलता है।

- He made **a gaffe**:
  He committed a blunder.
  उसने भारी भूल कर दी।

- There is **a technical hitch**:
  There is a technical problem.
  यह एक तकनीकी समस्या है।

- Do not believe **Tom, Dick and Harry**:
  Do not believe anybody or everybody.
  हर किसी पर विश्वास मत करो।

- He likes to **move in elite circles**:
  He likes the company of the rich and famous.
  उसे अमीरों के बीच रहना पसंद है।

- He is a **well-connected man**:
  He has a lot of influence.
  वह बहुत प्रभावशाली व्यक्ति है।

- You will have to **accept the gauntlet**:
  You must take up the challenge.
  तुम्हें यह चुनौती स्वीकार करनी होगी।

- You will not be able to **live down this insult**:
  You will not be able to get over/forget this insult.
  तुम इस अपमान को भूल नहीं पाओगे।

- **Put your money where your mouth is:**
  You must support your ideas/statements by putting down your own money on this.
  अपने पैसों को अपनी कमाई का जरिया बनाओ।

- Stop **griping** all the while:
  Stop complaining constantly.
  हर समय परेशानियों का रोना बंद करो।

- He is a **gritty** man:
  He is a man of firm character.
  वह एक चरित्रवान व्यक्ति है।

- She is his **sidekick**:
  She is his partner/special friend.
  वह उसकी करीबी दोस्त है। / वह उसकी अंतरंग मित्र है।

- **No guts, no glory**:
  If you do not take risks, you will never succeed.
  अगर आप खतरा नहीं उठाएँगे, आप सफल नहीं हो सकते।
- They are **birds of a feather**:
  They have similar interests/characteristics.
  वे एक जैसे हैं। / चोर-चोर मौसेरे भाई होते हैं।
- She is **bird-bained**:
  She is silly.
  वह मूर्ख है।
- He is **a birdwatcher**:
  His hobby is watching birds/he is fond of watching girls.
  उसे लड़कियों पर नज़र रखना अच्छा लगता है।
- This is **strictly for the birds**:
  This is not to be taken seriously.
  यह कोई गंभीर बात नहीं है।
- **Tell it to the birds**:
  I don't care/I am not interested.
  मुझे इसमें कोई रुचि नहीं है।
- He has **a lousy hand**:
  He writes very badly.
  वह बहुत ख़राब लिखता है।
- His **contribution was measly**:
  His contribution was worthless/insignificant.
  उसका योगदान नगण्य था।
- His claims are **all phoney**:
  His claims are all false.
  उसका दावा ग़लत था।
- He **reeks of** alcohol:
  He smells very strongly of liquor.
  उससे शराब की बदबू आती है।
- He was **drunk to the gills**:
  He was totally drunk.
  वह पूरी तरह से नशे में धुत था।

- He couldn't even **put one leg before the other**:
  He was so drunk he could barely walk.
  वह इतना पिए हुए था कि चलना भी उसके लिए मुश्किल था।
- You must **make the right pitch to** sell products:
  You must put the right points across to sell products.
  आपको अपने उत्पादन की बिक्री के लिए उसके गुण सामने रखने होंगे।
- I want this done **pronto**:
  I want this done immediately.
  ये काम मुझे अभी चाहिए।
- He is a **shady character**:
  He is a disreputable man.
  वह एक घटिया आदमी है।
- I was **stumped by** his argument:
  I was left speechless by his logic/argument.
  उसके तर्कों ने मुझे नि:शब्द कर दिया।
- You **give me a tinkle** in the evening:
  You can ring me up in the evening.
  मुझे शाम के समय फ़ोन करो।
- She is a **very touchy** character:
  She is an oversensitive person.
  वह अति संवेदनशील है।
- She is like a **touch-me-not**:
  She is very shy.
  वह बहुत शर्मीली है।
- Do you **believe all this tripe**?
  Do you believe all this rubbish?
  क्या तुम्हें इस बकवास पर यकीन है?
- He likes **to spin yarns**:
  He likes to tell lies/stories that are not true.
  उसे झूठी कहानियाँ गढ़ना पसंद है।
- He has **a yen** for expensive items:
  He likes costly things.
  उसे महँगी चीज़ें बहुत पसंद हैं।

- **This is not what I had bargained for:**
  This is not what I had expected.
  मुझे इसकी उम्मीद नहीं थी।
- He **blacked out**:
  He lost consciousness.
  वह अचेत हो गया।
- The crisis will soon **blow over**:
  The major trouble will get over soon.
  यह समस्या जल्दी ही हल हो जाएगी।
- You must **read the writing on the wall**:
  You must realise the seriousness of the situation.
  तुम्हें वक़्त की नज़ाकत को समझना होगा।
- The bird **broke into** a song:
  The bird began singing.
  चिड़िया ने चहकना शुरू कर दिया।
- He is a **jailbird**:
  He is in prison.
  वह कैद में है।
- They **bump off** their competitor:
  They killed their rivals.
  उन्होंने अपने प्रतिद्वंद्वियों को मार दिया।
- The film industry **called on** the government to reduce taxes:
  The film industry appealed to the government to lower tax rates.
  फिल्म उद्योग ने सरकार से करों में कमी करने की माँग की।
- The government **cracked down** upon the **protestors**:
  The government took firm action against the protestors.
  सरकार ने प्रदर्शनकारियों के ख़िलाफ़ कड़ी कार्यवाही की।
- This is all **balderdash**:
  This is all rubbish.
  ये सब बकवास है।
- All his plans **came unstuck**:
  All his plans failed.
  उसकी हर योजना असफल रही।

- The protests **petered out**:
  The protests gradually died down.
  विरोध प्रदर्शन धीरे-धीरे मृतप्राय हो गया।

- You must **call his bluff**:
  You must expose/challenge his lie.
  तुम्हें उसकी धोखेबाज़ी को सामने लाना होगा।

- The Americans believe in **gunboat diplomacy**:
  The Americans believe in the use of threats or the show of force to achieve their aims.
  अमरीकी लोग शक्ति के द्वारा अपना लक्ष्य प्राप्त करने में विश्वास रखते हैं।

- The police **flagged down** his car:
  The police signalled his car to stop.
  पुलिस ने उसे कार रोकने का इशारा किया।

- Do not **fly off the handle**:
  Do not lose your temper.
  गुस्सा न करो।/आपे से बाहर मत हो।

- The traders **jacked up** the prices:
  The traders increased the prices.
  व्यापारियों ने कीमतें बढ़ा दीं।

- He was **leafing through the magazine**:
  He was casually glancing at the pages of the magazine.
  वह पत्रिका के पन्ने पलट रहा था।

- You must **play ball**:
  You must cooperate.
  तुम्हें सहयोग करना होगा।

- You cannot **pull strings** for this job:
  You cannot use influence for this job.
  आप इस नौकरी को पाने के लिए अपने प्रभाव का प्रयोग नहीं कर सकते।

- There are **no strings attached** in this deal:
  There are no hidden conditions in this deal.
  इसमें कोई भी छिपी हुई शर्तें जुड़ी नहीं हैं।

- The actress was **roped in for** the **inauguration**:
  The actress was persuaded to attend the inauguration.
  उस अभिनेत्री को उद्घाटन समारोह में सम्मिलित होने के लिए मनाया गया।
- They will be keen **to settle scores**:
  They will be looking to take revenge.
  वे बदला लेने पर उतारू ज़रूर होंगे।
- You must **stay put** till I return:
  Please stay here itself till I come back.
  जब तक मैं न आऊँ आपको काम जारी रखना होगा।
- Please **take stock of the situation** every month:
  Please review the situation every month.
  कृपया हर महीने हालात का जायज़ा लीजिए।
- The government **wrote off the** losses of nationalised banks:
  The government cancelled (agreed to treat as irrecoverable) the losses of nationalised banks.
  सरकार ने राष्ट्रीकृत बैंकों के नुकसान को मान लिया।
- He is **fighting fit**:
  He is fully fit and healthy.
  वह पूरी तरह से चुस्त-दुरुस्त है।
- He loves **backseat driving**:
  He loves to dish out advice without having to accept the responsibility.
  वह बिना खुद कोई ज़िम्मेदारी उठाए, दूसरों को सलाह देने में बहुत आगे हैं।
- This was the **bone of contention** between them:
  This was the reason for the quarrel/dispute between them.
  इनके बीच झगड़े की जड़ यह है।
- Don't try to **hit me below the belt**:
  Don't try to use unfair tactics against me.
  मेरे ख़िलाफ़ ग़लत हथकंडे मत आज़माओ।
- This sentence is perfectly **legal tender**:
  This sentence is proper and correct.
  ये वाक्य पूरी तरह उपयुक्त है।

- She was **dressed to kill**:
  She was dressed in a very sexy, seductive outfit.
  इन कपड़ों में वह बहुत ही आकर्षक लग रही थी।
- No doubt this is a **feather in your cap**:
  This is undoubtedly an achievement for you.
  यह नि:संदेह तुम्हारे लिए एक उपलब्धि है।
- He doesn't even have a **ghost of a chance**:
  He stands no chance whatsoever.
  उसके पास कोई मौका नहीं है।
- The company has now **turned the corner**:
  The company is no longer making losses.
  अब कंपनी को नुकसान नहीं हो रहा है।
- The company is now **in the black**:
  The company is now making profits.
  कंपनी अब मुनाफ़ा कमा रही है।
- **She is a bombshell**:
  She is very sexy/attractive.
  वह बहुत ही आकर्षक है।
- He was given **marching orders**:
  He was dismissed from service.
  उसे नौकरी से निकाल दिया गया।
- They are **poles apart**:
  They have widely differing tastes/interests.
  वे एक-दूसरे से बिल्कुल अलग हैं।
- It was a **slip of the tongue**:
  It was an unintentional mistake while speaking.
  ये बोलने में गलती हो गई थी।
- **Come again**:
  Please repeat what you said, I did not hear you properly.
  कृपया दोबारा कहें, मैंने सुना नहीं।
- His **fat** is now **in the fire**:
  He is now going to get into trouble.
  उसका भविष्य अब संकट में है।

- Has that man **gone bananas**?
Has he gone mad?
क्या यह आदमी पागल है?

- Don't **let the cat out of the bag**:
Don't reveal the secret.
राज़ मत खोलो।

- He **pulled out all the stops**:
He did everything in his power.
उससे जो भी बन पड़ा उसने किया।

- Don't **put the cart before the horse**:
Don't reverse the logical order of things.
चीज़ों को उनकी सही दिशा में चलने दो।

- Does my name **ring a bell**?
Does my name sound familiar?
क्या मेरा नाम आपको सुना हुआ लगता है।

- Don't **take things lying down**:
Don't accept the situation meekly.
परिस्थितियों से घबराकर चुपचाप समझौता मत करो।

- He **sleeps like a log**:
He sleeps very soundly.
वह बहुत गहरी नींद में सोता है।

- You must **toe the line**:
You must follow the rules/norms.
आपको नियमों का पालन करना पड़ेगा।

- They will have to **fall in line**:
They will have to accept the norms, whether they like it or not.
उनको नियमों का पालन करना पड़ेगा, चाहे उन्हें पसन्द हों या ना हों।

- This is **in line with** standard practice:
This is in conformity/agreement with the norms.
यह सामान्य व्यवहार के अनुकूल है।

- Do not **skirt the issue**:
  Do not avoid the issue.
  विषय से मत हटो। / विषय से विषयांतर न हों।
- You must **gird up your loins**:
  You must prepare for energetic action.
  आपको उत्साह से जुटने के लिए तैयार होना होगा।
- You must **keep your ear to the ground**:
  You must keep yourself well informed about what is happening around you.
  तुमको अपने आपको चौकन्ना रखना होगा।
- We do not approve of **kite-flying**:
  We do not approve of false stories/practices.
  हम झूठी कहानियों पर यकीन नहीं करते।
- It **was an absolute howler**:
  It was a glaring mistake.
  वह एक बड़ी भूल थी।
- We will not **climb down from** our position:
  We will not retreat/withdraw from this position.
  हम अपनी बात से पीछे नहीं हटेंगे।
- Let us now **conclude matters**:
  Let us now end the matter.
  चलो, इस बात को यहीं ख़त्म करें।

Part-II

Dictionary of Phrasal Expressions

अंग्रेज़ी-हिन्दी अभिव्यक्ति कोश

A

Abandonment of claim : हक को छोड़ना
Abatement of duty : शुल्क में गिरावट / शुल्क में कमी
Abbreviation of above : उपरोक्त का संक्षिप्त रूप
Abbreviation of name : नाम का संक्षिप्त रूप
Abide by the rules : नियमों से बँधना / नियमों का पालन करना
Abiding conviction : पक्की धारणा / पूर्ण विश्वास
Ability to elicit co-operation : सहयोग लेने की सामर्थ्य
Ability to pay : भुगतान करने की क्षमता
Ability to plan and organise : योजना बनाने और संगठित करने की योग्यता
Ability to read and write : पढ़ने-लिखने की क्षमता
Abjure violence : हिंसा का त्याग करना
Able and willing : समर्थ और इच्छुक
Able-bodied unemployed : शरीर से समर्थ बेरोजगार
Able to get in well with : (किसी के) साथ मिलकर कार्य करने में सक्षम
Abnormal circumstances : असामान्य परिस्थितियाँ
Abnormal profit : असामान्य लाभ / बहुत लाभ
Abolition of untouchability : छुआछूत का अंत
Aboriginal tribes : आदिवासी जनजातियाँ / कबीलाई जनजातियाँ
About to take steps : कदम उठाने को तैयार
Above all : सबसे ऊपर / सबसे पहले
Above average : औसत से ऊपर / सामान्य से अधिक
Above board : खुल करके / खुल्लमखुल्ला / बिना बेईमानी के
Above cited : ऊपर दर्शाया गया / ऊपर दिखाया गया
Above defined : ऊपर परिभाषित किया गया
Above given : ऊपर दिया गया / उपरोक्त

Above mentioned : ऊपर वर्णित किया गया / ऊपर लिखा गया
Above noted : ऊपर दिया गया / ऊपर लिखा गया
Above par : औसत से अधिक
Above procedure : उपरोक्त प्रक्रिया
Above quoted : ऊपर उद्धृत किया गया / ऊपर कहा गया
Above quoted reference : उपरोक्त सन्दर्भ / उपरोक्त हवाला
Absence on---------regularised as leave due : दिनांक ---- की छुट्टी को देय छुट्टी के रूप में नियमित किया जाए
Absence without leave : बिना छुट्टी की अनुपस्थिति
Absence without permission : बिना अनुमति की अनुपस्थिति
Absent in spite of service of summons : सम्मन तामील होने पर भी अनुपस्थित
Absent without leave : बिना अवकाश अनुपस्थित
Absentee statement : अनुपस्थिति विवरण
Absolute acceptance : पूर्ण स्वीकृति / अंतिम स्वीकृति
Absolute and unconditional : निरुपाधि और बिना शर्त के
Absolute authority : परम प्राधिकारी
Absolute contraband : पूर्ण / सर्वथा निषिद्ध
Absolute discretion : पूर्ण विवेक / पूर्ण विवेकाधीन
Absolute estate : अबाधित संपदा
Absolute majority : पूर्ण बहुमत / स्पष्ट बहुमत
Absolute monopoly : सर्वथा एकाधिपत्य
Absolute necessities : परम आवश्यकताएँ
Absolute occupancy right : कब्जे का पूर्ण अधिकार
Absolute occupancy tenant : पूर्ण अधिवासी किरायेदार
Absolute owner : पूर्ण स्वामी
Absolute ownership : पूर्ण स्वामित्व
Absolute power : परम अधिकार / सत्ता
Absolute right : पूर्ण अधिकार
Absolute rule : निरपवाद नियम
Absolute title : परम उपाधि / परम पदवी

Absolute undertaking : पूर्ण व्यवसाय
Absolutely above : बिलकुल अलग / पूरी तरह परे
Absolutely correct : पूरी तरह सही
Absolutely necessary : पूरी तरह जरूरी
Absolutely transfer : पूरी तरह स्थानान्तरण
Absolutely upright and sound : बिलकुल खरा और शुद्ध
Absolutely vested : पूर्णरूप से मौजूद
Absolved of the responsibility : जिम्मेदारी से बरी / उत्तरदायित्व से मुक्त
Absorb in regular service : नियमित सेवा में रख लेना
Absorb salary in increments : वेतन वृद्धियों में सम्मिलित करना
Abstain from drinking : शराब न छूना
Abstention from voting : मतदान में भाग न लेना
Abstract book : सार पुस्तिका
Abstract of accounts : लेखा सार
Abstract of tender : निविदा / टेंडर का सार
Abstract statement of cases : मामलों का संक्षिप्त विवरण
Absurd argument : भद्दे तर्क
Abundant proof : प्रचुर प्रमाण
Abuse of official position : सरकारी पद का दुरुपयोग
Abuse of power : अधिकार / सत्ता का दुरुपयोग
Abusive language : गाली-गलौज / अपशब्द
Academic aptitude : शैक्षिक रुझान
Academic council : शिक्षण परिषद् / विद्या परिषद्
Academic discussion : बौद्धिक विचार विनिमय / बौद्धिक चर्चा
Academic qualification : शैक्षणिक योग्यता
Academic year : शिक्षा-वर्ष / शैक्षिक सत्र
Academy of fine arts : ललित कला अकादमी
Accede to one's demand : मांग पर सहमति
Accede to one's request : प्रार्थना की स्वीकृति
Acceding states : सम्मिलित होने वाले राज्य
Accelerated promotions : त्वरित पदोन्नतियाँ
Acceptance in principle : सैद्धांतिक स्वीकृति
Acceptance of responsibility : उत्तरदायित्व की स्वीकृति

Acceptance of tender : निविदा की स्वीकृति
Acceptance resolution : स्वीकृति का प्रस्ताव
Accepted as authentic : अधिप्रमाणित रूप में स्वीकृति
Accepted as correct : सही मानकर स्वीकृत
Accepted on trial basis : परीक्षण आधार पर स्वीकृति
Accepted provisionally : अस्थाई या अनंतिम रूप से स्वीकृत
Accepted, allocated and passed for payment : स्वीकृत, वितरित और भुगतान के लिए पास किया गया
Access to records : अभिलेखों तक पहुँच
Accessible document : सुगम दस्तावेज
Accessible place : सुगम स्थान
Accession book/ register : पंजीयन पुस्तिका
Accessory Licence : अतिरिक्त अनुज्ञप्ति / लाइसेंस
Accessory product : सहायक उत्पाद
Accident and health insurance : दुर्घटना और स्वास्थ्य बीमा
Accident and sickness benefit : दुर्घटना और बीमारी लाभ
Accident spot : दुर्घटना-स्थल
Accidental death benefit : दुर्घटनाजन्य मृत्यु लाभ
Accidental delay : आकस्मिक विलम्ब
Accidental fluctuation : आकस्मिक घट-बढ़
Accidental slip : आकस्मिक भूलचूक
Accommodating terms : सुविधाजनक शर्तें
Accommodation charges : रहने का किराया
Accompanying letter : संलग्न पत्र / साथ भेज गया पत्र
Accomplished fact : सिद्ध बात / प्रमाणित तथ्य
Accomplishment of purpose : उद्देश्य की पूर्ति / प्रयोजन सफल होना
Accord approval : कृपया --- को अनुमोदित करें
Accord priority : प्राथमिकता देना / प्राथमिकता दें
Accord sanction : स्वीकृति देना / स्वीकृति दें
According to convenience : सहूलियत के मुताबिक, सुविधानुसार
According to convention : परम्परा के अनुसार
According to facts : तथ्यों के अनुसार
According to his light : अपने दृष्टिकोण के अनुसार

According to law : कानून के मुताबिक
According to merit : योग्यता के अनुसार
According to report : जानकारी के अनुसार
According to rules in vogue : प्रचलित नियमों के अनुसार
According to seniority : वरिष्ठता के अनुसार
According to specification : विशिष्ट विवरण के अनुसार
According to speculation : अनुमान के अनुसार
According to stipulation : अनुबंध के अनुसार
According to the procedure prescribed : नियत प्रक्रिया के अनुसार
According to the terms of agreement : करार की शर्तों के मुताबिक
Accordingly it has been decided : तदनुसार ऐसा निर्णय किया गया है कि
Account brought to the : लेखा ...में लिया गया
Account for (to answer for) : के प्रति उत्तरदायी / का लेखा
Account for (to give a reason for) : का कारण बताना / की कैफियत देना
Account for (to render accounts) : का हिसाब-किताब देना / का लेखा देना
Account is being maintained : लेखा रखा जा रहा है
Account of activities : गतिविधियों का हिसाब-किताब / क्रियाकलापों का ब्यौरा
Account on in that behalf : लेखा ...की तरफ से प्रस्तुत
Account rendered : प्रस्तुत लेखा / लेखा प्रस्तुत किया गया
Accountable for : के प्रति उत्तरदायी
Accountant General : महालेखाकार
Accounting and procedure : लेखा-पद्धति और कार्यप्रणाली
Accounting year : लेखा वर्ष
Accounts code : लेखा संहिता
Accounts section : लेखा अनुभाग
Accredited press correspondent : मान्यता प्राप्त संवाददाता
Accruing from : जन्मा / से निकला हुआ
Accruing right : सही प्रस्तुति / सही निर्माण

Accumulation of capital : पूँजी संचय
Accuracy of statement : कथन का सत्य होना / विवरण का सही होना
Accurate reporter : सही रिपोर्टर
Accurately and fully : सही-सही और पूरी तरह से
Accurately done : सही तरह से किया गया
Accused was bailed out : आरोपी जमानत पर छूट गया था
Acid test : कठिन परीक्षा / अग्नि परीक्षा
Acknowledgement card : प्राप्ति-रसीद
Acknowledgement due : प्राप्ति आवश्यक
Acknowledgement in writing : लिखित में प्राप्ति
Acknowledgement maybe obtained : पावती भेजी जाए
Acknowledgement of source : सूत्र का उल्लेख
Acknowledgement receipt : पावती रसीद
Acquainted with the facts of the case : मामले के तथ्यों से अवगत / परिचित
Acquired or requisitioned : अर्जित या अधिग्रहीत
Acquisition of land : भूमि अधिग्रहण
Acquisition of property : संपत्ति का अर्जन
Acquit oneself : अपने कर्तव्य का पालन करना
Acquittance register : वेतन रजिस्टर / रसीदी रजिस्टर
Acquittance roll Pay day : वेतन लेखा-जोखा
Acreage allotment : एकड़वार आवंटन
Across the board increase : सपाट वृद्धि
Act a dash : रंग बाँधना
Act contrivance or device : कार्य, उपाय या युक्ति
Act in force : प्रवृत्त या प्रचलित अधिनियम
Act of bad faith : बुरी नीयत से काम करना / दुर्भावना से कार्य करना
Act of commission or omission : कार्य या कार्य-लोप / कृत-अकृत
Act of gallantry : वीरतापूर्ण कार्य
Act of God : ईश्वरीय कार्य / दैवयोग से होने वाली घटना

Act of indiscipline	: अनुशासन तोड़ने का कार्य
Act of indiscretion	: विवेकपूर्ण कार्य
Act of insubordination	: अनादर का कार्य / विद्रोह का कार्य
Act of justice	: विवेकपूर्ण कार्य
Act of misconduct	: दुर्व्यवहार का कार्य
Act of sabotage	: विध्वंस का कार्य
Act of trespass	: अनाधिकार प्रवेश का कार्य
Act of vandalism	: गुंडागर्दी
Act of violence	: हिंसक कार्य
Act under instructions	: निर्देश के अनुसार कार्य
Act within the scope	: परिधि के भीतर कार्य
Acting allowance	: कार्यकारी भत्ता
Acting appointment	: कार्यकारी / स्थानापन्न नियुक्ति
Acting as	: के रूप में कार्य करना / बनकर कार्य करना / करते हुए
Acting in good faith	: सद्भावना से कार्य करना / करते हुए
Acting in his discretion	: विवेक से कार्य करना / करते हुए
Acting in official capacity	: आधिकारिक तौर पर कार्य करना / करते हुए
Acting incumbent	: कार्यकारी पदाधिकारी
Acting on behalf of	: की तरफ से कार्य करना / करते हुए
Acting promotion	: कार्यकारी पदोन्नति
Acting within the scope of his authority	: अपने अधिकारक्षेत्र के भीतर कार्य करते हुए
Action as at `A' above	: के अनुसार कार्यवाही कीजिए
Action at once please	: कृपया त्वरित कार्यवाही करें
Action habits of	: क्रियामूलक आदतें
Action has already taken accordingly	: तदनुसार कार्यवाही की गई है
Action has not yet been initiated	: अभी तक प्रारम्भ नहीं किया गया है
Action is required to be taken early	: शीघ्र कार्यवाही की जाए
Action is under way	: कार्यवाही चल रही है

Action may be taken as proposed : यथा प्रस्तावित कार्यवाही की जाए
Action proposed to be taken : प्रस्तावित कार्यवाही की जाए
Action should be taken forthwith : तत्काल कार्यवाही की जाए
Action taken is valid : की गई कार्यवाही विधि-मान्य है
Action taken, thereon : उस पर की गई कार्यवाही
Action will in : क्रियान्वित इच्छाशक्ति
Actionable claim : कानूनी कार्यवाही योग्य दावा
Actionable wrong : अभियोज्य दोष
Active capital : सक्रिय पूँजी
Active consideration : सक्रिय रूप से विचार
Active habits : सक्रिय व्यवहार
Active officer : सक्रिय अधिकारी
Active partner : सक्रिय भागीदार / साझेदार
Active population : अर्जक जनसंख्या
Active resistance : सक्रिय प्रतिरोध
Acts and manuals : अधिनियम एवं नियमावली
Actual and probable expenditure : वास्तविक और संभावित व्यय / असली और संभावित खर्चे
Actual damage or loss : वास्तविक क्षति या हानि
Actual expenses incurred may be paid : वास्तविक व्यय का भुगतान किया जाए
Actual travelling expense : वास्तविक यात्रा व्यय
Actual wages : वास्तविक पारिश्रमिक / असली मजदूरी
Actually and voluntarily : वास्तव में और स्वेच्छा से
Actually employed : वस्तुतः नियोजित
Actually received : वस्तुतः प्राप्त
Actuals and targets : वास्तविक आंकड़े और लक्ष्य
Actuated by conscientious motives : सद्भाव से प्रेरित
Actus reus : दोषपूर्ण कार्य
Acute congestion : अत्यधिक भीड़भाड़
Acute mind : कुशाग्र बुद्धि

Acute shortage : नितांत अभाव / बहुत अधिक कमी
Ad alium diem : अन्य दिवस
Ad audiendum : सुनने के लिए
Ad certum diem : सुनिश्चित दिन
Ad hoc appointment : तदर्थ नियुक्ति
Ad hoc committee : तदर्थ समिति
Ad hoc indent : तदर्थ मांग पत्र
Ad hoc offer : तदर्थ प्रस्ताव
Ad hominem : व्यक्ति विशेष के लिए
Ad infinitum : निरवधि / अनंत काल तक
Ad interim injunction : अंतरिम निषेधाज्ञा
Ad litem : वाद कालीन प्रतिपालक / वादार्थ संरक्षक
Ad referendum on approval : अनुमोदन-अधीन जनमत संग्रह
Ad valorem : मूल्यानुसार, यथामूल्य
Adaptation to the circumstances : परिस्थितियों से समझौता
Adapted to our needs : हमारी आवश्यकताओं के प्रति अनुकूलन / समझौता
Additional assessment : अतिरिक्त मूल्यांकन
Additional fee : अतिरिक्त शुल्क
Additional funds : अतिरिक्त धन
Additional hands : अतिरिक्त सहयोग / अतिरिक्त कर्मचारी
Additional improvement or alteration : अतिरिक्त सुधार और परिवर्तन
Additional pay : अतिरिक्त वेतन
Additional profit : अतिरिक्त लाभ
Additional provision : अतिरिक्त प्रावधान
Additional requirements should be indicated : अतिरिक्त आवश्यकताएँ बताई जाएँ
Additions and betterments : परिवर्तन और सुधार
Address all concerned : सर्व-सम्बन्धित को लिखा जाए
Address and messages : अभिभाषण और संदेश
Address of the Governor : राज्यपाल का अभिभाषण

Address of welcome : स्वागत भाषण, अभिनन्दन पत्र
Addressed to : के नाम / को संबोधित
Addressograph machine : पतालेखी मशीन
Adequate accommodation : समुचित स्थान-सम्बन्धी सुविधा
Adequate compensation : यथोचित पारितोषिक
Adequate consideration : यथोचित प्रतिफल / विचार
Adequate data : समुचित आंकड़े / सामग्री
Adequate protection : यथोचित संरक्षण
Adequate provision : यथोचित प्रावधान
Adequate publicity : समुचित प्रचार
Adequate relief : पर्याप्त सहायता
Adequate remuneration : यथायोग्य पारिश्रमिक
Adequate security : यथोचित प्रतिभूति
Adequate step : यथोचित कार्यवाही
Adequate wages : पर्याप्त मजदूरी
Adhere to a rule too rigidly : नियम का अक्षरश: पालन करना
Adhere to earlier decision : पिछले निर्णय पर दृढ़ रहना
Adjournment motion : स्थगन प्रस्ताव
Adjournment of the House : सदन का स्थगन
Adjudication by arbitral award : विवाचन द्वारा अधिनिर्णय
Adjudication of dispute : विवाद का अधिनिर्णय
Adjust accounts : लेखों का समायोजन
Adjust progressively : धीरे-धीरे अभ्यस्त बनाना
Adjusted provisionally : अस्थायी रूप से समायोजित
Adjusted total income : समायोजित कुल आय
Adjusting operation : समायोजन संक्रिया
Adjusting the costs : व्यय का समायोजन करना
Adjustment account : समायोजन लेखा
Adjustment by transfer : अंतरण द्वारा समायोजन
Adjustment eventual : अंतिम समायोजन
Adjustment of rights : अधिकारों का समायोजन
Adjustment of suits : वादों का समायोजन
Administer oath : शपथ दिलाना

Administer warning : चेतावनी देना
Administration and control : प्रबंध और नियंत्रण
Administration convenience : प्रशासन सुविधा / प्रशासनिक सुविधा
Administration of justice : न्यायकरण / न्याय प्रशासन
Administration of the affairs : कार्यकलाप का प्रशासन
Administrative ability : प्रशासनिक योग्यता
Administrative action : प्रशासनिक कार्यवाही
Administrative approval may be obtained : प्रशासनिक अनुमोदन प्राप्त किया जाए
Administrative affairs : प्रशासनिक कार्य
Administrative authority : प्रशासनिक अधिकारी
Administrative cadre : प्रशासनिक संवर्ग
Administrative capacity : प्रशासनिक क्षमता
Administrative charge : प्रशासनिक प्रभार
Administrative Control : प्रशासनिक नियंत्रण
Administrative department : प्रशासनिक विभाग
Administrative expenses : प्रशासनिक व्यय
Administrative experience : प्रशासनिक अनुभव
Administrative framework : प्रशासनिक ढाँचा
Administrative functions : प्रशासनिक कार्य
Administrative head : प्रशासन प्रमुख / प्रशासनिक प्रमुख
Administrative lapse : प्रशासनिक भूलचूक
Administrative machinery : प्रशासन तंत्र
Administrative officer : प्रशासनिक अधिकारी
Administrative report : प्रशासनिक जानकारी
Administrative sanction : प्रशासनिक स्वीकृति
Administrative set up : प्रशासन व्यवस्था
Administrative staff : प्रशासनिक कर्मचारी
Administrative unit : प्रशासनिक इकाई
Admissibility of adjournment : काम रोको प्रस्ताव
Admissibility of allowance : भत्ते की स्वीकार्यता
Admissibility of claim : दावे की स्वीकार्यता
Admissibility of questions : प्रश्नों की ग्राह्यता

Admissible in proof : सबूत के लिए साक्ष्यग्राह्यता
Admissible under rules : नियमानुसार ग्राह्य
Admission fee : प्रवेश शुल्क
Admission of fact : तथ्य की स्वीकृति
Admission register : प्रवेश-पुस्तिका
Admission with permission : अनुमति लेकर ही अन्दर आएँ
Admit an application : आवेदन ग्रहण करना
Admit one : एक को प्रवेश करने दें
Admit one's mistake : अपनी गलती मान लेना
Admit to bail : जमानत पर छोड़ना / जमानत मंजूर करना / जमानत लेना
Admitted claim : स्वीकृत दावा
Admitted in evidence : साक्ष्य से लिया गया / साक्ष्य द्वारा प्राप्त किया गया
Adopted minutes : स्वीकृत कार्य-विवरण
Adopted son : गोद लिया बेटा
Adult franchise : वयस्क मताधिकार
Adult member : वयस्क सदस्य
Adulterated drugs : मिलावटी दवाएँ
Advance and its recovery : अग्रिम और उसकी वसूली
Advance arrangements are necessary : पूर्व-प्रबंध आवश्यक है
Advance Copy : अग्रिम प्रति
Advance from pay/P.F. is permissible : तनख्वाह / भविष्य-निधि से पेशगी दी जा सकती है
Advance guard : अग्रिम सैनिक टुकड़ी
Advance increment : अग्रिम वेतन वृद्धि
Advance money : अग्रिम धन
Advance notice : अग्रिम सूचना
Advance of pay : अग्रिम वेतन
Advance of T.A. : अग्रिम यात्रा भत्ता
Advance party : अग्रिम दल
Advance payment : अग्रिम भुगतान

Advance Tax : अग्रिम शुल्क
Advanced countries : उन्नत देश / विकसित देश
Advanced training : अग्रिम प्रशिक्षण
Advancing of money : रुपया उधार देना
Advantages obtained : प्राप्त किया गया लाभ
Adverse claimant : प्रतिकूल दावेदार
Adverse entry : प्रतिकूल प्रविष्टि
Adverse party : प्रतिपक्ष, विरोधी दल
Adverse remark : प्रतिकूल टिप्पणी
Adverse report : प्रतिकूल जानकारी
Adverse to the title : अधिकार के प्रतिकूल
Adversly affected : क्षतिग्रस्त
Advertised for sale : विक्रय के लिए विज्ञापित
Advertised post : विज्ञापित पद
Advertised tender : विज्ञापित निविदा
Advertising media : विज्ञापन माध्यम
Advice awaited : परामर्श प्रतीक्षित है
Advice of despatch : भेजने की सूचना
Advice of payment : भुगतान की सूचना
Advice or concurrence : सलाह या सहमति
Advise further development : आगे की प्रगति से अवगत कराएँ
Advise telegraphically : तार द्वारा सूचित करें
Advise that the transfer proposed would not be in order : को सूचित करें कि प्रस्तावित स्थानान्तरण नियमों के अनुकूल नहीं होगा
Advise the action taken : की गयी कार्यवाही से अवगत कराएँ
Advise the party that : पार्टी को सूचित करें कि
Advise this office of the result of the enquiry : इस कार्यालय को जाँच के परिणाम से अवगत कराएँ
Advisory and coordinating function : सलाह और समन्वय विषयक कार्य
Advisory board : सलाहकार मंडल / बोर्ड
Advisory Committee : सलाहकार समिति

Advisory council of employment : रोजगार सलाहकार परिषद्
Advisory council, Central : केन्द्रीय सलाहकार परिषद्
Advisory service : सलाहकार सेवा
Aerial survey : हवाई सर्वेक्षण
Affable manners : मधुर व्यवहार
Affairs of state : राज्य के कार्यकलाप
Affairs of undertaking : उपक्रम के कार्यकलाप
Affect materially : आर्थिक प्रभाव डालना
Affect shall be deemed : प्रभाव डालने वाली समझी जायेगी
Affidavit submitted by the employee is not in order : कर्मचारी द्वारा प्रस्तुत शपथपत्र नियमानुकूल नहीं है
Affirm the decision : निर्णय की पुष्टि करना
Affirmative agreement : सकारात्मक करार
Affirmative reply : सकारात्मक उत्तर / हामी भरना
Affix a seal : मोहर लगाना
Affix one's signature : हस्ताक्षर करना
Afford opportunities / facilities to : को अवसर / सुविधाएँ प्रदान करें
Aforesaid rules : पूर्वोक्त नियम
After adequate consideration : पर्याप्त विचार करने के उपरांत
After all : कुछ भी हो / बहरहाल
After care programme : बाद वाला देखभाल का कार्य
After careful consideration : सावधानी से विचार करने के उपरांत
After consultation with : से परामर्श के उपरांत
After discussion : विचार-विमर्श के उपरांत
After due deliberation : उचित विचार-विमर्श के उपरांत
After great persuation : बहुत समझाने के उपरांत
After issue : जारी होने के उपरांत
After Minister in charge has seen : सम्बन्धित विभाग के मंत्री के द्वारा देख लेने के उपरांत
After perusal : निरीक्षण के पश्चात / देख लेने के उपरांत
After proper examination : उचित परीक्षण के उपरांत

After taking into account : पर विचार करने के उपरांत

After taking into consideration of all aspects : सभी पहलुओं को मद्देनजर रखकर

After the expiry : के बाद / की समाप्ति पर

Against public interest : जनहित के विरुद्ध

Against the name : नाम के सामने

Against the rules : नियमों के विरुद्ध

Age certificate : आयु प्रमाणपत्र

Age entry : आयु की प्रविष्टि

Age group : आयु वर्ग / वय समूह

Age limit : आयु सीमा

Age of consent : विवाह की (अनुमति हेतु) आयु, सम्मति–वय

Age of relaxation : आयु–सीमा में छूट

Age of superannuating : निवर्तन / अधिवर्षिता की अवस्था

Agenda is sent herewith : कार्यसूची साथ भेजी गई है

Agenda will follow : कार्यसूची बाद में भेजी जायेगी

Aggregate marks : पूर्णांक / अंकों का पूर्ण योग

Aggravate the situation : स्थिति को गंभीर बनाना

Aggregate value : कुल समस्त मूल्य

Aggregate votes : कुल मत

Aggressive mob : आक्रामक भीड़

Aggrieved party : असंतुष्ट पार्टी

Agitational approach : आन्दोलनात्मक रवैया

Agreeable personality : रुचिकर व्यक्तित्व

Agreeable proposal : मानने योग्य प्रस्ताव

Agreed by the meeting : मीटिंग में स्वीकार किया गया

Agreed to Approach, cooperative सहयोगपूर्ण रवैये के प्रति स्वीकृति

Agreement clearing : सहमति द्वारा स्वीकृति

Agreement in writing : लिखित करार

Agreement is entered : करार हो गया

Agreement of indemnity : क्षतिपूर्ति का करार

Agreement shall not be discharged : करार प्रभावमुक्त नहीं होगा
Agreement to lease : पट्टे पर देने का करार
Agreement without consideration : प्रतिफल के बिना करार
Aid and advice : सहायता और परामर्श
Aid any title : किसी भी हक की मदद करना
Aided institution : सहायताप्राप्त संस्थान
Aided school : सहायताप्राप्त विद्यालय
Aims and objects : लक्ष्य और उद्देश्य
Airlift : विमान द्वारा पहुँचाना, वायुवहन
Air raid shelter : हवाई हमले से बचाव हेतु आश्रय स्थल
Alien resident : विदेशी
Aliens solo : अन्य की भूमि पर
Alive to his duties : अपने कर्तव्यों के प्रति सजग
Alive to his responsibility : अपने उत्तरदायित्व के प्रति सजग
All along satisfactory : पूर्ण संतोषजनक
All around : चारों तरफ
All clear signal : पूर्ण निर्बाध संकेत
All concerned to note : सभी संम्बन्धित व्यक्ति ध्यान दें
All correspondence relating to the matter should be placed on file : मामले से संम्बन्धित पूरा पत्र-व्यवहार फाइल में रखा जाए
All in all : सर्वेसर्वा
All material circumstances : सब तात्विक परिस्थितियाँ
All of a sudden : अचानक
All ostentations expenditure : सभी तड़क-भड़क वाले खर्चे
All out aid : चहुँमुखी सहायता
All out effort : भरसक प्रयत्न
All right/round able officer : सर्वथा योग्य अधिकारी
All rights reserved : सर्वाधिकार सुरक्षित
All round economy in expenditure is needed : किसी भी तरह के अतिरिक्त व्यय से बचें / पूर्णतया मितव्ययी रहें

All round improvement : सर्वतोन्मुखी सुधार
All rounder : सर्वगुण संपन्न
Alleged inability : कथित असमर्थता
Alleged misconduct : कथित दुर्व्यवहार
Alleged offender : कथित अपराधी
Alleged right : कथित अधिकार
Allied organisation : सहबद्ध संगठन
Allied subject : सहबद्ध विषय
Allocation of business : कामकाज का बँटवारा
Allocation of funds : धन का आवंटन
Allocation of taxes : करों का बँटवारा
Allocation of time : समय का बँटवारा / समय का निर्धारण
Allotment from the reserved quota : आरक्षित कोटे से आवंटन
Allotment of wagons : मालडिब्बों का आवंटन
Allotment placed at your disposal : आपको सौंपी गई रकम / आपको दी गई आवंटित राशि
Allow for : गुंजाइश रखना
Allow on appeal : अपील मंजूर करना
Allowances and honoraria : भत्ते तथा मानदेय
Allowed by law : विधिसम्मत / कानून के मुताबिक
Allowed to pass : निकल जाने दिया गया / जाने दिया गया
Alphabetical indexing : वर्णानुसार सूची निर्माण
Alteration in draft : प्रारूप में परिवर्तन
Alteration of areas : क्षेत्रों का परिवर्तन / क्षेत्रों में परिवर्तन
Alteration of rights : अधिकारों का परिवर्तन / अधिकारों में परिवर्तन
Alternative accommodation : वैकल्पिक आवास
Alternative draft : वैकल्पिक प्रारूप
Alternative longer route : वैकल्पिक लंबा मार्ग
Alternative tariff : वैकल्पिक शुल्क सूची
Although it is known : यद्यपि यह विदित है

Always well turned out : हमेशा चुस्त-दुरुस्त

Amalgamation of offices : कार्यालयों का एकीकरण

Ambiguous suggestion : अस्पष्ट सुझाव

Ambitious Scheme : महत्त्वाकांक्षी योजना

Amenable to control : नियंत्रण को मानने वाला

Amended claim has been received : संशोधित दावा प्राप्त हो गया है

Amended draft put up : संशोधित प्रारूप प्रस्तुत हुआ है

Amended to read as : अवलोकनार्थ संशोधित रूप

Amenities fund : सुख-सुविधा निधि

Amenities provided : प्रदत्त सुख-सुविधाएँ

Amicable settlement : मैत्रीपूर्ण समझौता

Amortization of debt : ऋण का परिशोधन / कर्जा चुकाना

Amount due for the quarter : तिमाही के लिए देय धनराशि

Amount hereby sanctioned : इस हेतु स्वीकृत की गई धनराशि

Amount of punishment : दंड की मात्रा

Amount of royalty : रॉयल्टी की धनराशि / लेखन का समय-समय पर आने वाला पारिश्रमिक

Amount over paid maybe calculated : अधिक भुगतान की गई राशि का हिसाब लगाया जाए

Amount proposed earlier can not be enhanced : पूर्व प्रस्तावित राशि में कोई वृद्धि नहीं की जा सकती

Amount realised : वसूल की गयी राशि

Analogus posts : एक समान पद / सादृश्य पद

Analysis of data : आंकड़ों का विश्लेषण

Analytical mind : विश्लेषणात्मक विचार

Anarchical tendencies : अराजक प्रवृत्तियाँ

Ancestral property : पैतृक संपत्ति

Ancillary activities : आनुषंगिक गतिविधियाँ

Ancillary industry : सहायक उद्योग

Ancillary services : सहायक सेवाएँ

Animal husbandry : पशुपालन

Animus dedicandi : समर्पण का आशय

Animus deserendi : अभित्याजन का आशय
Animus domini : आधिपत्य का आशय
Animus possidendi : कब्जे का आशय
Animus revertendi : प्रत्यागमन का आशय
Annexure to the letter : पत्र के साथ संलग्न
Announce by beat of drums : ढिंढोरा पीटकर घोषणा करना
Annual Accounts : वार्षिक हिसाब-किताब / सालाना लेखा
Annual closing : वार्षिक लेखा-पूर्णता
Annual dividend : वार्षिक लाभांश
Annual enumeration : वार्षिक गणना
Annual equated instalments : सालाना सामान किश्तें
Annual financial statement : वार्षिक वित्तीय विवरण
Annual general meeting : वार्षिक सामान्य बैठक
Annual indent : वार्षिक मांग-पत्र
Annual repairs : वार्षिक सुधार / वार्षिक मरम्मत
Annual review in progress : वार्षिक समीक्षा चल रही है
Annual verification on certificate : वार्षिक सत्यापन प्रमाणपत्र
Annual yield : वार्षिक उपज
Annual yield/income : वार्षिक आय / वार्षिक उपज
Annuity deposit scheme : वार्षिक जमा योजना
Annuity guaranteed for life : आजीवन गारंटी वाली वार्षिकी
Anonymous complaint : गुमनाम शिकायत
Answer all cases, generally : सभी मामलों पर ध्यान दिया जाए
Answer the charge : आरोप का उत्तर देना
Answerable to : के प्रति उत्तरदायी
Antagonistic attitude : विरोधी रवैया
Ante : पहले
Antedated cheque : पूर्व दिनांकित चेक
Anti-corruption measure : भ्रष्टाचार विरोधी उपाय / कदम
Anti-erosion measure : मिट्टी का कटाव रोकने के उपाय
Anti-inflationary measures : मुद्रा-स्फीति निरोधी उपाय
Anti-social elements : असामाजिक तत्व

Anti-strike legislation : हड़ताल विरोधी कानून
Anticipated cost : पूर्वानुमानित मूल्य
Anticipated expenditure : पूर्वानुमानित व्यय
Anticipated revenue : पूर्वानुमानित राजस्व
Anticipated shortfall : पूर्वानुमानित कमी
Anxious to learn : सीखने को उत्सुक / जानने को व्याकुल
Any contravention to this rule : इस नियम का कोई उल्लंघन
Any further delay : और कोई भावी विलम्ब
Any law made : बनाया गया कोई भी कानून
Any other law for the time being in force : कुछ समय के लिए लागू कोई अन्य कानून
Apart from this : इसके अतिरिक्त
Apparent error on the face of records : अभिलेखों में साफ दिखने वाली भूल
Apparent from the records : अभिलेख से साफ जाहिर है
Apparent on its face : देखने से ही जाहिर है
Appeal allowed : अपील स्वीकृत
Appeal be dismissed : अपील अस्वीकृत
Appeal does not lie : अपील नहीं की जा सकती
Appeal has been rejected : अपील रद्द की गई है
Appeal is dismissed with costs : खर्च सहित अपील रद्द की जाती है
Appeal is filed by : द्वारा अपील दायर की गई है
Appeal is rejected : अपील अस्वीकृत की जाती है
Appeal is time barred : अपील नियत समय के भीतर ही की जाए
Appeal lies : अपील संभव है
Appeal to the court : अदालत से अपील करना
Appeal was heard exparte : अपील एकतरफा हुई
Appealable decree : अपीली आज्ञा / अदालत की अपीली आज्ञा
Appear for interview : साक्षात्कार के लिए पधारें
Appears to be keen : उत्सुक प्रतीत होता है
Appellant has requested for a personal hearing : अपीलकर्ता ने निजी सुनवाई के लिए अनुमति मांगी है

Appellate authority : अपील अधिकारी
Appellate board : अपीली बोर्ड
Appellate decision : अपीली निर्णय
Appellate functions : अपीली कार्यवाही
Appellate jurisdiction : अपीली अधिकार-क्षेत्र
Appellate tribunal : अपीली अधिकरण
Appended herewith : साथ लगा है / संलग्न है
Appertaining thereto : तद्विषयक / उस विषय का
Applicable to : पर लागू होता है
Application for maintenance : भरण-पोषण के लिए प्रार्थना-पत्र
Application for order : आदेश हेतु आवेदन
Application for review : पुनरावलोकन हेतु आवेदन
Application has not been made in proper form : आवेदन ढंग से नहीं किया गया
Application made by a motion : प्रस्ताव द्वारा पारित आवेदन
Application maybe rejected : आवेदन अस्वीकृत किया जाए
Application of rules : नियमों का आवेदन
Apply for sanction : मंजूरी के लिए आवेदन कीजिये
Apply for withdrawal from P. F. : निर्वाह-निधि से राशि निकालने हेतु आवेदन दीजिये
Apply in writing : लिखित में आवेदन कीजिये
Appointed as referee : रेफरी के तौर पर नियुक्त
Appointed destination : निर्धारित गंतव्य
Appointed place : निर्धारित स्थान
Appointing authority : नियुक्ति-अधिकारी
Appointment is temporary and will not offer any title : नियुक्ति स्थायी नहीं है और कोई अधिकार प्रदान नहीं करती
Appointment of assets : संपत्तियों का बँटवारा
Appointment of casual nature : अनौपचारिक नियुक्ति / सादी नियुक्ति
Appointment of dates : तारीखों का निर्धारण
Appointment of liabilities : दायित्वों का आवंटन
Appointment of receiver : प्राप्तकर्ता की नियुक्ति
Appointment of responsibilities : उत्तरदायित्वों का बँटवारा
Appointment by way of : नियोजन के रूप में

Appreciation on prices : मूल्यों में वृद्धि
Apprehended loss : आशंकित हानि
Appropriate charge : समुचित प्रभार
Appropriate circulation : समुचित खपत / समुचित प्रसार
Appropriate sense of urgency : आवश्यक कार्य के महत्त्व की समुचित समझ
Appropriation account : विनियोजन लेखा
Appropriation bill : विनियोग विधेयक
Appropriation of funds : निधियों का विनियोजन
Appropriation of the revenue : आमदनी का विनियोजन
Approval is first sought : पहले स्वीकृति चाहिए
Approval maybe accorded : अनुमोदन प्रदान कर दिया जाए
Approved as per remarks in the margin : हाशिये में दी गयी टिप्पणी के अनुसार अनुमोदित
Approved as proposed : यथा प्रस्ताव अनुमोदित
Approved Service Certificate : अनुमोदित सेवा प्रमाणपत्र
Approved subject to the objections at 'A' : 'अ' पर उल्लिखित आपत्तियों के अधीन अनुमोदित
Approximate cost : लगभग लागत / लगभग व्यय
Apt to be careless occasionally : कभी-कभी लापरवाह हो जाते हैं
Apt to be loose about his utterances : बोलचाल में संयम खो देने की प्रवृत्ति है
Apt to loose his head : अक्सर बुद्धि नष्ट हो जाती है
Apt to physical progress of the work : कार्य की अनुमानित स्थूल प्रगति की सूचना
Arable land : कृषियोग्य भूमि
Arbitrary price : मनमानी कीमत
Arbitration agreement : मध्यस्थतापूर्ण अनुबंध
Arbitration board : मध्यस्थता मंडल
Arbitrator award : पंच निर्णय
Arbitrium est judicium : मध्यस्थ का निर्णय पंच
Arduous responsibility : दुष्कर उत्तरदायित्व
Area check register : क्षेत्रीय जांच पुस्तिका

Area covered by previous application : पूर्व आवेदन में निर्दिष्ट क्षेत्र
Area lender crops : फसली क्षेत्र
Area not cropped : वह क्षेत्र जिसमें फसल न बोई गई हो
Area per capita : प्रतिव्यक्ति क्षेत्र
Area under cultivation : कृषियोग्य भूमि
Argumentative matter : तर्कसंगत विषय
Arguments advanced : प्रस्तुत तर्क
Arising in the course of : के दौरान उत्पन्न होने वाला
Arising on a contract : समझौताजन्य
Arising on a guarantee : प्रत्याभूतिजन्य
Arising out of any proceedings : किन्ही कार्यवाहियों से पैदा हुआ
Arising out of confidence : विश्वास से उद्भूत
Arising out of the administration of this act : इस अधिनियम के प्रशासन से जन्म लेने वाला
Arising out of the same act : इसी कानून से पैदा होने वाला
Arising therefrom : से उद्भूत / से उत्पन्न
Armed and ammunitions : अस्त्र-शस्त्र
Armed hostilities : सशस्त्र संघर्ष
Arrange early disposal of the case : मामले के शीघ्र समाधान का प्रबंध करें
Arrange payment : भुगतान का प्रबंध करें
Arrange to regularise : नियमित करने का प्रबंध करें
Arrange to settle : निपटाने की व्यवस्था करें
Arranged in order of merit : योग्यतानुसार गुण-क्रम में व्यवस्थित
Arrangement maybe made : प्रबंध किया जाए
Arrangement of files : फाइलों का विन्यास
Arrear claim : बकाये का दावा
Arrear statement : बकाया विवरण
Arrears have been cleared off : बकाये का भुगतान हो गया है
Arrears of interest : ब्याज का बकाया
Arrears of land revenue : भू-राजस्व का बकाया
Arrival and departure : आगमन और प्रस्थान
Arrival report : आगमन की जानकारी

Arrived at, by agreement : अनुबंध द्वारा किया गया निर्णय / निपटान
Arrived at, no settlement is : कोई समझौता नहीं हुआ
Art objects : कला सम्बन्धी वस्तुएँ
Articles asked for : मांगी गई वस्तुएँ
Articles of association : संस्था की नियमावली
Articles of charges : आरोप की धाराएँ
Articles of dead stock : अविक्रय माल
Articles of stationery : लेखन-सामग्री
Artificial dearness : कृत्रिम महँगाई
Artificial pressure : कृत्रिम दबाव
As a gift : उपहारस्वरूप
As a last resort : अन्तिम विकल्प के तौर पर
As a matter of caution : सावधानी के तौर पर
As a matter of course : स्वाभाविक रूप से
As a matter of fact : दरअसल / यथार्थतः
As a precautionary measure : सावधानी के उपाय के रूप में
As a result of : के परिणाम के रूप में
As a rule : नियम के तौर पर / नियमतः
As a safeguard : सुरक्षा के तौर पर
As a special case : विशेष रूप में / विशेष रूप से
As a whole : समस्त रूप से / पूर्णतया
As above : जैसा ऊपर दिया गया है
As aforesaid : जैसा पहले कहा गया है / पूर्व कथनानुसार
As against : की तुलना में / के मुकाबले में
As against creditors : लेनदारों के विरुद्ध
As already pointed out : जैसा कि बताया जा चुका है
As an ad hoc measure : तदर्थ उपाय के रूप में
As an exception : एक अपवाद के तौर पर
As an exceptional case : एक अपवाद वाले मामले के तौर पर
As an experiment : एक प्रयोग के तौर पर
As and when : जब भी
As approved : जैसा कि अनुमोदित किया गया है

As arrears of land revenue : भू-राजस्व के बकाया के तौर पर

As before : पहले की तरह

As between him and them : जहाँ तक उसका और उनका सम्बन्ध है

As between third person : अन्य व्यक्तियों के बीच

As contained in the minutes above : जैसा कि ऊपर कार्य-विवरण में दिया गया है

As decided : जैसा कि निर्णय किया गया है / था

As defined : जैसा परिभाषित किया गया है / था

As described : जैसा कि वर्णन किया गया है

As desired, as hope : जैसी कि उम्मीद की गई है

As determinded : यथा निर्धारित

As directed : जैसा निर्देशित किया गया है / निर्देशानुसार

As discussed : जैसा विचार किया गया है

As enjoined : जैसा कि आदेश दिया गया है

As evidenced : जैसा कि सबूत है

As expeditiously as possible : यथासम्भव शीघ्रता के साथ

As explained in the foregoing para : जैसा कि पूर्ववर्ती पैरा में स्पष्ट किया गया है

As explained in your letter : जैसा कि आपके पत्र में बताया गया है

As far as circumstances permit : हालात के मुताबिक जहाँ तक मुमकिन है

As far as maybe : जहाँ तक हो सके

As far as permissible : जहाँ तक अनुमति मिल सके

As follows : जैसा कि आगे दिया गया है

As from appointed date : नियत तारीख से

As from appointed day : नियत दिन से

As furnished below : जैसा कि नीचे दिया गया है

As he thinks fit : जैसा कि उसे सही लगता है

As hereinafter defined : जैसा कि यहाँ उसके बाद परिभाषा दी गई है

As hereinafter directed : जैसा कि यहाँ उसके बाद निर्देश है

As hereinafter provided : इसमें इसके आगे दिए अनुसार

As hinted : इशारे के अनुसार

As hitherto : जैसा कि अभी तक देखा गया है / हुआ है

As if : मानो / जैसे

As it is : इस / इसी हालत में

As in force for the time being : जैसा कि उस समय लागू हो

As incidental to : आनुषंगिक रूप में

As indicated above : जैसा कि ऊपर बताया गया है

As is (usually) done : जैसा कि सामान्य तौर पर होता है

As is mentioned in : में जैसा वर्णित है

As is, where is : जैसा है, जहाँ है

As it stands : जैसा है

As laid down : यथा निर्धारित

As listed below : जैसा कि नीचे सूचीबद्ध रूप में दिया गया है

As may be mutually agreed : जैसा आपस में तय हो

As may be necessary upon : जैसी आवश्यकता हो

As maybe agreed upon : जैसा कि आपस में तय हो

As maybe considered expedient : जैसा कि उचित हो

As maybe deemed fit : जैसा कि सही लगे

As maybe just : जैसा कि न्यायसंगत हो

As maybe prescribed : जैसा कि विहित / नियत किया गया हो

As maybe recognized : जैसी मान्यता दी जाए

As maybe specified : जैसा निर्दिष्ट किया जाए

As notified : जैसा कि अधिसूचित किया गया है

As occasion require : अवसर के अनुसार

As originally enacted : जैसा मूल रूप में है

As part of the transaction : लेन-देन के अनुरूप

As per advice : सलाह / सूचना के अनुसार

As per concluding para : अन्तिम अनुच्छेद के अनुसार

As per item in the schedule : अनुसूची की मदों के अनुसार

As per list enclosed : साथ में दी गई सूची के अनुसार
As per noting : टिप्पणी के अनुसार
As per opinion of : के मतानुसार
As per orders on page ... : पृष्ठ...के आदेश के अनुसार
As per standard distribution list : मानक वितरण सूची के अनुसार
As per verbal order : मौखिक आदेश के अनुसार
As pointed out above : जैसा कि ऊपर संकेत किया गया है
As precisely possible : यथासम्भव ठीक-ठाक रूप में
As proposed : यथा-प्रस्तावित
As provided by law : कानून के मुताबिक
As recommended : जैसी कि सिफारिश की गई है
As recorded : जैसा दर्ज किया गया है
As required under, rules : नियमों के अनुरूप
As said by my predecessor : जैसा कि मेरे पूर्ववर्ती ने कहा है
As shown in diagram : जैसा कि आरेख में दिया गया है
As soon may-be : हो सकता है जल्दी ही
As soon may-be convenient : जितनी जल्दी सुविधापूर्वक हो सके
As soon practicable : जितनी जल्दी व्यावहारिक रूप से हो
As stipulated : जैसा कि तय हुआ था
As stood on ... : जैसा कि आग्रह किया गया था
As suggested above : जैसा कि ऊपर संकेत किया गया है / ऊपर दी गई सलाह के अनुसार
As surmised : जैसा कि अनुमान था
As tentative proposal : जैसा कि अस्थाई प्रस्ताव के अनुसार
As the case may-be : जैसा कि मामला हो / प्रकरण के अनुसार
As the circumstances of the case may require : जैसा प्रकरण की परिस्थितियों के लिए आवश्यक हो
As the matter stands : जैसी स्थिति है
As there is no clear vacancy : चूँकि कोई खाली जगह नहीं है
As to accounts : लेखाओं के विषय में
As usually done in such cases : जैसा कि इन मामलों में आमतौर पर होता है

As verbally instructed : जैसा कि मौखिक निर्देश दिया गया था
As you are no doubt aware : जैसा कि आपको बेशक पता है
Assembling of parts : पुर्जों का संयोजन
Assembly of persons : व्यक्तियों का जमाव
Assembly unlawful : विधि-विरुद्ध जमाव
Assertion of right : अधिकार का दावा
Assessed value : निर्धारित मूल्य
Assessing authority : निर्धारण अधिकारी
Assessment of the instalment : किश्त का निर्धारण
Assessment order : निर्धारण क्रम
Assets and liabilities : जायदाद और देनदारी / देना-पावना
Assign in writing : लिखित रूप में काम सौंपना
Assign interest : हित का समुदेशन करना
Assistance board : सहायक मंडल
Assistance in kind : अ-मौद्रिक सहायता करना
Assumption of charge : कार्यभार ग्रहण करना
Assumption of office : पद ग्रहण करना
Assurance of property : संपत्ति हस्तांतरण-पत्र
At a discount : कम भाव की दरों पर
At a glance : एक नजर में / प्रथमदृष्ट्या
At a premium : अधिमूल्य पर
At a stretch : एक साथ ही
At a time : एक समय पर
At all : बिलकुल / पूरी तरह
At all times : सभी समय पर
At an early date : पूर्व तिथि पर
At any time (hour) : किसी भी समय
At close quarters : नजदीक से
At consigner's expense : भेजने वाले के खर्चे पर
At fair price : सही कीमत पर
At flag 'A' : 'अ' पर चिह्नित
At Govt. expenses : सरकारी खर्चे पर
At his option : अपनी इच्छा से

At his own option : स्वयं अपनी इच्छा से
At his own request : उनकी निजी प्रार्थना पर
At his own risk : अपनी जिम्मेदारी पर
At large : स्वच्छंद / स्वतंत्र
At leisure : फुर्सत में
At liberty to withdraw : क्षतिपूर्ति हेतु स्वतंत्र
At or about any place : पर या किसी भी स्थान पर
At random : चाहे जैसे / किसी भी तरह से
At sight : नजर आते ही
At source : स्रोत पर
At the close of : की समाप्ति पर
At the close of month : महीने के समापन पर
At the commencement of : की शुरुआत पर
At the cost of : की कीमत पर
At the discretion of : के विवेक पर
At the disposal of : के अधीन
At the earliest opportunity : शीघ्रतम अवसर पर
At the foot : पद भाग में
At the maximum of the scale : वेतनमान के अधिकतम पर
At the pleasure of : के प्रसादानुसार
At the time mentioned above, : उपरोक्त समय पर
At times inclined to be rather sentimental : कभी-कभी भावुक हो जाने की प्रवृत्ति
At times used rather harsh words : कभी-कभी कुछ कड़े शब्दों का प्रयोग किया
At variance with : से भिन्न
At will : इच्छानुसार
At your convenience : आपकी सुविधानुसार
At your earliest convenience : आपकी सुविधानुसार जितनी जल्दी हो सके
At your end also : आपकी ओर से भी
Attachable proportion : कुर्की योग्य अनुपात
Attached herewith : साथ संलग्न

Attached office : संलग्न कार्यालय
Attached to : से जुड़ा हुआ
Attachment of salary : वेतन की कुर्की
Attain majority : बहुमत प्राप्त करना
Attain the age of : की आयु पर पहुँचना
Attainment of object : उद्देश्य की प्राप्ति
Attainment of qualification : योग्यता की प्राप्ति
Attend diligently to duties : कर्तव्यों का तत्परतापूर्वक पालन करना
Attend to : की परिचर्या करना / की देखभाल करना
Attend to duties, to : कर्तव्य करने के लिए उपस्थित रहना
Attested true copy : अनुप्रमाणित यथार्थ प्रति
Attributable causes : दिए जा सकने योग्य कारण
Auction notice : नीलामी की सूचना
Auction sale : नीलामी बिक्री
Auction the produce : उपज की नीलामी कीजिये
Auctioneering agreement : नीलामी करारनामा
Audience hall : सभा मंडप
Audio visual arts : दृश्य-श्रव्य कलाएँ
Audio visual publicity : दृश्य-श्रव्य प्रचार
Audit notes : लेखा परीक्षा टिप्पणियाँ
Audit objections : लेखा परीक्षा आपत्तियाँ
Audit of accounts : लेखों की संपरीक्षा
Audited accounts : परीक्षित लेखे
Austerity measures : मिताहार उपाय
Auter droit : पराधिकार
Authentic translation : प्रामाणिक अनुवाद
Authenticated copy : प्रामाणिक प्रति
Authenticity of the orders : आदेशों की प्रामाणिकता
Author of the trust : न्यासकर्ता
Authorisation letter with the specimen signature of the bearer : पत्रवाहक के नमूने के हस्ताक्षर से युक्त प्राधिकार-पत्र
Authorised capital : प्राधिकृत पूँजी
Authorised expenditure : प्राधिकृत व्यय

Authorised leave : प्राधिकृत छुट्टी

Authority competent to decide the case : निर्णय देने हेतु समर्थ अधिकारी

Authority competent to make payments : भुगतान करने हेतु समर्थ अधिकारी

Authority competent to sanction : स्वीकृति देने हेतु समर्थ अधिकारी

Autonomous body : स्वायत्त संस्था

Auxiliary service : सहायक सेवा

Avail of leave : छुट्टी का उपभोग करना

Avail oneself of the opportunity : अवसर का लाभ उठाना

Available capital : उपलब्ध पूँजी

Average both in quality and quantity : गुणवत्ता और मात्रा दोनों में औसत

Average competence : औसत क्षमता

Average merit : औसत गुण / औसत योग्यता

Average revenue : औसत आय

Average type, of : औसत दर्जे का

Averting a loss : नुकसान बचाना

Avoid being sentimental, should : भावावेश में न आया करें

Avoid the risk of : के खतरे से बचाना

Avoidable cause : परिहार्य / वर्जनीय कारण

Avoidable delay : परिहार्य / वर्जनीय विलम्ब

Avoidable extra expenditure : परिहार्य / वर्जनीय अतिरिक्त व्यय

Await further comments : आगे की टिप्पणियों की प्रतीक्षा करें

Await further report : आदेशों की प्रतीक्षा है

Await return of the employee from leave : कर्मचारी की वापसी की प्रतीक्षा करें

Awaiting orders : आदेशों की प्रतीक्षा है

Award costs : खर्च दिलवाएँ / खर्च दिलवाना

Aware of, be : का ज्ञान होना / की जानकारी होना

■■

B

Back journey : वापसी यात्रा
Back out : कदम पीछे लेना / मुकर जाना
Back page : पिछला पृष्ठ
Back reference (B. R.) : पूर्व-सन्दर्भ, पिछला हवाला
Back to work : काम पर वापसी
Background of the case : प्रकरण की पृष्ठभूमि
Bad and unwork manlike manner : बुरा और अकुशल / फूहड़
Bad blood : कटुता, बैर
Bad climate allowance : बुरी जलवायु का भत्ता
Bad conduct : दुर्व्यवहार
Bad debt : डूबा ऋण, अशोध्य ऋण
Bad faith : अ-सद्‌भावपूर्ण
Bad in law : कानूनी तौर पर अमान्य
Bad security : खराब प्रतिभूति
Bad temper : कटु स्वभाव
Bag and baggage : बोरिया-बिस्तर
Baggage allowance : सामान भत्ता
Bailable offence : जमानत योग्य अपराध
Balance accounts : शेष / बकाया निकालना
Balance brought forward : पिछला शेष
Balance has been struck : हिसाब-किताब कर लिया गया है
Balance in hand : अपने पास शेष
Balance of accounts, general : (समस्त) लेखाओं का शेष
Balance of convenience is in favour of : की अधिक सुविधा होगी
Balance of payments : बकाया भुगतान / अदायगी बाकी
Balance of trade : व्यापार शेष
Balance sheet : पक्का चिट्ठा / तुलन-पत्र
Balance to be completed : भुगतान पूरा करना है

Balanced budget : संतुलित बजट
Balanced development : संतुलित विकास
Ban on further promotion : भावी पदोन्नति पर रोक
Ban on further recruitment : भावी भरती पर रोक
Ban on the filling of posts : पद भरने पर रोक
Banking account : बैंक में खाता
Banking and treasury arrangement : बैंक कार्य और कोषागार प्रबंध
Banking institution : बैंकिंग संस्था
Banking transaction : बैंकिंग लेन-देन
Bar future employment : भविष्य की नियुक्ति बंद करें
Bar to interference : हस्तक्षेप पर रोक
Bar to proceedings : कार्यवाही पर रोक
Bare subsistence level : निर्वाह-मात्र स्तर
Barrage of questions : प्रश्नों की झड़ी / बौछार
Barred by any law : विधि द्वारा वर्जित / कानूनी मनाही
Barred by law : कानूनी तौर पर निषिद्ध
Barred by limitation : परिसीमा द्वारा बाधित
Barred by time : समय बाधित
Barrier clerk : नाका मुंशी
Base coin : खोटा सिक्का
Base level : आधार तल / आधार स्तर
Base line : आधार रेखा
Base year : आधार वर्ष
Based on actuals : वास्तविकताओं पर आधारित
Based on figures : आंकड़ों पर आधारित
Basic components : आधारभूत घटक
Basic pattern of education : शिक्षा का मूल रूप
Basic structure : आधारभूत ढाँचा
Basic wages : आधारभूत पारिश्रमिक
Basis of charge : प्रभार का आधार
Be cautious : सावधान रहिये
Be in (one's) bad books : किसी के द्वारा नापसंद होना

Be in addition to : के अतिरिक्त होना
Be overcome : सफल होना
Be that as it may : यथासंभव होना
Be void : खाली होना
Bear the cost : खर्चा उठाना
Bear true faith : सच्ची श्रद्धा रखना
Bearer cheque : वाहक चेक
Bearer of bond : वाहक बांड
Bearer security : वाहक प्रतिभूति
Bearing of question : प्रश्न से सम्बन्धित
Bearing on the subject : विषय से सम्बद्ध
Beat about the bush : इधर-उधर की बातें करना
Beat guard : गश्ती गारद
Beat the record : कीर्तिमान तोड़ना
Beaten track : बँधी लीक
Become enforceable : प्रवर्तनीय होना
Become inoperative : निष्क्रिय होना
Become vested : निहित होना
Becomes liable to : के प्रति उत्तरदायी होना
Becomes subject to any disqualification : किसी भी योग्यता से ग्रस्त हो जाना
Before his pay concurred in : उसके वेतन के सम्बन्ध में सहमति देने से पहले
Before issue : सौंपे जाने से पहले
Before said tally : उक्त बातचीत से पूर्व
Before such settlement : इस समझौते के पूर्व
Before taking his/her seat own title : अपना स्थान ग्रहण करने के पूर्व
Before the date of submission : जमा करने की तिथि के पूर्व
Before the expiry of : के समापन के पूर्व
Beg to be excused : क्षमाप्रार्थी हूँ / क्षमा कीजिएगा
Behind Schedule : निर्धारित कार्यक्रम से पीछे होना / चलना

Being cognizant : संज्ञान रखते हुए
Being concerned in any quarrel : जब वह किसी झगड़े से सम्बन्धित हो
Being in command : शासित होना
Believing in good faith : सद्‌भावनापूर्ण विश्वास करते हुए
Belong to the service : सेवा का अंग होना
Belonging to them in common : जो उनके साझे की है
Below par : कम मूल्य पर
Below par value : (कंपनी द्वारा) नियत की गई प्रतिभूति से कम
Bench and bar : न्यायाधीश और अधिवक्ता
Bends and corners : मोड़ और कोने
Beneficial and healthy use : लाभप्रद और अच्छा उपयोग
Beneficial effect : हितकर प्रभाव
Beneficial enjoyment : हितकर उपभोग
Beneficial interest : लाभकारी स्वार्थ
Beneficial to mankind : मानवता के लिए लाभदायी
Beneficial winding up : फायदे के लिए परिसमापन
Benefit assured by the rules : नियमों द्वारा दिए गए आश्वासन वाला फायदा
Benefit ceiling : सुविधा की उच्चतम सीमा
Benefit dependency : आश्रित सुविधा
Benefit fund : सुविधा निधि / लाभ राशि
Benefit of a class of persons : व्यक्तियों के किसी वर्ग का फायदा
Benefit of exception : अपवाद का लाभ
Benefit of public : आम जनता का हित
Benefit period : दी गई सुविधा की अवधि
Benefit show : सहायता प्रदर्शन
Benefit to the revenue : राजस्व का लाभ
Benevolent fund : हितकारी निधि
Besides this : इसके अतिरिक्त
Besides what has been stated above : उपरोक्त कथन के अतिरिक्त
Best adapted : उपयुक्ततम

Best endeavour : सर्वोत्तम प्रयत्न
Best fitted : सर्वाधिक उपयुक्त
Best judgement assessment : सर्वोत्तम विवेक बुद्धि के अनुसार निर्धारण
Best of ability : पूरी सामर्थ्य
Best of knowledge and belief : जहां तक जानकारी है और विश्वास है
Best of my judgement : अपनी सर्वोत्तम विवेक-बुद्धि से
Best of skill and ability : सर्वोत्तम कौशल और योग्यता
Best price obtainable : अधिकतम प्राप्य मूल्य
Best serve the interests of the public : जनता के हितों की सर्वोत्तम सेवा
Best terms : सर्वोत्तम शर्तें
Better accept the proposal : बेहतर होगा कि इस प्रस्ताव को मान लिया जाए
Better appreciation : समुचित आकलन
Better farming society : उन्नत कृषि समिति
Better government : सुशासन
Better implementation : बेहतर कार्यान्वयन
Better prevention : बेहतर रोकथाम
Better statement : बेहतर कथन
Better title : बेहतर अधिकार
Betterment tax : खुशहाली कर
Beyond a period of : एक समय के बाद
Beyond midnight : अर्धरात्रि के बाद
Beyond reasonable doubt : उचित संदेह से परे
Beyond the said period : कहे गए समय के बाद
Beyond the scope of authority : उसके अधिकार के विस्तार से परे
Beyond the scope of the agreement : करार की शर्तों से परे
Beyond the seas : सात समुन्दर पार / समुद्र पार
Biased opinion : पूर्वाग्रहयुक्त परामर्श
Bidding sheet : बोली-पत्र
Biennial gathering : द्विवार्षिक समारोह
Big majority : भारी बहुमत

Bilateral negotiations : द्विपक्षीय वार्ता
Bill (s) have been drawn : बिलों पर अदायगी ली जा चुकी है
Bill (s) maybe passed for payment : बिलों को भुगतान के लिए पास किया जाए
Bill cashed on : पर बिल का पैसा प्राप्त किया जा चुका है
Bill disbursed on : पर बिल का पैसा दिया जा चुका है
Bill has been paid : बिल का भुगतान किया जा चुका है
Bill has been scrutinised and found in order : बिल जाँचा गया और सही पाया गया है
Bill has been verified : बिल का सत्यापन कर लिया गया है
Bill head : बिल-शीर्ष
Bill is returned herewith : यहाँ बिल साथ में वापस किया जा रहा है
Bill of costs : खर्चे का बिल
Bill of entry : आगम-पत्र / प्रवेश-पत्र
Bill of exchange : विनिमय-पत्र / हुंडी
Bill of indemnity : क्षतिपूर्ति बिल
Bill of loading : लदान पत्र / लदान बिल
Bill of parcels : पार्सलों का बिल
Bill of rights : अधिकार-पत्र
Bill of sale : विक्रयाधिकार-पत्र
Bill of simple receipt : सादी रसीद वाला बिल
Bill outstanding : बचा हुआ बिल
Bill passed : पास किया जा चुका बिल
Bill pay, order : बिल भुगतान आदेश
Bill payable on demand : माँग देय बिल
Bill then pending : उस समय रुका हुआ बिल
Bill to be passed : पास करने हेतु बिल
Bills payable : भुगतान हेतु बिल
Binding agreement : बिलों का समझौता
Binding on : पर बिल
Binding upon : के ऊपर बिल

Bi-parte agreement : उभयपक्षीय करार / दोतरफा करार
Birth rate : जन्म-दर
Bitterness, to cause any : कटुता पैदा करना
Biweekly statement : अर्ध-साप्ताहिक विवरण
Black Marketing : कालाबाज़ारी
Blank cheque : खाली / कोरा चेक
Blanket price : एकमुश्त कीमत
Blighted area : गन्दी बस्ती, झोंपड़पट्टी
Blind alley position : बेतरक्की पद, उन्नतिहीन पद
Blocked account : निरुद्ध खाता
Blocked capital : निरुद्ध पूँजी
Blood and iron policy : कठोर नीति
Blue book : सरकारी रिपोर्ट / अधिकृत रिपोर्ट
Blue print : रूपरेखा
Board of conciliation : सुलह मंडल
Board of Revenue : राजस्व मंडल
Board of studies : पाठ्य समिति
Board, on : के फलक पर
Board's orders : मंडल के आदेश
Boarding and lodging : रहना-खाना
Bodily injury : शारीरिक चोटें
Bodily pain : शारीरिक दर्द
Bodily weakness : शारीरिक कमजोरी
Body corporate : निगमित निकाय
Body of the letter : पत्र का मुख्य भाग
Body of the persons : व्यक्तियों का निकाय
Body of the suspicious character : संदिग्ध व्यक्तियों का गिरोह
Body of the villagers : ग्रामीणों का समूह
Body, in : निकाय के रूप में
Bogus transaction : जाली लेन-देन
Bogus voucher : जाली वाउचर
Bona fide annual value : वास्तविक वार्षिक मूल्य

Bona fide error : सद्भाविक गलती
Bona fide payment : सद्भाव भुगतान
Bona fide possession : वास्तविक कब्जा
Bona fide resident : वास्तविक नागरिक
Bond-holder : बॉण्डधारक
Bone of contention : झगड़े की जड़
Bonus share : बोनस अंश
Book adjustment : खाता समायोजन
Book asset : बही जायदाद
Book circular : पुस्तक परिपत्र
Book debt : बही ऋण
Book of reference : सन्दर्भ-पुस्तिका
Book of transfer : अंतरण पुस्तिका
Book of treasury receipts : खजाना रसीद बुक
Book transaction : खाता लेन-देन
Book transfer : खाता-अंतरण
Books of the firm : कंपनी खाते
Borne on the books : बहीखाते में दर्ज
Borne on the cadre : कैडर में
Borne on the muster roll : मस्टर रोल में दर्ज
Borrow and repay method : उधार अदायगी प्रणाली
Borrowed funds : उधार ली गयी रकम
Both days inclusive : दोनों दिन मिलाकर
Bottle neck : अवरोध, रुकावट
Bound by law : विधि द्वारा आबद्ध
Bound for : को जाने वाला
Bound to accept : स्वीकार करने के लिए बाध्य
Bound to do that act : उस कार्य को करने के लिए आबद्ध
Bound to furnish : देने के लिए आबद्ध
Bound to prove : साबित करने के लिए आबद्ध
Boundary dispute : सीमा-विवाद
Branch is necessary : शाखा आवश्यक है
Branch of learning : शिक्षा की शाखा

Breach is continuing : लगातार भंग हो रहा है
Breach of agreement : करार भंग
Breach of canal : नहर की दरार
Breach of conditions : शर्तों को तोड़ना
Breach of contract : समझौते को तोड़ना
Breach of duty : कर्तव्य भंग
Breach of law : कानून तोड़ना
Breach of partnership : साझेदारी तोड़ना
Breach of peace : शान्ति भंग करना
Breach of trust : विश्वास भंग / विश्वासघात करना
Breach privilege : विशेषाधिकार भंग करना
Break down of administration : प्रशासन ठप्प पड़ जाना
Break in prices : कीमतें गिरना
Break in service : सेवा भंग
Break in service has been condoned : सेवा-क्रम में व्यवधान को क्षमा कर दिया गया है
Break into any : में अनधिकृत प्रवेश
Break of discipline : अनुशासन भंग
Break up : विघटन / विसर्जन
Breakage in transit : परागमन में
Bribery and corruption : रिश्वत और भ्रष्टाचार
Brief for the meeting : बैठक के लिए हिदायतें / सूचना
Brief history of the case is as follows : प्रकरण का संक्षिप्त इतिहास नीचे दिया गया है
Briefs for the meeting : मीटिंग के विचार-बिन्दु
Bring an action : कार्यवाही करना
Bring forward : प्रस्तुत करना
Bring into action : काम करना
Bring into commission : प्रवर्तन करना
Bring into force : लागू करना
Bring into notice : ध्यान में लाना
Bring into operation : काम में लाना
Bring round : मना लेना

Bring this to the notice of all : सबकी जानकारी में लाना
Bring to book : स्पष्टीकरण माँगना
Broad distinction : वृहद् अंतर
Broad outline : स्थूल रूपरेखा
Broad outlook : उदार दृष्टिकोण वाला
Broad sheet : बड़ा चिट्ठा
Broadcast crop : छिटका बोआई
Broadly classified : स्थूल रूप से वर्गीकृत
Broadly speaking : मोटे तौर पर कहा जाए तो
Broken period in service : खंडित सेवाकाल
Brought forward : पिछला जोड़
Brought over : आगे ले जाया गया / अगला जोड़
Brusque manner : रूखा व्यवहार
Budget estimate : बजट अनुमान / बजट गणना
Budget grants : बजट अनुदान
Budget proposals : बजट प्रस्ताव
Budget provision : बजट व्यवस्था
Budget provision exists : बजट में व्यवस्था है
Budget provision is not adequate : बजट व्यवस्था पर्याप्त नहीं है
Budget session : बजट सत्र
Budget speech : बजट भाषण
Budgetary allotment : बजट में आवंटन
Budgetary deficit : बजट में घाटा
Budgetary powers : बजट सम्बन्धी शक्तियाँ
Budgetary procedure : बजट सम्बन्धी प्रक्रिया
Budgetary surplus : बजटीय अधिशेष
Buffer stock : सुरक्षित भण्डार
Building division : निर्माण प्रभाग
Building grant : निर्माण अनुदान
Building material : निर्माण सामग्री
Built up area : निर्मित क्षेत्र
Built up reputation : अर्जित ख्याति

Bulk cases	:	अधिकांश प्रकरण
Bulk entry system	:	एकत्रित प्रवेश व्यवस्था
Bulk expenditure	:	अधिकांश व्यय
Bulk indent	:	थोक माँगपत्र
Bulk inspection	:	सामूहि क निरीक्षण
Bulk purchase	:	थोक खरीद
Bulk sale	:	थोक बिक्री
Bulk supplies	:	थोक प्रदाय
Bumper crop	:	अच्छी फसल
Burden of obligation	:	बाध्यता का बोझ
Burden of proof	:	बहुत सारे साक्ष्य
Bureau of information	:	सूचना ब्यूरो
Bureaucratic approach	:	नौकरशाही रवैया
Business Advisory Committee	:	व्यापार सलाहकार समिति
Business concern	:	व्यावसायिक प्रतिष्ठान
Business management	:	व्यवसाय प्रबंध
Business rules	:	कार्य संचालन नियम
Business sudden and urgent	:	अचानक और जरूरी कार्य
Business to be dealt with at the meeting	:	इस बैठक में उठाये जाने वाले कार्य
Business transaction	:	व्यापारिक लेन-देन
Busy season	:	व्यस्त रहने का समय
But nevertheless	:	लेकिन ...तो भी
But for	:	यदि ऐसा न होता तो
But not exceeding	:	किन्तु ...से अधिक नहीं
But not exceeding in any case	:	किन्तु किसी भी स्थिति में ....से अधिक नहीं
Buying and selling	:	खरीद और बिक्री / क्रय-विक्रय
By a certain date	:	नियत तिथि तक
By all means	:	हर तरह से
By and by	:	धीरे-धीरे / क्रमशः
By authority of	:	के अधिकार-क्षेत्र में
By beat of drums	:	ढिंढोरा पीटकर

By command of : के समादेश से
By dishonest means : गलत तरीकों से
By duly authorised agent : सम्यक रूप से प्राधिकृत एजेंट के द्वारा
By express delivery : तुरंत वितरण द्वारा
By far the best : कहीं अधिक श्रेष्ठ
By force : शक्ति द्वारा / दबाव डालकर
By general order : सामान्य आदेश के द्वारा
By goods train : मालगाड़ी के द्वारा
By habit : आदतन
By hand : हाथों से
By law : कानूनी तौर पर
By laws : कानून के मुताबिक
By means of : के द्वारा
By mistake : गलती से
By name : नाम लेकर
By necessary implications : आवश्यक विवक्षा से
By or on behalf of : की तरफ से
By order : के आदेश पर
By order of the Governor : राज्यपाल के आदेशानुसार
By ordinary telegram : सामान्य तार द्वारा
By post : पत्र द्वारा
By product : उप-उत्पाद
By proxy : परोक्ष रूप में
By regd post : रजिस्टर्ड पोस्ट से
By return of post : वापसी के पत्र द्वारा
By road : सड़क मार्ग से
By special messenger : विशेष दूत द्वारा
By special order : विशेष आदेश से
By subjecting : अधीन करके
By suppression : दबाकर
By the action : काम द्वारा
By the variance : फेरबदल करके
By way of amendment : सुधार करके

By way of damages	: नुकसानी के तौर पर
By way of etiquette	: शिष्टाचार के नाते
By way of exchange	: अदला-बदली करके
By way of penalty	: दंड-स्वरूप
By whatever form of words	: चाहे जिन शब्दों से
By words or action	: शब्दों या काम के द्वारा
By word of mouth	: वाचिक तौर पर

■■

C

Cabinet resolution : मंत्रिमंडल का प्रस्ताव
Cabinet responsibility : मंत्रिमंडल का उत्तरदायित्व
Cable gram : काबिल / समुद्री तार
Cadre authority : कैडर / संवर्ग प्राधिकारी
Cadre strength : कैडर सदस्य संख्या
Calculated to deceive : धोखा देने के प्रयोजन से
Calculated to deprive : से वंचित करने के उद्देश्य से
Calculated to embarrass : शर्मिन्दा करने के इरादे से
Calculation of means : साधनों की गणना
Calculations and rates checked : हिसाब और दरों की जाँच की गई
Call attention notice : ध्यानाकर्षण सूचना
Call back pay : विशेष कार्य वेतन / उपस्थिति वेतन
Call deposit (Demand deposit) : माँग जमा
Call for application : से आवेदन-पत्र की माँग
Call for information : जानकारी की माँग
Call for inspection : निरीक्षण की माँग
Call for Pay on demand : माँगी गयी तनख्वाह प्रदान करने की माँग
Call for report : रिपोर्ट की माँग
Call for such recommendations as are deemed fit : यथायोग्य सिफारिशों की माँग
Call for the file : फाइल की माँग
Call for the record : अभिलेख की माँग
Call in : वापस लेना
Call in pay : विशेष कार्य वेतन / उपस्थिति वेतन
Call in question : पर आपत्ति करना / पर संदेह करना
Call loan : माँग / कर्ज / शीघ्रावधि ऋण
Call money : माँग धन
Call off duty : काम बंद करना
Call out : बुलाना, सहायता के लिए बुलाना

Call out on service : सेवा हेतु बुलाना
Call up : बुलाना
Call up for training : प्रशिक्षण के लिए बुलाना
Call upon : निमंत्रित करना, बुलाना
Call upon to give evidence : साक्ष्य देने हेतु आमंत्रित करना
Call upon to show cause : कारण बताने का आदेश देना
Called by whatever name : जिस भी किसी नाम से उसे बुलाया जाए
Called on for hearing : सुनवाई के लिए बुलवाना
Calling over : तेज आवाज में पढ़ते हुए
Calling upon : अपेक्षा करने वाली
Callings Tax : आजीविका कर
Calls in arrears : बकाया माँग
Came to rescue : बचाव हेतु आये
Camera meeting : बंद कमरे में मुलाकात / बातचीत
Camp office : शिविर कार्यालय
Camping ground : शिविर कैम्प / कैम्प स्थल
Cancel the charge : अभियोग अस्वीकृति
Cancel the pardon : क्षमायाचिका अस्वीकृति
Cancellation clause : निरसन खंड
Cancellation of indent : क्षतिपूर्ति निरसन
Cancellation of nomination : नामांकन का रद्द होना
Cancelled draft : रद्द ड्राफ्ट
Cancelled refund authorised : अधिकृत रकम की वापसी रद्द की
Cannot be acceded to : स्वीकार्य नहीं है
Cannot stand together : साथ नहीं आ सकते / साथ नहीं हो सकते
Canons of taxation : कराधान के अधिनियम
Capable but bit slow : समर्थ किन्तु कुछ मंद
Capable by law : वैधानिक तौर पर समर्थ
Capable in difficult job : दुष्कर कार्य करने में समर्थ
Capable of correction : सुधार में समर्थ
Capable of delivery : परिदान करने में समर्थ

Capable of execution order : आदेश के पालन में समर्थ
Capable of meeting the charge : प्रभार को पूरा करने में समर्थ
Capacity of, in the : के बतौर
Capacity to pay wages : वेतन / पारिश्रमिक देने की क्षमता
Capital account : पूँजीगत लेखा
Capital appropriation : पूँजी विनियोजन
Capital at charge : ब्याज देय पूँजी
Capital budget : पूँजीगत बजट
Capital cost : पूँजीगत लागत
Capital credited as paid : पूँजी जिसे समादत्त के रूप में दिखा दिया गया है
Capital employed in business : कारोबार में लगी पूँजी
Capital expenditure : पूँजीगत व्यय
Capital formation : पूँजी संचय
Capital gains : पूँजीगत लाभ
Capital goods : पूँजीगत माल
Capital improvement : पूँजीगत उन्नयन
Capital inputs : पूँजी निविष्टियाँ
Capital outlay : लगी हुई पूँजी / पूँजी लागत
Capital payment : पूँजीगत अदायगी
Capital plant : पूँजी संयंत्र
Capital reserve : सुरक्षित पूँजी
Capital stock : मूल पूँजी
Capital structure : पूँजी संरचना
Capital works : पूँजी संकर्म
Capitalisation of profits : लाभों का पूँजीकरण
Capitalised value : पूँजीकृत मूल्य
Capitalistic economy : पूँजीवादी अर्थव्यवस्था
Capitation grant : प्रतिव्यक्ति अनुदान
Capitation Tax : प्रतिव्यक्ति कर
Capturing force : पकड़ने वाला बल
Card index : कार्ड सूची
Card trade : व्यापार कार्ड

Cardinal principle : मूल सिद्धांत
Care and caution : सावधानी और सतर्कता
Care and custody for the goods : माल की देखरेख और अभिरक्षा
Care and pains : सावधानी और परिश्रम
Care entrusted to him : देखरेख हेतु उसको सौंपा गया
Career master : व्यवसाय परामर्शदाता
Careful observance : सावधानी से पालन
Careless and incorrect report : असावधानीपूर्वक लिखी गयी और गलत रिपोर्ट
Carried down : अधोनत, तलशेष
Carried forward : अग्रनीत
Carried over effects : पूर्वावशिष्ट प्रभाव
Carry back of losses : पिछले लाभ से घाटा पूर्ति
Carry forward of losses : अगले लाभ से घाटा पूर्ति
Carry on business for profit : लाभ के लिए कारोबार चलाना
Carry out instructions ungrudgingly : बिना उज्र अनुदेशों का पालन करना
Carry out obligation : बाध्यता का पालन करना
Carry out orders : आदेशों का पालन करना
Carry weight : का प्रभाव पड़ना
Carrying interest : ब्याज पर, जिस पर ब्याज लगे
Carrying on activity for profit : लाभ हेतु गतिविधियाँ चलाना
Carrying out the provisions : उपबंधों को क्रियान्वित करना
Carrying over : आगे ले जाना
Case be remanded : प्रकरण लौटाया जाए / प्रतिप्रेषित किया जाए
Case file is put up below for perusal : प्रकरण फाइल अवलोकनार्थ प्रस्तुत की गई है
Case for disposal : प्रकरण निपटान हेतु
Case for order on : तारीख को आदेश के लिए पेशी
Case has been badly delayed : प्रकरण काफी विलंबित हो गया है
Case has been closed : प्रकरण समाप्त
Case is filed : प्रकरण दर्ज हो गया है

Case is not traceable : फाइल नहीं मिल रही है

Case is remanded for fresh disposal : पुनः कार्यवाही हेतु फाइल लौटाई जाती है

Case is resubmitted as directed on pre page : पिछले पृष्ठ पर दिये गए निर्देश के अनुसार प्रकरण फिर से प्रस्तुत किया जाता है

Case is to be reviewed : प्रकरण पर पुनर्विचार होना है

Case is under consideration : प्रकरण विचाराधीन है

Case maybe heard and decided in his absence : उसकी गैरहाजिरी में मामले की सुनवाई और फैसला किया जाए

Case maybe, processed in accordance with the extent orders : वर्तमान आदेश के अनुसार मामले पर कार्यवाही की जाए

Case should pend till : तक मामला रोका जाए

Cash and carry : थोक खरीद

Cash balance in hand : शेष रकम

Cash balance report : रोकड़ बाकी का विवरण

Cash crop : नकदी फसल

Cash equivalent : नकद समतुल्य

Cash in hand : पास की नकद रकम

Cash remittance : रोकड़ प्रेषण

Cash transaction : नकद लेन-देन

Cash under double lock : दो कुंजी वाले तालों में रखी नकद रकम

Cash value : नकद मूल्य

Cash wage : नकद पारिश्रमिक

Cast away : फेंक देना

Casting vote : निर्णायक मत

Casual and non-recurring nature : आकस्मिक और अनावर्ती प्रकृति

Casual employment : नैमित्तिक नियुक्ति

Casual labour : अनियत श्रमिक

Catalogue of books : पुस्तक-सूची

Catch crop : बीच की फसल

Catchment area : जल-ग्रहण क्षेत्र / आवाह-क्षेत्र
Category of amounts : रकम का प्रवर्ग
Category of securities : प्रवर्ग सूची
Cause (beyond the control of the employee) : (कर्मचारी के काबू के बाहर) कारण
Cause an election to be held : चुनाव कराना
Cause disturbance of public tranquility : जन-शान्ति में बाधा आना
Cause of collision : टकराव का मामला
Cause of exceptional nature, by any : असाधारण प्रकृति के कारण
Cause of Hindi : हिंदी का हित
Cause of Salvage : निस्तारण का मामला
Cause to be laid down : रखवाया जाना
Cause showing : कारण प्रदर्शित करना
Caused by : के कारण
Causes to be produced : कारण पेश करवाना
Causing grievous hurt : गंभीर चोट पहुँचाना
Causing restraint : अवरोध पैदा करना
Causing the loss : क्षति का कारण बनना
Causing the mortgage to be merged : बंधन का विलयन करना
Caution : सावधानी / चेतावनी
Caveat emptor : क्रेता सावधान रहें
Cease to be : न रहना / न होना
Cease to be enforceable : प्रवर्तनीय न रहना
Cease to be in force : लागू न रहना
Cease to be levied : उद्ग्रहीत नहीं किया जाना
Cease to be member : सदस्यता का समापन
Cease to exercise jurisdiction : अधिकारिता का प्रयोग न करना
Cease to exist : अस्तित्वहीन हो जाना / न रहना / न होना
Cease to have effect : प्रभाव समाप्त हो जाना
Cease to hold office : पद पर न रह जाना / अपदस्थ हो जाना

Cease to operate : प्रवृत्त न होना
Cease to reside : निवास न करना
Ceiling limit : अधिकतम सीमा
Ceiling price : अधिकतम मूल्य
Censure motion : निंदा प्रस्ताव
Censured for his ommission and false statement : अपनी चूक और मिथ्या कथन के लिए परिनिन्दित
Central revenue : केन्द्रीय राजस्व
Centralisation of administration : प्रशासन का केन्द्रीकरण
Cepi corpus : वह सशरीर पकड़ लिया गया है और अभिरक्षा में है
Ceremonial centre : समारोह केंद्र
Ceremonial parade : समारोह परेड
Certificate be amended : प्रमाणपत्र संशोधित किया जाए
Certificate by the competent authority is required : समर्थ अधिकारी का प्रमाणपत्र अपेक्षित है
Certificate of administration : प्रशासन का प्रमाणपत्र
Certificate of appeal : अपील का प्रमाणपत्र
Certificate of assumption of Charge : भार-ग्रहण प्रमाणपत्र
Certificate of committal : सुपुर्दगी का प्रमाणपत्र
Certificate of naturalisation : देशीकरण का प्रमाणपत्र
Certificate of practice : व्यवसाय का प्रमाणपत्र
Certificate of recognition : मान्यता का प्रमाणपत्र
Certificate of sale : बिक्री का प्रमाणपत्र
Certificate of share : शेअर का प्रमाणपत्र
Certification mark : प्रमाणीकृत चिह्न
Certified extract : प्रमाणित उद्धरण
Certified that the amount of the bill has been disbursed to proper persons : प्रमाणित किया जाता है कि बिल की रकम का भुगतान सही व्यक्तियों को कर दिया गया है
Cessation of act : कार्य का बंद होना
Cessation of approval : अनुमोदन की समाप्ति

Cessation of force : बल-प्रयोग की समाप्ति
Cessation of motion : गतिहीनता
Cessation of profession : व्यवसाय का बंद होना
Cessation of work/act : कार्य अवरोध
Challenged officer : वह अफसर जिसके विषय में आक्षेप किया गया हो
Challenged vote : आक्षेपित मत
Channel of communication : संचार माध्यम
Character and antecedents : चरित्र और पूर्व-वृत्त
Character of agent : अभिकर्ता की हैसियत
Character-roll : चरित्रपंजी
Character-roll warning : चरित्रपंजी चेतावनी
Charge a property : संपत्ति को भारित करना
Charge allowance : कार्यकार भत्ता
Charge for service : सेवार्थ प्रभार
Charge imperfect : अपूर्ण आरोप
Charge of impersonation : प्रतिरूपण का आरोप
Charge of insubordination : आदेश की अवहेलना का आरोप
Charge of like nature : समान प्रकृति का भार
Charge of tax : कर प्रभारण
Charge report : कार्यभार रिपोर्ट
Charge sheet has been read out and explained to the employee Entry made upon a charge : आरोपपत्र कर्मचारी को पढ़कर सुना और समझा दिया गया है
Charge to capital : पूँजी खर्च में डालना
Charge with liability : दायित्व का भार सौंपना
Charge with notice : सूचना आरोपित करना
Charged erroneous : गलत आरोप
Charged expenditure : प्रभारित व्यय
Charged with : का भार रखते हुए / का आरोप लगाते हुए
Charged with liability : दायित्व से भारित
Charged with notice : सूचना आरोपित

Charitable allowance : पुण्यार्थ भत्ता

Charitable and religious endowments : पुण्यार्थ तथा धार्मिक अक्षय निधि

Chase the case : मामले की प्रगति बनाए रखें

Cheapest route : सबसे सस्ता रास्ता

Cheat by personation : प्रतिरूपण द्वारा छल

Cheque is realised : चेक भुन गया है

Check measurement : माप परीक्षण

Check register : जाँच रजिस्टर

Check weighment : जाँच के रूप में तौलना

Chest money : तिजोरी रोकड़ा / तिजोरी में सुरक्षित पैसा

Chief Auditor : मुख्या लेखा परीक्षक

Chief Protocol : नयाचार प्रमुख

Chief Rector : मुख्य कुलाधि सचिव

Chief whip : मुख्य सचेतक

Child mortality rate : शिशु मृत्युदर

Chronological order : कालक्रमानुसार

Circle office : मंडल कार्यालय

Circular in draft : प्रारूप परिचालित करना

Circulate : प्रचलित होना / प्रचार पाना

Circulate and then file : सबको दिखाकर फाइल कर दिया जाए

Circulate the precis : संक्षेपिका सबको प्रेषित की जाए

Circulation : प्रचार-प्रसार / संचरण

Circulation of currency : मुद्रा संचालन

Circulation policy : प्रसार नीति / विक्रय नीति

Circumstances attending death : वे परिस्थितियाँ जिनमें मृत्यु हुई

Circumstances that exist : वे परिस्थितियाँ जो विद्यमान हैं

City compensatory allowance : नगर प्रतिकार भत्ता

Civic interest : नागरिक हित

Civil action : सिविल कार्यवाही / अर्थविवाद

Civil affairs : नागरिक कार्य

Civil area : नगरीय क्षेत्र
Civil case : दीवानी मुकदमा
Civil contempt : सिविल अवमानना
Civil disobedience movement : सविनय अवज्ञा आंदोलन
Civil law : दीवानी कानून
Civil Liability : नागरिक दायित्व
Civil offence : नागरिक / दीवानी अपराधी
Civil proceedings : दीवानी कार्यवाहियाँ
Civil process : नागरिक प्रक्रिया
Civil rights : नागरिक अधिकार
Civil supply : नागरिक आपूर्ति
Claim as right : अधिकार रूप में माँगना
Claim deduction : कटौती का दावा करना
Claim is excessive/ unreasonable : दावा जरूरत से काफी ज्यादा है
Claim is time barred : दावा समयबाधित है
Claims of privilege : विशेषाधिकार का दावा
Claims paid : चुकाए जा चुके दावे / भुगतान कर दिए गए दावे
Claims to be on trial : विचारार्थ दावे
Clandestine (y) removal : छिपाकर हटाया जाना
Classification of posts : पदों का वर्गीकरण
Classified account : वर्गीकृत लेखा
Classless society : वर्गहीन समाज
Clause by clause : खंडशः
Clean and accurate accounts : स्पष्ट और सही लेखा
Clean and concise : स्पष्ट और संक्षिप्त
Clean cultivation : घास-पातरहित कृषि
Clean days : पूरे दिन / पूर्ण दिन
Clean it is quite evident : ऐसा अक्सर देखा जा रहा है / ऐसा प्रायः हो रहा है
Clean notice of a week : एक हफ्ते की स्पष्ट सूचना
Clean thinker : स्पष्ट विचारक

Clearance of goods : माल की निकासी
Clearing a bill : बिल समाशोधन
Clearing agent : निकासी अभिकर्ता
Clearing house : समाशोधन गृह
Clearly worded proposal : स्पष्ट शब्दों में कहा गया प्रस्ताव
Clerk of court : न्यायालय का अधीक्षक / पेशकार
Close and effective supervision : सूक्ष्म और कारगर पर्यवेक्षण
Close arrest : बंदी / गिरफ्तारी
Close of evidence : साक्ष्य की समाप्ति
Close watch is being kept on the case : मामले पर बारीक नजर राखी जा रही है
Closed holiday : अवकाश दिवस
Closed motion : समापन प्रस्ताव
Closer supervision : निकटतर पर्यवेक्षण
Code of practice : व्यवहार संहिता
Codification of rules : नियमों का संहिताकरण
Co-extensive with the duration of : उसकी अवधि उतनी ही होगी जितनी कि
Cognate expression : सजातीय अभिव्यक्ति
Cognizable case : संज्ञेय प्रकरण
Cognizable offence : संज्ञेय अपराध
Collaboration of, in : के साथ / के सहयोग से
Collateral agreement : संपार्श्विक समझौता
Collateral credit : जमानती उधार
Collateral heir : संपार्श्विक उत्तराधिकारी
Collateral security : संपार्श्विक प्रतिभूति
Collection of arrears : बकाये की वसूली
Collection of dues : प्राप्य राशियों की वसूली
Collection of revenue : राजस्व का संग्रहण
Collector of revenue : राजस्व संग्राहक / राजस्व कलेक्टर
Colour of office : पदाभास
Colour of process, under : उचित कार्यवाही के नाम पर

Colour of trust : न्यायाभास
Columns provided in the form : फार्म में दिए गए कालम / खाते
Combination, acting in : मिलकर कार्य करते हुए
Combined finance and revenue accounts : सम्मिलित वित्त तथा राजस्व लेखे
Come in the way of : के मार्ग से बाधित होना
Come into contact with : के संपर्क में आना
Come into force : प्रवृत्त होना / लागू होना
Come into operation : चालू होना / प्रवर्तन में आना
Come into position : स्थिति में आना
Come into possession : कब्जे में आना
Come to an end : समाप्त होना
Come under charge : कम दाम में लेना / कम दाम में होना
Command greatest measure of intelligibility : अधिक-से-अधिक मात्रा में समझने योग्य व्यक्ति
Command respect : सम्मान का अधिकारी होना
Commanded area : प्रभावित क्षेत्र
Commands and injunctions : समादेश और व्यादेश
Commendable work : सराहनीय कार्य
Commensurate with labour : पारिश्रमिक / परिश्रम के अनुसार
Commercial intelligence : वाणिज्यिक आसूचना
Commercial undertaking : वाणिज्यिक उपक्रम
Commission of an act : कार्य का किया जाना
Commission of an offence : अपराध करना
Commission of murder : हत्या करना
Commission of the act charged as an offence : अपराध समझे जाने वाला कार्य करना
Commit default : व्यतिक्रम करना
Commit for trial : विचारण के लिए सुपुर्द करना
Commit indiscretions : अविवेकपूर्ण कार्यों को करना
Commit to jail : कारागार के सुपुर्द करना
Committal proceedings : अर्पण की कार्यवाहियाँ
Committed to the court of sessions : सेशन सुपुर्द

Committee on public undertaking : लोक उपक्रम समिति

Committee on ways and means : उपाय और साधन समिति

Common goods : सामान्य वस्तुएँ

Common irregularities : सामान्य अनियमितताएँ

Common object : सामान्य उद्देश्य

Common regulation : सामान्य विनियम

Common understanding : सामान्य समझ

Communicate displeasure : अप्रसन्नता व्यक्त करना

Communicate with press : प्रेस से संपर्क करना

Communication of acceptance : प्रतिग्रहण की सूचना

Communication received : प्राप्त सूचना

Communication referred to in the P.U.C. does not appear to have been received in this office : ऐसा प्रतीत होता है कि विचाराधीन पत्र में उल्लेख किया गया पत्र इस कार्यालय को प्राप्त नहीं हुआ है

Communication referred to public : जनसाधारण को संसूचित करना

Commutation of pension : पेंशन का संराशिकरण

Commutation of rights : अधिकारों का रूपांतरण

Commuted leave : परिवर्तित छुट्टी

Commuted value of pension : पेंशन का संराशिकृत मूल्य

Comparable employment : सदृश नियोजन

Comparative rate schedule : तुलनात्मक दर अनुसूची

Compared by : ने मिलान किया / ने तुलना की

Compassionate allowance : अनुकम्पा भत्ता

Compassionate gratuity : अनुग्रह धन

Compendium of standing orders : स्थायी आदेशों का सार संग्रह

Compensation for wrong : दोष का प्रतिकार

Compensation to workmen : कामगारों को मुआवजा

Competent and reliable person : सक्षम और विश्वसनीय व्यक्ति

Competent authority may kindly decide : सक्षम अधिकारी कृपया निर्णय दें

Competitive rates : प्रतियोगी दरें

Compilation of accounts : लेखाओं का संकलन
Complementary to each other : एक-दूसरे के पूरक
Complementary work : पूरक कार्य
Complete decontrol : पूर्ण विनियंत्रण
Completed accounting period : संपूरित लेखा कालावधि
Compliance of judgement : निर्णय का अनुपालन
Compliance report : अनुवर्तन रिपोर्ट
Compliance with orders is still awaited : आदेश के अनुपालन की अभी प्रतीक्षा है
Compliment, as a : सम्मानस्वरूप
Complimentary remark : प्रशंसात्मक उक्ति
Comply with the order : आदेश का पालन कीजिये
Comply with the requirements : जरूरतें पूरी की जाएँ
Composed of : से मिलकर बना हुआ
Composition for duty : शुल्क के लिए प्रशमन
Composition of offences : अपराधों का आपसी निपटारा
Compound a case : मुकदमे में समझौता करना
Comprehensive questionnaire : व्यापक प्रश्नावली
Comprised in : में समाविष्ट
Compulsory acquisition : अनिवार्य अर्जन
Compulsory grant : अनिवार्य अनुदान
Compulsory notification of vacancies : रिक्तियों की अनिवार्य अधिसूचना
Computation of net profits : शुद्ध लाभों की संगणना
Computation of time : समय की संगणना
Concentration of efforts : प्रयासों का संकेंद्रीकरण
Concentration of industries : उद्योगों का संकेंद्रीकरण
Concerned section : सम्बन्धित विभाग
Conciliation proceeding : सुलह कार्यवाही
Conclusions of the conference : सम्मलेन के निष्कर्ष
Conclusive and final : निश्चयात्मक और अंतिम
Conclusive evidence : निर्णायक साक्ष्य
Concrete proposal : ठोस प्रस्ताव

Concurrence for the creation of the following posts is require : निम्नलिखित पदों के निर्माण के लिए सहमति चाहिए

Concurrence for the extension of the following posts : निम्नलिखित पदों की अवधि बढ़ाने के लिए सहमति अपेक्षित है

Concurrence has been obtained : सहमति प्राप्त कर ली गई है

Concurrence of the finance branch is necessary : वित्त शाखा की सहमति आवश्यक है

Concurrent finding : एक ही निष्कर्ष

Concurrent jurisdiction : समवर्ती क्षेत्राधिकार

Concurrent list : समवर्ती सूची

Concurring vote : सहमति वोट

Condemned goods : अनुपयोगी सामान

Condition and contract of sale : विक्रय की शर्तें और संविदा

Condition of previous publication : पूर्व प्रकाशन की शर्त

Condone the delay : विलम्ब हेतु क्षमा करना

Conduct is questionable : आचरण आपत्तिजनक है

Conduct of business : कार्य संचालन / कामकाज करना

Conduct of elections : निर्वाचनों का संचालन

Conduct of public business : सार्वजनिक कारोबार का संचालन

Conduct rules : आचरण के नियम

Confer on : पर विचार-विमर्श करना

Confer power : शक्ति प्रदान करना

Confer with : के साथ विचार-विमर्श करना

Conferred by : द्वारा प्रदत्त

Conferred by charter : चार्टर द्वारा प्रदत्त

Conferring the power : शक्ति प्रदान करने वाला

Confidential capacity : गोपनीय हैसियत

Confidential character roll : गोपनीय चरित्र पुस्तिका

Confidential communication : गोपनीय सूचना / गोपनीय सन्देश

Confined to discussion : चर्चा तक सीमित

Confirm the transfer : स्थानान्तरण की पुष्टि करना

Confirmation in the grade : श्रेणी में पुष्टि

Confirmation of a govt. servant : सरकारी कर्मचारी का स्थायीकरण
Confiscated amount : जब्त की गई राशि
Confused in dealing with complex matters : जटिल मामलों में किंकर्त्तव्यविमूढ़
Congested area : घनी बस्ती
Connect previous papers : पिछले कागजात नत्थी करें
Connecting reference : सम्बंधित हवाला / सम्बंधित सन्दर्भ
Conscientious officer : अन्तःपरायण अधिकारी
Consecutive sentence : लगातार दंडादेश
Consecutive terms : लगातार अवधियाँ
Consensus ad idem : एक ही बात पर एक ही अर्थ में मतैक्य
Consequence of non-attendance : अनुपस्थित रहने के परिणामस्वरूप
Consequence of, in : के परिणाम का / के परिणाम में
Consequent change : परिणामी परिवर्तन
Consequent events : अनुवर्ती घटनाएँ
Consequent upon : के परिणामस्वरूप
Consequently it has been decided that : अतः यह निश्चय किया गया है कि
Consider the finding idle money : निष्क्रिय धनराशि को प्राप्त करने पर विचार करें
Considerable assistance : यथेष्ट सहायक होना
Considerable economy : यथेष्ट मितव्ययिता
Considerable magnitude : पर्याप्त बड़े पैमाने पर
Considerable scope for improvement : सुधार के लिए पर्याप्त गुंजाइश
Considerable time : पर्याप्त समय
Considerably delayed cases : पर्याप्त रूप से विलंबित प्रकरण
Consideration for guarantee : प्रत्याभूति हेतु विचारार्थ
Consideration of services : सेवाओं का प्रतिफल
Consideration transferee for : सप्रतिफल अन्तरिति
Consideration valuable : मूल्यवान विचार / प्रतिफल
Considered opinion : सुविचारित राय

Consign to records : अभिलेखागार में रखिये
Consignment note : प्रेषण नोट / पत्र
Consistent view : स्थिर विचार / अविचल विचार
Consistent with the provisions : उपबंधों से संगत के अनुसार
Consolidated annual accounts : समेकित वार्षिक लेखे
Consolidated fund : संचित निधि / समेकित निधि
Consolidated pay : संचित वेतन
Consolidated report : समेकित रिपोर्ट / समेकित विवरण
Consolidated report may be furnished : समेकित रिपोर्ट प्रस्तुत करें
Consolidated revenue : समेकित राजस्व
Consolidated statement : समेकित विवरण
Consolidation of holdings : चकबंदी
Conspicuous place : सहज दृश्य स्थान
Conspicuously notified : सुस्पष्टतः अधिसूचित
Constant study : बराबर अध्ययन / सफल अध्ययन
Constituted a quorum : कोरम पूरा हुआ
Constituted by law : विधिवत गठित
Constituted by or under : के द्वारा या अधीन गठित
Constitution of a committee : समिति का गठन
Constitution of an authority : प्राधिकरण का गठन
Constitutional crisis : संवैधानिक समस्या
Constitutional deadlock : संवैधानिक गतिरोध
Constitutional reason : संवैधानिक कारण
Construction of documents : दस्तावेज का अर्थान्वयन
Construction of structure : संरचना का निर्माण
Construction of will : वसीयत का अर्थ लगाना
Construction sub-division : निर्माण उपसंभाग
Constructive criticism : रचनात्मक आलोचना
Constructive possession : आन्वयिक कब्जा
Constructive view, take a : रचनात्मक दृष्टि से विचार करना
Construed accordingly : तद्नुकूल अर्थ लगाया जाना
Consultation Consumerate with : के साथ आनुपातिक रूप में रखना

Consultation with ... is necessary : से परामर्श करना आवश्यक है
Consumption has increased : खपत बढ़ गई है
Contact the informer : सूचना देने वाले से संपर्क कीजिये
Contemplated action : सोची गई कार्यवाही
Contention is not correct : तर्क ठीक नहीं है
Contention is untenable : तर्क में बल नहीं है
Contents of Book : पुस्तक की विषय-सूची
Contents of document : दस्तावेज की विषयवस्तु
Contents of memorandum : ज्ञापन की विषयवस्तु
Contents of proclamation : उद्घोषणा की विषयवस्तु
Contesting the petition : अर्जी का विरोध करना
Contiguous area : निकटवर्ती क्षेत्र
Contingency fund : आकस्मिकता निधि
Contingency may arise : आकस्मिक स्थिति पैदा हो सकती है
Contingent and prospective liabilities : समाश्रित तथा भावी दायित्व
Contingent bill : आकस्मिक बिल
Contingent charges : आकस्मिक / प्रासंगिक प्रभार
Contingent nature : आकस्मिक प्रकार
Contingent on : पर निर्भर
Contingent on impossible events : असंभव घटनाओं पर समाश्रित
Contingent register : फुटकर खर्च रजिस्टर
Contingent use : संभावित उपयोग
Continuance of attachment : कुर्की का चालू रहना
Continuance of office : पद पर बने रहना
Continue in force : प्रवृत्त रहना / बना रहना
Continue in possession : कब्जा बने रहना
Continued concentration : निरंतर एकाग्रता
Continued to do good work : निरंतर अच्छा कार्य करता रहे
Continues to be approved : अनुमोदन कायम है
Continues to be recognized : मान्यता कायम है
Continuing breach : लगातार किया जा रहा उल्लंघन

Continuing default : व्यतिक्रम चालू रहना
Continuing guarantee : अनवरत गारंटी / प्रत्याभूति
Continuing offence : निरंतर होने वाला अपराध
Continuous line of communication : संचार की जारी लाइन
Contra balances : दुतरफा शेष
Contraband goods : विनिषिद्ध माल
Contraband trade : विनिषिद्ध व्यापार
Contract be reformed : संविदा में सुधार किया जाए
Contract contingencies : नियत आकस्मिक व्यय
Contract for sale : विक्रय की संविदा
Contract in good faith : सद्भावपूर्वक संविदा / ठेका
Contract maybe terminated : ठेका समाप्त कर दिया जाए
Contract rate : संविदा दर
Contract supply system : संविदा पूर्ति पद्धति / ठेके पर पूर्ति की पद्धति
Contravenes the provision of : के उपबंधों का उल्लंघन करना
Contravention of rules : नियमों का उल्लंघन करना
Contribute largely : पर्याप्त योगदान देना
Contribution for leave and pension : छुट्टी और पेंशन के लिए अंशदान
Contributory provident fund : अंशदायी भविष्य निधि
Control of goods : माल पर नियंत्रण
Controlled area : नियंत्रक क्षेत्र
Controlled circulation : नियंत्रक प्रसार
Controlling power : नियंत्रक शक्ति
Controversy as to right : अधिकार के सम्बन्ध में विवाद
Convenient despatch : सुविधानुसार प्रेषण
Convenient head : सुविधाजनक शीर्ष
Convenient speed : सुविधाजनक शीघ्रता
Conventional law : पारंपरिक विधान / कानून
Conventional rights : परम्परागत अधिकार
Conversant with : से परिचित

Convey your financial concurrence approval : अपनी वित्तीय सहमति / अनुमोदन की सूचना दें

Conveyance allowance : वाहन भत्ता

Convocation address : दीक्षांत भाषण

Cool and collected : प्रशांत और स्थिर

Cool and dependable : प्रशांत और निर्भरयोग्य

Cooperation movement : सहकारिता आन्दोलन

Cooperative efforts : सहकारिता के प्रयास

Cooperative land mortgage bank : सहकारी भू–बंधक बैंक

Coopted member : सहयोजित सदस्य

Co-partnership deed : सहभागीदार विलेख / डीड

Cope with the work : काम करने में समर्थ होना

Copied by : ने प्रति तैयार की

Copy applied for : के लिए मांगी गई प्रति

Copy enclosed for ready reference : तत्काल हवाले / सन्दर्भ के लिए प्रति साथ भेजी गई है

Copy of the letter referred to above is sent herewith : उल्लिखित पत्र की प्रति इसके साथ संलग्न है

Copy together with 5 spares is forwarded to : पांच अतिरिक्त प्रतियों सहित प्रति प्रेषित है

Copy with a spare copy forwarded to : अतिरिक्त प्रति के साथ प्रतिलिप प्रेषित

Core programme : मूल कार्यक्रम

Corporate body with perpetual succession : शाश्वत उत्तराधिकार प्राप्त निगमित निकाय

Corpus delicti : अपराध सार

Corpus possessions : कब्जाधीन वस्तु

Correct demarcation : ठीक सीमांकन

Correct edition : संशोधित संस्करण

Corrected to date : आज तक संशोधित

Correction of errors : भूल सुधार

Correctional services : सुधारात्मक सेवाएँ

Corrective measures : सुधार हेतु उठाये जाने वाले कदम

Correctly maintain : सही-सही रखना

Correspond with : के सदृश होना / के अनुरूप होना / से पत्राचार करना

Correspondence resting with your memo No. : आपके ज्ञापन-पत्र पर रुका हुआ पत्र-व्यवहार

Correspondence section : पत्र-व्यवहार अनुभाग

Corresponding amount : तत्समान रकम

Corresponding appointment : तत्समान नियुक्ति

Corresponding entry : तत्सम्बन्धी प्रविष्टि

Corresponding functionary : तत्समान कर्मचारी

Corresponding jurisdiction : समरूपी अधिकारक्षेत्र

Corresponding official : तत्समान अधिकारी

Corresponding provision : तत्समान उपबंध

Corrigendum maybe put up : शुद्धि-पत्र प्रस्तुत किया जाए

Cost accounts : लागत लेखा

Cost at his own : स्वयं अपने खर्चे पर

Cost investigation : लागत अन्वेषण

Cost maybe debited : लागत काट ली जाए

Cost of acquisition : अर्जन की लागत

Cost of living index number : जीवन-निर्वाह व्यय सूचकांक

Cost of relief : सहायता का खर्च

Cost price : लागत मूल्य

Counter charge : प्रत्यारोप

Counter productive : प्रति-उत्पादक

Counter signature : प्रति-हस्ताक्षर / प्रमाणीकरण के हस्ताक्षर

Counterfeit coin/stamp : जाली सिक्का / मुद्रा

Countermand of payment : भुगतान रद्द करना

Counterpart : प्रतिरूप

Counterpart of a lease : पट्टे का प्रतिलेख

Countervailing duty : प्रतिशुल्क

Countervailing force : प्रतिरोधी शक्ति

Counting Coup d'etat : बलात राज्य परिवर्तन

Course common : सामान्य अनुक्रम
Course of business : कारोबार का अनुक्रम
Course of dealing : व्यवहारचर्या
Course of employment : नियोजन का अनुक्रम
Course of exchange : विनिमय का अनुक्रम
Course of instruction : प्रशिक्षण का अनुक्रम
Course of in the : की चर्या में, के अनुक्रम में
Course of justice : न्याय का क्रम
Course of practical training : व्यावहारिक प्रशिक्षणक्रम
Course of trial, in the : विचारण के अनुक्रम में
Course of transit : अभिवहन का अनुक्रम
Court immediately below : ठीक नीचे का न्यायालय
Court immediately superior : ठीक वरिष्ठ न्यायालय
Court of competent jurisdiction : सक्षम अधिकारितायुक्त न्यायालय
Court of confirmation : पुष्टिकरण का न्यायालय
Court of equal jurisdiction : समान अधिकारिता वाला न्यायालय
Court of lowest grade : सबसे नीची श्रेणी का न्यायालय
Court of revision : पुनरीक्षण न्यायालय
Court of sessions : सेशन न्यायालय
Court of wards : प्रतिपालक अधिकरण / कोर्ट ऑफ वार्ड्स
Court revenue : राजस्व न्यायालय
Court subordinate : अधीनस्थ न्यायालय
Court superior : वरिष्ठ न्यायालय
Courteous in manner : व्यवहार में भद्र, सौजन्यपूर्ण
Courtesy and etiquette : सौजन्य और शिष्टाचार
Cover note sealed : सील किया हुआ कवर नोट
Credentials committee : प्रत्यय-पत्र समिति
Credit advice : जमा सूचना
Credit and thrift society : उधार और बचत समिति
Credit certificate : साख प्रमाणपत्र
Credit facilities : ऋण सुविधाएँ
Credit note : जमा / साख-पत्र

Credit of the person : व्यक्ति की विश्वसनीयता
Credit sale : उधार बिक्री
Credit scroll, daily : दैनिक जमा सूची
Credit service : साख सेवा
Credit society : उधार समिति
Credit system : उधार पद्धति
Credited into : समादत्त मानी जाकर जमा कर ली गयी
Credited to treasury : सरकारी खजाने में जमा की गयी
Criminal breach of trust : आपराधिक विश्वास भंग
Criminal contempt : आपराधिक अवमान
Criminal force : आपराधिक बल
Criminal intimidation : आपराधिक अभित्रास
Criminal jurisdiction : दंड क्षेत्राधिकार
Criminal liability : आपराधिक दायित्व
Criminal misappropriation : आपराधिक दुर्विनियोग
Criminal proceedings : फौजदारी कार्यवाही
Criminal process : आपराधिक आदेशिका
Critical faculty : आलोचनात्मक शक्ति
Cross checking : दो-तरफ जाँच / प्रति-परीक्षण
Cross decree : प्रति-आदेश
Cross objection : प्रत्याक्षेप
Cross reference : प्रति निर्देश / प्रति-सन्दर्भ
Cross road, at : चौराहे पर
Crushing defeat : जबरदस्त हार
Cultivate greater control, should : अधिक नियंत्रण रखना सीखें
Culturable area : कृषियोग्य क्षेत्र
Cultural relations : सांस्कृतिक सम्बन्ध
Cumbersome task : दुष्कर कार्य
Cumculative benefit : संचयी लाभ
Cumculative effect : संचयात्मक प्रभाव
Cumculative punishment : आकलित दंड
Currency of the post expires on : पद की अवधि को समाप्त होती है

Currency officer : मुद्रा अधिकारी
Current condition prevailing : वर्तमान परिस्थिति में
Current day : साधारण दिन / आज
Current duties : वर्तमान कर्तव्य-भार
Current liability : वर्तमान दायित्व
Current use : चालू उपभोग
Cursory glance : सरसरी नजर
Custodia legis : विधि अभिरक्षा
Custody having the force of law : विधि का बल रखने वाली
Custody of court : न्यायालय की अभिरक्षा
Custody of property : समाप्ति अभिरक्षक
Custody of records : अभिलेखों की अभिरक्षा
Custody of the law : विधि की अभिरक्षा
Custody of the minor : अवयस्क की अभिरक्षा
Custom of service : सेवा रूढ़ि
Customary bonus : रूढ़िगत बोनस
Customary concession : रूढ़िगत रियायत
Customary law : रूढ़िगत विधि
Customary manner : रूढ़िगत प्रकार
Customary mode : रूढ़िगत ढंग
Cut already imposed on entertainment and hospitality fund should, be scrupulously enforced : मनोरंजन और अतिथि सत्कार पर पहले से की गई कटौती कड़ाई से लागू की जानी चाहिए
Cut motion : कटौती प्रस्ताव

■■

D

Daily average number : दैनिक औसत संख्या
Daily average of cases disposed of : निपटाए गए मामलों का दैनिक औसत
Daily rated worker : दैनिक मजदूरी करने वाला कर्मकार
Dairy farming : दुग्ध उद्योग / डेरी उद्योग
Damage and deficiency (D.D.) : क्षति एवं कमी सम्बन्धी सन्देश
Damaged and unserviceable stores : टूटा-फूटा और अनुपयोगी सामान
Damages consequential : परिणाम में होने वाला नुकसान
Damages for breach of contract : संविदा भंग से होने वाला नुकसान
Damages for non-delivery : अवितरण से होने वाला नुकसान
Damages pecuniary : आर्थिक नुकसान
Damages special : विशेष नुकसान
Danger of being wasted : अपव्यय होने का खतरा
Dangerous epidemic disease : भयंकर संक्रामक रोग
Dangerously inflammable substance : खतरनाक रूप से ज्वलनशील
Date line : दिनांक-रेखा
Date next following : अगली आने वाली तारीख
Date of application : आवेदन की तारीख
Date of arrival : आगमन की तारीख
Date of closing : बंद करने की तारीख
Date of communication of notice : सूचना देने की तारीख
Date of execution : निष्पादन की तारीख
Date of issue : जारी किये जाने की तारीख
Date of maturity : परिपक्वता की तारीख
Date of occurrence : घटना की तारीख
Date of presentation : उपस्थापित किये जाने की तारीख
Date of publication of notice : सूचना के प्रकाशन की तारीख
Date of the pass may be extended : पास की तारीख बढ़ा दी जाए

Date stamp : तारीख की मुहर
Day by day : दिन-प्रतिदिन
De facto guardian : वास्तविक संरक्षक
De jure guardian : विधितः संरक्षक / कानूनन संरक्षक
De novo : नए सिरे से
Dead card : बेकार कार्ड
Dead letter office : पुनः प्रेषण केंद्र
Dead rent : बंद किराया
Dead stock : बिना बिका
Deal with appeal : अपील पर कार्यवाही करना
Deal with emergencies : आपातकालिक स्थितियों का सामना करना
Deal with the same : उसे ही निपटाना
Dealing between the parties : पक्षकारों के बीच व्यवहार
Dealing in any manner : किसी भी रीति में व्यवहार करना
Dealing with such applications : ऐसे आवेदनों का निपटान
Dealing with the matters : विषयों के सम्बन्ध में
Dealing with, person having : जिसका --- से व्यवहार है
Dealings have been good : व्यवहार अच्छा रहा
Dealt with in the report : रिपोर्ट में चर्चित
Dealt with, shall be : से व्यवहार करना / कार्यवाही करना / विचार करना / निपटाना
Debarred of right : अधिकार से विवर्जित
Debit against : नामे डालना
Debit balance : नामे शेष है
Debit side : नामे
Debitable to leave account : छुट्टी के हिसाब में लिखा जाने वाला
Debited to the head... : शीर्ष -- के अंतर्गत व्यय में डाला गया
Debited to the profit and loss : लाभ और हानि के अंतर्गत डाला गया
Debt charges : ऋण सम्बंधित व्यय
Decentralisation of industries : उद्योगों का विकेंद्रीकरण
Deception, in consequence of : प्रवंचना के परिणामस्वरूप

Deceptive practices : प्रवंचक व्यवहार
Decide on merits : गुण-दोष के अनुसार निर्णय करना
Decided on/at high level : उच्च स्तर पर निर्णीत
Decision, leading : अग्र-निर्णय
Declaration of acceptance of office : पद ग्रहण की घोषणा
Declaration of any trust : किसी न्यास की घोषणा
Declaration of fidelity : विश्वस्तता की घोषणा
Declaration of public policy : लोकनीति की घोषणा
Declaration of title : हक की घोषणा
Declare a witness hostile : साक्षी को प्रतिकूल घोषित करना
Declare null and void : निरर्थक और प्रभावहीन घोषित करना
Declare on oath : सशपथ घोषित करना
Declare the confidence : विश्वास घोषित करना
Declared goods : घोषित माल / सामान
Declared provision : घोषित उपबंध
Decorum lack of : शालीनता का अभाव
Decreasing cost : घटता मूल्य
Decree absolute : आत्यंतिक डिक्री
Decree appellate : अपीली डिक्री
Decree for damages : नुकसान की डिक्री
Decree for ejectment : बेदखली के लिए डिक्री
Decree for maintenance : भरण-पोषण की डिक्री
Decree for payment of money : धन के भुगतान किये जाने की डिक्री
Decree holder : डिक्री प्राप्त / लेनदार
Decree in appeal : अपील में डिक्री
Decree of the first court : प्रथम न्यायालय की डिक्री
Decree shall agree with the judgment : डिक्री निर्णय के अनुरूप होगी
Decree shall follow : के अनुसरण में डिक्री होगी
Deed of further charge : भार का विलेख
Deemed to accrue : प्राप्य समझा जाए
Deemed to be arise : के रूप में समझा जाए

Deemed to have been dissolved/received : प्राप्त समझा जाए

Defalcation and losses : गबन और हानियाँ

Default imprisonment in : व्यतिक्रम के बदले में कारावास

Default is remedied व्यतिक्रम का उपचार कर दिया गया है

Defeat of title : हक की गलती / अधिकार की त्रुटि

Defeat or irregularity not to vitiate proceedings : दोष या अनियमित कार्यवाही को दूषित न करें

Defeat the ends of justice : न्याय के उद्देश्य को समाप्त करना

Defeat the object of law : विधि का उद्देश्य समाप्त होना

Defeat the provision : उपबंधों को समाप्त करना

Defect, latent : अप्रकट खराबी

Defective title : त्रुटिपूर्ण अधिकार

Defence right of private : व्यक्तिगत प्रतिरक्षा का अधिकार

Deferred annuity : आस्थगित वार्षिकी

Deferred benefit : आस्थगित फायदा

Deferred dividend : आस्थगित लाभांश

Deferred expenditure : आस्थगित व्यय

Deferred payment : आस्थगित भुगतान

Defiance of law : कानून की अवज्ञा

Deficiency of assets : गुणों में कमी

Deficiency of values : मूल्य में कमी

Deficit area : कमी वाला क्षेत्र

Deficit budget : घाटे का बजट

Deficit economy : घाटे की अर्थव्यवस्था

Deficit financing : घाटे की वित्तव्यवस्था

Deficit pockets : कमी वाले भाग

Define the scope : संभावना निश्चित करना

Definite basis : निश्चित आधार

Deflation of currency : मुद्रा अवस्फीति

Defray expences : व्यय चुकाना

Degree of care and deligence : सावधानी और तत्परता की मात्रा

Degree of control : नियंत्रण की मात्रा

Delay are chronic : विलम्ब की आदत बन गई है

Delay causes much difficulty in the compilation of : देर के कारण संकलन में बहुत कठिनाई होती है

Delay in returning the file is regretted : फाइल के लौटाने में हुए विलम्ब के लिए खेद है

Delay in submission of the case is regretted : प्रकरण को प्रस्तुत करने में हुए विलम्ब के लिए खेद है

Delayed beyond the period prescribed : विदित अवधि से अधिक विलम्ब

Delayed refunds : विलंबित प्रतिदाय

Delayed tender : विलंबित टेंडर

Delaying the execution : निष्पादन में विलम्ब करना

Delegate his office : अपने पद को प्रत्यायोजित करना

Delegated authority : प्रत्यायोजित अधिकारी

Delegated legislation : प्रत्यायोजित बिधान

Delegation of powers : शक्तियों का प्रत्यायोजन

Deliberative body : विचारण निकाय

Delimitation of constituencies : निर्वाचन क्षेत्रों का सीमाकरण

Delimitation order : परिसीमन आदेश

Delinked, file has been : फाइल अलग कर दी गई है

Delivery end : निकासी सिरा

Delivery of dak : डाक वितरण

Demand for grants : अनुदानों की मांग

Demand payable on : मांग पर देय

Demand security : प्रतिभूति मांगना / जमानत मागना

Democratic planning : लोकतंत्रीय आयोजन

Denial of execution : निष्पादन का प्रत्याख्यान

Deny the knowledge of : की जानकारी होने से इनकार करना

Department may please see for comments : विभाग कृपया टिप्पणी हेतु देख लें

Department may see the preceding note with reference to their query : विभाग अपनी पूछताछ के सन्दर्भ में इससे पहले वाली टिप्पणी देखें

Department will be advised accordingly : विभाग को तद्नुसार सूचित कर दिया जाएगा

Departmental accounts : विभागीय लेखे
Departmental action in progress : विभागीय कार्यवाही की जा रही है
Dependent relations : आश्रित सम्बन्ध
Deposit of title deeds : हक-विलेखों का निक्षेप
Deposit of will : वसीयतों का निक्षेप
Deposited in record room : रिकॉर्ड कक्ष में जमा किया गया
Depreciation account : मूल्यह्रास लेखा
Depreciation allowance : मूल्यह्रास भत्ता
Depreciation charges : मूल्यह्रास प्रभार
Depreciation fund : मूल्यह्रास निधि
Depressed class : दलित वर्ग
Deprivation of appointment : नियुक्ति से वंचन
Deprived of a right : अधिकार से वंचित
Deputation of citizens : नागरिकों का प्रतिनिधिमंडल
Deputation of officers on short term contract : अधिकारियों की छोटे समय के कार्य के लिए नियुक्ति
Deputy Chairman : उपाध्यक्ष
Deputy Chief ,Whip : उपमुख्य-सचेतक
Dereliction of duty : कर्तव्य विमुखता
Derive interest : हित प्राप्त करना
Derive of title : हक प्राप्त करना
Derogate from powers : का अधिकार घटाना
Descendant lineal : पारंपरिक वंशज
Deserted site : उजाड़ बस्ती
Deserve promotion out of turn : बारी आने से पहले पदोन्नति का पात्र है
Deserves every encouragement : सब प्रकार के प्रोत्साहन के योग्य है
Designated purchaser : अभिहित क्रेता
Designated trade just now : अभी-अभी का अभिहित व्यवसाय
Desirable type of worker in all respect : सर्वरूपेण वांछित कार्यकर्ता
Despatch book : प्रेषण-पुस्तक
Despatch note : प्रेषण-पत्र

Despatch practicable : साध्य शीघ्रता
Detached outlook : तटस्थ दृष्टिकोण
Detached service : तटस्थ सेवा
Detached view : तटस्थ विचार
Detailed account : विस्तृत विवरण / ब्यौरेवार लेखा
Detailed contingent bill : ब्यौरेवार आकस्मिक विपत्र
Detailed examination of all points : सभी विचार बिन्दुओं का सविस्तार परीक्षण
Detailed particulars maybe furnished : विस्तृत विवरण भेजा जाए
Details of expenditure and sanction thereto have not been furnished to : व्यय का ब्यौरा और उसकी स्वीकृति को प्रस्तुत नहीं किया गया है
Detention cell : निरोध कोठरी
Detention home : निरोध गृह
Detention in transit : अभिवहन / मार्ग में निरुद्ध
Detention order : निरोधादेश
Detention preventive : निवारक निरोध
Determination by retirement : निवर्तन द्वारा पर्यवसान
Determination of attachment : कुर्की का अवसान
Determination of conditions of service : सेवा शर्तों की अवधारण
Determination of interest (Law) : (कानूनी) हित का पर्यवसान
Determination of lease : पट्टे का पर्यवसान
Determination of question : प्रश्न का अवधारण
Determination of the court : न्यायालय का अवधारण
Determination points of : अवधारण के लिए प्रश्न
Determine by lot : समूह द्वारा निर्धारित करना
Determine issue of fact : तथ्य विवादक अवधारित करना
Determine the appeal : अपील का अवधारण करना
Determine the boundary : सीमा निश्चित करना
Determine the objection : आक्षेप का अवधारण करना
Determined action : निश्चयात्मक कार्य
Determined as : जैसा निर्धारित

Determined by lot : समूह द्वारा निर्धारित
Determining the jurisdiction : अधिकारिता का निश्चय करते हुए
Determining the value of land : भूमि का मूल्य अवधारण
Deterrent punishment : निवारक दंड
Detrimental action : अहितकर कार्य
Detrimental in the interest of : के हित में हानिकारक
Detrimental in the public interest : जनहित में हानिकारक
Detrimental in the security : सुरक्षा की दृष्टि से हानिकारक
Detrimental to the interest of : के हित में हानिकारक
Devaluation of currency : मुद्रा का अवमूल्यन
Develop symptoms : लक्षण विकसित होना
Development block : विकास खंड
Development charges : विकास प्रभार
Development of character and abilities : चरित्र और योग्यताओं का विकास
Deviation from : से विचलन
Devoid of : से रहित
Dies-non : अकार्य-दिवस
Difference matter in : मतभेद का विषय
Differential scale : अन्तरीय मान
Differential schedule : भेद-दर्शक अनुसूची
Dignified in his dealings : अपने व्यवहार में गरिमापूर्ण
Dilatory by habit : आदतन विलम्ब करने वाला
Dilatory motion : विलंबकारी प्रस्ताव
Diminish value or utility : मूल्य या उपयोगिता का कम होना
Diplomatic agent : राजनयिक अभिकर्ता
Diplomatic privileges : राजनयिक विशेषाधिकार
Dire necessity : अत्यंत आवश्यकता
Directed as : जैसा निर्देश किया गया है
Directed I am : मुझे निर्देश किया गया है
Directed to appear : उपस्थित होने का निर्देश
Direction and control of : का निर्देशन और नियंत्रण
Directly employed : सीधा नियोजित

Directly produced : सीधा उत्पादित
Directly take benefit : सीधा फायदा लेना
Director may please see for approval : निदेशक कृपया अनुमोदन हेतु देख लें
Disability disadvantages of the proposal out weight the advantages : प्रस्ताव से लाभ की तुलना में हानि अधिक है
Disallow claim : दावे को नामंजूर करना
Disallow deduction : कटौती को नामंजूर करना
Discharge a debt : ऋण चुकाना
Discharge a decree : डिक्री का उन्मोचन
Discharge by payment : भुगतान द्वारा दायित्व मुक्ति
Discharge of arrears : बकाया का उन्मोचन
Discharge of debt : ऋण का उन्मोचन
Discharge of public functions : लोक-कार्यक्रमों का उन्मोचन
Discharge of the liability : दायित्व से उन्मोचित
Discharged from liability : दायित्व से उन्मोचित
Discharged from obligation : बाध्यता से उन्मोचित
Disciplinary lay off : अनुशासनिक जबरदस्ती छुट्टी
Disclaim responsibility : उत्तरदायित्व अस्वीकार करना
Disclose bound to : प्रगट करने को बाध्य
Disclose fully and truly : पूर्णतया और ठीक-ठीक प्रगट करना
Disclosure true : सत्य का प्रगटन
Discontinue the public use : सार्वजनिक उपयोग को रोकना
Discrepancy may be reconciled : विसंगति का निपटारा हो सकता है
Discretion of court : न्यायालय का विवेक
Discretionary duties : विवेकपूर्ण / विवेकाधीन कर्तव्य
Discretionary grant : विवेकाधीन अनुदान
Discretionary power : विवेकाधिकार
Discussion, during the course of : विचार-विमर्श / चर्चा के दौरान
Disgraceful conduct : लज्जास्पद आचरण
Dishonest concealment : बेईमानी से छुपाना

Dishonest misappropriation of property : सम्पत्ति का बेईमानी से दुरुपयोग
Dishonoured cheque : अस्वीकृत चेक
Dislocation of work : काम में गड़बड़
Dismiss with costs : खर्चे सहित खारिज करना
Dismissal statement : बर्खास्तगी विवरण
Disorderly behaviour : अनियमित व्यवहार
Disorderly conduct person : उपद्रवी व्यक्ति
Disparity in rates : दरों में असमानता
Dispassionate opinion : निष्पक्ष / निरपेक्ष राय
Dispel doubts : संशय दूर करना
Dispense with normal procedure : सामान्य प्रक्रिया का त्याग करना
Dispense with services : नौकरी से अलग करना
Dispense with the proof : साबित किये जाने से अभिमुक्ति देना
Displaced person : विस्थापित व्यक्ति
Display drive : अभिप्रेरणा शक्ति का परिचय देना
Disposal by confiscations : अधिहरण द्वारा व्ययन / निपटान
Disposal by delivery : प्रदान द्वारा व्ययन / निपटान
Disposal by destruction : विनाश द्वारा निपटान
Disposal list : निपटान सूची
Disposal of business : काम निपटाना
Disposal of cases be expedited : मामले शीघ्र निपटाए जाएँ
Disposal of property : संपत्ति का व्ययन / संपत्ति की बिक्री
Disposal of routine work : नेमी कार्य का निपटारा
Disposals quick : अविलम्ब निपटान करना है
Disposed of : निपटा देना / से छुटकारा पाना
Dispute the claim : दावे का विरोध करना
Disqualified, will be declared : अनर्ह घोषित किया जाएगा
Disregarding the facts : तथ्यों की उपेक्षा के साथ / तथ्यों की उपेक्षा करते हुए
Disrepute, bring : बदनाम करना
Dissemination of information : सूचना प्रसार
Dissolution of society : संस्था / समिति का विघटन

Distinct claim : सुस्पष्ट दावा
Distinct consideration : सुस्पष्ट प्रतिफल / सुस्पष्ट रूप से विचार करना / ध्यान देना
Distinct expertise : सुस्पष्ट विशेषज्ञता
Distinct from : से भिन्न / से अलग
Distinction adverse : प्रतिकूल विभेद
Distinction in : में विशेष योग्यता / से भेदभाव / अलगाव
Distinguish oneself : अपनी विशिष्टता दिखाना
Distinguished guest : विशिष्ट अतिथि
Distinguished service : विशिष्ट सेवा
Distress call : सहायता की पुकार
Distressed and destitute : दुखी और निराश्रित
Disturbance Diversion to non-agricultural purpose : गैर-किसानी कामों के लिए उपयोग में लाना
Division of labour : श्रम विभाजन
Divisions of time : समय के प्रभाग
Do the needful : जो आवश्यक है वो करें
Docketing of papers : कागजात के डाकेट करना
Document of title : हक का दस्तावज
Documentary evidence : दस्तावेजी साक्ष्य
Documentary proof : दस्तावेजी सबूत
Does not seem to have been received in this office : इस कार्यालय में प्राप्त हुआ नहीं जान पड़ता है
Does not seem to stand to reason : तर्कसंगत नहीं जान पड़ता है
Doli incapax : अपराध करने में अक्षम
Domestic concern : घरेलू मामला
Domestic hygiene : घरेलू सफाई
Domicile by birth : जन्म से नागरिक / जन्म से अधिवासी
Domicile of : अधिवास
Dominated the will : इच्छा को अधिशासित करना
Done with due care : आवश्यक सतर्कता से किया गया / पर्याप्त सतर्कता से किया गया

Dormant capital : निष्क्रिय पूँजी
Double account : दोहरा हिसाब
Double crop : दुहरी फसल
Double dealing : दुरंगी चाल / दुहरा व्यवहार
Double entry : दोहरी प्रविष्टि
Double jeopardy : दोहरा संकट
Double role : दोहरी भूमिका
Down period : कार्यबंदी अवधि
Draft acknowledgement letter put up : प्राप्ति पत्र का प्रारूप प्रस्तुत है
Draft amendment : संशोधन प्रारूप
Draft as amended maybe issued : संशोधित प्रारूप अनुमोदन के लिए प्रस्तुत है
Draft as amendment is put up for approval : संशोधित प्रारूप अनुमोदन के लिए प्रस्तुत है
Draft as directed by ... is submitted for approval : के निर्देशानुसार प्रारूप संशोधन हेतु प्रस्तुत है
Draft circular put up for signature : परिपत्र का मसविदा हस्ताक्षर हेतु प्रस्तुत है
Draft constitution : संविधान का प्रारूप
Draft maybe amended accordingly : तद्नुसार संशोधित किया जाए
Draft reply : उत्तर का प्रारूप / मसविदा
Draft scheme : योजना का प्रारूप / मसविदा
Draft submitted for approval : अनुमोदनार्थ प्रारूप प्रस्तुत है
Drafted as directed : निर्देशानुसार लिखा गया / प्रस्तुत किया गया
Drafting and noting : प्रारूप लेखन और टिप्पणी
Drainage system : जल-निकास व्यवस्था
Draw increment : वेतन-वृद्धि लेना
Draw inference : अनुमान करना
Draw up the finding : निष्कर्ष को लेखबद्ध करना
Drawal of arrear : पिछला हिसाब लेना
Drawback claim : वापसी का दावा

Driving power : अभिप्रेरणा शक्ति
Drop in prices : कीमतों में गिरावट
Dry cultivation : अभिसिंचित कृषि
Dry farming : बरानी खेती
Dry promotion : सूखी तरक्की / लाभ-रहित पदोन्नति
Dual government : दोहरा शासन / दोहरी सरकार
Due account of : का उचित लेखा
Due administration : सम्यक प्रशासन
Due and proper account : सम्यक और उचित लेखा
Due authority : सम्यक प्राधिकार
Due balance : सम्यक संतुलन
Due care and caution : सम्यक सावधानी और सतर्कता
Due consideration shall be given : सम्यक ध्यान रखा जाएगा
Due course : सम्यक अनुक्रम
Due interest : अपेक्षित रुचि / दिलचस्पी
Due notice : सम्यक सूचना / उचित नोटिस
Due observance : सम्यक अनुपालन
Due performance of agreement : करार का उचित पालन
Due to dislocation of the traffic : यातायात के अव्यवस्थित होने के कारण
Due to non-receipt : न मिलने के कारण
Due to omission : चूक के कारण
Due to oversight : ध्यान न रहने के कारण
Duly account for : सम्यक रूप से हिसाब देना
Duly authorised in that behalf : उस विषय में प्राधिकृत
Duly complied : उचित रीति से पालन किया गया
Duly conferred : सम्यक रूप से प्रदत्त
Duly convicted : सम्यक रूप से दोष सिद्ध किया गया
Duly disposed of : सम्यक रूप से निपटान किया गया
Duly done : उचित रीति से किया गया / सम्यक रूप से किया गया
Duly elected : सम्यक रूप से चयन किया गया
Duly empowered : सम्यक रूप से सशक्त किया गया

Duly established : सम्यक रूप से स्थापित / सिद्ध किया गया
Duly examined : सम्यक रूप से परीक्षित
Duly executed : सम्यक रूप से निष्पादित किया गया
Duly exercised : सम्यक रूप से प्रयोग किया गया
Duly filled in : सम्यक रूप से भरा गया
Duly instituted : सम्यक रूप से संस्थित
Duly performed : सम्यक रूप से किया गया / कार्यान्वित किया गया
Duly presented : सम्यक रूप से प्रस्तुत किया गया / उपस्थित किया गया
Duly proved : सम्यक रूप से सिद्ध किया गया / साबित किया गया
Duly published : सम्यक रूप से प्रकाशित
Duly qualified : यथोचित योग्यता वाला
Duly recorded : सम्यक रूप से अभिलिखित
Duly sanctioned : विधिवत मंजूर किया गया
Duly stamped : सम्यक रूप से स्टाम्प लगाया गया
Duly verified : विधिवत सत्यापित
Duplicating machine : डुप्लीकेट करने वाली मशीन
During the pendency of the case : प्रकरण विचाराधीन रहने के दौरान
During the period under review : समीक्षाधीन अवधि में
During the pleasure of : के प्रसाद पर्यन्त
Duty bond : कर्तव्यबद्ध
Duty burden : कर्तव्यभार / शुल्क का भार
Duty certificate : कर्तव्य प्रमाणपत्र
Duty exemption : शुल्क छूट / शुल्क माफी
Duty is over, before : कर्तव्यकाल समाप्त होने के पूर्व
Duty off : कर्तव्य-समय समाप्त
Duty schedule : कर्तव्य-सूची

E

Each and every	: प्रत्येक
Eager to get things moving	: काम चलता रहे इसके लिए उत्सुक
Earlier transfer	: पूर्वतर अन्तरिति
Earliest possible opportunity	: यथासंभव सुअवसर
Early action in the matter is requested	: प्रकरण पर शीघ्र कार्यवाही अपेक्षित है
Early orders are solicited	: शीघ्र आदेश प्रार्थित हैं
Early reply is solicited	: शीघ्र उत्तर भेजने की प्रार्थना है
Early reply will be highly appreciated	: यदि उत्तर शीघ्र भेज दें तो बड़ी कृपा होगी
Earmarked funds	: निर्धारित निधि
Earned leave granted	: अर्जित अवकाश स्वीकृत
Earning dependents	: कमाने वाले आश्रित
Ease loving	: आरामतलब
Easements annexed thereto	: उससे संलग्न सुखभोग
Easily obtainable	: सरलता से प्राप्य
Easily one of the best	: निस्संदेह, सर्वोत्तमों में से एक
Easy access	: आसानी से प्रवेश / सुलभ प्रवेश
Easy terms	: आसान शर्तें
Economic activity	: आर्थिक गतिविधि
Economic affairs	: आर्थिक विषय / मामले
Economic analysis	: आर्थिक विश्लेषण
Economic boycott	: आर्थिक बहिष्कार
Economic breakdown	: आर्थिक व्यवस्था-भंग
Economic collaboration	: आर्थिक सहयोग
Economic incentive	: आर्थिक प्रोत्साहन
Economic investigator	: आर्थिक अन्वेषक
Economic self-sufficiency	: आर्थिक आत्मनिर्भरता
Economic services	: आर्थिक सेवाएँ
Economic survey	: आर्थिक सर्वेक्षण

Economical rate : मितव्ययी दर
Economy cut : मितव्ययी कटौती
Economy measures : किफायत के उपाय
Economy of time : समय की मितव्ययिता
Economy report : मितव्ययिता रिपोर्ट
Economy slip : किफायती पर्ची
Educationally unqualified : शैक्षिक अनर्ह / शैक्षिक रूप से अयोग्य
Effect alternation : परिवर्तन करना
Effect carrying into : क्रियान्वित करना
Effect from such date, with : इस तारीख से लागू
Effect give : प्रभावी करना / लागू करना
Effect reduction : कमी करना
Effect shall have : प्रभावशील होगा / लागू होगा
Effect to that : उस भाव का / उस प्रभाव का
Effect with immediate : तत्काल प्रभाव से लागू
Effecting action : प्रभावी कार्यवाही
Effecting arrangement : प्रभावी व्यवस्था
Effecting blockade : असरदार नाकेबंदी
Effecting carrying out : प्रभावी रूप से कार्यान्वयन करना
Effecting control : प्रभावी नियंत्रण
Effecting escape : निकल भागना
Effecting steps should be taken to clear the arrears : शेष कार्य के निपटान के लिए कारगर उपाय किये जाएँ
Effecting strength : वास्तविक सामर्थ्य
Efficiency bar : दक्षता रोध
Efficiency cum performance : दक्षता तथा निष्पादन
Efficient conduct of the affairs : कार्यकलापों का दक्ष संचालन
Efficient discharge of functions : कार्यों का दक्षतापूर्ण निष्पादन
Efficient instructions : अच्छा शिक्षण-प्रशिक्षण
Efficient lighting : पर्याप्त रौशनी
Efficient performance of functions : कार्यों का कुशल प्रदर्शन
Efficiently done : दक्षता से किया गया

Either by name or by virtue of office : या तो नाम से या पदाभिधान से

Either conditionally or unconditionally : या तो सशर्त या बिना शर्त के

Either generally or in specified classes of cases : साधारणतया या मामलों के विशिष्ट वर्गों में

Either of the expressions : दोनों में से कोई भी अभिव्यक्ति

Either party : दोनों में से कोई भी एक पक्ष

Either wholly or in part : सम्पूर्ण या आंशिक

Ejected from : से बेदखल किया गया / से निष्कासित किया गया

Elect for pensionary benefits : पेंशन के लाभों हेतु चयन करना

Elect to proceed without suit : वाद के बिना चलाने का चयन

Elect to receive the pension : पेंशन लेने का चयन करना

Elect to receive the profit : लाभ लेने का चयन

Election fever : चुनावी सरगर्मी

Election in prospect : भावी निर्वाचन / भावी चुनाव

Election papers : चुनाव सम्बन्धी कागजात

Election priority : निर्वाचन प्राथमिकता

Election tactics : चुनावी हथकंडे

Election to the : के लिए निर्वाचन

Electoral roll : निर्वाचन नामावली

Electoral understanding : चुनाव समझौता

Electric installation : विद्युत् संस्थापन

Elicit cooperation : सहयोग प्राप्त करना

Eliciting public opinion : जनमत जानना

Eligibility is certified : पात्रता प्रमाणित है

Eligibility to office : पद के लिए पात्रता

Elimination of records : अभिलेख नष्ट / समाप्त करना

Elucidate the reasons : कारण समझाइये

Embarrassing position : परेशानी / उपहासास्पद स्थिति

Embezzlement of public money : सरकारी धन का गबन

Embody in the document : दस्तावेज में सन्निविष्ट करना

Emergency certificate : आपात प्रमाणपत्र
Emergency measures : आपातकालीन उपाय
Emergency proclamation of : आपातकाल की उद्घोषणा
Emergent meeting : आपात बैठक
Emigrant control : उत्प्रवास नियंत्रण
Emigrant population : उत्प्रवासी जनसंख्या
Eminently deserves promotion : सर्वथा प्रोन्नति के पात्र हैं
Eminently suitable : विशिष्टतया उपयुक्त
Employees federation : कर्मचारी महासंघ
Employer's contribution : नियोजक का अंशदान
Employment oriented : नियोजन / रोजगारपरक
Empowered to : के लिए शक्ति-प्राप्त
En bloc transfers : सामूहिक स्थानान्तरण
En clair telegram : शब्दबद्ध तार
En route : मार्ग में / रास्ते में
Enacted as follows : निम्नलिखित रूप से अधिनियमित
Enclosed statement : संलग्न विवरण
Enclosures as follows : सहपत्र नीचे दिए अनुसार
Encouragement of industry : उद्योग को प्रोत्साहित करना
Encouragement on Govt. lands : सहकारी भूमि का अधिग्रहण
Encumbered estate : भारग्रस्त संपदा
End of the week : सप्ताहांत में
Endorsed warrant : पृष्ठांकित वारंट
Endorsement No. : पृष्ठांकन क्रमांक
Endorsement put up for signature : पृष्ठांकन हस्ताक्षर हेतु प्रस्तुत
Endorsement transfer of : टिप्पणी का उतारा जाना
Endowment insurance : बंदोबस्ती बीमा
Ends of justice : न्याय के उद्देश्य
Energy and drive : ऊर्जा और अभिप्रेरणा शक्ति
Energy and imagination, with more : और अधिक स्फूर्ति और कल्पना के साथ
Enforce a partition : विभाजन कराना

Enforce a trust : न्यास का प्रवर्तन करना
Enforce attendance : उपस्थिति के लिए विवश करना
Enforce direction : निदेश का प्रवर्तन करना
Enforce discipline : अनुशासन का पालन करना
Enforce for the benefit of : के लाभ हेतु लागू करना
Enforced absense : अनुपस्थिति के लिए विवश करना
Enforcement of orders : आदेशों को लागू करना
Enforcement staff : प्रवर्तन अमला / स्टाफ
Enforcing claim : दावा लागू करना
Engaged in a disorder : उपद्रव में लगा
Engagement diary : कार्य डायरी
Engagement of labour : मजदूर लगाना
Engagement proposed : प्रस्तावित व्यस्तता
Engrossed in details : ब्योरे में तल्लीन
Enhanced land revenue : बढ़ा हुआ भू-राजस्व
Enhanced rent : बढ़ा हुआ किराया
Enjoy confidence of the people : जनता का विश्वास प्राप्त करना
Enjoy good reputation of integrity : इनकी निष्ठा सर्वथा विख्यात है
Enjoyment of the right of use : उपभोग के अधिकार का उपयोग
Enlarge or extend : वृद्धि या विस्तार करना
Enlarge the time : समय को बढ़ाना
Enlarged jurisdiction : बढ़ाया गया क्षेत्राधिकार
Enlist support : समर्थन प्राप्त करना
Enormous adventures : अनेक दुस्साहस के कार्य
Enquire into the case and report early : प्रकरण की जाँच करें और शीघ्र रिपोर्ट दें
Enquire the present position of the case : मामले की मौजूदा स्थिति का पता लगाएँ
Enquiries made reveal that : जाँच से पता चला है कि
Enquiry has been ordered : जाँच के आदेश दिए गए
Enquiry has not been held in a proper manner : जाँच उपयुक्त ढँग से नहीं हुई
Enquiry into a charge : किसी आरोप की जाँच

Enquiry may be completed : जाँच पूरी की जाए

Enquiry should be completed and report submitted without delay : जाँच पूरी करके रिपोर्ट अविलम्ब प्रस्तुत की जाए

Enrolled person : भरती किया गया व्यक्ति

Ensuing year : आगामी वर्ष

Ensure full enjoyment of leisure : खाली समय का पूर्ण उपयोग सुनिश्चित करना

Ensure prompt and speedy implementation : त्वरित और द्रुत गति से लागू किया जाना / सुनिश्चित किया जाए

Ensure public safety : जन-सुरक्षा सुनिश्चित की जाए

Ensure that rules are properly observed in future : यह सुनिश्चित किया जाए कि भविष्य में नियमों का उचित पालन हो

Entailed, expenses : (पर) हुए व्यय

Entailing disqualification : जिससे योग्यता समाप्त होती है

Enter by force : जबरदस्ती घुसना

Enter in register : रजिस्टर में चढ़ाना

Enter into an agreement : करार / समझौता करना

Enter into bond : बंधपत्र लिखना

Enter into engagement : वचनबद्ध करना

Enter into partnership : भागीदार बनना

Enter into possession of interest : हित का कब्जा कर लेना

Enter into service : सेवा में प्रवेश करना

Enter on defence : प्रतिरक्षा प्रारम्भ करना

Enter on reference : निर्देश पर कार्य आरम्भ करना

Entered as on : तक दर्ज किया गया

Entertain an application : आवेदन-पत्र स्वीकार करना

Entertain erroneous opinion : गलत राय बनाना

Entertain the claim : दावा ग्रहण करना

Entertain upon an office : पद ग्रहण करना

Entertain upon duty : कर्तव्य ग्रहण करना

Entirely optional : सर्वथा वैकल्पिक

Entitled as of right : साधिकार हकदार

Entitled to : का हकदार होना / का अधिकारी होना
Entitled to act : कार्य करने के लिए हकदार होना
Entitled to avoid : शून्यकरण का हकदार होना
Entitled to benefit : फायदा पाने का हकदार
Entitled to compensation against : से मुआवजा / प्रतिकार पाने का हकदार होना
Entitled to possession : कब्जे का हकदार
to retain : प्रतिधारण का हकदार
Entries have been checked and verified : प्रविष्टियों की जाँच कर हस्ताक्षर कर दिया गया है
Entrust with duty : कर्तव्य सौंपना
Entrusted to his care : देखरेख के लिए सौंपा गया
Entrusted with the functions : कार्य सौंपे गए
Entrustment of certain function : कुछ कार्य सौंपना
Entry in leave account : छुट्टी लेखा में प्रविष्टि
Ephemeral role : अल्पकालिक पंजी
Equal division of opinion : राय रखने वालों की संख्या बराबर
Equal in all respects : हर तरह से बराबर
Equal protection of law : समान कानूनी संरक्षण
Equal treatment to all castes : सभी जातियों के प्रति समान व्यवहार
Equality of opportunity : अवसर की समानता
Equality of votes : मतों की समानता / मत बराबर होना
Equally divided in opinion : राय में बराबर बनते हुए
Equally efficacious relief : समान प्रभावकारी अनुतोष
Equivalent to : के सामान / के तुल्य / के समकक्ष
Erratic in temperament : अस्थिर स्वभाव के
Erroneous entry : गलत प्रविष्टि
Erroneous views : गलत दृष्टिकोण / खामी वाले नजरिए
Error apparent on the face of the record : अभिलेख से स्पष्टतया प्रकट भूल
Error in writing : लिखने में गलती / लेखन की गलती
Error is regretted : गलती का अफसोस है / भूल के लिए खेद है

Error of form : प्रारूपिक त्रुटि / प्रारूपिक गलती
Error of omission : भूल-चूक
Errors and omissions expected : भूल-चूक लेनी-देनी
Errors and their rectification : त्रुटियाँ और उनका सुधार
Essential commodity : आवश्यक वस्तु
Essential services : अनिवार्य सेवाएँ / आवश्यक सेवाएँ
Essential term : आवश्यक निबंधन
Essentiality certificate : अनिवार्यता प्रमाणपत्र
Establish a charge : आरोप सिद्ध करना
Establish title : हक स्थापित करना
Established by the constitution : संविधान द्वारा स्थापित
Established practice : सुस्थापित प्रथा
Established procedure : सुस्थापित प्रक्रिया
Establishing right : अधिकार सिद्ध करना
Establishment bill : स्थापना बिल
Establishment charges : स्थापना / व्यय प्रभार
Establishment section : स्थापना अनुभाग
Estate duty : संपदा शुल्क
Estimate is under preparation : प्राक्कलन तैयार किया जा रहा है
Estimated liability : प्राक्कलित दायित्व
Estimated value : अनुमानित मूल्य
Estimates committee : प्राक्कलन समिति
Estimates of expenditure : व्यय-प्राक्कलन
Estimates should be completed in all respect : प्राक्कलन हर तरह से पूर्ण किया जाना चाहिए
Estimating, in : प्राक्कलन करने में
Estimation has been excessive : प्राक्कलन बहुत बढ़ा-चढ़ाकर किया गया है
Evade duties : कार्यों को टालना
Evade the payment of tax : कर की अदायगी से बचना
Evasion in : अपवंचन करके
Evasion of process : प्रक्रिया से बचना

Evasive denial : वाक्-छलपूर्ण प्रत्याख्यान
Evasive replies : टालू उत्तर
Evenly balanced : सुसंतुलित
Eventually this is bound to happen : अंततः यह तो होना ही है
Ever since : तभी से
Every encouragement should be given : सब तरह से प्रोत्साहन दिया जाए
Every now and then : बार-बार, जब-तब
Eviction proceedings : बेदखली की कार्यवाही
Evidence adduced guts : दिया गया साक्ष्य
Evidence giving : साक्ष्य प्रदान
Evidence is closed : साक्ष्य की समाप्ति हो गई है
Evidence of distinctiveness : सुभिन्नता का साक्ष्य
Evidence of life : जीवन के लक्षण
Evidence of title : हक का साक्ष्य
Evident advantage : सुव्यक्त लाभ
Evidentiary fact : साक्ष्यिक तथ्य
Evil repute : कुख्यात
Ex facie : स्पष्ट रूप में / सहज स्वरूप से
Ex gratia : अनुग्रह धन
Ex gratia payment : अनुग्रही भुगतान
Ex post facto : कार्योत्तर / भूत-लक्ष्यी प्रभाव
Ex post facto sanction : कार्योत्तर मंजूरी
Ex-serviceman : भूतपूर्व-सैनिक
Ex turpi causa : अधम कार्य से
Exact nature : यथावत प्रकृति
Exact reference : ठीक-ठाक हवाला / निर्देश
Exactly this is what was stated there : बिलकुल यही कहा गया
Examination and certification : परीक्षा और प्रमाणीकरण
Examination of films : फिल्मों का परीक्षण
Examination report : परीक्षा-रिपोर्ट विवरण

Examine the proposals in the light of observation at : 'क' पर व्यक्त विचारों को दृष्टि में रखते हुए प्रस्तावों की जाँच कीजिये
Examined and countersigned : परीक्षित और प्रतिहस्ताक्षरित
Ex-cadre post : संवर्ग बाह्य पद
Except according to procedure established : तय की हुई प्रक्रिया को छोड़कर
Except as expressly provided : स्पष्ट रूप से उपबंधित स्थिति को छोड़कर
Except as otherwise provided : अन्यथा उपबंधित स्थिति को छोड़कर
Except for special reasons : विशेष कारणों के सिवाए
Except for the purpose of : के प्रयोजन के उद्देश्य के अतिरिक्त
Except with the consent : की सहमति के बिना
Except with the previous sanction : की पूर्व स्वीकृति से ही
Exception to the rule : इस नियम के अलावा
Exceptional and emergent cases : असामान्य और आपाती मामले
Exceptional calibre : असामान्य चरित्रवान
Exceptional circumstances : असाधारण परिस्थितियाँ
Exceptional grant : आपवादिक अनुदान
Exceptional hardship : असाधारण कष्ट
Exceptional measures : विशेष उपाय, असाधारण कार्यवाही
Excess fare ticket : अतिरिक्त भाड़ा टिकट
Excess is due to : अधिकता का कारण यह है कि
Excess of his power, in : अपनी शक्तियों के बाहर
Excess over allotment : आवंटन से अधिक राशि
Excess shall be disregarded : आधिक्य हिसाब में नहीं लिया जाएगा
Excess shall be refunded : अधिक रकम वापस कर दी जायेगी
Excesses and savings : अधिक व्यय और बचत
Exchange below par : अवमूल्य पर विनिमय
Exchange facilities : विनिमय की सुविधाएँ
Exchange of population : आबादी की अदला-बदली
Exchange of views : वैचारिक आदान-प्रदान
Excluding the charges : खर्चों को छोड़कर

Exclusive jurisdiction : अनन्य आधिकारिता
Exclusive possession : एकमात्र कब्जा
Exclusive privilege : एकमात्र विशेषाधिकार
Exclusively for : केवल ----के लिए
Excute the work order : कार्य-आदेश का पालन कीजिये
Executed in good faith : सद्भावनापूर्ण निष्पादन हुआ
Executed instrument in writing : निष्पादित लिखित
Execution of a deed : विलेख का निष्पादन
Execution of act : अधिनियम को कार्यान्वित करना
Execution of contract : संविदा / ठेका निष्पादन
Execution of decree : डिक्री का निष्पादन
Execution of documents : दस्तावेजों का निष्पादन
Execution of duty : कर्तव्य करना , निभाना
Execution of public duty : लोक कर्तव्य का निष्पादन
Execution of warrant : वारंट का निष्पादन
Execution proceeding : निष्पादन कार्यवाही
Executive ability : कार्य सम्पादन की योग्यता
Executive bent of mind : कार्यपालक प्रवृत्ति
Executive order : कार्यपालक आदेश / अधिशासी आज्ञा
Executive power : कार्यपालक शक्ति
Executive staff : कार्यपालक कर्मचारीगण
Exemplary manner : अनुकरणीय नीति
Exemplary punishment : शिक्षाप्रद दंड
Exempli gratia (e.g.) : उदाहरण के लिए, जैसे
Exempted employee : छूट दिए गए कर्मचारी
Exempted from attachment : कुर्की से छूट प्राप्त
Exercisable from time to time : जिसका समय-समय पर प्रयोग किया जा सकता है
Exercise absolute discretion : आत्यंतिक विशेषाधिकार का प्रयोग करना
Exercise due discretion : उचित स्वविवेक का प्रयोग करना
Exercise initiative : स्वप्रेरणा का प्रयोग करना
Exercise of discretion : स्वविवेक का प्रयोग करना

Exercise of functions : गतिविधियों का संचालन
Exercising jurisdiction, person : अधिकारिता का प्रयोग करने वाला व्यक्ति
Exhaustive inspection : व्यापक निरीक्षण
Exhaustive report : परिपूर्ण / विशद प्रतिवेदन
Exhibit good understanding : अच्छी समझ का परिचय देना
Exhibit number : प्रदर्श क्रमांक
Exhibited in the accounts : लेखाओं में दिखाया गया है
Exigencies of administrative work : प्रशासकीय कार्य की अत्यावश्यकताएँ
Exigencies of public service : लोकसेवा की आवश्यकताएँ
Existence of customs : रूढ़ि / परिपाटी का अस्तित्व
Existence of designs : परिकल्पना का अस्तित्व
Existence of entry : प्रविष्टि का अस्तित्व
Existence of mortgage : बंधक का अस्तित्व
Existence of public right : जनाधिकार का अस्तित्व
Existing consideration : विद्यमान प्रतिफल
Existing organisation : विद्यमान संगठन
Existing patent : विद्यमान पेटेंट
Ex-parte : एकपक्षीय / इकतरफा
Ex-parte assessment : एकपक्षीय निर्धारण
Ex-parte decision : एकपक्षीय निर्णय
Ex-parte injunction : एकपक्षीय निषेधाज्ञा
Ex-parte order : एकपक्षीय आदेश
Expedient for the end of justice : न्याय के उद्देश्यों की पूर्ति के लिए समीचीन
Expedient in the public interest : लोकहित में समीचीन
Expedite action : शीघ्र कार्यवाही करें / कार्यवाही में शीघ्रता करें
Expedite submission of report : रिपोर्ट शीघ्र भिजवाने की व्यवस्था करें
Expeditious disposal : शीघ्र निपटान
Expeditious settlement of claims : दावों का शीघ्र निपटारा
Expenditure including the bill : बिल सहित व्यय

Expenditure incurred bona fide : सद्भावपूर्वक किया गया व्यय
Expenditure is excessive : व्यय अत्यधिक है
Expenditure is recurring : व्यय आवर्ती है
Expenditure is within budgetary allotment : व्यय बजट आवंटन के भीतर है
Expenditure met from revenue : राजस्व में किया गया व्यय
Expense of, at the : की हानि करके
Expenses entailed on him : उस पर हुआ व्यय
Experiment to be tried : प्रयोग किया जाना
Experimental measure : प्रयोगात्मक उपाय
Expiring laws continuance bill : नियम / कानून की अवधि समाप्त होने पर बिल जारी रहेगा
Explain the circumstances under which : वे परिस्थितियाँ बताइये जिनके कारण
Explain why disciplinary action should not be taken against you : बताइये कि आपके विरुद्ध अनुशासनात्मक कार्यवाही क्यों न की जाए
Explained in your memorandum : आपके ज्ञापन में स्पष्ट किया गया
Explanation be called for : स्पष्टीकरण माँगा जाए
Explanation from the defaulter maybe obtained : बकायेदार से स्पष्टीकरण माँगा जाए
Explanatory of conduct : आचरण को स्पष्ट करने वाला
Explanatory of facts : तथ्यों को स्पष्ट करने वाला
Explicit agreement : स्पष्ट समझौता
Explicitly told : स्पष्टतया बता दिया गया
Export credit guarantee : निर्यात उधार गारंटी
Express contract : अभिव्यक्ति संविदा
Expression local : स्थानीय शब्द प्रयोग
Expression of opinion : मताभिव्यक्ति
Expressly provided : स्पष्टतः उपबंधित
Extend assistance : सहायता करना / मदद देना
Extend time : समय बढ़ना / समय बढ़ाना
Extension methods : विस्तार-विधियाँ
Extension of delivery date : सुपुर्दगी की तारीख का बढ़ना

Extension of posts : पद का विस्तारीकरण
Extension services : नौकरियों का विस्तारीकरण
Extensive cultivation : विस्तृत / सघन कृषि
Extent of recognition : मान्यता का विस्तार
Extenuating circumstances : उपशामक परिस्थितियाँ
Extinct tribe : लुप्त प्रजातियाँ
Extinction of rights : अधिकारों निर्वापन
Extinction of trust : न्यास का निर्वापन
Extra duty allowance : अतिरिक्त कार्यभत्ता
Extra mural employment : बाहरी रोजगार
Extra ordinary gazette : असाधारण राजपत्र
Extra ordinary leave : साधारण अवकाश
Extra ordinary leave without allowances : बिना भत्तों की असाधारण छुट्टी
Extra ordinary meeting : असाधारण बैठक
Extra ordinary session : असाधारण सत्र
Extra territorial offence : राज्य-क्षेत्र से बाहर हुआ अपराध
Extracts taken : सार ले लिया गया
Extraneous matter : असंगत विषय
Extra-ordinary powers in the case of emergency : आपात स्थिति में असाधारण शक्तियाँ
Extravagance in living in habitable condition : रहन-सहन में फिजूलखर्ची
Extravagant expenditure : फिजूल खर्च
Extremely narrow scope : अत्यंत संकीर्ण दायरा

■■

F

Fabricated evidence : गढ़ा हुआ साक्ष्य
Fabricating false evidence : मिथ्या साक्ष्य गढ़ना
Fabrication false documents : जाली दस्तावेज बनाना
Face value : अंकित मूल्य
Facilitating commission of offence : अपराध करने को आसान बनाना
Facilities are not available : सुविधाएँ उपलब्ध नहीं हैं
Facsimile signature : प्रतिकृति हस्ताक्षर
Fact-finding committee : तथ्यान्वेषी समिति
Fact in issue : विवादग्रस्त तथ्य
Fact of minority : अवयस्कता का तथ्य
Fact of public nature : लोकप्रकृति का तथ्य
Fact question of : तथ्य का प्रश्न
Factor affecting : प्रभाव डालने वाली बातें
Facts admitted : स्वीकृत तथ्य
Facts and figures : तथ्य तथा आंकड़े
Facts constituting the offence : अपराध गठित करने वाले तथ्य
Facts of the case in brief are as follows : संक्षेप में मामले के तथ्य इस प्रकार हैं
Facts of the case may kindly be furnished : प्रकरण सम्बन्धी तथ्य प्रस्तुत किये जाएँ
Fag end : बिलकुल अंत
Failing any indication : कोई संकेत न होने पर
Failing which : जिसके न होने पर / जिसके न किये जाने पर
Failing which serious action will be taken : जिसके न होने पर गंभीर कार्यवाही की जायेगी
Fails without sufficient cause : पर्याप्त हेतु के बिना असफल रहता है
Failure in duty : कर्तव्यपालन में असफलता
Failure of consideration : प्रतिफल की असफलता

Failure of constitutional machinery : संवैधानिक तंत्र विफल हो जाना
Failure of crops : फसलें बिगड़ जाना / अपेक्षित फसलें न होने पर
Failure of device : प्रयुक्ति की असफलता
Failure of interest : हित की निष्फलता
Failure of issue : संतान का न होना
Failure of justice : न्याय का न हो पाना / न्याय न दिया जा पाना
Failure of prior interest : प्राथमिक हित की निष्फलता
Failure of proof of an offence : अपराध का सबूत न होने पर
Failure to apply : आवेदन करने में असफलता
Failure to comply : अनुपालन में असफलता
Failure to deliver returns : विवरण देने में असफलता / जमा करने में असफलता
Failure to give surety : प्रतिभूति देने में असफल रहना
Failure to submit returns : विवरण भेजने में असफल रहना
Fair and accurate report : उचित और सही रिपोर्ट / उचित और सही जानकारी
Fair and correct summary : निष्पक्ष और सही संक्षेप
Fair and equitable distribution : उचित और समान वितरण
Fair and just : उचित और न्यायसंगत
Fair and reasonable : उचित और तर्कसंगत
Fair comment : उचित टीका-टिप्पणी
Fair compensation : उचित प्रतिकर
Fair copy : विशुद्ध प्रतिलिपि
Fair knowledge : अच्छा ज्ञान
Fair minded officer : निष्पक्ष अधिकारी
Fair price shops : उचित मूल्य की दुकानें
Fair proportion of the expense : व्यय का उचित अनुपात
Fair weather roads : खुले मौसम की सड़कें
Fairly good degree of capability : काफी अच्छी योग्यता
Fairly satisfactory : साधारणतया संतोषजनक

Fairly sound in judgement : फैसला सामान्यतया ठीक
Fait accompli : संपन्न कार्य
Faith acting in good : सद्भावपूर्वक
Faith in bad : असद्भावपूर्वक
Faithfully performance : निष्ठापूर्वक कार्य / निष्ठापूर्वक पालन
Fall due : देय होना
Fall in line with : के अनुसार कार्य करना
Fall through : निष्फल होना
Fall within the control : नियंत्रण में आना
Fallacious argument : दोषपूर्ण दलील
False accounts : झूठा हिसाब-किताब
False accusation : झूठा आरोप
False defence : मिथ्या प्रतिवाद
False impression : भ्रांत धारणा
False light : भ्रामक प्रकाश
False measure : मिथ्या नाप
False personation : मिथ्या प्रतिरूपण करना
False statement : मिथ्या कथन / झूठा बयान
False suggestion : मिथ्या सुझाव
False warranty : मिथ्या वारंटी
False weights : खोटे बाँट
Falsely implicated : झूठा फँसाया गया
Falsely personate : मिथ्या प्रतिरोपण
Falsely suggest : मिथ्या उपलक्षण
Falsification of accounts : हिसाब का मिथ्याकरण
Famine stricken : अकालग्रस्त
Far reaching effect : दूरगामी प्रभाव
Fault-finding : दोषारोपण / दोष निकालने वाला
Faux pas (indiscreet speech or action) : सामाजिक भूल / अशिष्टता
Favourable attitude : अनुकूल रुख
Favourable balance : अनुकूल शेष
Fear or favour. : भय या पक्षपात

Fearless in giving advice : परामर्श देने में निडर
Feasibility report : साध्यता रिपोर्ट
Feasibility study : साध्यता सम्बन्धी अध्ययन
Features essential : सारभूत लक्षण
Feedback : परिष्करण / परिमार्जन / परिशोधन
Feeling expressed in the meeting : बैठक में व्यक्त भावना
Feeling of ill will : शत्रुता की भावना
Felo de se : आत्मघाती
Fictitious loss : काल्पनिक हानि
Fictitious payee : फर्जी अदाकर्ता
Fidelity bond : विश्वस्तता बंधपत्र
Fidelity guarantee bond : निष्ठा गारंटी बीमा
Field agency : क्षेत्रीय अभिकरण
Field appointment : क्षेत्र नियुक्ति
Field oriented : क्षेत्र-केन्द्रीय / क्षेत्र अभिमुख
Fifth ultimo : गत महीने की पाँचवीं तारीख
Figure for the corresponding period of the last year : पिछले वर्ष की इसी अवधि के आंकड़े
Figure head : चित्र शीर्ष / नाममात्र का प्रमुख
Figures do not tally : आंकड़े मेल नहीं खाते
Figures have been compiled and shown in attached statement : आंकड़े संकलित कर दिए गए हैं और संलग्न विवरण में दिए गए हैं
File (in question) is place' below : अपेक्षित फाइल नीचे रखी है
File 'A' eliminated May be filed : फाइल (क) कर दी गई है
File 'A' partly eliminated : फाइल (क) रूप से कर दी गई है
File a suit : मुकदमा दायर करना
File an affidavit : शपथपत्र प्रस्तुत करना
File an appeal : अपील दायर करना
File an application : आवेदन प्रस्तुत करना
File board : फाइल बोर्ड
File classification system : फाइल वर्गीकरण पद्धति

File has been delinked : फाइल अलग कर दी गई है

File in play (action) : कार्याधीन फाइल / (इस) फाइल पर कार्य हो रहा है

File is not readily traceable : फाइल अभी नहीं मिल रही है

File is under submission : फाइल अधिकारी के पास है

File may be referred to ministry...for comments : फाइल टिप्पणी हेतु मंत्रालय को भेजी जाए

File movement register : फाइल संचालन रजिस्टर

Files are indexed : फाइलों को सूचीबद्ध कर दिया गया है

Filing return : विवरण प्रस्तुत करना

Filing system : फाइल पद्धति

Fill the office : पद को भरना

Fill up gaps : खाली स्थान भरना

Final bill is not on prescribed form : अंतिम बिल निर्धारित फार्म पर नहीं है

Final concurrence is accorded : अंतिम सहमति दी जाती है

Final decision when arrived at will be communicated : अंतिम निर्णय हो जाने पर सूचित

Final decree : अंतिम डिक्री

Final disposal : अंतिम निपटान

Final evidence : अंतिम साक्ष्य

Final order : अंतिम आदेश

Final pension : पक्की पेंशन

Final reply will follow : अंतिम उत्तर भेज दिया जाएगा

Final withdrawal : अंतिम धनाहरण / अंतिम प्रत्याहार / अंतिम सम्बन्ध विच्छेद

Finally disposing of the matter : मामले को अंतिम रूप से निपटाते हुए

Finally exempt : अंतिम रूप से छूट देते हुए

Finance Department may kindly be requested to reconsider : कृपया वित्त विभाग से पुनर्विचार हेतु अनुरोध किया जाए

Finance Department may please see for concurrence : वित्त विभाग कृपया सहमति हेतु देख ले

Financial accommodation : वित्तीय स्वीकार्य

Financial administration : वित्तीय प्रशासन

Financial bearing : वित्तीय प्रभाव

Financial concurrence : वित्तीय सहमति

Financial concurrence of the following post is necessary : नीचे दिए गये पद हेतु वित्तीय सहमति आवश्यक है

Financial concurrence to the proposal is awaited : प्रस्ताव पर वित्तीय सहमति प्रतीक्षित है

Financial implications of the proposal made by duly, vetted by A/C are furnished : द्वारा बनाए गए प्रस्ताव के वित्तीय फलितार्थ प्रस्तुत किये जा रहे हैं जिनकी लेखा विभाग ने विधिवत जाँच कर ली है

Financial irregularity : वित्तीय अनियमितता

Financial management and control : वित्तीय प्रबंध और नियंत्रण

Financial obligation : वित्तीय भार / वित्तीय बाध्यता

Financial position : वित्तीय स्थिति

Financial propriety : वित्तीय स्वामित्व

Financial reporting : वित्तीय जानकारी देना

Financial statement : वित्तीय विवरण

Financial stock taking : वित्तीय स्थिति की जाँच

Find surety : प्रतिभूति देना

Finding arrived at : दिया निष्कर्ष पर पहुँचा गया है

Finding given : निष्कर्ष निकाला गया / निकाला गया निष्कर्ष

Finding in the affirmative : सकारात्मक निष्कर्ष / अनुकूल निष्कर्ष

Finding in the negative : नकारात्मक निष्कर्ष / प्रतिकूल निष्कर्ष

Finding made : किया गया निष्कर्ष

Finding of the Enquiry Officer : जाँच अधिकारी का निष्कर्ष

Fine workmanship : शिल्प कौशल

Fined Rs. : रुपये जुर्माना किया गया

Fire protection and control : अग्नि सुरक्षा और नियंत्रण

Fire service : अग्निशमन सेवा

Firm by being more : अधिक दृढ़ होकर

First come first served : जो पहले आये वो पहले पाए

First count : प्रथम गणना / प्रथम गिनती
First detected : पहले पहल पता चला
First hearing : पहली सुनवाई
First in rank : पंक्ति में प्रथम
First schedule : प्रथम अनुसूची
Fit and proper person : उपयुक्त व उचित व्यक्ति
Fit and safe : उपयुक्त और निरापद
Fit for accelerated promotion : त्वरित प्रोन्नति योग्य
Fit for confirmation : समर्थन योग्य
Fit for trial : परीक्षण के योग्य
Fit its keeping fit : ये दुरुस्त है
Fit memo : आरोग्य प्रमाणपत्र
Fit state of health : ठीक स्वास्थ्य
Fit to be heard : सुनवाई के योग्य
Fix a date for meeting : मुलाकात के लिए तारीख मुकर्रर करें / मिलने के लिए समय नियत करें
Fix up responsibility : उत्तरदायित्व निर्धारित करें
Fix up some date : कोई तारीख तय करें
Fixation of ceiling : अधिकतम सीमा नियत
Fixation of pay : वेतन निर्धारण
Fixation of responsibility : उत्तरदायित्व का निर्धारण
Fixed assets : स्थायी आस्तियाँ / स्थायी संपदा
Fixed boundary : नियत सीमा
Fixed dimensions : नियत विस्तार
Fixed structure : स्थिर संरचना
Fixtures and fittings : जुड़ी हुई वस्तु और उपस्कार
Flag 'A' : पताका 'क'
Flair for executive work : प्रबंध कार्य की सहज वृत्ति
Flat denial : सीधी स्वीकारोक्ति
Flat rate : समान दर
Floating capital : अस्थायी पूँजी
Flow irrigation : बहाव सिंचाई
Fluctuation in agricultural development : कृषि विकास में उतार-चढ़ाव

Fly from justice : न्याय से भागना
Fly leaf : कोरा पन्ना
Flying visit : तूफानी दौरा
Fodder crops : चारा फसलें
Follow in : अंत तक पीछा करना
Follow the orders : आदेशों का पालन करना
Follow the procedure : प्रक्रिया का अनुसरण करना
Follow up cultivation : अनुवर्ती कृषि
Follow up negotiation : अनुवर्ती बातचीत
Following day : अगले दिन
Following facts : अग्रलिखित तथ्य
Following in his steps : अनुकरण करना
Following is an extract of : बोर्ड के आदेश का उद्धरण नीचे दिया गया है
Food position : खाद्य स्थिति
Foot at the : पद-भाग से
Footing, separate and independent : पृथक और स्वतंत्र आधार
For a certain sum : एक नियत राशि हेतु
For a continuous period : की निरंतर समय तक / हेतु
For administrative approval : कृपया प्रशासनिक अनुमोदन करें
For all concerned please : सभी सम्बन्धित लोगों के लिए
For all that : बावजूद इन सबके
For and against : पक्ष और विपक्ष में
For and on behalf of : के लिए उनकी ओर से
For any reason : किसी कारण से
For carrying out the purpose of : के प्रयोजन को पूरा करने के लिए
For compliance : अनुपालन के लिए
For concurrence : सहमति के लिए
For disposal according to law : कानूनी तरीके से निपटान के लिए
For disposal or report : व्यवस्था या प्रतिवेदन के लिए
For each year of completed service : पूरी हुई सेवा के प्रत्येक वर्ष के लिए
For early compliance : शीघ्र अनुपालन हेतु शीघ्र अनुपालन करें

For early remarks	: शीघ्र टिप्पणी हेतु / शीघ्र टिप्पणी दें
For enquiry and report	: जाँच और रिपोर्ट हेतु दें
For examination and report in due course	: परीक्षा और रिपोर्ट निश्चित समय के भीतर दें
For facility of reference	: सन्दर्भ की सुविधा के लिए
For favour of doing the needful	: आवश्यक कार्यवाही हेतु
For favour of necessary action	: उचित कार्यवाही हेतु / कृपया आवश्यक कार्यवाही करें
For filing into the case concerned	: सम्बंधित मामले के साथ नत्थी करने के लिए
For financial concurrence	: वित्तीय सहमति के लिए
For furnishing information	: जानकारी / सूचना देने के लिए
For good and satisfactory reasons	: संतोषजनक और पर्याप्त कारणों से
For gross negligence on your part	: आपकी तरफ से घोर असावधानी के कारण
For immediate attention	: तत्काल कार्यवाही हेतु
For information and guidance	: सूचना और मार्गदर्शन हेतु
For my part	: जहाँ तक मेरा सम्बन्ध है
For non-residential purposes	: निवासेत्तर प्रयोजनों के लिए
For obvious reasons	: स्पष्ट कारणों से
For onward transmission	: आगामी प्रसारण हेतु
For order please if the papers may be handed over to...	: कृपया ---- को पेपर्स दिए जाने का आदेश जारी करें
For orders if the credit be deposit	: कृपया आदेश दें कि क्या ------ के खाते में डाल दिया जाए
For orders please if the claim maybe repudiated	: कृपया आदेश दें कि क्या दावा अस्वीकार कर दिया जाए
For orders please whether security deposit of Rs. ... be returned to the contractor	: कृपया आदेश दें कि क्या ठेकेदार को -----रुपये की जमानत लौटा दी जाए
For orders please, if action maybe taken on the lines indicated above	: कृपया आदेश दें कि क्या अग्रलिखित अनुसार कार्यवाही की जाए

For orders, if this maybe procured through local purchases	: कृपया स्थानीय खरीद से उपलब्ध कराने हेतु आदेश जारी करें
For particular purpose in question	: सम्बंधित विशिष्ट प्रयोजन हेतु
For perusal and return	: पढ़कर / देखकर लौटाएँ / पढ़कर या देखकर लौटाने हेतु
For precedent, please see	: उदाहरण हेतु कृपया --------- देखें
For preserving peace	: शांति बनाए रखने हेतु
For ready reference	: तत्काल हवाले के लिए
For reasons explained above	: उपरोक्त कारणों के स्पष्टीकरण हेतु
For reasons now explained	: अब स्पष्ट किये गए कारणों से
For reasons stated in	: में बताये गए कारणों से
For reasons unconnected with	: से असम्बद्ध कारणों से
For remarks and return	: कैफियत के साथ लौटाए जाने के लिए
For service and return	: तामील करने और लौटाने के लिए
For signature please	: कृपया हस्ताक्षर करें / हस्ताक्षर के लिए
For spot enquiry	: स्थल पर जाँच हेतु
For suitable action	: समुचित कार्यवाही करें / समुचित कार्यवाही हेतु
For sympathetic consideration	: सहानुभूतिपूर्वक विचार करने के लिए
For that matter	: जहाँ तक उसका सम्बन्ध है
For the considering of	: के विचारार्थ
For the ends of justice	: न्याय के उद्देश्यों की पूर्ति के लिए
For the first time	: पहली बार
For the general good	: सबकी भलाई के लिए / सर्वसाधारण के हित के लिए
For the issue of another process	: दूसरी आदेशिका भेजने के लिए
For the nonce	: तत्समय / इसी बार
For the purpose of	: के उद्देश्य से
For the reasons now explained we concur with the proposal	: अब जो कारण बताये गए हैं उन पर विचार करने के बाद हम इस प्रस्ताव पर सहमति देते हैं

For the rest : बाकियों के लिए
Force in : प्रवृत्त
Force of law : कानून / कानून की शक्ति
Force persuasive : आग्रही बल
Forced by economic necessity : आर्थिक आवश्यकता के दबाव में
Foregoing debt : पूर्वगामी ऋण
Foregoing deposition : पूर्ववर्ती अभिसाक्ष्य
Foregone conclusion : पहले से निकाला गया निष्कर्ष
Foreign agent : विदेशी अभिकर्ता
Foreign dignitary : विदेशी उच्चाधिकारी
Foreign trade : विदेशी व्यवसाय
Forest offence : वन अपराध
Forest product : वन उत्पाद
Forfeited to government : सरकार को समापहरण
Forfeiture of property : संपत्ति का समापहरण
Forfeiture of seniority : ज्येष्ठता का समापहरण
Forfeiture of service : सेवाकाल का समापहरण
Forfeiture ordered : जब्ती का आदेश दिया
Forgery of document : कागजों की जालसाजी
Form a conjecture : अनुमान लगाना
Form a document, reduced to : दस्तावेज के रूप में लेख का न्यूनीकृत
Form a quorum : निर्दिष्ट संख्या की पूर्ति
Form an opinion : राय बनाना
Form and practice : रीति और परिपाटी
Form defective in point of : प्रारूपिक दृष्टि से त्रुटिपूर्ण
Form of a memorandum with : ज्ञापन के रूप में
Form of a notice : सूचना का प्रारूप
Form of order : आदेश का प्रारूप
Form of procedure : प्रक्रिया का स्वरूप
Form of return : विवरणी का प्रारूप
Form of security : प्रतिभूति का स्वरूप
Form of tender : निविदा का प्रारूप
Form of the charge : आरोप का प्रारूप

Form of the warrant : वारंट का प्रारूप
Formal approval is necessary : औपचारिक नियमित अनुमोदन आवश्यक है
Formal character : औपचारिक प्रकार
Formal charge : यथारीति आरोप
Formal deed : जाब्ते का विलेख
Formal document : जाब्ते का दस्तावेज
Formal sanction : औपचारिक स्वीकृति
Formal trial : औपचारिक विचारण
Formal warning : यथारीति चेतावनी
Formation of cliques : गुटबंदी
Former court : पूर्ववर्ती न्यायालय
Former employment : पूर्व नियोजन
Fortnightly reminders : पाक्षिक स्मरणपत्र
Fortuitous event : आकस्मिक घटना
Forward contract : अग्रिम संविदा
Forwarded and recommended : सिफारिश के लिए अग्रेषित
Forwarded for immediate compliance : तत्काल अनुपालन के लिए अग्रेषित
Forwarded for information and necessary action : सूचना और आवश्यक कार्यवाही के लिए अग्रेषित
Forwarded in due course : सम्यक अनुक्रम में भेजा गया
Forwarding letter : अग्रेषण पत्र
Forwarding note : अग्रेषण नोट / टिप्पणी
Foul, to get : अटक जाना
Found guilty of : का दोषी पाया जाना
Founded upon separate and distinct facts : पृथक और भिन्न तथ्यों पर आधारित
Fraction of a year : वर्ष का भाग
Fragmentation of holdings : जोत विखंडन
Frame of suit : वाद की विरचना
Framing of a charge : आरोप लगाना
Fraud by concealment : छिपाव द्वारा कपट
Fraudulent breach of trust : कपटपूर्ण न्यास भंग

Fraudulent dealing : कपटपूर्ण संव्यवहार
Fraudulent intention : कपटपूर्ण इरादा
Fraudulent mark : कपटपूर्ण संकेत
Fraudulent person : कपटपूर्ण व्यक्ति
Fraudulent preference : कपटपूर्ण प्राथमिकता
Free and voluntary consent : स्वतंत्र और स्वैच्छिक सहमति
Free competition : खुली प्रतियोगिता
Free consent : स्वतंत्र सहमति
Free from any defect : सर्वथा दोषरहित
Free from encumbrances : भार-मुक्ति / भाररहित
Free furnished residence : सज्जित आवास गृह
Free goods : सज्जित सामान
Free issue : सज्जित अंक
Free of charge : आरोपमुक्त
Free of cost : मूल्य मुक्त
Free pass : तैयार पास
Free passage : तैयार मार्ग
Free sale, for : विक्रय हेतु तैयार
Free sample : तैयार नमूना
Free Zone : तैयार क्षेत्र
Freedom and dignity (in condition of) : स्वतंत्रता और प्रतिष्ठा
Freedom from want : आवश्यकता से मुक्ति
Freedom of conscience : चेतना की स्वतंत्रता
Fresh proclamation : नई उद्घोषणा
Fresh receipt (F.R.) : नई आवती
Fresh receipt is for information for the present : नई आवर्ती अभी सूचना के लिए है
Fresh security : नई प्रतिभूति
Friendly disposition : मैत्रीपूर्ण मनोवृत्ति
Frivolous argument : निरर्थक दलील
From his own knowledge : स्वयं अपने ज्ञान से
From previous page : पिछले पृष्ठ से
From rank : अग्र पंक्ति

Fulfil the promise : वादा निभाना

Fulfilment of obligation : बाध्यता की पूर्ति करना

Fulfilment of contract : संविदा की पूर्ति करना

Full and true account : पूर्ण और सत्य विवरण

Full and true schedule : पूर्ण और सत्य अनुसूची

Full bench : पूर्ण न्यायपीठ

Full extent possible : संभावित पूर्ण मात्र

Full force and effect : पूर्ण शक्ति और प्रभाव

Full understanding of the circumstances : परिस्थितियों को पूर्णतया समझना

Fully and effectually : पूर्णतया और प्रभावी तौर पर

Fully paid share : पूर्ण प्रदत्त अंश

Fully paid up : पूरी तरह भुगतान किया हुआ

Fully vouched contingencies : पूर्ण प्रामाणिक आकस्मिक व्यय

Functional constituency : व्यावसायिक निर्वाचनक्षेत्र

Functions and powers : कार्य और शक्तियाँ

Functus duties : मूल कर्तव्य

Functus officio : पदकारी निवृत्त / समाप्ताधिकार

Fund apportionment : निधि प्रभाजन

Fund may be provided by re-appropriation : पुनार्विनियोग द्वारा निधि की व्यवस्था

Fundamental rights : मौलिक / मूल अधिकार

Funded debt : निधिबद्ध ऋण

Funds will be asked for : रकम माँगी जायेगी

Funds will be made available : रकम उपलब्ध कराई जायेगी

Furnish fresh security : नई प्रतिभूति देना

Furnish information : जानकारी देना

Furnish your definite , instructions : अपने निश्चित निर्देश दें

Furnishing a security on : पर सुरक्षा प्रदान करें

Further action maybe awaited : अगले कदम / अगली कार्यवाही की प्रतीक्षा करें

Further communication will follow : आगे पत्र भेजा जाएगा

Further correspondence in this respect may please be addressed to ...	: इस सिलसिले में कृपया इस पते पर पत्र-व्यवहार करें
Further destination	: अतिरिक्त निरोध
Further orders will follow	: आगे आदेश भेजे जायेंगे
Further particulars	: अगले विवरण / अगली जानकारियाँ / अतिरिक्त विशिष्टियाँ
Further Proceedings	: आगे की कार्यवाहियाँ
Further report may be awaited	: अगली रिपोर्ट प्राप्त होने की प्रतीक्षा करें
Further sentence	: अगला दंडादेश
Further such action as may be necessary	: अगले यथाआवश्यक कदम उठाये जाएँ
Future disposal	: भावी व्यवस्था / भावी निपटान

■■

G

Gain considerably : बहुत कुछ सीखना
Galloping inflation : तेजी से बढ़ती मुद्रास्फीति
Gazette notification : राजपत्र अधिसूचना / गजट सूचना
Gazetted officer of enforcement : राजपत्रित प्रवर्तन अधिकारी
Gazetted service : राजपत्रित सेवा
Gear up : तैयार होना / तैयार करना
General abstract of results : परिणामों का सामान्य सार
General acceptance : सामान्य स्वीकृति
General average loss : साधारण औसत हानि
General average sacrifice : साधारण औसत त्याग
General character : साधारण प्रकृति
General convenience : सामान्य सुविधा
General discussion : सामान्य वैचारिक आदान-प्रदान
General disposition : साधारण प्रवृत्ति
General exception : सामान्य अपवाद
General Normal term of office : कार्यालय की का सामान्य अवधि
General object of management : प्रबंध का सामान्य आदेश
General Order of a nature : सामान्य प्राकृतिक विधान
General public, utility of : सामान्य जनसुविधा
General service : सामान्य सेवा
General set up : सामान्य व्यवस्था
General supervision : साधारण अधीक्षण / साधारण पर्यवेक्षण
General well-being : सामान्य कल्याण
Genuine firm : असली फर्म / असली कंपनी
Genuine hardship : वास्तविक कठिनाइयाँ
Genuine text just adequate : प्रामाणिक पाठ
Get lost sight of : आँखों से ओझल हो जाना / ध्यान से निकल जाना
Get schemes executed : योजनाओं पर कार्य करवाएँ

Get to the bottom of : की तह तक जाएँ
Gets on well with his colleagues : अपने सहकर्मियों के साथ अच्छा घुलना-मिलना
Getting in : अपने भार साधन में लेना
Gift deed : दानपत्र
Gift of movable property : चल संपत्ति का दान
Gift over : परिवर्ती दान
Gist of the proposals : प्रस्ताव का सारांश
Give a good account of himself : अपनी योग्यता का अच्छा परिचय देना
Give a satisfactory account on oneself : अपने बारे में संतोषजनक विवरण देना
Give credence to : पर विश्वास करना
Give due weight to : पर्याप्त महत्त्व देना
Give evidence on oath : शपथ पर साक्ष्य देना
Give in : मन लेना
Give retrospective effect : भूतलक्षी रूप से प्रभावी करना
Give rise to : से पैदा होना
Give up : छोड़ देना / हार मान लेना
Give validity : विधि मान्यता प्रदान करना
Given gratis : मुफ्त दी गयी
Given under my hand : मुझे दी गई (जिम्मेदारी काम)
Glaring disparity : अत्यधिक असमानता
Glaring mistake : बड़ी भूल / बड़ी गलती
Glib tongue, to have a : ज्यादा बोलना
Glossary of terms : पारिभाषिक शब्द-संग्रह
Go slow strike : धीरे काम करो हड़ताल
Go slow tactics : विलंबकारी हथकंडे
Goad officers to work hard : अधिकारियों को परिश्रम की प्रेरणा दो
Good conscience : शुद्ध अंतःकरण
Good credit : अच्छी साख
Good debt : खरा ऋण
Good faith, in : सद्भाव से
Good grasp : अच्छी पकड़ / अच्छा ज्ञान

Good information : अच्छी जानकारी
Good insight : अच्छी अंतदृष्टि
Good law : मान्य विधि / स्वीकार कानून
Good offices : सत्प्रयास
Good order : सुव्यवस्था
Good sense : विवेक / सद्बुद्धि
Good service : अच्छी सेवा
Good title : कानूनी हक
Goods in transit : रास्ते में का सामान
Goods liable to confiscation : अधिहरण योग्य सामान
Goodwill mission : सद्भावना मिशन
Government consider that : सरकार समझती है कि
Government dues : सरकारी शोध्य / सरकारी पावना
Government estate : राज संपदा
Government securities : सरकारी प्रतिभूतियाँ
Government servant conduct rules : सरकारी कर्मचारी आचरण नियमावली
Govt. (are) pleased to accord sanction : शासन मंजूरी देता है
Govt. (are) pleased to approve of your proposal : शासन आपके प्रस्ताव का अनुमोदन करता है
Grace day of : अनुग्रह दिवस / कृपा कर दिया गया दिन
Gradation list : पदक्रम सूची
Grade inferior : अवर श्रेणी / निचला क्रम
Grade pay : ग्रेड वेतन / पदक्रम वेतन
Grading Fair : श्रेणी साधारण
Grading inspector : श्रेणीकरण निरीक्षण
Grain advance : अनाज अग्रिम
Grant and expenditure statement : अनुदान और व्यय वितरण
Grant in lieu of : के बदले में अनुदान / की जगह पर अनुदान देना
Grant injunction : व्यादेश देना

Grant of special pay : विशेष दिन का अनुदान
Grant-in-aid : सहायता अनुदान
Gratification as a motive : हेतु के रूप में परितोषण
Gratification by corrupt or illegal means : भ्रष्ट या अवैध साधनों द्वारा परितोषण
Gratification Pecuniary : धन सम्बन्धी परितोषण
Gratis copy : निःशुल्क प्रति
Gratuitous advice : मुफ्त सलाह
Gratuitous relief : निःशुल्क सहायता
Gratuity fund : उपदान निधि
Grazing ground : चारागाह
Great devotee to his duty : अत्यधिक कर्तव्यनिष्ठ
Greatest common advantage : सर्वाधिक सामान्य लाभ
Grievous disease : गंभीर रोग
Grievous hurt : गंभीर चोट
Grip over rules and regulations, perfect : नियमों और विनियमों पर पूर्ण अधिकार
Gross abuse : भारी दुरुपयोग
Gross amount : कुल रकम, सकल राशि
Gross assets : सकल परिसंपत्ति
Gross error : भारी गलती
Gross impertinence : घोर धृष्टता
Gross income : सकल आय
Gross mismanagement : भारी अव्यवस्था
Gross neglect : घोर उपेक्षा
Gross returns : कुल प्रत्यागमन
Gross revenge : बड़ा बदला
Grossly inaccurate : बिलकुल गलत
Grossly insubordinate : अत्यधिक अधीनता
Ground of defence : प्रतिरक्षा का आधार
Grounds of public policy : लोकनीति का आधार
Grounds of suspicion : संदेह के कारण
Guarantee bond : गारंटी बांड / गारंटी पत्र / प्रत्याभूति पत्र

Guarantee commission : प्रत्याभूति आयोग
Guarantee continuing : चलन प्रत्याभूति / गारंटी
Guarantee contract of : प्रत्याभूति की संविदा
Guard file : गार्ड फाइल
Guard of honour : सैनिक सलामी
Guardian ad litem : वादार्थ संरक्षक
Guardian de facto : वस्तुतः संरक्षक
Guilty intention : दूषित आशय / दोषपूर्ण आशय
Guilty knowledge : दूषित ज्ञान / दोषपूर्ण ज्ञान
Guilty of laches : अतिविलम्ब का दोषी
Gun licence renewed from : बन्दूक के लाइसेंस का नवीनीकरण तारीख ------ से किया गया

■■

H

Habeas corpus : बंदी प्रत्यक्षीकरण
Habit of making criticism : आलोचना करने की आदत
Habitation area : आवासीय क्षेत्र
Habitual criminal : आदतन अपराधी
Habitual defaulter : आदतन कर्जदार
Habitual indebtedness : आदतन कर्जदारी
Had better taken Finance devision's advise : वित्त विभाग से परामर्श कर लेना बेहतर होगा
Had exceeded orders : आदेशों का अतिक्रमण किया
Had to be dropped : को छोड़ देना पड़ा
Half average pay leave : अर्ध औसत वेतन अवकाश
Half daily allowance not admissible : आधा दैनिक भत्ता देय नहीं है
Half mast : आधा झुका
Half pay leave : आधा वेतन वाला अवकाश
Halting allowance : ठहरने का भत्ता
Hand in : हाथ में मौजूद
Handbill : पर्चा / विज्ञप्ति / इश्तहार
Handbook : पुस्तिका
Handingover certificate : हस्तांतरण प्रमाणपत्र
Hand-note : रुक्का / हस्तांक-पत्र
Handover charge : कार्यभार सौंपना
Hand-to-hand fight : आमने-सामने की लड़ाई
Handle file firmly : फाइल का निपटान दृढ़तापूर्वक किया जाए
Handled the situation : स्थिति सम्भाल ली
Handling charges : उठाने-रखने का व्यय
Handling problems satisfactorily : समस्याओं को संतोषजनक ढंग से सम्भालना
Handwriting document : हस्तलिखित दस्तावेज

Happening of an event : घटना का घटित होना

Happening of an uncertain event : अनिश्चित घटना का घटना

Harbouring an offender : किसी अपराधी को आश्रय देना

Harbours a sense of grief : दुखी रहता है

Hard currency : दुर्लभ मुद्रा

Hard headed : व्यवहार-कुशल / समझदार

Hard labour : कठिन परिश्रम

Hard manual work : कठोर शारीरिक श्रम

Hard-working hand : परिश्रमी व्यक्ति

Harmonious relation with his colleagues : अपने सहकर्मियों से मधुर सम्बन्ध

Has a clear record of service to his credit : उसका सेवावृत्त निष्कलंक है

Has applied for manual transfer : से परस्पर तबादले के लिए अर्जी दी है

Has been accustomed to absenting unauthorisedly : अनधिकृत रूप से अनुपस्थित रहने का अभ्यस्त

Has been dealt with suitably : समुचित कार्यवाही की जा रही है

Has been exonerates : दोषमुक्त कर दिया गया है

Has been screened : क्या इसकी जाँच हो चुकी है?

Has few equals : कुछ ही लोग इनकी समानता कर सकते हैं

Has his own way of doing things : कार्य करने का उसका अपना ढँग है

Has made a varying statement on different occasions : विभिन्न अवसरों पर अलग-अलग बयान दिया है

Has made himself indispensable : अपरिहार्य बन गया है

Has no comments to make : कोई टिप्पणी नहीं करनी है

Has not been pursued properly : समुचित धयान नहीं दिया गया है

Has put in an application for leave : अवकाश के लिए आवेदन किया है

Has reason to believe : विश्वास करने का कारण है

Has reported sick : बीमारी की अर्जी भेजी है

Has sense of urgency : आवश्यकता को महत्त्व देते हैं
Has sent a rejoinder : प्रत्युत्तर भेज दिया है
Hasty in action : काम में जल्दबाज है
Hatred or contempt : घृणा अथवा अनादर
Haulage charges : ढुलाई खर्चा
Have effect accordingly, shall : का तदनुरूप प्रभाव होगा
Have full grip over : पूर्ण नियंत्रण
Have recourse to : का सहारा लेना
Have the force of law, shall : विधि / कानून की ताकत रहेगी
Have the same force : वही प्रभाव होगा
Have you gone through the papers : क्या आपने कागजात देख लिए हैं?
Haves and have-nots : पैसेवाले और गरीब लोग
Having come to know it is felt that : जानकार इस निष्कर्ष पर पहुँचे
Having jurisdiction : अधिकार क्षेत्र में हो
Having regard to all the circumstances of the case : प्रकरण की सभी परिस्थितियों को ध्यान में रखते हुए
Having regard to the facts stated above : उपरोक्त तथ्यों को ध्यान में रखते हुए
Having regard to the merits of the case : प्रकरण के गुण-दोषों को ध्यान में रखकर
Having solemnly resolved : दृढ संकल्पित होकर
Hazard to the community, without : समाज को संकट में डाले बिना
Hazardous act : जोखिम वाला काम
He can be approached : उस तक पहुँच हो सकती है
He disowns ownership : वह उसके स्वामित्व से इनकार करता है
He has been repeatedly told : उसे बार-बार बताया गया है
He is Indispensable : उसके बिना काम नहीं चल सकता
He may be warned to be careful in future : उसे भविष्य में सतर्क रहने की चेतावनी दी जाए
He resents correction : वह सुधार पसंद नहीं करता है

He was censured : उसकी निंदा की गई थी
Head note : शीर्ष टिप्पणी
Head of account : लेखा-प्रमुख
Head of charge : आरोप का शीर्ष
Head of revenue : राजस्व शीर्ष
Head of the gang : गिरोह का मुखिया
Headquarters of district : जिला मुख्यालय
Health and well-being : स्वास्थ्य और कल्याण
Heard and finally decided : सुना और अंतिम रूप से निर्णय किया गया
Heard in person : व्यक्ति की सुनवाई की
Hearing was adjourned : सुनवाई स्थगित कर दी गई
Hearing Heat of passion : भावावेश
Hearing motion : समावेदन की सुनवाई
Heavy industry : भारी उद्योग
Heavy transport : भारी यातायात
Heir apparent : प्रत्यक्ष उत्तराधिकारी
Heir-at-law : कानूनी वारिस
Heir in possession : सकब्जा वारिस
Heir presumptive : संभावित वारिस
Held in abeyance : रोककर रखा गया है
Held in esteem, by all : सभी लोगों द्वारा आदर प्राप्त
Held in trust : न्यास के रूप में रखा गया है
Henceforth : अब से आगे
Hereafter : इसके बाद
Hereby : इसके द्वारा / एतदद्वारा
Hereby acknowledged : इसके द्वारा प्राप्ति स्वीकार की जाती है
Hereditary office : आनुवंशिक पद
Hereditary tenant : मौरूसी किरायेदार / किसान
Herein above described : जिसका इसमें ऊपर उल्लेख किया गया है
Herein provided for : इसमें दिए अनुसार / इसमें उपबंधित
Hereinafter : इसके उपरान्त / इसके आगे

Hereinafter provided : इसके उपरान्त उपबंधित
Hereinbefore : इसके पहले
Hereunder : आगे चलकर
Hesitant to trust anybody : किसी पर विश्वास करने में हिचकिचाने वाला
High contracting party : उच्च संविदाकारी पक्षकार
High order, of a very : बहुत उच्चकोटि का
High order, probable : उच्चकोटि का
High Power Committee : उच्चाधिकार समिति
High priority : उच्च प्राथमिकता
High road/ way : राजमार्ग / शहरों को जोड़ने वाली बड़ी सड़क
High sense of duty : कर्तव्यनिष्ठता की भावना
High standard of public taste : लोक रुचि का उच्च स्तर
High way, public : राजमार्ग / लोकमार्ग
Higher dignitaries : उच्चतर प्रतिष्ठित व्यक्ति
Highest character : अत्यंत उच्च चरित्र वाला
Highest duty : अधिकतम शुल्क
Highly improbable : अत्यंत असंभावित
Highly objectionable : अत्यंत आपत्तिजनक
Hill allowance : पर्वतीय भत्ता
Hilly country : पहाड़ी प्रदेश / पहाड़ी क्षेत्र
Hire charges : भाड़ा
Hire purchase agreement : भाड़ा क्रय करार
His conduct should be watched till that time : उस समय तक उसके आचरण पर निगाह रखी जाए
His explanation maybe obtained and put up : उसका स्पष्टीकरण प्राप्त कर प्रस्तुत किया जाए
His name is not borne in seniority list : उसका नाम वरिष्ठता सूची में नहीं आया है
His relations both with those above and below him are cordial : अपने से सभी बड़े और छोटों से उसका मधुर सम्बन्ध है
His request is in order : उसकी प्रार्थना नियमसंगत है

Hoarding and profiteering : जमाखोरी और मुनाफाखोरी
Hold a high opinion : ऊँची धारणा रखना
Hold a joint interest : संयुक्त हित रखना
Hold a meeting : बैठक करना
Hold a property : संपत्ति धारण करना
Hold a seat : स्थान ग्रहण करना
Hold an office of profit : लाभ का पद धारण करना
Hold briefs : वकालत करना/पक्ष लेना
Hold charge : प्रभारी होना
Hold correspondence : पत्राचार करना
Hold in abeyance : रोककर रखना
Hold in trust : न्यास के रूप में धारित करना
Hold lien on post : पद पर पुनः ग्रहणाधिकार
Hold out : प्रस्तुत करना
Hold over : रोक लेना / स्थगित करना
Hold over for life : आजीवन रोक रखना
Hold up : रोकना / स्थगित करना
Home consumption : देश में उपयोग / घर में उपयोग
Home travel concession : गृह-यात्रा रियायत
Honorary associate : सम्मानिक सहयोगी
Honorary capacity : अवैतनिक हैसियत
Honorary degree : मानार्थ उपाधि
Honorary fellow : सम्मानिक अध्येता
Honoris causa : सम्मानार्थ
Honour a bill/draft : हुंडी स्वीकारना
Honour for : आदरार्थ
Honour payment for : आदर के लिए संदाय
Honourably acquitted : सम्मानार्थ बरी
Honourably inefficient : बिलकुल निकम्मा
Horticulture operation : बागवानी संक्रियाएँ
Hospital leave : अस्पताल में दाखिल होने के लिए छुट्टी
Hostile witness : पक्षद्रोही गवाह

House allowance in lieu of free quarter is admissible : निःशुल्क क्वार्टर के बदले (कर्मचारी को) मकान भत्ता दिया जा सकता है

House building advance : गृह निर्माण अग्रिम

House Cessation of membership : सदस्यता स्थगन

House has been vacated : मकान खाली कर दिया गया है

House of people : लोक सभा

House patient : अन्तर्वास रोगी

House rent allowance : मकान किराया भत्ता

House search : घर की तलाशी

House tax : गृह कर

House trespass : गृह-अतिक्रमण

Housing allowance in lieu of rent : किराए के बदले में मकान किराया भत्ता

How the matter stands : मामला किस स्थिति में है

Hypothecation of goods : सामान को बंधक रखने का कार्य

■■

I

I am directed to : मुझे निर्देश गया है कि
I am directed to say (state) : मुझे कहने के लिए कहा गया है कि
I am to add : मुझे यह भी कहना है / मुझे यह भी लिखना है
I am to enquire : मुझे यह पूछना है / जानना है
I am to say : मुझे कहना है
I fully endorse the remark : मैं अभियुक्ति का पूर्ण समर्थन करता हूँ
I have been directed to ask you : मुझे आपसे पूछने के लिए कहा गया है कि
I have been directed to form you : मुझे आपको बताने के लिए कहा गया है कि
I have been directed to request you : मुझे आपसे प्रार्थना करने को कहा गया है कि
I have known Shr...for the last two years : मैं श्री ------ से पिछले दो सालों से परिचित हूँ
I have no further comments : मुझे और कुछ नहीं कहना है
I have no instruction the matter : इस विषय पर मुझे और कोई निर्देश नहीं दिया गया है / नहीं देना है
I have no knowledge : मुझे इसकी कोई जानकारी नहीं है
I have not the least hesitation holding : मैं किसी हिचक के बिना इस निर्णय पर पहुँचा हूँ कि
I have not yet received any reply from your end : मुझे आपकी तरफ से कोई जवाब नहीं आया है
I have satisfied myself : मैं इससे संतुष्ट हूँ / मैंने अपना समाधान कर लिया है
I have satisfied myself that the employee is not at fault : मैं समझ गया हूँ कि इस कर्मचारी का कोई दोष नहीं है
I have to thank you for assistance the matter : इस विषय पर आपके हेतु धन्यवाद

I have your attention to this important fact : मैं इस महत्त्वपूर्ण तथ्य के प्रति आपका ध्यान दिलाना चाहता हूँ

I proceed ex parte : मैं एकतरफा आगे बढ़ रहा हूँ

I regret to inform : मुझे यह बताते हुए अफसोस है

I reiterate my former comments : मैं अपने पूर्व कथन को दोहराता हूँ

I see no reason to interfere : मुझे नहीं लगता कि इसमें किसी तरह के दखल की आवश्यकता है

I shall be grateful : मैं आपको धन्यवाद दूँगा

I shall be highly obliged : मैं आपका अनुग्रहीत होऊँगा

I solicit your orders : आपका आदेश प्रार्थनीय है

I wish to inform you that : मैं आपको बताना चाहता हूँ कि

Identical case in every particular : हर एक विशिष्ट में समरूप

Identical scales of pay : समान वेतनमान

Identical time scale : समान उच्च वेतनमान

Identical with : तदनुरूप है / वैसा ही है

Identify certificate : पहचान प्रमाणपत्र

Identify of handwriting : हस्तलेख की मान्यता

Identify of informant : इत्तला देने वाले का नाम / पहचान

Identify of the author : रचयिता का परिचय

Identify of the partner : पक्षकार की पहचान

If agreed to, he will be advised accordingly : यदि आप सहमत हों तो उन्हें तदनुसार सूचित कर दिया जाएगा

If agreed to, papers will be filed : यदि आप सहमत हों तो कागजात फाइल कर दिए जाएँगे

If and whenever : जब भी कभी

If and in so far as : यदि और जहाँ तक

If and when : यदि और जब

If any deviation is noticed the same will be viewed seriously approved, a letter will be sent on the above lines : यदि अनुमति दी गई तो इस विषयक पत्र प्रेषित किया जाएगा

If approved, remarks will be called for from the employee : यदि अनुमति दी गई तो कर्मचारी से कैफियत मानी जायेगी

If approved, sale value will be refunded : यदि अनुमति दी गई तो विक्रय मूल्य लौटा दिया जाएगा

If approved, the employee will be advised accordingly : यदि अनुमति दी गई तो तो कर्मचारी को तदनुसार परामर्श दिया जाएगा

If deemed fit : यदि सही प्रतीत हुआ

If ignorance of law : कानून न जानना

If ignored, shall be : पर ध्यान नहीं दिया जाएगा

If it is otherwise in order, the proposal maybe accepted : यदि प्रस्ताव अन्यथा नियमसंगत हो तो उसे स्वीकार किया जाए

If necessary : यदि आवश्यक हो

If quorum is not available : यदि कोरम पूर्ण न हो / यदि गणपूर्ति न हो

If required : यदि जरूरत पड़ी

If satisfied after due enquiry even if he agrees : यदि यथोचित जांच से समाधान हो जाए

If the requisite information is expedited : यदि आवश्यक जानकारी की गति बढ़ाई जाती है तो

If the state of work permits : यदि कार्य की स्थिति को देखते हुए उचित हो

If you will kindly look into this : यदि कृपा कर आप इसे देख लें

Ill gotten money : अवैध कमाई

Ill health : खराब स्वास्थ्य

Ill treat : दुर्व्यवहार

Illegal gratification : अवैध परितोषण

Illegal omission : अवैध लोप

Illegality of the strike : हड़ताल की अवैधता

Illegible writing : अपाठ्य लिखावट

Illicit cultivation : अवैध खेती

Illustrative list : निदर्शी सूची

Immaterial allegation : तथ्यहीन आरोप

Immaterial issue : आधारहीन मामला

Immediate annuity due : तत्काल देय वार्षिकी
Immediate compliance : तत्काल पालन
Immediate disposal of the file is required : फाइल को तत्काल निपटाया जाए
Immediate employer : आसन्न नियोक्ता
Immediate execution immediate delivery : तुरंत प्रदान की कार्यवाही
Immediate gain : तात्कालिक लाभ
Immediate measure : तुरंत उपाय / तात्कालिक कदम
Immediate official superior : अव्यवहित पदीय वरिष्ठ
Immediate presence of, in the : की उपस्थिति में
Immediate prevention : त्वरित रोकथाम
Immediate slip : तुरंत पर्ची
Immediate vicinity : ठीक निकट
Immediately after : तुरंत बाद
Immediately before : तुरंत पहले
Immediately before the appointed date : नियत की गई तारीख के ठीक पहले
Immediately following : अगला ही / अगला आने वाला ही
Immediately on passing : पास होते ही / पारित होते ही
Immediately preceding : के ठीक पहले / से ठीक पहले
Immediately preceding year : ठीक पूर्ववर्ती वर्ष
Immediately succeeding : ठीक बाद का / ठीक बाद में
Immemorial usage : स्मरणतीत प्रथा
Immigrant population : आप्रवासी जनसंख्या
Immovable property : अचल संपत्ति
Immune from : से सुरक्षित
Immune from process of courts of law : अदालती कार्यवाही से सुरक्षित
Impact point : प्रभाव बिंदु
Impede any person : किसी व्यक्ति के समक्ष अड़चन डालना
Imperfect (erroneous) charge : अपूर्ण आरोप / गलत आरोप
Imperfect in form : प्रारूप की दृष्टि से अपूर्ण
Implementation cell : कार्यान्वयन विभाग

Implementing the agreement : करार लागू करना
Implication of rule : नियम का निहितार्थ
Implied agreement : निहित करार
Implied authority : निहित प्राधिकार
Implied consent : निहित स्वीकृति
Implied contract : निहित विवक्षा / निहित संविदा
Implied promise : विवक्षित / निहित वायदा
Implied term : निहित शर्त
Implied undertaking as to title : हक के बारे में विवक्षित परिवचन
Implied warranty : विवक्षित वारंटी
Impose fine : जुर्माना करना / कर अधिरोपित करना
Imposition of duties : शुल्क अधिरोपित करना
Imposition of penalty : शास्ति का अधिरोपण
Imposition of tax : कर का अधिरोपण
Impound a document : दस्तावेज को परिबंधित करना
Impracticable suggestion : अव्यावहारिक सुझाव
Imprest account : अग्रदाय लेखा
Imprest holder : अग्रदायधारी
Imprest money : अग्रदाय धनराशि
Imprisonment till the rising of court : न्यायालय उठने तक कैद
Improper acceptance : अनुचित प्रतिहरण / अनुचित रूप से स्वीकार करना
Improper admission of evidence : साक्ष्य का अनुचित ग्रहण
Improper description : अनुचित वर्णन
Improper employment : अनुचित नियोजन
Improper language : अनुचित भाषा
Improper rejection : अनुचित अस्वीकृति
Improper way joined improperly : अनुचित रूप से साथ आना
Improve the standard : स्तर में सुधार कीजिये
Improvement is gratifying : सुधार संतोषजनक है
Improvised arrangement : सुधरी हुई व्यवस्था

In a body : सब मिलाकर / सामूहिक रूप से
In a level headed way : संतुलित ढँग से
In a most satisfactory manner : पूर्ण संतोषजनक ढंग से
In a round about way : गोलमाल ढँग से
In a route manner : नेमी रूप से
In a summary way : संक्षेप में / संक्षिप्त रूप में
In abeyance : स्थगित
In accordance with his colleagues : उसके सहकर्मियों के अनुसार
In accordance with prescribed channels : विहित प्रणाली के अनुसार
In accordance with the provision made that behalf : इस निमित्त किये गए उपबंध के अनुसार
In accordance with the requirements : आवश्यकताओं के अनुसार
In acknowledge receipt of : की पावती भेजते हुए
In action : कर्म में / संघर्ष में / कार्यरूप में
In addition to : के अतिरिक्त / के साथ-साथ
In aid of : की सहायता से
In all respects : हर तरह से
In amplification of : का विस्तार करते हुए
In an exemplary manner : अनुकरणीय रीति से
In an existing vacancy : विद्यमान रिक्त पद पर
In an honorary capacity : अवैतनिक रूप से
In anticipation of your approval : आपके अनुमोदन की प्रत्याशा में
In any case : किसी भी हालत में
In any event : किसी भी स्थिति में / हर हालत में
In any form : किसी भी रूप में
In any material point : किसी तात्विक बात के सम्बन्ध में
In any respect : किसी भी तरह से
In any special case : किसी विशेष मामले में
In bad faith : बुरे इरादे से
In breach of his official duties : संविदा भंग करते हुए
In Camera : कैमरे में

Incapable of giving evidence : साक्ष्य देने में असमर्थ
In case it appears : अगर ऐसा लगे तो
In case of difference : मतभेद होने की दशा में
In case of doubt : संदेह होने की दशा में
In case of failure : असफलता की दशा में
In case of need : आवश्यकता की दशा में
In case of urgency : अति आवश्यकता की दशा में
In certain cases : कुछ मामलों में
In certain respects : कुछ विषयों में
In circulation : प्रसार में / सबको दिखाया जाए
In collaboration with : के सहयोग से
In compliance with your request : आपकी प्रार्थना को स्वीकार करते हुए
In confirmation of : की पुष्टि के रूप में
In conformity with rules : नियमों के अनुरूप
In consideration of : के प्रतिफल स्वरूप
In consistent therewith : से असंगत
In consultation with : के परामर्श से
In contact with : के संपर्क से
In contuation of : के आगे, के सिलसिले में, के क्रम में
In contravention of : के विपरीत, के प्रतिकूल
In correspondence with : से पत्र-व्यवहार में
In course of checking : जाँच के दौरान
In course of discussion : चर्चा के दौरान
In course of duty : काम के दौरान
In default of agreement : करार के अभाव में
In default of appearance : उपस्थित होने के व्यतिक्रम में
In default of bail : जमानत न होने की दशा में
In default of payment : भुगतान न करने की दशा में
In defence of : के बचाव में
In defiance of : की अवज्ञा करते हुए
In derogation of : के अल्पीकरण की दशा में
In descendg order : गिरते क्रम में

In discharge of his duties : अपने कर्तव्य के पालन में
In disorderly fashion : अव्यवस्थित रूप में
In due course of law : विधि के सम्यक अनुक्रम में
In due time : सम्यक समय में
In duplicate : दो प्रतियों में
In each case : हर मामले में
In effect : प्रभावशील / लागू
In efficient hand : अदक्ष कर्मचारी
In either of which cases : दोनों दशाओं में से हर एक के मामले में
In evasion of : का अपवंचन करके
In excess of his powers : अपनी शक्तियों से अधिक
In excess of the award : पंचाट से अधिक
In exercise of : के प्रयोग में / के उपयोग में / का प्रयोग (उपयोग) करते हुए
In exercise of the powers conferred by section : धारा ----- द्वारा प्रदत्त शक्तियों का उपयोग करते हुए
In extensive form : विस्तृत रूप में
In extension : सविस्तार
In fair measure : पर्याप्त मात्रा में
In fairness : न्याय / औचित्य की दृष्टि से
In figures : संख्या में
In force : लागू
In full : पूरा / पूरी तरह
In full and final payment : पूरा और पक्का भुगतान
In furtherance of work : काम को आगे बढ़ाने के लिए
In good circumstances : अच्छी परिस्थितियों में
In good faith for consideration : सद्भावपूर्ण और सप्रतिफल
In good health : स्वस्थ
In good order : सुव्यवस्थित / अच्छी हालत में
In good spirit : सद्भावना में
In his discretion : अपनी समझ में / अपने विवेकानुसार
In his judgement : उसके निर्णय में

In his own interest : उसके अपने हित में
In his present duties : अपने विद्यमान कर्तव्यों में
In implementing the decision : निर्णय को कार्यान्वित करने में
In issue : विवाद्य
In lieu of : के स्थान पर / के बदले में / की जगह
In like manner : समान रीति से / उसी तरह / उसी प्रकार
In memorium : स्मृति में
In modification of : का संशोधन करते हुए
In money : धन रूप में
In moral to public policy : लोकनीति के विरुद्ध
In obedience to : की आज्ञा का पालन करते हुए
In occupation : अधिभोगी
In official capacity : पद / अधिकारी की हैसियत से
In open court : खुली अदालत में
In operation : अमल में / प्रवर्तन में
In order of merit : योग्यता क्रम में
In order of preference : अधिमान के क्रम में
In order of priority : प्राथमिकता के आधार पर
In order to avoid delay : विलम्ब से बचाव हेतु
In order to ensure that : को पक्का करने के लिए
In order to obtain : प्राप्त करने के लिए
In order to safeguard against : से बचाव के लिए
In other respects : अन्य बातों में
In partial modification : आंशिक परिवर्तन करते हुए
In perpetuity : सदैव / सदा के लिए
In personal capacity : व्यक्तिगत तौर पर
In personam : व्यक्तिगत बँधी
In pla language : सीधी भाषा में
In posse : संभव
In possession of : के कब्जे में
In preference to : की अपेक्षा / के समक्ष / के सामने

In prescribed manner : विहित ढँग से
In present : वर्तमान में
In present of : की प्रस्तुति के दौरान
In priority to other duties : दूसरे कर्तव्यों की अपेक्षा प्राथमिकता में
In proper perspective : सही परिप्रेक्ष्य में
In proper sequence : ठीक अनुक्रम में
In proportion to : के अनुपात में
In prosecuting of : को सजा देते हुए
In pursuance of : का काम करते हुए / पर बढ़ते हुए
In quadruplicate : चार प्रतियों में
In question : प्रश्नों के घेरे में
In regular order : नियमित क्रम में
In rem : सर्व बंधी
In representative capacity : प्रतिनिधि के रूप में
In respect thereoff : के विषय में / के बारे में
In reverse direction : उल्टी दिशा में
In separate parts : अलग-अलग हिस्सों में
In sextuplicate : छह प्रतियों में
In similar circumstances : समान परिस्थितियों में
In so far as they are consistent with the provisions : जहाँ तक वे उपबंधों से सुसंगत हों
In so much as : यहाँ तक कि क्योंकि
In specie : मुद्रा में / वास्तु रूप में
In spirit as well as letter : तत्वतः और अक्षरशः
In spite of a thorough search : भलीभाँति ढूँढ़ने पर भी
In spite of handicaps : बाधाओं के होते हुए भी
In spite of repeated remember : बार-बार याद दिलाने के बाद भी
In spite of the fact : इस तथ्य के बावजूद
In subversion of : लगातार अनुक्रम से
In succession : लगातार / अनुक्रम से
In supersession of : का अधिक्रमण करते हुए
In terms of money : पैसे के रूप में
In that respect : उस तरह से

In the absence of any rules : किसी भी नियम की अनुपस्थिति में

In the alternative : के विकल्प में

In the background of : की पृष्ठभूमि में

In the case of : की हालत में

In the circumstances of : की परिस्थितियों में

In the concluding para : समाप्त करने वाले अनुच्छेद में

In the course of duty : कर्तव्य कर्म के दौरान

In the course of the suit : मुकदमे के दौरान

In the course of trial : विचारण के दौरान

In the discharge of official duties : आधिकारिक कर्तव्य के दौरान

In the estimation : अनुमान के अनुसार

In the event of : की घटना होने पर

In the execution of office : ऑफिस में काम करते हुए

In the exercise of : का प्रयोग करते हुए

In the existing vacancy : मौजूदा खाली जगह में

In the field : कार्यक्षेत्र में

In the following manner : दिए गए हिसाब से / आगे बताये गए तरीके से

In the interest of justice : न्याय के हित में

In the manner hereafter appearing : इसमें आगे बतलाई गई विधि से

In the manner provided : दिए गए तरीके से

In the mean time following remarks will be passed the register : इस बीच रजिस्टर में निम्नलिखित कैफियत

In the meanwhile : इसी दौरान / इसी बीच

In the nature of surety : प्रतिभूति के रूप में

In the ordinary course of business : कारोबार के सामान्य अनुक्रम में

In the performance of his duties : अपने कर्तव्यों के पालन में

In the prevailing circumstances : वर्तमान परिस्थितियों में

In the same interest : एक ही हित में

In the same way : एक ही तरह से / एक ही विधि से / एक ही रास्ते में
In this behalf : इसके लिए / इसके निमित्त / इस विषय में
In this state of affairs : इस परिस्थिति में
In this view of the matter : मामले के इस नजरिए के अनुसार
In token of : प्रमाणस्वरूप / प्रतीकस्वरूप
In token of the fact : तथ्य के प्रमाणस्वरूप
In token there of : उसी के प्रतीकस्वरूप
In toto : कुल मिलाकर / संपूर्णतः
In trust : न्यास के रूप में
In vain : बेकार / व्यर्थ / निष्फल
In view of : के दृष्टिकोण में
In view of circumstances stated above : उपरोक्त परिस्थितियों को नजर में रखकर
In view of the changed policy : बदली हुई नीति को दृष्टि में रखकर
In view of the present exigencies of work to deal with : कार्य करने की वर्तमान आवश्यकताओं को ध्यान में रखते हुए
In view of what has been stated above : उपरोक्त कथन को दृष्टि में रखकर
In violation of : का अतिक्रमण करके
In witness where of : जिसके साक्षी स्वरूप
In writing under his hand, order : स्वहस्ताक्षरित लिखित आदेश द्वारा
Inability to agree : सहमत न हो पाने की स्थिति में
Inaccurate figures : गलत आंकड़े
Inaccurate particulars : गलत विवरण
Inadequate consideration : अपर्याप्त प्रतिफल
Inadequate funds : अपर्याप्त धन
Inadmissible evidence : अग्राह्य साक्ष्य
Inadvertently overlooked : असावधानी से छूट गया
Inadvertently received : असावधानी से ली गई
Incentive scheme : प्रोत्साहन योजना
Incidental charges : प्रासंगिक भार / खर्चा

Incidental damages : आनुषंगिक हानि / नुकसान
Incidental order : प्रासंगिक आदेश / प्रासंगिक व्यवस्था
Incidentally it may be observed : प्रसंगवश यह कहा जा सकता है
Incidentally it maybe pointed out that : प्रसंगवश यह उल्लेखनीय है
Incited mob : उत्तेजित भीड़
Incoming telegram : आने वाला टेलीग्राम
Incompatible with : से बेमेल / से मेल न खाने वाला
Incompetent hands : अक्षम कर्मचारी
Inconclusive debate : अधूरी बहस
Inconclusive proof : अनिश्चयात्मक साक्ष्य
Inconsistent : असंगत / परस्पर-विरोधी
Inconsistent not : से असंगत नहीं
Inconsistent with the facts : तथ्यों से असंगत
Inconsonance with : से असंगति
Incorporated in the draft : प्रारूप में सम्मिलित / मसविदे में शामिल
Incorrect totalling : गलत जोड़
Incorrectly granted : गलती से अनुदत्त
Increasing the liability : दायित्व को बढ़ाना
Increment deferred by... days leave without pay : दिन की बिना छुट्टी के कारण
Increment in sub-grade granted : मूल ग्रेड में वेतन वृद्धि मंजूर की गई
Incumbent original : मूल पदधारी
Incumbent upon, to be : के लिए लाजमी / आवश्यक होना
Indefinite expression : अनिश्चयार्थ कथन
Indefinite payment : अनिश्चयात्मक भुगतान
Indefinite period : अनिश्चयात्मक अवधि
Indefinite time : अनिश्चयात्मक समय
Indelible ink : अमिट स्याही
Indemnity contract of : क्षतिपूर्ति की संविदा
Indemnity to administration bodies : प्रशासनिक निकायों की क्षतिपूर्ति

Indent item : माँगपत्र मद
Indent register : मांगपत्र पुस्तिका
Indentor's instructions : मानकर्ता की हिदायतें
Indentured labour : करारबद्ध श्रमिक
Independent charge : स्वतंत्र भार
Independent discretion : स्वतंत्र विवेक
Independent evidence : स्वतंत्र साक्ष्य
Independent note : स्वतंत्र टिप्पणी
Independent opinion : स्वतंत्र राय
Index card : सूचक कार्ड
Indication of the identity : पहचान का उपदर्शन
Indifferent attitude : उदासीन भाव
Indigenous production : देशी उत्पादन
Indigent circumstances : निर्धनावस्था
Indispensable for existence : अस्तित्व के लिए अपरिहार्य
Individual cases will be decided on merits : प्रत्येक पर उसके गुण-दोषों के आधार पर निर्णय दिया जाएगा
Individual inspection : व्यक्तिगत निरीक्षण
Indoor patient : भरती हुआ रोगी
Indulgence shown by you : आपने जो अनुग्रह किया है
Industrial depression : औद्योगिक मंदी
Industrial establishments : औद्योगिक प्रतिष्ठान
Industrial state : औद्योगिक क्षेत्र
Industrial undertaking : औद्योगिक उपक्रम
Ineligible for : के लिए अपात्र
Inevitable payment : अपरिहार्य भुगतान
Inference suggested : इंगित अनुमान
Inferior goods : घटिया माल
Inferior quality : घटिया किस्म / घटिया गुणवत्ता
Infirm person : बीमार व्यक्ति
Inflated rate of pay : वेतन की बढ़ी हुई दर
Inflationary trends : मुद्रास्फीति की प्रवृत्ति
Informal discussion : अनौपचारिक विचार-विमर्श

Information has already been obtained from the office concerned : सम्बन्धित कार्यालय से सूचना पहले ही माँग ली गई है
Information has been sent under this office letter No. : इस कार्यालय के पत्र संख्या ----- के अधीन सूचना पहले ही भेजी जा चुकी है
Informed of : की जानकारी दी गई
Inherent defect : अन्तर्निहित त्रुटि
Inherent lacuna : अन्तर्निहित कमी
Inherent power : अन्तर्निहित शक्ति
Inheritance tax : उत्तराधिकार कर
Inherited property : विरासत में मिली संपत्ति
Initial account : प्रारम्भिक लेखा
Initial capital : प्रारम्भिक पूँजी
Initial constitution : प्रारम्भिक गठन
Initialled by : द्वारा आद्याक्षरित
Initiative on his own : स्व-प्रेरणा पर
Injunction perpetual : शाश्वत व्यादेश
Injunction prohibitory : प्रतिषेधात्मक व्यादेश
Injure character : शील को दोष लगाना / चरित्रहीनता का आरोप
Injure party : क्षतिग्रस्त पक्ष
Injurious effect : हानिकारक प्रभाव
Injury personal : वैयक्तिक क्षति
Injury to life : जीवन को क्षति
Inquire in camera : बंद कमरे में जाँच
Inquire into the office : कार्यालय में जानकारी प्राप्त करें
Inquiring into the case has been completed : मामले की पड़ताल पूर्ण हो गई है
Inquiry on oath : शपथ पर जाँच
Inquiry preliminary : प्रारम्भिक जाँच
Insanitary dwelling : अस्वास्थ्कर आवास
Insertion in document : दस्तावेज में जोड़ना
Insignificant amount : नगण्य राशि

Insolvent circumstances : दिवालिए की परिस्थितियाँ
Insolvent debtor : दिवालिया कर्जदार
Inspect the spot : स्थल का निरीक्षण कीजिये
Inspection after execution : निष्पादन के पश्चात निरीक्षण
Inspection at site inspection report : स्थल पर निरीक्षण रिपोर्ट
Inspection Book : निरीक्षण पुस्तिका
Inspection house : निरीक्षण गृह
Inspire respect : श्रद्धा का भाव जागृत करना
Inspiring confidence : विश्वास जागृत करना
Instalment actually in default : वह किश्त जिसके सम्बन्ध में वास्तव में व्यतिक्रम हुआ है
Instance in the first : प्रथमदृष्ट्या
Instance in this : इस मामले में
Instant death : तत्काल मृत्यु
Instant hurt : तत्काल चोट
Instance of, at that : की प्रेरणा पर / के अनुरोध पर
Instantaneous action : त्वरित कार्यवाही
Instigated by : द्वारा उकसाया गया
Institute a suit : वाद चलाना / मुकदमा शुरू करना
Institute an enquiry : जाँच चलाना / जाँच शुरू करना
Institute prosecution : अभियोजन चलाना
Instruction phase : निर्देश का समय
Instructions are solicited : कृपया अनुदेश दें / हिदायत दी जाए
Instructions were issued but these have not been acted upon : हिदायतें दी गई थीं पर उन पर अमल नहीं किया गया
Instrument creating a power of attorney : मुख्तारनामा अर्जित करने वाली लिखत
Instrument of gift : दान की लिखत
Instrument of trust : न्यास की लिखत
Insulting language : अपमानजनक भाषा
Insurance general : साधारण बीमा
Insurance life : जीवन बीमा

Insured letter : बीमा किया हुआ पत्र
Insured on : बीमा किया गया
Integral part : अभिन्न अंग
Integrated development : एकीकृत विकास
Integrated unit : समाकलित इकाई
Integrity is beyond doubt : सत्यनिष्ठा संदेह से परे है
Intellectual attainment : बौद्धिक उपलब्धि
Intend to engage : लगाने का इरादा रखना
Intended leave : आशायित छुट्टी / अपेक्षित अवकाश
Intended lessee : आशायित पट्टेदार
Intended marriage : आशायित विवाह
Intended resolution : आशायित संकल्प
Intended trustee : आशायित न्यासी
Intending purchaser : आशायित क्रेता
Intensive cultivation : गहन खेती
Intensive drive : गहन प्रयास / गहन अभियान
Intention contrary opposed to (of being) : (से) प्रतिकूल आशय
Inter alia : अन्य वस्तुओं के साथ-साथ
Inter connected : अन्दर से जुड़ा हुआ / आपस में सम्बन्धित
Interest accrued : प्रोद्भूत / एकत्रित हुआ ब्याज
Interest created : सृष्टि-हित / हित की सृष्टि
Interest is vested : हित निहित है
Interest of Govt. : सरकारी हित / सरकारी उद्देश्य
Interest of justice : न्याय-हित
Interest of labour : श्रमिक-हित / श्रम-हित
Interest subsisted : हित विद्यमान था / हित निहित था
Interim agreement : अंतरिम समझौता / अंतरिम करार
Interim arrangement : अंतरिम प्रबंध
Interim award : अंतरिम पंचाट
Interim casual vacancy : अंतरिम आकस्मिक रिक्ति
Interim custody : अंतरिम अभिरक्षा

Interim forum : अंतरिम मंच
Interim Govt. : अंतरिम सरकार
Interim information : अंतरिम जानकारी / अंतरिम सूचना
Interim order : अंतरिम आदेश / अंतरिम व्यवस्था
Interim payment/relief : अंतरिम भुगतान
Interim reply maybe given : अंतरिम उत्तर भेज दिया जाए
Interim report : अंतरिम रिपोर्ट / अंतरिम जानकारी
Intermediate Loan : मध्यकालिक कर्ज
Intermediate person : मध्यवर्ती व्यक्ति
Intermediate station : मध्यवर्ती स्टेशन
Internal administration : आंतरिक प्रशासन
Internal audit : आंतरिक लेखा परीक्षा
Internal finance : आंतरिक वित्त
International understanding : अंतर्राष्ट्रीय सद्‌भावना
Interpretation clause : निर्वचन खंड
Interpreted and admitted correct : निर्वचन के उपरान्त ठीक समझा गया
Interpreted service : विच्छिन्न सेवा
Interruption in service : सेवा में व्यवधान
Intersectional movement register : अंतरानुभागीय संचलन रजिस्टर
Intersectional references : अंतरानुभागीय पत्राचार
Intervening area : अंतरवर्ती क्षेत्र
Intervening period : बीच की अवधि
Intimate knowledge : आंतरिक जानकारी
Intimation of acceptance : स्वीकृति की सूचना / जानकारी
Intimation to us, under : हमारे लिए सूचना / जानकारी
Intoxication, state of : नशे की हालत
Intra vires : शक्ति के अधीन / अधिकाराधीन
Intricate matter : पेचीदा मामला
Intricate problems : पेचीदा समस्याएँ
Intrinsic value : वास्तविक मूल्य
Introduction to the book : पुस्तक की भूमिका / का परिचय

Intrude upon the privacy : एकांत में बाधा डालना / गोपनीयता समाप्त करना
Invalidation of proceedings : कार्यवाहियों का अमान्यकरण
Inventory of furniture : फर्नीचर की सूची
Inventory of the property : संपत्ति तालिका
Investment value : निवेश मूल्य
Invitation of tender over the phone : फोन पर टेंडर मांगना
Inviting a reference to : का हवाला देते हुए
Inviting your attention to : की तरफ आपका ध्यान आकर्षित करते हुए
Involve a risk to the life : जीवन जोखिम में डालना
Involves any connection : किसी प्रकार का सम्बन्ध अंतर्ग्रस्त है
Involving question of policy : में नीति का प्रश्न निहित है
Inward entry : आवक प्रविष्ठी
Inward register : आवक पुस्तिका / आवक रजिस्टर
Inward returns : आवक विवरणियाँ
Irrecoverable amount : न वसूल की जा सकने वाली रकम
Irrelevant to the issue : मामले से असंगत / विषय से असम्बद्ध
Irrespective of : का विचार किये बिना
Irrespective of the fact : इस बात के होते हुए भी
Irrespective of whether or not : हाँ या न के बिना भी / हाँ या न को नजरंदाज करके
Irresponsible words : अनुत्तरदायी शब्द / अनुत्तरदायी बात
Irrevocable decision : अटल निर्णय
Irrigation cess : सिंचाई उपकर
Irritable temper : चिड़चिड़ा मिजाज
Is a very vital point in the case : प्रकरण / विषय में बहुत महत्त्वपूर्ण बिंदु है
Is frequently the case : अकसर ऐसा होता है
Is gradually picking up : धीरे-धीरे (काम) समझ रहे हैं
Is hereby informed : एतद्द्वारा सूचित किया जाता है / जानकारी दी जाती है

Is not permitted by the rules : नियमों के अनुसार अनुमति नहीं दी जा सकती

Is not reasonably practicable : युक्तियुक्त रूप से व्यवहार्य नहीं है

Is referred to : को निर्दिष्ट है

Is requested to pursue the note : से अनुरोध है कि टिप्पणी का अवलोकन करें और तदनुसार कार्यवाही करें

Is reverted to h substantive post : उन्हें अपने मूल पद पर लौटाया जाता है

Is self explanatory : स्वतः स्पष्ट है

Is set aside : अलग रखा जाता है / रद्द किया जाता है

Is without jurisdiction : न्यायाधिकार नहीं है

Issue a precept : आज्ञा-पत्र निकालना

Issue as amended : यथा संशोधित जारी करें

Issue call for tenders : टेंडर मंगवाइये

Issue immediate reminder : स्मरण-पत्र तत्काल भेजिये

Issue note : विवरण जारी कीजिए

Issue notice to the : को सूचना भेजिए

Issue of fact : तथ्य विवाद्यक

Issue of permit : आज्ञापत्र जारी करना

Issue of process : आदेशिका जारी करना

Issue of store : सामान देना

Issue of this is authorised : इसको जारी करने की अनुमति है

Issue reminder urgently : तुरंत अनुस्मारक भेजें

Issue telegraphic instructions : तार से अनुदेश भेजिए

Issue warning : चेतावनी जारी कीजिये / भेजिए

Issues agreed upon : विवाद्यक जिन पर स्वीकृति हो गई है

Issues are settled : विवाद्यक स्थिर किये गए हैं

Issues have been framed : विवाद्यक तैयार किये गए हैं / की रचना की गई है

Issues of the case : मामले के विवाद्यक / वाद्पद

Issuing concern : निर्गमन करने वाला समुत्थान

It could be visualised : इसे निर्गमित करते हुए / जारी करते हुए

It gives us pleasure to inform you	: आपको सूचित करते हुए हमें हर्ष है
It has been discoverd	: इसे देखा जा सकता है
It has since been decided	: ऐसा पाया गया है
It is a matter of regret / maybe regretted	: ये खेद का विषय है
It is a side issue	: और अब यह निश्चित किया गया है
It is an open secret that	: यह मूल विषय नहीं है
It is conceded	: यह रहस्य सबको पता है
It is desirable	: यह मान लिया गया है
It is for consideration whether	: ऐसी अपेक्षा की जाती है / यह वांछनीय है
It is for orders whether	: अतः यह विचारणीय है कि क्या
It is further requested	: यह भी प्रार्थना है
It is hereby agreed	: इसके द्वारा यह करार किया जाता है
It is implied	: आशय यह है
It is irregular and can not be covered by any stretch of interpretation of the rules	: यह अनियमित है और चाहे जिस तरह व्याख्या की जाए इसे न्यायसंगत नहीं ठहराया जा सकता
It is natural that	: यह स्वाभाविक है
It is not proposed to hold an open enquiry in this case	: इस प्रकरण में खुली जाँच करने की अनुमति नहीं है
It is notified for general information	: आम सूचना हेतु इसे अधिसूचित किया जाता है
It is obligatory	: यह अनिवार्य है
It is presumed that	: यह धारणा है कि
It is regretted that	: खेद है कि
It is suggested that	: यह सुझाव दिया जाता है कि
It is understood	: मालूम हुआ है कि
It is unreasonable to insist on the	: पर जोर देना अनुचित है
It is within the powers	: यह अपने अधिकार में है
It leaves no margin	: इसमें कोई गुंजाइश नहीं

It may further be added : आगे यह जोड़ा जा सकता है / आगे यह कहा जा सकता है

It may pointed out that : यह बताया जाए कि

It maybe recollected : आपको याद होगा कि

It shall be lawful : यह विधिसम्मत होगा

It was manipulated : जोड़-तोड़ भिड़ा लिया गया था

It will be greatly appreciated : बड़ी कृपा होगी

It will be highly appreciated बड़ी कृपा होगी

It will be inexpedient : यह समीचीन नहीं होगा / यह उचित नहीं होगा

It will be necessary to obtain following particulars : नीचे लिखे ब्यौर प्राप्त करना आवश्यक होगा

It will be remembered : यह स्मरणीय है

It will be seen : यह देखने में आता है कि

It would be incumbent upon : के लिए यह आवश्यक होगा

It would be noticed : यह देखने योग्य है कि

Item in suspense : अनिश्चयपूर्ण मद

■■

J

Jealously : ईर्ष्यापूर्वक
Job classification : कार्य वर्गीकरण
Joinder of causes of action : वाद हेतुकों का संयोजन
Joinder of charges : आरोपों का संयोजन
Joinder of parties : पक्षकारों का संयोजन
Joining time allowance : पद ग्रहणकाल भत्ता
Joining time pay : पद ग्रहण अवधि वेतन
Joint annuity : संयुक्त वार्षिकी
Joint application : संयुक्त आवेदन-पत्र
Joint attestation : संयुक्त अनुप्रमाणन
Joint concurrence : संयुक्त सहमति
Joint consultation : संयुक्त परामर्श
Joint contract : संयुक्त संविदा
Joint decree : संयुक्त डिक्री
Joint decree holder : संयुक्त डिक्रीदार
Joint direction : संयुक्त निदेश
Joint enquiry has been ordered : संयुक्त जाँच का आदेश दिया जा चुका है
Joint hands : संयुक्त जनबल / कर्मचारी
Joint holder : संयुक्त धारक
Joint liabilities : संयुक्त दायित्व
Joint meeting : संयुक्त बैठक / अधिवेशन
Joint occupation : संयुक्त अधिभोग
Joint parties : संयुक्त पक्षकार
Joint personal security : संयुक्त व्यक्तिगत प्रतिभूति
Joint promisor : संयुक्त वचनदाता
Joint resolution : संयुक्त संकल्प / संयुक्त प्रस्ताव
Joint sitting : संयुक्त बैठक
Joint tenants : संयुक्त किरायेदार
Jointly concerned : संयुक्त तौर पर सम्बन्धित

Jointly owe : संयुक्त देनदार
Journal of proceedings : कार्यवाही रोजनामचा
Journey unauthorised : अनधिकृत यात्रा
Judgement dissenting : विसम्मत निर्णय
Judgement delivered to hear : सुनने के लिए निर्णय सुनाया गया
Judgement is not rhyme with the facts : निर्णय तथ्यों से मेल नहीं खाता
Judicial award : न्याय अधिनिर्णय
Judicial balance and steadiness : न्याय सम्बन्धी संतुलन और स्थिरता
Judicial custom : न्यायिक आचार
Judicial duty : न्यायिक कर्तव्य
Judicial formulation of law : विधि की न्यायाधीशों द्वारा रचना
Judicial lock up : न्यायिक कारावास
Judicial office : न्यायिक पद
Judicial pronouncement : न्यायिक निर्णय
Judicial record : न्यायिक अभिलेख
Judicial reference : न्यायिक निर्देश
Judicial separation : न्यायिक विच्छेद
Judicial sobriety : न्यायिक गाम्भीर्य
Judicial stamp : न्यायिक मुद्रांक
Judicial work of high order : उच्चकोटि का न्यायिक कार्य
Judicially interpreting : न्यायिक निर्वचन करते हुए
Judicious taxation : विवेकसम्मत कराधान
Junior time scale : अवर समयमान
Jurisdiction appellate : अपीली अधिकारिता
Jurisdiction barred : विचाराधिकार की रोक
Jurisdiction inferior : अवर अधिकारिता
Jurisdiction not vested in it by law : अधिकारिता जो कानूनसम्मत नहीं है
Jurisdiction superior : वरिष्ठ अधिकारिता
Jurisdictional basis : कानूनी आधार
Jurisdictional purpose : अधिकारिता का प्रयोजन
Jury man : जूरी सदस्य

Jus ad rem : अपूर्ण अधिकार
Jus cavile : सिविल कानून
Jus tertii : पर व्यक्ति का अधिकार
Just and convenient : न्यायसंगत और सुविधापूर्ण
Just and equitable : न्यायसंगत और साम्यिक
Just and expedient : न्यायसंगत और सामयिक
Just and reasonable : उचित और युक्तिसंगत
Just excuse : न्यायसंगत क्षमायाचना
Just cause : न्यायसंगत कारण
Just moderate : प्रायः साधारण
Justice of the case : मामले में न्याय
Justice, equality and conscience : न्याय, समता और शुद्ध अंतःकरण
Justification for the proposal : प्रस्ताव का औचित्य
Justified the trust reposed in : व्यक्त विश्वास के योग्य प्रमाणित हुए

■■

K

Keen interest : उत्साहपूर्ण रुचि
Keen mind : तीक्ष्ण बुद्धि
Keep abreast of the times : समय के साथ रहिये
Keep alert : सावधान रहिये
Keep in abeyance : स्थगित रखा जाए
Keep in close touch with : के साथ निकट संपर्क बनाये रखिये
Keep in confinement : बंद करके रखिये / परिरोध में रखिये
Keep in force : प्रवृत्त रखिये
Keep in good order : सुव्यवस्थित रखिये
Keep in peace : शान्ति रखिये
Keep in suspense : दुविधा में रखना / राज रखना
Keep pending : विचाराधीन रखा जाए / रोक के रखिये
Keep service before self : स्वार्थ से सेवा को अधिक महत्त्व दीजिये
Keep this in view : इसे ध्यान में रखिये
Keep up the progress : प्रगति बनाए रखिये
Keep with the file : फाइल के साथ रखा जाए
Keeping in view : ध्यान में रखते हुए
Kept pending, maybe : रोक के रखा जाए / विचाराधीन रखा जाए
Kept with the file : फाइल के साथ रखा जाए
Key industry : प्रमुख उद्योग
Key map : मूल नक्शा
Key point : मूल बिंदु
Key post : मुख्य पद
Kind, in : वस्तु के रूप में
Kindly accord concurrance : कृपया सहमति प्रदान करें
Kindly acknowledge receipt : कृपया पावती भेजिए
Kindly advice, if the claim maybe treated as closed : कृपया सूचित करें कि क्या प्रकरण समाप्त समझा जाए

Kindly direct them to this office : कृपया उन्हें इस कार्यालय में भेजिए

Kindly expedite reply : कृपया शीघ्र उत्तर दीजिये

Kindly instruct further : कृपया आगे अनुदेश दें

Kindly look into it : कृपया इसे देख लें

Kindly record essentiality certificate : कृपया अनिवार्यता प्रमाणपत्र दें

Kindly refer to my D.O. letter : कृपया मेरे अर्धसरकारी पत्र देखें

Kindly return the bills : कृपया बिल वापस भेजें

Kindly review the case : कृपया प्रकरण पर पुनर्विचार करें

Knocked down : बोली मंजूर / खतम की

Know how job well : काम की अच्छी जानकारी रखना

Knowingly and unlawfully : जानबूझकर और अवैध रूप से

Knowingly and wilfully : जानते हुए और जानबूझकर

Knowledge and belief, to the best of : अधिकतम जानकारी और विश्वास के अनुसार / जहाँ तक पता है और विश्वास है

Knowledge of facts : तथ्यों की जानकारी

Known defects : ज्ञात दोष

know-how : जानकारी / सुविज्ञता

Knows to be false : मिथ्या होने का ज्ञान है

■■

L

Label affixed : लगाया गया लेबल
Laborious task : श्रमसाध्य कार्य
Labour Appellate Tribunal : श्रम अपील अधिकरण
Labour colony : श्रमिक बस्ती
Labour dispute : श्रमिक विवाद
Labour intensive industry : श्रमप्रधान उद्योग
Labour involved in gathering information : जानकारी एकत्र करने में लगने वाली मेहनत
Labour productivity : श्रम उत्पादकता
Labour tribunal : श्रम अधिकरण
Labour turnover : श्रम आवर्त
Lacking behind : पीछे छूटा हुआ
Lacking initiative and drive : अभियान चलाने और अभिप्रेरणा का अभाव
Lacking of decision in firmly applying rules : नियमों को दृढ़ता से लागू करने की निर्णय क्षमता का अभाव
Laid down : निर्धारित
Laid down in Para ... : पैराग्राफ ------- में दिए गए / बताये गए
Laid down procedure maybe followed : बतायी गयी / निधारित कार्यविधि को अपनाया जाए
Land arable : कृषियोग्य भूमि
Land holding : भू-धारण
Land of tenure : पट्टेदारी वाली भूमि
Land record : भू-अभिलेख
Land slide : भूमि-स्खलन
Landed property : भू-संपत्ति
Language commonly understood : सामान्यतः समझी जाने वाली भाषा
Lapse of Government : सरकार का चले जाना

Lapse of grant : अनुदान का व्यपगत होना
Lapse of time : समय बीतना
Lapsed sanction : व्यपगत मंजूरी
Lapsing of deposit : जमा का व्यपगमन
Largely engaged : अत्यधिक व्यस्त
Last audited : अंतिम संपरीक्षित
Last before that time : उस समय से ठीक पहले
Last mentioned : अंत में उल्लिखित
Last preceding : ठीक पहले की / ठीक पहले वाला
Last preceding census : अंतिम पूर्ववर्ती जनगणना
Later act : बाद वाला अधिनियम
Later created right : बाद का अधिकार
Later reference : बाद का हवाला
Law-abiding : कानून को मानने वाला / विधिपालक
Law administrably court : न्यायालय द्वारा प्रशासित विधि
Law and order disturbances : कानून और व्यवस्था सम्बन्धी उपद्रव
Law and practice : विधि और प्रथा
Law in force : लागू कानून
Law of evidence : साक्ष्य का कानून
Law of limitation : परिसीमा विधि
Law of nature : प्रकृति का नियम
Law of the land : देशी कानून / देश का कानून
Lawful apprehension : विधि के अनुसार पकड़ा गया
Lawful authority : वैध प्राधिकारी
Lawful capture : वैध प्रग्रहण
Lawful charge : विधिपूर्ण प्रभार
Lawful consideration : विधिपूर्ण प्रतिफल
Lawful debt : विधिपूर्ण ऋण
Lawful discharge of duty : विधिपूर्ण कर्तव्य निर्वहन
Lawful excuse : विधिपूर्ण कारण / वैध कारण
Lawful ground : न्यायसंगत
Lawful impediment : वैध अड़चन
Lawful manner : विधिपूर्ण / वैध प्रकार

Lawful object : विधिपूर्ण उद्देश्य
Lawful sentence : वैध दंडादेश
Lawful thing : वैध बात
Lawfully procured : विधिवत प्राप्त किया
Lawsuit : वाद / मुकदमा
Lay a foundation stone : शिलान्यास करना
Lay claim to : पर दावा जताना
Lay down : रख देना / निर्धारित करना
Lay down the law : विधि अधिकथित करना
Lay down the procedure : प्रक्रिया अधिकथित करना
Lay hands on : पकड़ना / हड़पना
Lay off : कामबंदी / अस्थायी छँटनी
Lay off, retrenchment and closure : कामबंदी, छँटनी और बंद किया जाना
Lay on the table of the : सदन के पटल पर रखना
Laying down rule : नियम निर्धारित करना
Laying Out : बिछाया जाना
Lead a witness : साक्षी से सूचक प्रश्न करना
Leading article : अग्र लेख
Leading counsel : मुख्य कौंसिल
Leading mark : मुख्य चिह्न
Leading personalities : मुख्य व्यक्ति
Leading question : सूचक प्रश्न
Lean year : मंदा साल
Lease hold : पट्टे पर
Lease hold nature, of : पट्टेधारी के स्वरूप की
Lease without term : निरवधि पट्टा
Least possible delay : जहाँ तक हो कम से कम विलम्ब
Leave account : छुट्टी लेखा
Leave admissibility certificate : छुट्टी स्वीकार्यता प्रमाणपत्र
Leave admissible : अनुज्ञेय अवकाश
Leave asked for maybe sanctioned : मांगी गई छुट्टी मंजूर की गई
Leave at his credit : उसके हिसाब में जमा छुट्टी

Leave availed of : ली गयी छुट्टी
Leave is due at his credit : उसके हिसाब में जमा छुट्टी
Leave of court : न्यायालय की स्वीकृति
Leave of the House : सदन की अनुमति
Leave on average pay : औसत वेतन छुटी
Leave on private affairs : निजी काम के लिए छुट्टी
Leave preparatory to retirement : सेवानिवृत्ति पूर्व छुट्टी
Leave reserve : छुट्टी रिजर्व
Leave reserve staff : छुट्टी रिजर्व कर्मचारी
Leave salary : अवकाश वेतन
Leave salary and pension contribution : अवकाश वेतन और पेंशन अंशदान
Leave taken in conjuntion : एक ही क्रम में ली गई छुट्टी
Leave to appeal : अपील के लिए अनुमति
Leave to disclaim : दावा त्याग करने की अनुमति
Leave to issue execution : निष्पादन को जारी रखने की अनुमति
Leave vacancy : अवकाश रिक्ति
Ledger of stock : स्टॉक लेजर खाता
Legacy for beneficiaries : हितधारियों के लिए वसीयत
Legal character : विधिक स्वरूप
Legal condition : वैध शर्त
Legal defect : विधिक त्रुटि
Legal incapacity : वैध असमर्थता
Legal obligation : कानून प्रदत्त जिम्मेदारी
Legal remembrancer : विधि परामर्शी
Legal representative : विधिक प्रतिनिधि
Legal tender : विधिक संविदा
Legally bound to appear : हाजिर होने के लिए वैध रूप से आबद्ध
Legally bound to do : करने के लिए वैध रूप से आबद्ध
Legally compellable : वैध रूप से विवश किया जाना आदि
Legally competent : विधिसक्षम व्यक्ति
Legally evicted : वैध रूप से बेदखल किया गया

Legible handwriting : सुवाच्य लिखाई
Legislative business : विधायी कार्य
Legislative capacity : विधायी हैसियत
Legislative powers : विधायी शक्तियाँ
Legislative procedure : विधायी कार्यविधि
Legitimate origin : आरम्भ से ही वैध
Length of notice : सूचना की कालावधि
Less than adequate : पर्याप्त से कम
Less than proportional to : के अनुपात से कम
Let us wait for sometime : कुछ समय प्रतीक्षा की जाए
Lethal weapon : घातक हथियार
Letting value : भाड़ा मूल्य
Letting value of land : भूमि का भाड़ा मूल्य
Level headed officer : संतुलित पदाधिकारी
Level of prices : मूल्य स्तर
Levied by attachment : कुर्की द्वारा उद्ग्रहीत
Levy a tax : कर उगाहना
Levy of cess : उपकर उगाहना
Lex tallienis : प्रतिषेध विधि
Liabilities and assets : दायित्व और परिसंपत्तियाँ
Liabilities lawfully incurred : विधितः उठाये गए दायित्व
Liability limited : परिसीमित दायित्व
Liability of a capital nature : पूँजी की प्रकृति वाला दायित्व
Liable for debts : ऋणों का देनदार
Liable of account : हिसाब का देनदार
Liable to attachment : कुर्की के दायित्व के अधीन
Liable to be apprehended : पकड़े जाने के दायित्व के अधीन
Liable to be confiscated : जब्त किये जाने लायक
Liable to be punished : दंडनीय
Liable to disciplinary action : अनुशासनात्मक कार्यवाही के योग्य
Liable to fine : जुर्माने से दंडनीय
Liable to pay : शुल्क देने का भागी
Liable to pay the duty : शास्ति का दायी

Liable to penalty : सजा पाने योग्य
Liable to termination on one week's notice : एक सप्ताह के नोटिस पर समाप्त किया जा सकता है
Liable Liaison officer : संपर्क अधिकारी
Liable Libellous matter : अपमान लेखीय सामग्री
Liable Lie from, no appeal shall : से कोई आपत्ति नहीं होगी
Lien on post : पद पर पुनः अधिकार
Lien right of : धारणा अधिकार
Lieu thereof, in : उसके बदले में
Life annuity : आजीवन वार्षिकी
Light house : प्रकाश स्तम्भ
Light responsibility : हलकी जिम्मेदारी
Like sanction : वैसी ही मंजूरी
Likeable officer : पसंद के लायक पदाधिकारी
Likely to adversely effect : प्रतिकूल प्रभाव पड़ने / डालने की संभावना
Limit, time : समय सीमा
Limited by guarantee : प्रतिभूति से सीमित
Limited by notice : सूचना से परिसीमित
Limited by this act : इस धारा से परिसीमित
Limited concern : सीमित देयता प्रतिष्ठान
Limited risk : दायित्व का खतरा
Limited tender : दायित्व संविदा
Line of action : कार्य की दिशा
Line of communication : संचार की दिशा
Linguistic minorities : भाषाई अल्पसंख्यक
Link language : संपर्क भाषा
Link the file : फाइल जोड़ें / संयुक्त करें
Linked file : सम्बद्ध फाइल
Linked file is kept below : सम्बद्ध फाइल नीचे लगी है
Liquidated damages : परिनिर्धारित / निर्धारित हर्जाना
Liquidated demand : निर्धारित मांग

Liquidation of debt : ऋणसमापन
Lis pendeus : विचाराधीन वाद / चल रहा मुकदमा
List of business : कार्य-सूची
Litera legis : विधि के शब्द
Livestock development : पशुधन विकास
Living wage : निर्वाह मजदूरी
Loans and advances : उधार तथा अग्रिम
Local act : स्थानीय अधिनियम
Local expression jurisdiction : स्थानिक शब्द प्रयोग
Local fund accounts : स्थानीय निधि लेखा
Local limit : स्थानीय सीमा
Locate the irregularities : अनियमितताओं का पता लगाएँ
Lodge an account : लेखा दाखिल करना
Lodge objection in writing : लिखित आपत्ति दाखिल करना
Lodge suit : मुकदमा करना
Lodging charges : आवास व्यय
Long delays : अधिक विलम्ब
Long hand judgement : हस्तलिपि में निर्णय
Long over due : बहुत पहले से अपेक्षित / निर्धारित समय से अधिक हो जाना
Long range planning : दीर्घावधि योजना
Long standing complaint : दीर्घकालिक शिकायत
Look after the work : काम देखें
Loose about utterances : बोलचाल में संयम का अभाव
Loss in transit : मार्ग में खो जाना
Loss is not due to negligence, carelessness or dishonesty on the part of any staff : किसी कर्मचारी की असावधानी या बेईमानी के कारण यह नुकसान नहीं हुआ है
Loss occasioned by neglect : लापरवाही / असावधानी से हुई हानि
Loss of office : पद-हानि
Loss sustained : हुई हानि / हानि उठाई गई
Losses may be written off : नुकसान को बट्टेखाते में डाला जाए

Lot of delay has occurred in the disposal of this case : इस प्रकरण को निपटाने में काफी विलम्ब हो गया है

Lower division : निम्न श्रेणी

Lower in rank : पंक्ति में निम्नतर

Lower limit : निचली सीमा

Lower selection grade : निम्न प्रवर क्रम

Lower stage in time scale : समयमान में निचली अवस्था

Lowest quotation : सबसे कम भाव

Lucid and precise : स्पष्ट और ठीक

Lucrative offer : लाभदायक प्रस्ताव

Lurking doubt : मामूली संदेह

Lying to credit : जमाखाते में पड़ी

■■

M

Made it quite clear : यह बिलकुल स्पष्ट कर दिया गया है
Made to order : आर्डर से बनाया गया
Magistrate committing : सुपुर्द करने वाला जज
Maintain grip over staff : कर्मचारियों पर पकड़ रखना
Maintain proper account : उचित हिसाब रखना
Maintenance and repairs : रखरखाव और मरम्मत
Maintenance of discipline : अनुशासन बनाए रखना
Major and minor work : प्रधान तथा गौण कार्य
Major head : मुख्य शीर्ष
Majority of not less than two third : दो-तिहाई से कम बहुमत नहीं
Make a memorandum : ज्ञापन बनाना
Make a note : नोट करना
Make a partition : याचिका बनाना
Make an assertion : निश्चयपूर्वक कहना
Make apology : माफी माँगना
Make available : सुलभ कराना
Make award : पंचाट देना
Make away with : लेकर भाग जाना
Make best of one's capacities : अपनी सामर्थ्य का यथाशक्ति उपयोग करना
Make contract : संविदा करना
Make default in performance of duty : कर्तव्यपालन में चूक करना
Make due provision : सम्यक व्यवस्था करना
Make good : चुका देना / पूरा करना
Make good the deficiency : कमी पूरी करना
Make good the loss : हानि की पूर्ति करना
Make head way : प्रगति करना / प्रशस्त करना
Make interim arrangement : अंतरिम व्यवस्था करना

Make public	: लोकविदित करना
Make special note of the decision	: इस निर्णय को विशेष रूप से नोट कर लें
Make the minutes	: कार्यावृत्त तैयार करना
Make up his deficiencies	: अपनी कमियों को दूर करना
Make use of	: का इस्तेमाल करना
Making good of the sum	: पूरी धनराशि देना
Mala in se	: स्वतः दोषपूर्ण
Malicious act	: द्वेषपूर्ण कार्य
Malus usuo	: कुप्रथा
Man-hours	: कार्य के घंटे
Manage himself	: अपनी देखभाल करना
Mandays lost	: नष्ट श्रमदिन
Manipulation of accounts	: हिसाब में जोड़तोड़ करना
Manner and form	: रीति और रूप
Margin money scheme	: सीमान्त धन योजना
Margin of deviation	: अंतर की मात्रा
Marginal note	: हाशिये की टिप्पणी
Marginal utility	: सीमान्त उपयोगिता
Marginally noted	: हाशिये में नोट किया गया
Marine survey	: समुद्री सर्वेक्षण
Mark of honour	: सम्मान का प्रतीक
Mark of injury	: क्षति चिह्न
Marking and sorting	: चिह्न लगाना और छाँटना
Mass picketing	: सामूहिक धरना
Massive demonstration	: विराट प्रदर्शन
Master of details	: सूक्ष्म विवरण देने में प्रवीण
Matching contribution	: समरूप अभिदाय
Material alteration	: सारभूत परिवर्तन
Material change	: सारभूत परिवर्तन
Material circumstances	: अहम् परिस्थितियाँ
Material defect	: तात्विक त्रुटि
Material error	: तात्विक त्रुटि

Material fact : सारवान तथ्य
Material feature : सारवान बात
Material form : सारवान रूप
Material information : अहम् सूचना
Material irregularity : सारवान अनियमितता
Material part : अहम् भाग
Material proposition : अहम् प्रतिपादन
Material question : अहम् प्रश्न
Material resources : अहम् संसाधन
Material statement : अहम् कथन
Material time : अहम् समय
Materially affect : तात्विक रूप से प्रभाव डालना
Materially false : तात्विक रूप से गलत
Materially increase : तात्विक वृद्धि होना
Materially interfere : तत्वतः विघ्न डालना
Materially leave on full pay : पूर्ण वेतन पर प्रसूति अवकाश
Matter and style : विषय और शैली
Matter connected therewith : तत्सम्बन्ध विषय
Matter has already been considered : मामले पर विचार किया जा चुका है
Matter has been examined : मामले की जाँच की गई है
Matter in difference : मामले पर मतभेद
Matter is receiving attention : मामले पर ध्यान दिया जा रहा है
Matter is under correspondence : मामले के सम्बन्ध में पत्र-व्यवहार चल रहा है
Matter is under disposal : मामले का निपटारा हो रहा है
Matter of a routine nature : सामान्य ढंग का प्रकरण
Matter of extreme urgency : विशेष शीघ्रता का प्रकरण
Matter of fact statement : तथ्य कथन
Matter of public nature : जनहित का विषय
Matter under reference : निर्देशाधीन विषय
Matured claim : परिपक्व दावा
May a reference be made to : क्या ---- को लिखा जाए

May be admitted	:	प्रविष्ट किया जा सकता है
May be admitted to bail	:	जमानत की जाए
May be alter the destination	:	क्या गंतव्य बदल दिया जाए
May be alter the route	:	क्या रास्ता बदला जाए
May be called	:	बुलाया जाए / कहा जाए
May be commenced	:	प्रारम्भ किया जाए
May be dealt with	:	बरती जाए
May be debited to	:	नामे डाला जाए
May be deferred to	:	को हटाया जाए
May be disposed of	:	बेचा जाए / निपटाया जाए
May be excused	:	माफ किया जाए
May be filed	:	फाइल किया जाए
May be law determined	:	विधि द्वारा अवधारित करें
May be obtained	:	प्राप्त किया जाए
May be perused	:	विहित किया जाए
May be prescribed	:	विहित किया जाए
May be reckoned as	:	लेखबद्ध किया जाए
May be requested to clarify	:	स्पष्ट करने के लिए निवेदन किया जाए
May be reverted to the former post	:	पिछले पद पर परावर्तित कर दिया जाए
May call for	:	माँगा जा सकता है
May charge the amount	:	रकम चार्ज की जा सकती है
May deem necessary	:	आवश्यक समझें
May fix	:	नियम कर सकेगा
May glance through	:	पर निगाह डाल लें
May kindly accord sanction	:	कृपया स्वीकृति प्रदान करें
May kindly see for remark	:	कृपया देखकर अपना विचार दें
May perhaps feel inclined to consider the proposal favourably	:	कदाचित प्रस्ताव पर अनुकूल दृष्टि से विचार करना चाहें
May plead	:	अभिवचन कर सकेगा
May please furnish the requisite information	:	कृपया निर्दिष्ट सूचना भेजें

May please see before issue : जारी होने के पहले कृपया देख लें

May please see with reference to marginal 'A' : कृपया हाशिये के (क) के सन्दर्भ में देखें

May prove : साबित कर सकेगा

May take steps : कार्यवाही कर सकेगा

May the proposal be accepted : क्या प्रस्ताव स्वीकार कर लिया जाए

Means by all : निस्संदेह / अवश्यमेव

Means ends relationship : साधन-साध्य सम्बन्ध

Means of livelihood : आजीविका के साधन

Means of living : आजीविका के साधन

Medical charges : चिकित्सा व्यय

Medical relief : चिकित्सा - सहायता

Mediocre in ability : मध्यम योग्यता वाला

Medium current liabilities : चालू दायित्वों का निर्वाह करना

Medium term credit : मध्यावधि उधार

Meet liabilities : दायित्वों की पूर्ति करना

Meet the end of justice : न्याय का उद्देश्य पूरा होना

Member in charge : प्रभारी सदस्य

Member secretary : सदस्य सचिव

Memo of minor points : गौण विषयों का ज्ञापन

Memo under reference : निर्देशाधीन ज्ञापन

Memoranda of documents : दस्तावेजों का ज्ञापन

Memorandum book : याददाश्त पुस्तक

Memorandum of a body : निकाय का ज्ञापन

Memorandum of an agreement : करार का ज्ञापन

Memorandum of appeal : अपील का ज्ञापन

Memorandum of substance : सार का ज्ञापन

Menial establishment : चतुर्थ श्रेणी स्थापना

Mentioned above overhead expenses : उपरोक्त सीमा से अधिक व्यय

Mere supposition : कल्पना मात्र

Merged states : विलीन राज्य

Merger of grades : ग्रेडों का विलयन

Merit tempered with seniority : योग्यता प्रधान ज्येष्ठता गौण
Meriting consideration : विचार करने योग्य
Meritorious service : सराहनीय सेवा
Merits and demerits : गुण और दोष
Merits of performance : प्रस्तुति के गुण-दोष
Mesne profits : अंतःकालीन लाभ
Metalled road : पक्की सड़क
Method of compulsion : विवश करने का साधन
Method of disposal : निपटारे की रीति
Method of instruction : शिक्षण का तरीका
Mileage allowance : मील भत्ता
Minimum living wage : न्यूनतम निर्वाह मजदूरी
Minor deviation : मामूली अंतर
Minor head : गौण शीर्ष
Minor irrigation : लघु सिंचाई
Minor schemes : लघु योजनाएँ
Minus item : ऋणात्मक मद
Minute of dissent : विसम्मति टिप्पणी
Minutes of sitting : बैठक का कार्यवृत्त
Minutest details : सूक्ष्मतम विवरण
Misappropriated amount : दुर्विनियोजित राशि
Misappropriated of accounts : लेखा दुर्विनियोजन
Miscarriage of justice : न्याय की हत्या
Miscellaneous general services : विविध सामान्य सेवाएँ
Miscellaneous register : प्रकीर्ण रजिस्टर
Misconception of fact : तथ्य का भ्रम
Misrepresentation of facts : तथ्यों की गलतबयानी
Missionary spirit : सेवा भाव
Misstatement be rectified : गलत विवरण सुधार लिया जाए
Mistake under a : भूल में / भूल से
Mixed economy : मिश्रित अर्थव्यवस्था
Mode of life : जीवन का ढंग

Mode of proceeding : कार्यवाही का ढंग
Moderate ability : मध्यम योग्यता
Moderate means : सीमित साधन
Modus operandi : कार्यप्रणाली
Modus vivendi : निर्वाह रीति / जीवनचर्या
Monentary fund : मुद्राकोष
Monentary grant : आर्थिक अनुदान
Monentary limit : आर्थिक सीमा
Money credited to public accounts : लोक लेखाओं में जमा धन
Money decree : धन डिक्री
Money out of consolidated fund : संचित निधि से धन
Money paid receipt : भुगतान की रसीद
Monopoly price : एकाधिकार कीमत
Moral and material abandonment : नैतिक और भौतिक त्याग
Moral convenient : अधिक सुविधाजनक
Moral rectitude : आचार-विचार की शुद्धता
Moral turpitude : नैतिक अधमता
Mortgage by conditional sale : सशर्त विक्रय बंधक
Mortgaged simple : सादा बंधक
Motion for consideration : विचारार्थ प्रस्ताव
Motion moved : प्रस्ताव प्रस्तुत हुआ
Motion of adjournment : स्थगन प्रस्ताव
Motion of thanks : धन्यवाद प्रस्ताव
Movable court : चालित न्यायालय
Move a court : मुकदमा चलाना
Move a resolution : प्रस्ताव रखना
Much time has elapsed : काफी समय बीत गया है
Multifarious duties : बहुमुखी कर्तव्य
Multiparty system : बहुदलीय पद्धति
Multiracial council : नगर पालिका
Multiracial funds : नगरपालिका धन

Multiracial society : बहुजातीय समाज
Mushroom growth : सहसा वृद्धि / अति-वृद्धि
Must be rigidly adhered to : कड़ाई के साथ पालन किया जाए
Muster roll : उपस्थिति नामावली
Mutation proceedings : नामांतरण कार्यवाहियाँ
Mutatis mutandis : यथोचित परिवर्तनों सहित
Mutilated bill : कटा-फटा बिल
Mutual aid pact : परस्पर सहायता समझौता

■■

N

Naked power : पशु शक्ति / अनियंत्रित
Name card : नाम पर्ची
Narrative of the case : प्रकरण का तथ्य वर्णन
Narrow majority : बहुत थोड़ा बहुमत
National awakening : राष्ट्रीय जागरण
National extensional development block : राष्ट्रीय विस्तार विकास खंड
National income : राष्ट्रीय आय
National integration : राष्ट्रीय एकता
National sample survey : राष्ट्रीय नमूना सर्वेक्षण
National savings scheme : राष्ट्रीय बचत योजना
National spirit : राष्ट्रीय भावना
Nationalization of industry : उद्योग का राष्ट्रीयकरण
Natural deposit : प्राकृतिक निक्षेप
Natural justice : प्राकृतिक न्याय
Natural order : नैसर्गिक व्यवस्था
Natural phenomenon : नैसर्गिक घटना
Natural presumption : सहज धारणा
Natural resources : प्राकृतिक संसाधन
Naturalisation of aliens : विदेशियों का देशीकरण
Nature and character : प्रकृति और लक्षण
Nature and composition : प्रकृति और गठन
Nature of Interest : हित का स्वरूप
Nature and degree of the offence : अपराध की प्रकृति और मात्रा
Nature of act : कार्य की प्रकृति
Nature of agency : अभिकरण की प्रकृति
Nature of causes : कारणों की प्रकृति
Nature of commission : कमीशन का प्रकार
Nature of proceeding : कार्यवाही की प्रकृति
Nature of the allegation : आरोपों का स्वरूप

Nature of the case : मामले की प्रकृति
Nature of the claim : दावे की प्रकृति
Nature of the transaction : संव्यवहार की प्रकृति
Nature of the work : कार्य का स्वरूप
Naughty problems : विकट समस्या
Near at hand : पास में
Nearest to one third : एक-तिहाई के करीब
Nearly resembles : निकट सादृश्य है
Nearness of kin : जातक सम्बन्ध की निकटता
Necessary correction maybe carried out : आवश्यक संशोधन कर लिया जाए
Necessary data : आवश्यक आंकड़े
Necessary draft put up : अपेक्षित प्रारूप प्रस्तुत है
Necessary provisions have been made : आवश्यक उपबंध बना दिए गए हैं
Necessary report is still awaited : अपेक्षित रिपोर्ट की अभी तक प्रतीक्षा है
Needed for public purpose : लोक प्रयोजन हेतु आवश्यक
Needs amendment : संशोधन की आवश्यकता है
Needs close : बंद करने / रोकने की आवश्यकता है
Needs more of push : अधिक प्रेरणा की आवश्यकता है / अधिक जोर लगाने की जरूरत है
Needs no comments : टिप्पणी की आवश्यकता नहीं है
Negative reply : नकारात्मक उत्तर
Neglect of duty : कर्तव्य की उपेक्षा
Negligible quantity : अपने वैध कर्तव्यों की उपेक्षा करते हुए
Negotiable instrument : क्रय-विक्रय योग्य साखपत्र
Negotiable receipt : बेचनी रसीद
Negotiated contract : बातचीत से तय ठेका
Negotiation agreement : बातचीत से तय समझौता
Neither nor : न --- और न ही
Neither party : कोई भी पक्षकार नहीं
Nemo : कोई नहीं

Nested sampling : सैंपलिंग समूह / एकत्रित सैंपलिंग
Net amount payable Rs. : शुद्ध देय राशि
Net fixed assets : शुद्ध आय
Net loss : शुद्ध हानि
Net price : शुद्ध मूल्य
Net proceeds : शुद्ध आगम
Net result : अंतिम लाभ / अन्तिम परिणाम
Never grudges extra work : अतिरिक्त कार्यों के लिए कभी आनाकानी नहीं
Nevertheless : ऐसा होने पर भी / तथापि
New dimension : नया आयाम
New ground of claim : दावे के नए आधार
New items of expenditure : व्यय के नए मद
New procedure has been introduced : नया कार्य-स्वरूप लागू किया गया है
New trial : नया विचारण
Newly installed : नया लगाया गया
Newly set up : नए चलाये गए / नए बनाए गए
News and views : समाचार और विचार
Next below rule : तदन्तर निम्न नियम
Next day afterwards : ठीक अगले दिन
Next following : ठीक नीचे लिखा / ठीक अगला आने वाला
Next hearing has been fixed for : अगली सुनवाई ---- को होगी
Next hereinafter mentioned : इसके ठीक बाद वर्णित
Next increment in the officiating post is due : स्थानापन्न पद पर अगली वेतन वृद्धि देय
Next of rank : पंक्ति में ठीक नीचे
Next of seniority : वरिष्ठता में ठीक इसके नीचे
Next preceding : ठीक पहले का
Next succeeding : ठीक बाद का
Next succeeding day : ठीक अगला दिन
No action required : कोई कार्यवाही आवश्यक नहीं

No action seems to be called on our part	:	हमें कार्यवाही की आवश्यकता नहीं है
No admission	:	प्रवेश निषिद्ध
No admission except on official business	:	कार्यालयीन कार्यों के अतिरिक्त प्रवेश वर्जित
No appeal shall lie from	:	की अपील न होगी
No change is considered necessary	:	कोई परिवर्तन आवश्यक नहीं
No citizen shall be ineligible	:	कोई नागरिक अपात्र नहीं हो
No dated on the subject quoted above	:	विषय पर तिथि अंकित नहीं है
No decision has so far been taken in the matter	:	इस विषय में / प्रकरण में अभी तक कोई निर्णय नहीं लिया गया है
No delay call	:	अविलम्ब आवश्यकता
No demand certificate	:	बेबाकी पत्र / बेबाकी प्रमाणपत्र
No entry for vehicles	:	गाड़ियों का प्रवेश वर्जित
No exact precedent is available	:	कोई सुस्पष्ट पूर्व उदाहरण नहीं मिलता
No execution shall be issued	:	कोई भी निष्पादन जारी नहीं किया जाएगा
No funds are available	:	रकम उपलब्ध नहीं है
No further action is called for	:	कोई अगली कार्यवाही आवश्यक नहीं
No loss-profit basis	:	न हानि न ही लाभ के आधार पर
No maxima or minima have been laid down	:	कोई अधिकतम या न्यूनतम सीमा निर्धारित नहीं की गई है
No profit-loss	:	कोई लाभ-हानि नहीं
No reason to doubt	:	संदेह का कोई कारण नहीं
No reference available	:	कोई सन्दर्भ उपलब्ध नहीं
No reference is coming	:	पिछला निर्देश नहीं मिल रहा
No such representation has been received	:	इस तरह कोई अभ्यादन नहीं मिला है
No timely follow up action was taken	:	यथासमय अनुवर्ती कार्यवाही नहीं की गई
No travelling allowance will be allowed	:	यात्रा भत्ता स्वीकृत नहीं किया जाएगा

No work strike : कार्य-हड़ताल की अनुमति नहीं
Nomadic tribe : भ्रमणकारी जनजाति
Nominal inspection : नाममात्र का निरीक्षण
Nominated member : नामांकित सदस्य
Nomination paper : नामांकन पत्र
Non-aggression treaty : अनाक्रमण संधि
Non-appearance : अनुपस्थिति
Non-bailable offence : असंज्ञेय अपराध
Non-committal answer : गोलमोल उत्तर
Non-compliance of these orders will be severely viewed in future : इन आदेशों का पालन न होने पर भविष्य में कड़ी कार्यवाही की जायेगी
Non-confidential record : अगोपनीय अभिलेख
Non-controversial : निर्विवाद
Non-delivery advice : वितरण न होने की सूचना
Non-disclosure : प्रगट न किया जाना
Non-divisible expenditure : अविभाज्य व्यय
Non-edible : अखाद्य
Non-essential services : अनावश्यक सेवाएँ
Non-exempted goods : छूट-रहित सेवाएँ
Non-fulfilment : पालन न किया जाना
Non-gazetted : अराजपत्रित
Non-govt. delegate : गैर-सरकारी प्रतिनिधि
Non-judicial : गैर-न्यायिक
Non-ministerial : अलिपिक वर्गीय
Non-observance of rule : नियम का अपालन
Non-official : गैर-सरकारी
Non-official bill : अशासकीय बिल
Non-party Government : निर्दलीय शासन
Non-payment certificate : गैर-अदायगी प्रमाणपत्र
Non-pensionable : पेंशन रहित
Non-performance : न किया जाना
Non-plan expenditure : गैर-योजना खर्च
Non-practising allowance : प्रेक्टिस बंदी भत्ता

Non-production : अनुत्पादन
Non-productive consumption : अनुत्पादी उपभोग
Non-recurring expenditure : अनावर्ती व्यय
Non-recurring grant : अनावर्ती अनुदान
Non-resident interest : अनिवासी हित
Non-satisfaction : असंतुष्टिपूर्ण
Non-selection post : अप्रवरण पद
Non-statutory : अपरिनियत / गैरकानूनी
Non-technical post : गैर-तकनीकी पद
Non-violent resistance : अहिंसक प्रतिरोध
Non-working day : अवकाश का दिन
Not appearing in public : जो लोक समक्ष नहीं आती
Not forming part of : का हिस्सा न होने वाला
Not in vogue : चलन में नहीं है
Not inconsistent with any of the provisions : जो किसी उपबंध से असंगत न हों
Not later than : के बाद नहीं
Not less than : से कम नहीं
Not more than one : एक से अधिक नहीं
Not only this ...but also : मात्र ये नहीं लेकिन ये भी ----
Not otherwise provided for : जिसके सम्बन्ध में अन्य उपबंध न हो
Not payable before 1st of the next month : अगले माह की पहली तारीख के पूर्व भुगतान नहीं
Not subject to the jurisdiction : की अधिकारिता के अधीन नहीं
Not to be tolerated : सहा नहीं जाएगा
Not to yield to pressure : दबाव में नहीं आना
Not traceable : पता नहीं चलता
Not transferable : अहस्तान्तरणीय
Nota Bene (N.B.) : विशेष ध्यान दीजिये
Note and return : नोट करके वापस करें
Note of dissent : असहमति / विसम्मति टिप्पणी
Note of refusal : अस्वीकृति की टिप्पणी
Noted and returned : नोट किया गया और वापस भेजा गया

Noted below	: नीचे दिया गया / नीचे लिखा गया
Noted for future guidance	: भावी मार्गदर्शन हेतु नोट कर लिया गया
Noted thanks	: धन्यवाद टिप्पणी
Notes and orders at page ...	: पृष्ठ -------- पर दिए गए आदेश और टिप्पणियाँ
Notes on pages ...ante	: पिछले पृष्ठ ------- पर की गई टिप्पणियाँ
Nothing hereinafter contained	: इसकी कोई भी बात प्रभाव नहीं डालेगी
Nothing in clause 2 shall effect ...	: खंड 2 की किसी भी बात का ---- पर प्रभाव नहीं होगा
Nothing in this article shall apply to	: पर इस अनुच्छेद की कोई बात लागू नहीं होती
Nothing in this article shall prevent...	: इस अनुच्छेद की किसी बात से ---- में बाधा नहीं होती
Nothing in this clause shall be construed	: इस खंड की किसी बात का यह अर्थ नहीं लगाया जाएगा
Nothing shall derogate from the power of Parliament	: कोई बात संसद की शक्ति का अल्पीकरण नहीं करेगी
Nothing substantial	: कोई खास बात नहीं
Notice inviting tenders	: टेंडर मंगाने की सूचना
Notice of admission case	: मामले की स्वीकृति की सूचना
Notice of demand	: मांग की सूचना
Notice of deposit	: निक्षेप की सूचना
Notice of discharge	: सेवा-मुक्ति की सूचना
Notice server	: नोटिस तामील करना
Notification declaring forests reserved	: वनों को रक्षित घोषित करने वाली अधिसूचना
Notified area	: अधिसूचित क्षेत्र
Notified by proclamation	: उद्घोषणा द्वारा अधिसूचित
Notified for general information	: जनसाधारण वाली जानकारी हेतु अधिसूचित

Noting and drafting : टिप्पणी और मसविदा / टिप्पणी और प्रारूप-लेखन

Noting on (Pre) page 3 ante recall the case : पीछे पृष्ठ 3 की टिप्पणी इस मामले का स्मरण कराती है

Notwithstanding any rule : किसी नियम के बावजूद भी

Notwithstanding anything : किसी भी चीज के बावजूद भी

■■

O

Oath of secrecy : गोपनीयता की शपथ
Obedience to law : कानून का पालन
Obedience to summons, in : सम्मन का पालन
Obiter dictum : इतर उक्ति / प्रासंगिक उक्ति
Obituary notice : निधन सूचना
Objects and reasons : उद्देश्य और कारण
Object beneficial to mankind : आक्षेप को मान लिए जाने पर
Object of any description : किसी भी तरह का उद्देश्य
Object of body : शरीर का भाग
Object of financing : फाइनेंस का विषय
Object of legislation : कानून का विषय
Object of public utility : जनसुविधा का विषय
Objection being sustained : आक्षेप को मान लिया गया
Objection is taken : आक्षेप मंजूर किया गया
Objectionable it is highly : यह बहुत आपत्तिजनक है
Objections have been dealt with : आपत्तियों पर विचार कर लिया गया है
Objective examination : वस्तुनिष्ठ परीक्षण
Objective resolution : उद्देश्यों का कथन
Objective study : वस्तुपरक अध्ययन
Obligation to give information : सूचना देने का दायित्व
Obligation under : बाध्यता के अधीन
Obligatory attendance : अनिवार्य उपस्थिति
Obligatory between parties : पक्षकारों के बीच आबद्धकारी
Obligatory duties : अनिवार्य कर्तव्य
Obligatory expenses : अनिवार्य व्यय
Obligatory functions : अनिवार्य कार्य
Oblige himself to pay : देने के लिए अपने को बाध्य करना
Obliged to answer : उत्तर देने को बाध्य
Observance of rules : नियमों के प्रति सतर्क

Observation post : निगरानी चौकी
Observation to be made : प्रेक्षण किया जाना
Observations made above : उपरोक्त विचार
Observe and follow orders : आदेशों का अनुपालन और अनुसरण करना
Observer delegate : प्रेक्षक प्रतिनिधि
Obsolete pattern : अप्रचिलित प्रकार
Obstructions caused : उत्पन्न बाधाएँ
Obtain declaration : घोषणा-पत्र प्राप्त करें
Obtain evidence : साक्ष्य अधिप्राप्त करना
Obtain formal sanction : औपचारिक स्वीकृति प्राप्त करना
Obtain signature : हस्ताक्षर प्राप्त करना
Obtained by fraud : धोखे से प्राप्त करना
Obvious error : स्पष्ट गलती
Obvious mistake : स्पष्ट गलती
Obvious partiality : स्पष्ट पक्षपात
Occasional checks : यदा-कदा होने वाली जाँच
Occasioned by negligence : उपेक्षाजनित
Occasioned thereby : उसके कारण हुई
Occupancy tenant : मौरूसी काश्तकार
Occupational survey : व्यवसायगत सर्वेक्षण
Occupying so much space : काफी जगह घेरे हुए
Occurrence of vacancy : पद-रिक्त होना
Octroi barrier : चुंगी चौकी / नाका
Octroi duty : चुंगी / प्रवेश कर
Odd number : विषम संख्या
Of a formal character : औपचारिक प्रकार का
Of a high standard : उच्चस्तरीय
Of and from the same : उसके बारे में और उससे
Of any description : किसी भी प्रकार का
Of either sex : किस भी लिंग का
Of even number : इसी संख्या का
Of full age : पूर्ण आयु का

Of great significance : बहुत महत्त्व का
Of highly technical nature : बहुत ही तकनीकी किस्म का
Of his own accord : उसके अपने ढँग का
Of inferior quality : बुरी गुणवत्ता वाला
Of no avail : निष्फल / व्यर्थ / कोई फायदा नहीं
Of no effect : प्रभावहीन
Of rare competence : विशेष योग्यता वाला
Of the same nature : उसी ढँग का
Offence affecting the human body : मानव शरीर पर प्रभाव डालने वाला अपराध
Offence is a continuing nature : अपराध चालू रहने वाला है
Offence under section ... is clearly established : धारा ----- के अधीन अपराध साफ तौर पर सिद्ध हो चुका है
Offensive action : आक्रामक कार्यवाही
Offensive expressions : अप्रिय कटु वचन
Offensive language : अप्रिय भाषा / कटु भाषा
Offer insult : अपमान करना
Offer objection : आपत्ति करना
Offer of mediation : मध्यस्थता का प्रस्ताव करना
Offer remarks : विचार प्रकट करना / अभियुक्ति देना
Office accommodation : कार्यालय के लिए स्थान / कार्यालय द्वारा दिया गया स्थान
Office consider that : कार्यालय के विचार में
Office copy and fair copy for signature : हस्ताक्षर हेतु कार्यालय प्रति और स्वच्छ प्रति
Office elective : निर्वाचन पद
Office expenses hours : कार्यालय व्यय
Office head of : कार्यालय प्रमुख
Office is to be abolished : पद उत्सादित होना है
Office manual : कार्यालय नियम पुस्तिका
Office may note it carefully : कार्यालय कृपया इसे सावधानीपूर्वक नोट कर लें
Office may please examine : कार्यालय कृपया इसकी जाँच करें

Office memorandum : कार्यालय ज्ञापन
Office of distinction : विशिष्ट पद
Office of issue : निर्गम कार्यालय
Office of profit : लाभ पद
Office proposes : कार्यालय का प्रस्ताव है
Office put up its fair copies for approval : कार्यालय द्वारा स्वच्छ प्रति प्रस्ताव हेतु दी गई
Office to note and comply : कार्यालय कृपया ध्यान दें और अनुसरण करें
Office to take action : कार्यालय कार्यवाही करें
Office will put up draft : कार्यालय प्रारूप प्रस्तुत करेगा
Officer Commanding : कमान अधिकारी
Officer in command : कमान अधिकारी / मुख्य अधिकारी
Officer of average merit : औसत योग्यता का अधिकारी
Officer on special duty : विशेष कर्तव्याधीन अधिकारी
Officer receiving charge : कार्यभार प्राप्त करने वाला अधिकारी
Officer specially empowered : विशेषतः सशक्त अधिकारी
Offices with future : होनहार अधिकारी
Offices good : सत-प्रयत्न
Official chief : आधिकारिक प्रमुख
Official communique : सरकारी विज्ञप्ति
Official decorum : शासकीय शिष्टाचार
Official liquidator : सरकारी समापक
Official list : सरकारी सूची
Official mark : शासकीय चिह्न
Official reception : सरकारी स्वागत / स्वागत-समारोह
Official statistics : सरकारी आंकड़े
Official superior : पदीय वरिष्ठ
Official version : सरकारी कथन
Officiating appointment : स्थानापन्न नियुक्ति
Officiating arrangements proposed : प्रस्तावित स्थानापन्न व्यवस्था
Officiating pay : स्थानापन्न वेतन

Officiating promotion : स्थानापन्न प्रोन्नति

Officiating service : स्थानापन्न सेवा

Often times right : बहुधा ठीक

Omission to frame a charge, effect of : आरोप विरचित न करने का प्रभाव

Omit from the list : सूची में छोड़ देना

Omitted to be done : करने से छूट गया

On a certain day : किसी निश्चित दिन

On a conviction : दोष-सिद्धि पर

On a limited scale : सीमित मात्रा में

On a point of law : विधि के प्रश्न पर

On account of ill health : अस्वास्थ्य के कारण

On account of payments : भुगतान के कारण / संदाय के कारण

On account of reass given above : उपरोक्त कारणों से

On all fours : सादृश्य / अनुरूप

On an ad hoc bases : तदर्थ आधार पर

On an average : औसत के आधार पर

On and from the date of : इस तिथि ---- पर और इसके बाद से

On bended knees : घुटने टेककर

On ceasing to be such member : ऐसे सदस्य न रहने पर

On compassionate grounds : दया के आधार पर

On conviction : दोष सिद्ध किये जाने पर

On deputation : प्रतिनियुक्ति पर

On file please : कृपया मिसाल के साथ प्रस्तुत करें

On good Cause shown : अच्छा हेतुक दर्शित करने पर

On his account : उसके हिसाब में

On its face : देखते ही

On its merits : उसके गुण-दोष देखकर

On no account : किसी भी अवस्था में नहीं

On or about : को या उसके आसपास

On perusal of the application : आवेदन-पत्र देखने पर

On presentment : प्रस्तुत करने पर
On probati of good conduct : सदाचरण की परिवीक्षा पर
On reasable ground : युक्तिसंगत आधार पर
On receipt of your reply : आपका उत्तर प्राप्त होने पर
On relief by : के द्वारा प्रयुक्त किये जाने पर
On scrutiny into the matter : मामले की छानबीन करने पर
On the face of the application : आवेदन देखते ही
On the face of the record : अभिलेख को देखते ही
On one hand : एक तरफ
On the other hand : दूसरी तरफ
On the part of the candidate : अभ्यर्थी की तरफ से
On the pretext of : के बहाने से
On the subject noted above : उपरोक्त विषय पर
On the table of the House : सदन के पटल पर
On their own initiative : उनकी अपनी पहल से
Onus of proof : सिद्ध करने का दायित्व
Onward despatch : आगे भेजना
Open arrest : खुली गिरफ्तारी
Open court : खुला न्यायालय
Open delivery : खुली सुपुर्दगी
Open general licence : निर्बाध आम लाइसेंस
Open part file : खंड फाइल खोलें
Operation Execution phase : प्रवर्तन कार्यान्वयन अवधि
Operation of fund : निधि की संक्रिया
Operation of law, by : विधि प्रवर्तन
Operation of plan : योजना प्रवर्तन
Operation of rules : नियम प्रवर्तन
Operation of schemes : योजनाओं का प्रवर्तन
Operation shall prevail : प्रवर्तन प्रभावी होगा
Operative part : प्रभावी भाग / प्रवर्ती अंश
Opportune moment : उपयुक्त समय
Opportunity to be heard : सुनवाई का अवसर
Oppress any person : किसी व्यक्ति को सताना

Optimistic estimate : आशावादी अनुमान
Optimum condition : अनुकूलतम अवस्था
Optimum point : अनुकूलतम बिंदु
Optimum utilisation : अनुकूलतम उपयोगिता
Option left to you : आपके पास शेष विकल्प
Option of, at the : का विकल्प
Oral account : मौखिक वृत्तांत
Order communicated : आदेश भेज दिया गया
Orders are solicited : आदेश प्रार्थित है
Order incidental : आनुषंगिक आदेश
Order is passed, before : आदेश पारित किये जाने से पूर्व
Order is restored : शान्ति कायम की गई है
Order maybe issued : आदेश जारी कर दिया जाए
Order not to pay : भुगतान न करने का आदेश
Order of attachment : कुर्की का आदेश
Order of detention : निरोध का आदेश
Order of merit : गुणानुक्रम / योग्यताक्रम
Order of nature : प्रकृति की व्यवस्था
Order of performance : पालन का क्रम
Order of precedence : पूर्वता क्रम
Order of preference : अधिमान क्रम
Order of priority : प्राथमिकता क्रम
Order of time, in : समय क्रमानुसार
Order passed on appeal : अपील पर दिया गया आदेश
Orderly proceedings : व्यवस्थित कार्यवाहियाँ
Ordinary and additional powers : सामान्य और अतिरिक्त शक्तियाँ
Ordinary call : साधारण आवश्यकता
Ordinary course : मामूली अनुक्रम
Ordinary course of business : कामकाज का मामूली अनुक्रम
Ordinary course of official duty : पदीय कर्तव्य का मामूली अनुक्रम
Ordinary repair : मामूली मरम्मत
Organise on sound footing : ठोस आधार पर संगठित करना

Organizing qualities : संगठन गुणवत्ता
Oriental studies : प्राच्य विद्या
Original return in : मूल रूप से लौटाया जाता है
Ostensible means of subsistence : निर्वाह के ज्ञात साधन
Other side's version in another form : दूसरे पक्ष का कथन दूसरे रूप में
Otherwise than : से अन्यथा
Otherwise than in clerical capacity : लिपिकीय हैसियत से भिन्न हैसियत में
Otherwise than on a police report : पुलिस रिपोर्ट पर से अन्यथा
Otherwise transferred : अन्यथा अंतरित
Out of agency : अधिकरण से
Out of control points : नियंत्रण बिन्दुओं से
Out of turn : लीक से हटकर / बिना पारी आये
Out of turn allotment : बिना पारी आवंटन
Out of turn promotion : बिना पारी की पदोन्नति
Out of turn certificate : बिना पारी का प्रमाणपत्र
Outbreak of disease : रोग फैलना
Outbreak of hostilities : शत्रुता पैदा होना
Outfit allowance : वर्दी भत्ता
Outgoing file : जानेवाली फाइल
Outgoing member : पद छोड़ने वाला सदस्य
Outgoing partner : बाहर जाने वाला भागीदार
Outlay on the plan : योजना पर होने वाला व्यय
Outlay capital : पूँजी परिव्यय
Outlying area : बाहरी क्षेत्र
Outstanding devotion to duty : उत्कृष्ट कर्तव्यनिष्ठा
Outstanding liability : बकाया दायित्व
Outward register : जावक रजिस्टर
Outward return : जावक विवरणियाँ
Over a period of time : एक समय के भीतर
Over and above the (limit) : सीमा से अधिक

Over board, thrown	: बाहर फेंक दिया गया
Over commission	: अधिशासी कमीशन
Over riding decision	: अभिभावी निर्णय
Over riding effect	: अध्यारोही प्रभाव
Over rule	: विरुद्ध व्यवस्था देना
Overall deficit	: कुल घाटा
Overhead and general charges	: ऊपरी और सामान्य व्यय
Overhead cost	: ऊपरी लागत
Overstay of leave	: छुट्टी से अधिक ठहरना
Overwhelming proof	: अति-सबल प्रमाण
Owing to	: के कारण
Own motion	: स्व-प्रेरण
Owning authority	: मालिक / प्राधिकारी

■■

P

Package programme : एकमुश्त कार्यक्रम

Page for perusal and orders please : कृपया पृष्ठ देखें और आदेश दें

Pages consequently numbered : क्रमवारी पड़े हुए पृष्ठ

Pagination has not been done correctly : पृष्ठ संख्या ठीक नहीं डाली गई है

Paid and cancelled : भुगतान किया और रद्द किया

Paid by transfer : अंतरण द्वारा भुगतान

Paid off : भुगतान कर दिया गया

Paid out of fund : निधि से दिया गया

Paid up capital : समादत्त पूँजी

Paid up holding : समादत्त धृति

Paid up value : प्रदत्त मूल्य

Pains and sufferings : पीड़ा और यातना

Pains to take particular : विशेष कष्ट उठाना

Panel of experts : विशेषज्ञों का समूह

Paper for disposal : निपटान के लिए कागजात

Paper transaction : कागजी लेन-देन

Papers do not appear to have been received : ऐसा प्रतीत नहीं होता कि कागजात प्राप्त हुए हैं

Papers have been amalgamated : कागजात मिला दिए गए हैं

Papers maybe passed on to : कागजात ----- को भेज दिए जाएँ

Papers please : कृपया कागजात प्रस्तुत करें

Papers submitted : कागजात प्रस्तुत हैं

Par at : सम मूल्य पर

Par excellence : उत्कृष्ट / श्रेष्ठ

Paramount consideration : सर्वोपरि ध्यान

Parent cadre : मूल संवर्ग

Parent department : मूल विभाग संवर्ग

Part file : खंड फाइल

Part of, forming Form part of, shall : फाइल के हिस्से किये जाएँ
Part owner : आंशिक स्वामी
Part performance : आंशिक प्रस्तुति
Part with : से अलग होना
Part with the possession : स्वामित्व से अलग होना
Partial loss : आंशिक हानि
Particular in : विशेष रूप से
Particular person call : उद्दिष्ट व्यक्ति काल
Particular value : उद्दिष्ट मूल्य
Particulars give : विवरण दें
Particulars with full : पूरे विवरण सहित
Partly in order : अंशतः ठीक
Partner in : में भागीदार
Party in person : स्वयं पक्षकार
Party-in-power : सत्तारूढ़ दल
Party prosecuting suit : वाद चलाने वाला पक्षकार
Party to a submission : निवेदन का पक्षकार
Party to a suit : वाद का पक्षकार
Party to the proceeding : कार्यवाही का पक्षकार
Pass down : निकलना
Pass judgement : निर्णय देना
Pass on : आगे बढ़ा देना
Pass sentence : दंडादेश देना
Passed before a final order : अंतिम आदेश पारित किये जाने से पूर्व
Passed for Rs. : रुपये मंजूर किये गए
Passing of : चला देना
Passing of a bill : विधेयक पारित होना
Passing off : पारण पारित होना
Passing out parade : समापन परेड
Passing phase : अस्थायी अवस्था
Passive resistance : निष्क्रिय प्रतिरोध
Past command : भूतपूर्व समादेश

Past precedents : पूर्व उदाहरण
Patch work : छुटपुट काम
Patent office : पेटेंट कार्यालय
Paternal land : पैतृक भूमि
Patrol inspection : चालित - निरीक्षण
Pattern cropping : फसल क्रम
Paucity of finance : वित्त की कमी
Pauper appeals : अकिंचन अपीलें
Pauper suit : अकिंचन वाद
Pay adequate attention : यथेष्ट ध्यान देना
Pay substantive : अधिष्ठाई वेतन
Payable to order : आदेशानुसार देय
Peace public : जन-शान्ति
Peacetime economy : शांतिकालिक अर्थव्यवस्था
Pecuniary jurisdiction : धन सम्बन्धी अधिकारिता
Pecuniary liability : धन सम्बन्धी दायित्व
Pecuniary loss : धन सम्बन्धी हानि
Pecuniary penalty : धन सम्बन्धी शास्ति / जुर्माना
Pecuniary resources : धन सम्बन्धी साधन
Pecuniary reward : धन सम्बन्धी पुरस्कार
Penal code : दंड संहिता
Penal interest : दंडस्वरूप ब्याज
Penal servitude : सपरिश्रम कारावास
Penultimate paragraph of the note : टिप्पणी का अन्तिम से पहला उपात्य / पैरा
Penalty for contravention of certain orders : कुछ आदेशों के उल्लंघन के लिए दंड
Penalty or punishment : शास्ति या दंड
Penalty stipulated for : अनुबद्ध शास्ति
Pendency of a case : मामले का लंबित होना
Pensionary charges : पेंशन सम्बन्धी प्रभार
Per annum : प्रति वर्ष
Per bearer : पत्रवाहक द्वारा

Per capita : प्रतिव्यक्ति
Per contra credit : दूसरी और जमा
Per diem : प्रति दिन
Per diem of absence : गैरहाजिरी की मियाद / अनुपस्थिति की अवधि
Per se : स्वतः / अपने में स्वभावतः
Peremptory Summons : बाध्यकारी समन
Perform the obligations : बाध्यताओं को पूरा करना
Perform the work in public : इस कृति को सार्वजनिक रूप से प्रस्तुत करना
Performance of conditions : शर्तों का पालन
Performance of functions : कृत्यों का पालन
Performance of promise : वायदे का पालन
Performed specifically : पालन विनिर्दिष्टतः किया गया
Peril of life : प्राणों का खतरा
Period begins to run : काम का समय शुरू होता है अब
Period of dissolution : विघटन की अवधि
Period of limitation : परिसीमन अवधि
Periodic features in the process : कार्यवाही के दौरान आने वाली विभिन्न घटनाएँ
Periodical blocks : नियतकालिक खंड
Perishable nature : नश्वर प्रकृति
Permanent advance : स्थायी अग्रिम
Permanent lessee : स्थायी पट्टेदार
Permanent sense of grudge : स्थायी विद्वेष
Permissible maximum : अनुज्ञेय अधिकतम सीमा
Permissible upper limit : अनुज्ञेय ऊपरी सीमा
Permissible Perpetual : पहले और बाद में जोड़ने की अनुमति
Perpetual lease : शाश्वत पट्टा
Perpetual settlement : शाश्वत बंदोबस्त
Perpetual succession : स्थायी उत्तराधिकार / निरंतर क्रम
Perpetuate the memory : स्मृति कायम रखना
Perpetuity, transfer in : शाश्वत रूप में अंतरण

Persistent negligence : लगातार उपेक्षा

Persistently make default : बार-बार व्यतिक्रम करना

Persisting in refusal : इनकार पर अड़े रहना

Person aggrieved : व्यथित व्यक्ति

Person alleging himself to be the owner : अपने को स्वामी कहने वाला व्यक्ति / स्वामित्व जताने वाला

Person claiming under him : उसके अधीन होने का दावा करने वाला व्यक्ति

Person competent to act on his behalf : उसकी तरफ से कार्य करने के लिए सक्षम व्यक्ति

Person in : स्वयं

Persona non grata : अवांछनीय / अस्वीकार्य व्यक्ति

Personal hearing : व्यक्तिगत सुनवाई

Pertinent matter : सम्बद्ध बातें

Petition of appeal : अपील की अर्जी

Petty cash receipts : खुदरा रोकड़ रसीदें

Petty construction : छोटे-मोटे निर्माण

Petty time barred claim : मियाद के बाद आया हुआ छोटा-मोटा दावा

Physical verification of stock : स्टॉक का वास्तविक सत्यापन

Picking up well : काम अच्छी तरह सीख रहे हैं

Piece and bonus plan : उजरत और लाभांश योजना

Piece rate basis, on : मात्रनुपाती दर पर

Piece work : उजरती काम

Piece worker : उजरती कामगार

Piecemeal planning : खंडशः आयोजन

Pilot studies : आरंभिक अध्ययन

Pilot survey : प्रायोगिक सर्वेक्षण

Pious obligation : पुनीत कर्तव्य

Place at file : फाइल पर रखें

Place him under suspension : उसे निलंबित करें

Place of occurrence : घटना का स्थान

Place under suspension : निलंबित करना

Places of public resort : जन सैरगाह स्थल

Plain speaking : स्पष्टवादी

Plaintiff failed to appear : वादी उपस्थित नहीं हुआ

Plan expenditure : योजना व्यय

Planning and method : योजना और ढँग

Plea advanced by him : उसके द्वारा प्रस्तुत तर्क

Plea of guilty : दोषी होने का अभिवचन

Plea taken by the employee is not acceptable : कर्मचारी द्वारा दिया गया तर्क मान्य नहीं है

Plead guilty : अपराध स्वीकार करना

Pleasant to deal with : उसके साथ काम करने में प्रसन्नता है

Please adduce evidence : कृपया साक्ष्य प्रस्तुत कीजिये

Please arrange to spare Shri ... at the earliest : कृपया श्री ---- को यथाशीघ्र भारमुक्त करने की व्यवस्था करें

Please bring : कृपया लाइए

Please call for : कृपया बुला लें

Please carry out the orders : कृपया आदेशों का पालन करें

Please circulate and file : कृपया घुमाकर फाइल करें

Please classify : कृपया वर्गीकरण करें

Please compare with your specifications : कृपया अपने विवरण से तुलना करें

Please comply before due date : कृपया पहले से इसका पालन किया जाए

Please discuss : चर्चा कीजिये / कृपया चर्चा करें

Please examine : कृपया जाँच कीजिये

Please expedite : कृपया शीघ्र निपटाइए

Please expedite compliance : कृपया शीघ्र अनुपालन करें

Please explain : कृपया स्पष्ट करें

Please fix the date and time of the meeting : कृपया मिलने का समय और स्थान तय करें

Please frame charge sheet with statement of facts : तथ्यों के विवरण के साथ आरोपपत्र तैयार करें

Please furnish previous papers of the case : कृपया मामले के पुराने कागजात प्रस्तुत करें

Please give priority to : कृपया --- को प्राथमिकता दें

Please handover charge : कृपया कार्यभार सौंपें

Please inform accordingly : कृपया तदनुसार सूचना दें

Please investigate and report : कृपया जाँच करें और जानकारी दें

Please issue reminder : कृपया अनुस्मारक भेजें

Please make a special note of this decision : कृपया इस निर्णय को विशेष रूप से नोट कर लें

Please note down on the notice board : कृपया नोटिस बोर्ड पर लिख लें

Please note in the register : कृपया रजिस्टर में लिख लें

Please obtain on personal contact : कृपया व्यक्तिगत संपर्क स्थापित करके प्राप्त करें

Please obtain the explanation : कृपया जवाब-तलब करें

Please prepare precis of the case : कृपया मामले की संक्षेपिका प्रस्तुत करें

Please put up case file : कृपया मामले की फाइल प्रस्तुत करें

Please put up draft reply : कृपया उत्तर का प्रारूप प्रस्तुत करें

Please put up papers early : कृपया कागजात अविलम्ब प्रस्तुत करें

Please put up the case with previous papers : कृपया प्रकरण को पूर्व पत्रों के साथ प्रस्तुत करें

Please put up with previous papers : कृपया पूर्व पत्रों के साथ प्रस्तुत करें

Please quote authority : कृपया प्राधिकार प्रस्तुत करें

Please recast draft as discussed : कृपया चर्चानुसार ड्राफ्ट का पुनर्लेखन करें

Please reconcile the discrepancy in the entries : कृपया असंगति का समाधान करें

Please refer to this office memo under reference : कृपया इस कार्यालय का निर्देशित ज्ञापन देखें

Please reply by return and oblige : कृपया लौटती डाक से उत्तर देकर अनुग्रहीत करें

Please reply forthwith : कृपया अविलम्ब उत्तर दें

Please report : कृपया रिपोर्ट / जानकारी देखें

Please see me : कृपया मुझसे मिलें

Please see overleaf : कृपया पिछला पृष्ठ देखें
Please see the preceding notes : कृपया पिछली टिप्पणी देख लें
Please see the undersigned : कृपया अधोलिखित व्यक्ति को प्रेषित करें
Please send a copy of your letter : कृपया अपने पत्र की प्रति भेजें
Please send alternative proposals : कृपया वैकल्पिक प्रस्ताव भेजें
Please sign in Hindi : कृपया हिंदी में हस्ताक्षर करें
Please sign the certificate below : कृपया प्रमाणपत्र पर नीचे हस्ताक्षर करें
Please state definite reasons : कृपया निश्चित कारण बताइये
Please state for the information of the : कृपया ---- की जानकारी के लिए बताइये
Please submit explanation on or before : कृपया तारीख ----- को या इसके पहले स्पष्टीकरण दें
Please submit preliminary report : कृपया प्राथमिक रिपोर्ट प्रस्तुत करें
Please submit without further delay : कृपया अविलम्ब प्रस्तुत करें
Please take delivery : कृपया पार्सल छुड़ा लीजिये
Please take special note of : कृपया विशेष ध्यान रखें कि
Please turn over : कृपया पलटें (पृष्ठ)
Please verify : कृपया सत्यापन करें
Pleased to withdraw : प्रसन्नतापूर्वक वापस लेते हैं
Pledged as security : प्रतिभूति के रूप में गिरवी रखी गई
Plenary session : पूर्ण अधिवेशन
Plus and minus amendments : धन-ऋण संशोधन
Plus and minus memoranda : धन-ऋण ज्ञापन
Point at issue : विचारणीय प्रश्न / वाद प्रश्न
Point of determination : अवधारण हेतु प्रश्न
Point of law : विधि की बात / कानूनी तथ्य
Point of order : व्यवस्था प्रश्न
Points of substance : सार की बातें

Point to point adjustment : बिन्दुवार समायोजन
Police grid system : पुलिस ग्रिड व्यवस्था
Policy question : नीतिगत प्रश्न
Policy statement : नीतिसम्बन्धी वक्तव्य
Polished youth : सुसंस्कृत व्यक्ति
Polite in manners : व्यवहार में नम्र
Political sufferer : राजनैतिक पीड़ित
Poll shall be taken : मतदान होगा
Popular aspirations : लोक आकांक्षाएँ
Portion marked 'A' : (क) चिह्नित भाग
Position in life : जीवन में स्थिति
Position of disadvantage : हानिकर स्थिति
Position of management : प्रबंध का पद
Position will ease : स्थिति सुधर जायेगी
Possess considerable drive and initiative : पर्याप्त उपक्रमण और अभिप्रेरणा विद्यमान है
Possible remained unfilled for the reason : पद खाली रहने का कारण यह है
Possible right : संभव अधिकार
Possible script (P.S.) : पुनश्च / पश्च लेख
Possible substantive : अधिष्ठाई / मूल पद
Possible the item into the register : यह मद रजिस्टर में दर्ज कीजिये
Posted in due course : सम्यक अनुक्रम में डाक में डालना
Postpone further proceeding : आगे की कार्यवाहियाँ स्थगित
Potential infringement : संभाव्य अतिलंघन
Power in his : उसकी शक्ति में
Power of revision : पुनरीक्षण की शक्ति
Power to assume management : प्रबंध हाथ में लेने की शक्ति
Power to exempt : छूट देने की शक्ति
Power to legislate : विधि निर्माण की शक्ति / कानून बनाने की ताकत
Power to prohibit commission of public nuisance : सार्वजनिक उपद्रव को रोकने की शक्ति

Power to summon : बुलाने की शक्ति

Power to suspend execution of orders : आदेशों के निष्पादन को स्थगित करने की शक्ति

Powers vested implied meaning : निहित अधिकार

Practice and procedure : पद्धति और प्रक्रिया

Practice normally prevailing : सामान्यतः प्रचलित प्रथा

Practice of country : देश का चलन

Practise deception : प्रवंचना करना

Praiseworthy and meritorious work : प्रशंसनीय और उत्कृष्ट कार्य

Pre-eminently deserves promotion : प्रोन्नति के लिए सर्वाधिक योग्य है

Pre-requisite : पूर्वापेक्षित

Pre-supposed reason : पूर्वकल्पित कारण

Precarious financial position : अनिश्चित वित्तीय स्थति

Precautionary measures : सावधानी के उपाय

Precedent interest : पूर्ववर्ती हित

Preceding notes : पूर्वगामी टिप्पणियाँ

Precepts, legal : विधिक नियम

Precis at flag `A' explains the point at issue : पताका (क) पर दी गई संक्षेपिका विशेष प्रश्नों को स्पष्ट करती है

Precise account : यथार्थ विवरण

Precise knowledge : यथार्थ ज्ञान

Precise meaning : यथारूप अर्थ

Precise term of notice : सूचना के यथावत शब्द

Precisely expressed : ठीक-ठीक अभिव्यक्त

Precision of experiment : प्रयोग की यथार्थता

Predecessor in office : पूर्व पदाधिकारी

Predecessor in title : हक का पूर्वाधिकारी

Predecessor's decision : पूर्वाधिकारी का निर्णय

Predetermined specification : पूर्वनिर्धारित विवरण

Prefer an appeal : अपील करना

Prefer appeal against an order : आदेश के विरुद्ध अपील करना

Prefer belated claim to the post : किसी पद के लिए देर से दावा करना
Preferential payment : अधिमानी संदाय
Preferential right : अधिमानी अधिकार
Preferential treatment : अधिमानी उपचार / अधिमानी व्यवहार
Prejudice of, to the : के प्रतिकूल / के लिए हानिकारक
Prejudicial to : के प्रतिकूल / के लिए हानिकारक
Prejudicial to public safety : जनसुरक्षा के प्रतिकूल
Preliminary advice : प्राथमिक परामर्श
Preliminary decree : प्राथमिक डिक्री
Preliminary report : प्राथमिक जानकारी / प्राथमिक सूचना
Premature discovery : समयपूर्व प्रकटीकरण
Preparation of easibility report : साध्यता रिपोर्ट तैयार करना
Preparation of working plan : योजना तैयार करना
Preparatory to retirement : सेवानिवृत्ति से पहले
Prepartition claims : विभाजन से पहले के दावे
Prerogation of mercy : दया का परम अधिकार
Prerogative writs, high : उच्च परमाधिकार याचिका
Prescribed arrangement : विहित इंतजाम
Prescribed by law : विधि विहित
Prescribed form : विहित / निर्धारित फार्म
Prescribed manner : निर्धारित ढँग / विहित रीति
Prescribed person : विहित व्यक्ति
Prescribed standard : विहित मानदंड
Prescribed time limit : विहित समयसीमा
Presence and hearing in the : उपस्थिति में और सुनते हुए
Present an appeal : अपील प्रस्तुत करना
Present his/her case : अपना पक्ष प्रस्तुत करना
Present in the proceeding : प्रक्रिया में उपस्थित
Presentation of records : अभिलेखों की प्रस्तुति
Presentation of results : निर्णय की प्रस्तुति / फैसला देना
Preservative treatment : परीक्षणात्मक उपचार
Preserve peace : शान्ति बनाए रखें
President's assent : राष्ट्रपति की अनुमति

President's proclamation : राष्ट्रपति की उद्घोषणा
Press a claim : दावे पर जोर देना
Press and platform : समाचारपत्र और सभा
Press communique : प्रेस-विज्ञप्ति
Press copy : प्रेस प्रति
Press handout : प्रेस पत्र
Press party : पत्रकार दल
Press representative : प्रेस-प्रतिनिधि
Pressure of work : काम का दबाव
Presume, may : उपधारण कर सकेगा
Presumption is confirmed : धारणा की पुष्टि हो जाती है
Presumption is correct : धारणा सही है
Presumption of fact : तथ्य की उपधारणा
Presumption of law : विधि की उपधारणा
Presumption pay : प्रकल्पित वेतन
Prevent offences : अपराधों का निवारण करना
Prevention of harm : अपहानि का निवारण
Prevention of shortage : कमी को रोकना
Preventive detention : निवारक नजरबंदी
Preventive measure : निवारक उपाय
Preventive service : निवारक सेवा
Previous acquittal : पूर्व दोषमुक्ति
Previous and later references : पिछले और बाद के हवाले
Previous authority : पूर्व प्राधिकार
Previous order : पिछले आदेश
Previous papers put up as desired : निर्देशानुसार पिछले कागजात प्रस्तुत हैं
Previous sanction is necessary : पूर्व स्वीकृति आवश्यक है
Previous service : पिछली सेवा
Previous station : पिछला पद-स्थान
Priced publication : समूल्य प्रकाशन
Prima facie evidence : प्रथमदृष्ट्या साक्ष्य
Prima facie proof : प्रथमदृष्ट्या साक्ष्य

Primarily agent : प्राथमिक अभिकर्ता
Primarily education : प्राथमिक शिक्षा
Primarily employer : प्रधान नियोजक
Primarily in person : स्वयं मालिक
Primarily instrument : मूल लिखत
Primarily Managing agency : प्रधान प्रबंध अभिकरण
Primarily quality : प्राथमिक गुणवत्ता
Primarily rule : प्राथमिक नियम
Primarily unit : प्राथमिक इकाई
Printing and stationery : मुद्रण तथा लेखन सामग्री
Priority indent : अग्रता माँगपत्र
Priority marking : अग्रता अंकन / प्राथमिकता अंकन
Priority under the law : विधि के अधीन अग्रता
Privacy, intrude upon the : एकान्तता का अतिक्रमण करना
Private defence, right of : व्यक्तिगत प्रतिरक्षण का अधिकार
Private in : एकांत में
Privilege leave : रियायती छुट्टी
Privilege motion : विशेषाधिकार प्रस्ताव
Privileged communication : विशेषाधिकार प्राप्त संसूचना
Privileges Committee : विशेषाधिकार समिति
Privy Purse : प्रिवी पर्स / राजभत्ता
Privy to the offence : अपराध से संसर्गित
Prize bond : इनामी बॉण्ड
Probable cause for believing : विश्वास हेतु संभावित कारण
Probable consequence : अधिसंभाव्य परिणाम
Probable date of departure : के प्रस्थान की संभावित तारीख
Probation of good conduct : सदाचरण की परिवीक्षा
Procedural due process of law : प्रक्रिया सम्बन्धी सम्यक विधि व्यवस्था
Procedural matters : प्रक्रियात्मक मामला / प्रक्रियात्मक विषय
Procedural rules : कार्यविधिक नियमावली
Procedure laid down : निर्धारित कार्यविधि / तय प्रक्रिया
Procedure or practice : कार्यवाही या प्रक्रिया

Procedure should be strictly adhered to : कार्यविधि का कड़ाई से पालन होना चाहिए
Procedure to be adopted : अपनाई जाने वाली प्रक्रिया
Proceed to hear : सुनने के लिए अग्रसर होना
Proceed suit shall : वाद आगे चलेगा
Proceeding be stayed : कार्यवाही रोकी जाए
Proceedings of meeting : अधिवेशनों की कार्यवाही
Proceeds of fines : जुर्माना के आगम
Process of counterfeiting : कूटकरण की प्रक्रिया
Process the case for settlement : निपटान के लिए फाइल तैयार करें
Process under control : कार्यवाही नियंत्रण में
Process under colour of : कार्यवाही के नाम पर
Processing data : आंकड़े प्रक्रमण
Proclaimed offender : उद्घोषित अपराधी
Proclaiming by beat of drum : मुनादी के द्वारा उद्घोषित करना
Procuring a fit person : योग्य व्यक्ति को प्राप्त करना
Procuring property by fraud : धोखाधाड़ी करके संपत्ति हासिल करना
Produce of land : भूमि की उपज
Produced as evidence : साक्ष्य प्रस्तुत करना
Production of documents : दस्तावेजों को प्रस्तुत करना
Production of produce : उपज को पेश करना
Productivity centre : उत्पादकता केंद्र
Productivity test rate : उत्पादकता परीक्षण दर
Profit and loss account : लाभ-हानि लेखा
Profit sharing scheme : लाभ वितरण योजना
Profitable character : लाभदायी स्वरूप
Profits in lieu of : के बदले में लाभ
Proforma account : कच्चा लेखा
Programme of activities : गतिविधियों का कार्यक्रम
Progressive development : उत्तरोत्तर विकास
Progressive total : आनुक्रमिक / प्रगामी योग
Prohibitory order : निषेधाज्ञा

Prolonged default : निलंबित व्यतिक्रम
Prominent position : प्रमुख स्थान
Promises alternative : वैकल्पिक वचन
Promises of public action : लोक कार्यवाही का वचन
Promises of secrecy : गुप्त रखने का वचन
Promises set of : वचन संवर्ग
Promises very well : काफी होनहार लगते हैं
Promote feelings of enmity : शत्रुता की संभावनाएँ प्रवर्तित करना
Promotion of public health : लोक स्वास्थ्य का संप्रवर्तन
Promotion posts : पदोन्नति पद
Pronouncement, authoritative : प्रामाणिक निर्णय
Pronouncing an order : आदेश सुनाना / आज्ञा देना
Proof conclusive : निश्चयात्मक सबूत
Proper accounts : उचित हिसाब / सही लेखे
Proper footing, on : उचित आधार पर
Proper service, handed to : समुचित सेवा में सौंपा गया
Proper spacing : ठीक तरह से जगह छोड़ना
Properly defined : उचित रूप से परिभाषित
Properly drawn up : समुचित रूप से तैयार किया गया
Properties of distribution : संपत्तियों का वितरण
Property passing upon death : रिक्त संपत्ति
Property return : संपत्ति लौटाई गई
Property title in : संपत्ति में स्वामित्व
Proportional representation : आनुपातिक प्रतिनिधित्व
Proportionate cost : आनुपातिक लागत
Proportionate sample : आनुपातिक नमूना
Proposal has been vetted and concurred by : प्रस्ताव देख लिया है और उससे सहमत है
Proposal is in order : प्रस्ताव नियमसंगत है / प्रस्ताव ठीक है
Proposal lacks : प्रस्ताव में कमी है
Proposal required to be vetted by finance branch : प्रस्ताव पर वित्त शाखा की सहमति आवश्यक है

Proposal to arrange direct purchase of material is agreed to : सामग्री की सीधी खरीद की व्यवस्था का प्रस्ताव स्वीकार लिया गया है
Proposal was welcomed : प्रस्ताव का स्वागत किया गया था
Propose to pass an order : आदेश देने के लिए प्रस्ताव करते हैं
Proposed amalgamation : प्रस्तावित एकीकरण
Proprietary of order : आदेश का औचित्य
Proprietary rights : स्वामित्व के अधिकार
Pro-rata share : आनुपातिक हिस्सा / यथायोग्य भाग
Pros and cops : आगा-पीछा
Prospecting for : के लिए पूर्वेक्षण
Prospective candidate : भावी अभ्यर्थी
Protect the interest : हित का संरक्षण
Protect the sovereignty : स्वतन्त्रता या प्रभुसत्ता का संरक्षण
Protection of action : कार्यवाही के लिए संरक्षण
Protection of title : स्वामित्व का संरक्षण
Protest, under : आपत्तिपूर्वक
Prove to immediate help : बहुत और त्वरित सहायक साबित होना
Provided always that : परन्तु सदा ही यह कि
Provided as : यथा उपबंधित
Provided further that : परन्तु यह और कि
Provided that : बशर्ते कि
Provided that nothing in this clause shall be construed as : परन्तु इस खंड की किसी बात का यह अर्थ नहीं किया जाएगा कि
Provision for exclusion : अपवर्जन के लिए उपबंध
Provision to roster for all recruitment and promotion categories : सभी भरती और पदोन्नति वाली कोटियों के लिए रोस्टर व्यवस्था
Provisional agenda : अनंतिम कार्यसूची
Provisional estimates : अनंतिम प्राक्कलन
Provisional List : अस्थायी सूची
Provisional order : अस्थायी आदेश
Provisional receipt : कच्ची रसीद
Provisional recognition : अस्थायी मान्यता

Provisions shall apply mutatis mutandis to	:	उपबंध यथोचित परिवर्तन सहित ---- पर लागू होंगे
Proviso to this rule	:	इस नियम के साथ शर्त
Provocation, grave and sudden	:	गंभीर और अचानक प्रकोपन
Proximo	:	आगामी महीने की
Public accounts	:	लोक लेखा
Public action	:	लोक कार्यवाही
Public address	:	सार्वजनिक भाषण
Public capacity	:	सार्वजनिक हैसियत
Public character	:	सार्वजनिक स्वरूप का
Public company	:	सार्वजनिक कंपनी
Public enters freely	:	लोग बेरोकटोक आ-जा सकते हैं
Public function	:	सार्वजनिक समारोह
Public has access judgment of the	:	लोगों को आने की स्वतन्त्रता है
Public matter	:	लोक विषयक
Public nature	:	लोक प्रकृति
Public notice	:	जन-सूचना / आम सूचना
Public notification	:	सार्वजनिक अधिसूचना
Public order	:	जन-आदेश / लोक-व्यवस्था
Public records	:	लोक लेखे
Public right	:	जन-अधिकार
Public safety	:	जन-सुरक्षा
Pull down	:	ढहाना
Pull on well	:	अच्छा सम्बन्ध रखना
Pull up	:	डाँट-डपट करना
Punctiliousness about rules and regulations	:	नियमों और विनियमों के प्रति निष्ठा
Punitive tax	:	दंडात्मक कराधान
Purchase may be approved	:	क्रय अनुमोदित किया जाए
Purporting to be done	:	किये जाने के लिए के लिए अभिप्रेरित
Purporting to be made	:	बनाने के लिए अभिप्रेरित
Purporting to be written	:	लिखे जाने के लिए अभिप्रेरित

Put a draft reply accordingly : तदनुसार उत्तर का प्रारूप प्रस्तुत किया जाए

Put into commission : चालू करें

Put up connected papers : सम्बन्धित दस्तावेज प्रस्तुत करें

Put up for orders please : आदेशों के लिए प्रस्तुत है

Put up notes : टिप्पणी देना

Put up papers immediately : अविलम्ब दस्तावेज प्रस्तुत करें

Put up reference : सन्दर्भ प्रस्तुत करें

Put up requisition : माँग प्रस्तुत करें

Put up the papers at once : कागजात तुरंत प्रस्तुत करें

■■

Quadruplicate, in	: चार प्रतियों में
Qualification chart	: योग्यता चार्ट / अर्हता सूची
Qualification prescribed	: विहित योग्यताएँ
Qualifications essential	: शैक्षणिक योग्यताएँ
Qualified for reappointment	: पुनर्नियुक्ति के लिए योग्य
Qualified ownership	: सीमित स्वामित्व
Qualified support	: सापेक्ष आधार
Qualifying clause	: विशेषक खंड
Qualifying date	: अर्हता की तारीख
Qualifying examination	: योग्यता परीक्षा
Qualifying premium	: अर्हक प्रीमियम
Qualifying service	: विशिष्ट सेवा
Quality attainable	: प्राप्य गुण
Quality control	: गुणवत्ता नियंत्रण
Quality marking	: कोटि अंकन
Quantum of	: की मात्रा
Quantum of remuneration	: पारिश्रमिक की मात्रा
Quarantine leave	: संगरोध छुट्टी
Quarterly ending on	: तिमाही
Quarterly return	: तिमाही / त्रैमासिक विवरण
Quarterly statement	: तिमाही / त्रैमासिक विवरण
Quash the order issued	: जारी किये गए सन्देश को रद्द किया जाए
Quash the proceeding	: कार्यवाही रद्द करें
Quasi-judicial	: अर्ध-न्यायिक
Quasi-permanent	: अर्ध-स्थायी
Querry has been raised	: प्रश्न उठाया गया है
Question be now put	: अब प्रश्न रखा जाए
Question in	: विचाराधीन / विवादास्पद
Question in dispute	: विवादग्रस्त प्रश्न

Question in issue : विवादित प्रश्न
Question of fact : तथ्य का प्रश्न
Question of law : विधि का प्रश्न
Question of mixed law and fact : विधि और तथ्य मिश्रित प्रश्न
Question of procedure : प्रक्रिया सम्बन्धी प्रश्न
Question of propriety : औचित्य का प्रश्न
Question out of the : प्रश्न ही नहीं उठता / असंभव
Question raised by : द्वारा उठाया गया प्रश्न
Question shall be referred : प्रश्न ---- के पास भेजा जाए
Questionable antecedents : संदिग्ध पूर्ववृत्त
Questionable conduct : संदिग्ध व्यवहार
Questionable tactics : संदिग्ध चालें
Questionnaire has been framed : प्रश्नावली तैयार कर ली गई है
Questionnaire may kindly be returned duly filled : कृपया प्रश्नावली को भरकर लौटा दें
Quick and peaceable possession : निर्बाध और शान्तिपूर्ण कब्जा
Quick as lightning : बिजली के समान तेज
Quick assets : शीघ्र विक्रय परिसंपत्ति
Quick disposal : तुरंत निपटान
Quick yielding project : शीघ्र फलदायी योजना
Quickness in disposal of case : मामलों के निपटान में शीघ्रता
Quiet type of worker : शान्ति प्रकृति के कार्यकर्ता
Quinquennial groups : पंचवर्षीय समूह
Quinquennial report : पंचवर्षीय रिपोर्ट
Quo warranto : अधिकार पृच्छा
Quorum for meeting : बैठक के लिए गणपूर्ति
Quorum is not present : गणपूर्ति नहीं हुई है
Quotation of firm is reasonable : फार्म की दर उचित है
Quotations received : प्राप्त हुए भाव
Quote reference : सन्दर्भ बताएँ
Quoted below : नीचे उद्धृत / निम्नलिखित / नीचे दिया गया
Quoting reference : सन्दर्भ देते हुए ■■

R

Racial tension : प्रजातीय तनाव
Radical planning : आमूलचूल परिवर्तनवादी योजना
Radical reform : आमूलचूल सुधार
Radio adaptation : रेडियो रूपांतरण
Radio message : रेडियो सन्देश
Raids, border : सीमा छापे
Railway fare : रेलवे किराया
Railway receipt : रेल-रसीद
Railway risk rate : रेल जोखिम दर
Railway safety : रेल सुरक्षा
Railway warrant : रेल वारंट
Rain water : बरसात का पानी
Raise army : सेना जुटाना
Raise loan : उधार लेना
Raise substantially the same issue : तत्वतः उसी प्रश्न को उठाना
Raise the amount : रकम जुटाना
Raised and maintained : बनाए गए और ठीक रखे गए
Raised the plea : यह दलील पेश की
Random effects : यदा-कदा होने वाले प्रभाव
Random fluctuations : कभी-कभार होने वाला उतार-चढ़ाव
Random permutation : कभी-कभार का आमूल परिवर्तन
Random sampling : नमूने की जाँच
Rank and file : साधारण सैनिक / सिपाही
Rank equally : एक समान होना
Rank not inferior : अनिम्न पंक्ति
Rash act : दुस्साहसपूर्ण कार्य
Rate contract : दर ठेका / संविदा
Rate in force : लागू दर / चालू दर
Rate schedule : दर अनुसूची

Rateable property : करयोग्य संपत्ति
Rateably contribute : आनुपाती अभिदाय करना
Rateably distributed : आनुपातिक रूप से वितरित
Rather lethargic : कुछ सुस्त
Ratification of special appointment : विशेष नियुक्तियों का अनुसमर्थन
Ratification of treaty : संधि का अनुसमर्थन
Rating of quality : गुणवत्ता का स्तरीकरण
Ratio chart : अनुपात-चार्ट
Ratio decidendi : निर्णय-आधार
Rational and coordinated development : युक्तिसंगत तथा समन्वित विकास
Rational answer : युक्तिसंगत उत्तर
Rational judgment : युक्तिसंगत निर्णय
Rationalization of industry : उद्योगों का युक्तिकरण
Reach an accord : एकमत होना
Reactionary forces : प्रतिक्रियावादी शक्तियाँ
Read with : से पढ़ें / के साथ पढ़ें
Readiness to be in : तैयार रहना
Readmission of the appeal : अपील का पुनः ग्रहण किया जाना
Ready cash : नकदी रोकड़
Ready money : नकद धन
Ready reckoner : शीघ्र गणक
Real or exchangeable value : वास्तविक या विनिमय मूल्य
Real person : असली व्यक्ति
Realisable assets : वसूली योग्य आस्तियाँ
Realisable value : वसूली योग्य मूल्य
Realisation of bills : बिलों की वसूली
Reappropriation of funds : निधियों का पुनर्विनियोजन
Rearrange the papers : कागजात को फिर से तरतीब से जमाइये
Reason of age, by : आयु के कारण
Reason of any emergency, by : किसी आपत्ति के कारण
Reason of inability : असमर्थता के कारण

Reason to believe : मानने का कारण / विश्वास करने का कारण
Reason to suspect : संदेह का कारण
Reasonable and proper : युक्तिसंगत और उचित
Reasonable apprehension : युक्तिसंगत आशंका
Reasonable belief : युक्तिसंगत विश्वास
Reasonable compromise : उचित समझौता
Reasonable expenses : यथोचित व्यय
Reasonable ground of suspicion : संदेह का उचित आधार
Reasonable measure : समुचित उपाय
Reasonable notice : यथोचित सूचना
Reasonable opportunity : यथोचित अवसर
Reasonable remuneration : उचित पारिश्रमिक
Reasonable wear and tear : उचित टूट-फूट
Reasons on which the order is based : जिस कारण पर यह आदेश आधारित है
Reasons which so far have been adduced : अब तक जो कारण बताये गए हैं
Reassessment of value : मूल्य का पुनर्निर्धारण
Rebut on inference : अनुमान का खंडन करना
Rebuttable presumption : खंडनीय धारणा
Rebutting evidence : खंडनकारी साक्ष्य
Recalculated rate : फिर से गणना कर निकाली गई दर
Recall and reexamine : पुनः बुलाना और पुनः परीक्षण करना
Recall from leave : अवकाश से वापस बुलाना
Recapitulation of facts : तथ्यों का सार कथन
Receipient of benefits : लाभ प्राप्तकर्ता
Receipt book : रसीद बही / प्राप्ति पुस्तिका
Receipt certificate : प्राप्ति प्रमाणपत्र
Receipt has been acknowledged : पावती भेज दी गई है
Receipt has been issued : रसीद दे दी गई है
Receipt in a complaint, on : परिवाद / शिकायत प्राप्त करने पर

Receipt in acknowledgement : पावती रसीद
Receipt in consideration : प्रतिफल की रसीद
Receipt register : प्राप्ति पंजी (रजिस्टर)
Receipt itemised : मदवार रसीद
Receipts and disbursement : प्राप्तियाँ और संवितरण
Receipts and recoveries : प्राप्तियाँ और वसूलियाँ
Receivable in evidence : साक्ष्य में लिए जाने योग्य
Receive sentence : दंडादेश पाना
Receiver has been appointed : रिसीवर (लेने वाला) नियुक्त कर दिया गया है
Receiving Centre : प्राप्ति केंद्र
Reception committee : स्वागत समिति
Reciprocal arrangement : पारस्परिक व्यवस्था
Reciprocal basis : पारस्परिक आधार
Reciprocal buying : दोतरफा खरीददारी
Reciprocal promise : व्यतिकारी वचन / दुतरफा वादा
Reciprocal provision : व्यतिकारी उपबंध
Reciprocal treatment : पारस्परिक व्यवहार
Reckonable service : हिसाब में रखने वाली सेवा / गिनी जाने योग्य सेवा
Reckoned as absence : अनुपस्थित गिना जाना
Reclaiming land : भूमि को ठीक करना
Reclamation of land : भूमि का उद्धार
Reclamation of waste land : बंजर भूमि का उद्धार
Recognise an agreement in : लिखित करार को मान्यता देना
Recognition already granted will be withdrawn : पहले दी गई मान्यता वापस ली जायेगी
Recognized agent : मान्यताप्राप्त अभिकर्ता / एजेंट
Recognized better : अधिक मान्यता
Recognized by law : कानून द्वारा मान्य
Recognized holiday : मान्यताप्राप्त अवकाश दिवस
Recommendations made by the committee : कमिटी द्वारा सुझाए गए प्रस्ताव
Recommendatory certificate : सिफारिशी प्रमाणपत्र

Recommended for favourable consideration : अनुकूल विचार के लिए सिफारिश की जाती है
Reconcile the accounts : लेखा ठीक कीजिये
Reconciliation of accounts : लेखा समाधान
Reconciliation statement : समाधान विवरण
Reconstituted committee : पुनर्गठन समिति
Record a finding : निष्कर्ष अभिलिखित करना
Record an order : आदेश अभिलिखित करना
Record maintain : अभिलेख करना
Record of rights : अधिकार-अभिलेख
Record proceeding : कार्यवाही का अभिलेख
Record room : अभिलेख-कक्ष
Record shall show : अभिलेख दर्शित करेगा / अभिलेख में दर्शित होगा
Record the reasons in writing : कारणों को लेखबद्ध कीजिये
Recorded as certified : अभिलिखित कर लिया जाए कि प्रमाणित है
Recording of data : आंकड़ों का अभिलेखीकरण
Recording of files : फाइलों का अभिलेखीकरण
Recourse to, have : आश्रय लेना
Recovery of debt reconciliation instalment : ऋण समाधान किश्त की वसूली
Recovery of dues : देय राशियों की वसूली
Recovery of loss : नुकसानों की वसूली
Recruiting roll : भरती की तालिका
Rectification of register : रजिस्टर का परिशोधन
Rectify the mistake : गलती को सुधारों
Recurring and non-recurring grants : आवर्ती और अनावर्ती अनुदान
Recurring charges : आवर्ती प्रभार
Recurring deposits : आवर्ती निक्षेप
Recurring period : आवर्ती अवधि
Recurring right : आवर्ती अधिकार
Recusancy, in the case : अवज्ञा जारी रहने की दशा में

Red hat priority demand : अति-प्राथमिकता मांग
Red tapism : लाल फीताशाही
Redeem the goods : माल का मोचन करना
Redemption charges : मोचन प्रभार
Redemption fund : विमोचन निधि
Redemption of a bond : बॉण्ड (बंध-पत्र) का मोचन
Redemption of mortgage : बंधक मोचन
Redemption value : मोचन मूल्य
Redressal of grievances : शिकायतों का निवारण
Reduce in rank : पदावनति करना
Reduce the refund : प्रतिदाय में कमी करना
Reduce to a lower grade : निम्नतर श्रेणी में अवनत करना
Reduce to a minor offence : घटाकर छोटा अपराध करना
Reduction in pay for inefficiency : अयोग्यता के कारण वेतन में कमी
Reduction of staff : कर्मचारियों में कमी करना
Redundant staff : अनावश्यक कर्मचारीगण
Refer endorsement : पृष्ठांकन के सन्दर्भ में
Refer the matter ...for orders : आदेश हेतु प्रकरण --- को भेजा जाता है
Reference is invited to : सन्दर्भ मंगाया जाता है
Reference notes on pre page : पिछले पृष्ठ पर टिप्पणी के सन्दर्भ में
Reference register : सन्दर्भ पुस्तिका
Reference to your office letter No. ... : आपके कार्यालय पत्र क्रमांक ---- के सन्दर्भ में
Reference with : के प्रति निर्देश
Reference your note on pre page : पूर्व पृष्ठ पर आपकी टिप्पणी के सन्दर्भ में
Referred to as : के नाम से निर्दिष्ट
Refixation of pay : वेतन का पुनर्नियतन
Refixing rent : किराया फिर से तय करना
Reformation of criminals : अपराधियों का सुधार
Reformist zeal : सुधारवादी उत्साह

Refresher course : पुनश्चर्या पाठ्यक्रम
Refund of freight : भाड़े की वापसी
Refund of revenue : राजस्व का प्रतिदाय / राजस्व वापसी
Refund the excess amount : अतिरिक्त रकम वापस करना
Refusing to allow : अनुमति खारिज करते हुए
Refutation of charges : आरोपों का खंडन
Regained the duties : कर्तव्य / पद पर वापसी की
Regard shall be had to : का ध्यान रखा जाए
Regarding letter under reference : संदर्भाधीन पत्र के बारे में
Regarding the captioned subject : उपर्युक्त विषय के सन्दर्भ में
Register a case : मामला दर्ज कीजिये
Register of appeals : अपील दाखिल करना
Register of births : जन्म रजिस्टर
Registered acknowledgement due : पंजीकृत स्वीकृत अपेक्षित है
Registered instrument : पंजीकृत लिखत
Registering authority : पंजीकरण प्राधिकारी
Registrable document : पंजीकरण हेतु दस्तावेज
Regretted, the proposal cannot be agreed to : खेद है प्रस्ताव स्वीकार नहीं किया जा सकता
Regular course of business : कार्य के नियमित क्रम से
Regular establishment : नियमित स्थापना
Regular occupation : नियमित उपजीविका / सामान्य व्यवसाय
Regular performed : नियमित रूप से संपादित किया गया
Regular service should be taken into account : नियमित सेवा पर विचार करना चाहिए
Regularisation of excesses : अतिव्यय को नियमित करना
Regulating the conditions of service : सेवा की शर्तों का विनियमन करना
Regulating the procedure : प्रक्रिया विनियमित करना
Regulations frame thereunder : उसके अधीन बनाए गए विनियम

Regulatory measures : विनियामिक कदम / विनिमयकारी कार्यवाही

Rehabilitation of displaced person : विस्थापित व्यक्तियों का पुनर्वास

Rehearing of the suit : वाद की पुनः सुनवाई करना

Reimbursed entitled to be : प्रतिपूर्ति पाने का अधिकारी

Reinstated in service : नौकरी बहाल की गई

Reissue of notice : फिर से सूचना देना

Rejection memo : अस्वीकृति ज्ञापन

Relates to : से सम्बंधित

Relating to Connected papers : तत्संबंधी कागजात वाला / से जुड़ा हुआ

Relating to the period in question : विवादास्पद अवधि के विषय में

Relative change : सापेक्ष परिवर्तन

Relative degree of responsibility : उत्तरदायित्व की अपेक्षित मात्रा

Relative frequency : सम्बन्धित आवृत्ति

Relative priorities : सम्बन्धित प्राथमिकताएँ

Relative rank : अपेक्षित रैंक

Relative seniority : सापेक्ष वरिष्ठता

Relatively low cost : तुलनात्मक दृष्टि से कम लागत / कीमत वाली

Release from responsibility : उत्तरदायित्व से निर्मुक्त करना

Release of offenders on probation : अपराधियों को परिवीक्षा पर छोड़ देना

Relevance of facts : तथ्यों की सुसंगति

Relevant extract : सम्बंधित सार / सम्बंधित उद्धरण

Relevant orders are flagged : संगत आदेशों पर पर्ची लगा दी गई है / संगत आदेश चिह्नित कर दिए गए हैं

Relief and rehabilitation : सहायता और पुनर्वास

Relief cannot be arranged : एवजी का प्रबंध नहीं हो सकता

Relief of distress : कष्ट की राहत

Relief shall not be given : राहत नहीं दी जायेगी

Relief that maybe claimed : अनुतोष जिसका दावा किया जा सकेगा
Relieved of responsibility : उत्तरदायित्व से मुक्त करना
Religious or charitable foundation : धार्मिक या खैराती प्रतिष्ठान
Relinquish charge : कार्यभार छोड़ना
Relinquishment due : शोध देय
Relinquishment in force : शोध प्रभावी होना
Relinquishment in full force, effect and virtue : पूर्णतः प्रवृत्त प्रभावी बलशील होना
Relinquishment of claim : दावे का त्याग
Relinquishment of possession : स्वामित्व का त्याग / कब्जा छोड़ना
Relinquishment Remain : अनुकाल्पतः निर्भर करना
Remainder of the period : अवधि का स्मरण-पत्र
Remainder of the term : शर्त का स्मरण-पत्र
Remaining provisions : बची हुई शर्तें
Remand the case : मामले का प्रतिप्रेषण करना
Remarkable fact : उल्लेखनीय तथ्य
Remarkable it is : यह उल्लेखनीय है
Remarks column : अभियुक्ति का खाना
Remarks of adverse nature : प्रतिकूल अभियुक्तियाँ / कथन
Remedy, eventual : अंतिम उपचार
Remission of rent : किराए की माफी
Remit a sentence : सजा माफी
Remit to the court : न्यायालय के पास भेजना
Remittance charges : प्रेषण व्यय
Remote advantage : परोक्ष फायदा
Removal of doubts : संदेह का निराकरण
Render an account : हिसाब देना
Render defective account : गलत हिसाब देना
Render due accounts : सही हिसाब देना
Render ineffective : प्रभावहीन बना देना
Render oneself liable to punishment : दंड का भागी बन जाना
Renewal and repairs : नवीनीकरण और मरम्मत

Renewed efforts : नए सिरे से कोशिशें

Renewed this maybe : इसका नवीनीकरण किया जाए

Renounce a claim : दावा छोड़ना

Reopen agreement : करार पुनर्जीवित करना

Reorganisation of office : कार्यालय का पुनर्गठन

Repatriation of : का स्वदेश लौटना

Repeated warnings have had no effect upon him : बार-बार चेतावनी देने का उस पर कोई असर नहीं हुआ

Reply already sent vide my letter no. ... : उत्तर भेजा जा चुका है मेरा तारीख --------- का पत्र देखें

Reply at once : तुरंत उत्तर दें

Reply is awaited from : से उत्तर की प्रतीक्षा है

Reply is under issue today : उत्तर आज भेजा जा रहा है

Reply may be sent as per draft put up infringement of performing right : प्रस्तुत प्रारूप के अनुसार उत्तर भेज दिया जाए

Reply memo : जवाबी ज्ञापन

Reply not received in spite of repeated reminders : बार-बार स्मरण-पत्र भेजने पर भी उत्तर प्राप्त नहीं हुआ

Reply overdue : जवाब में बहुत देरी हो गई है

Reply specially on the evidence : साक्ष्य पर विशेषतया उत्तर देना

Reply to our communication at Serial No. 8 has not been received : हमारे पत्र क्रमांक 8 का उत्तर अभी तक प्राप्त नहीं हुआ है

Reply was sent to the party accordingly : पार्टी को तदनुसार उत्तर भेज दिया गया था

Reply will be sent on the above lines : उपरोक्त अनुसार ही प्रेषित किया जाएगा

Report compliance immediately : अनुपालन कर तुरंत सूचित करें

Report for duty : कर्तव्य पर उपस्थित होना

Report has not been scrutinized in your office : आपके कार्यालय में रिपोर्ट की छानबीन नहीं की गई है

Report the fact : तथ्य की रिपोर्ट करना
Report under the hand : स्वहस्ताक्षरित रिपोर्ट
Representation in good faith : सद्भावनापूर्वक अभ्यावेदन
Represantation in writing : लिखित अभ्यावेदन
Representative in interest : हित प्रतिनिधि
Reprimand for indifference : लापरवाही के लिए फटकारना
Reproduced, prominently : प्रमुख रूप से उद्धृत किये गए
Reproductive capacity : पुनरुत्पादन क्षमता
Reproductive debt : पुनरुत्पादक ऋण
Repugnant to the context : सन्दर्भ के विरुद्ध, प्रसंग के प्रतिकूल
Repute, of : ख्यातिप्राप्त
Request cannot be met with : प्रार्थना स्वीकार नहीं की जा सकती
Require personal sanction of : की वैयक्तिक मंजूरी अपेक्षित है
Required information is being obtained from : आवश्यक जानकारी प्राप्त की जा रही है
Required information is furnished herewith : आवश्यक जानकारी यहाँ जुटाई गई है
Required information may please be : कृपया आवश्यक जानकारी प्राप्त करें
Required to be ratified : सुधार हेतु आवश्यक
Requires modification : संशोधन की आवश्यकता है
Requisite abilities : आवश्यक योग्यताएँ
Requisite act : आवश्यक कार्य
Requisite files are placed below : आवश्यक फाइल्स यहाँ नीचे रखी गईं हैं
Requisite information : आवश्यक सूचना
Requisite information has already been given : आवश्यक सूचना पहले ही दी जा चुकी है
Requisite time for obtaining copy of the judgement : फैसले की प्रति प्राप्त करने हेतु आवश्यक समय
Requisition of land : भूमि का अधिग्रहण
Rescued from drowning : डूबने से बचाया गया
Reserve judgement : निर्णय बाद में दिए जाने के लिए छोड़ना

Reserve Police : रिजर्व पुलिस / आरक्षित पुलिस
Reserve ratio : आरक्षित अनुपात
Reserves and surpluses : आरक्षितियाँ और अधिशेष
Residential premises : आवासीय परिसर
Residential quarter : आवासीय गृह
Residual income : अवशिष्ट आय
Residuary power : अवशिष्ट अधिकार
Residuary power of legislation : अवशिष्ट विधि निर्माण अधिकार
Resign his office : पद से त्यागपत्र देना
Resolution published in the gazette : राजपत्र में प्रकाशित संकल्प
Respondent in the case : वाद में प्रतिवादी
Responding entry : प्रतिवेदन प्रवेश / प्रतिवेदन आवती
Responsibility should be fixed : दायित्व दिया जाए / जिम्मेदारी ठहराई जाए
Responsive to advice and instructions : परामर्श और अनुदेशों के प्रति ग्रहणशील
Rest with the court alone should : केवल उस न्यायालय के हाथ ही रहेगा
Restraining order : अवरोधक आदेश
Restricted interpretation : सीमित निर्वाचन
Restricted leave : सीमित अवकाश
Resubmitted as desired : आदेशानुसार पुनः प्रस्तुत है
Result of reference to ... is awaited : को भेजे गए पत्र के परिणाम की प्रतीक्षा है
Resulting from : से पैदा होने वाली / से होने वाला
Resume duties : काम फिर सम्भाल लें
Resume of the case : मामले का सारवृत्त
Resume of the case is given in ensuring para below : मामले का सारवृत्त आगे के पैरा में दिया जा रहा है
Resume possession : कब्जा रखे रहना
Resume proceedings : कार्यवाही पुनः आरम्भ कीजिये
Resumption of charge : कार्यभार पुनः सम्भाल लेना
Resumption of talks : फिर से वार्ता प्रारम्भ करना

Retain lien : पुनः ग्रहणाधिकार बनाए रखना

Retain possession : कब्जा बनाए रखना

Retrenched personnel : छँटनी किये गए कर्मचारी

Retrospective effect : भूतलक्षी प्रभाव

Retrospective effect cannot be given to this sanction : इस मंजूरी को भूतलक्षी प्रभाव नहीं दिया जा सकता

Return and forfeiture of deposits : जमा रकम की वापसी और जब्ती

Return in question is blank : सम्बंधित विवरण रिक्त है

Return of file may be awaited : फाइल की वापसी की प्रतीक्षा की जाए

Return on investment : लगी पूँजी पर लाभ

Return thereto : तत्संबंधी विवरण

Returned candidate : निर्वाचित अभ्यर्थी

Returned duly endorsed : उचित रीति से पृष्ठांकित करके लौटाया

Returned for want of certificate of assumption of charge : कार्यभार ग्रहण करने का प्रमाणपत्र न होने के कारण लौटाया गया

Returned for want of payee's receipt : रुपया पाने वाले की रसीद न होने से लौटाया गया

Returning officer : निर्वाचन अधिकारी

Revalidation of assets : परिसंपत्तियों का पुनर्मूल्यन

Revealing the path : पथ प्रदर्शन करते हुए

Revenue and capital expenditure : राजस्व और पूंजीगत व्यय

Revenue proceeding : राजस्व कार्यवाही

Revenue process : राजस्व आदेशिका

Revenue settlement : राजस्व बंदोबस्त

Reversion to a lower : पोस्ट निचले पद पर प्रत्यावर्तन (पदावनति)

Reverted to substantive post : मूल पद पर प्रत्यावर्तित

Review keep under : पुनरावलोकन करते रहना

Reviewing the control limits : नियंत्रण सीमाओं का पुनरावलोकन

Revised draft memorandum is put up as by : की इच्छानुसार ज्ञापन का परिशोधित प्रारूप प्रस्तुत है

Revised memo is put up as ordered : आदेशानुसार सम्बंधित ज्ञापन प्रस्तुत है
Revised return : सम्बंधित विवरण
Revised tender : संशोधित टेंडर / संशोधित निविदा
Revision maybe undertaken : परिशोधन / पुनरावृत्ति की जाए
Revive the case : मामले को फिर से उठाया जाए
Revocation of guarantee : गारंटी का प्रतिसंहरण
Richly deserves promotion : पूर्णतया पदोन्नति का पात्र है
Right as of : साधिकार
Right claimed in common : अधिकार हेतु सामान्यतः दावा
Right in personam : व्यक्तिसम्बन्धी अधिकार
Right in rem : कार्यसम्बन्धी अधिकार
Right of audience/hearing : सुनवाई का अधिकार
Right of lien : धारणाधिकार
Right of pre-emption : अग्र-क्रयाधिकार / पूर्व क्रयाधिकार
Right to appeal : अपील का अधिकार
Right to fair trial : उचित विचारण का अधिकार
Right to future : मेंटेनेंस भावी भरण-पोषण का अधिकार
Right to hold situation : ओहदे को धारण करने का अधिकार
Rightful claimant : सही दावेदार
Rigid bent of mind : अनम्य मनोवृत्ति
Rigidity in : कठोरता से
Rigorous : कठोर / सश्रम
Ripe and sound experience : परिपक्व और ठोस अनुभव
Rise in price : महँगाई / मूल्य वृद्धि
Rising of court : न्यायालय का उठना
Rival claims : प्रतिपक्षी दावे / विरोधी दावे
Road under repair : सड़क सुधार चल रहा है
Robust common sense : प्रबल व्यवहार बुद्धि
Rough calculation : मोटा हिसाब
Rough draft : कच्चा मसविदा / कच्चा प्रारूप
Rough estimate of the expenditure involved : प्रत्याशित व्यय का मोटा अनुमान
Rough weather : खराब मौसम

Rounded off as one	: एक मानकर गिन लिया गया
Routine test of a routine nature	: नेमी ढंग का नेमी परीक्षण / सामान्य दैनिक परीक्षण
Routine work	: दैनिक कार्य
Rule of law	: विधिसम्मत शासन
Rule was not enforced rigidly	: दृढ़ता से लागू नहीं किया गया था
Rules applicable to the case	: प्रकरण में में लागू नियम
Rules framed under section no	: धारा क्रमांक ------ के अधीन बनाए गए नियम
Rules of general application	: सब पर लागू होने वाले नियम
Rules of procedure	: कार्यविधि नियम
Rules shall prevail	: नियम अभिभावी होंगे
Rules will be strictly adhered to	: नियम कड़ाई से पालित होंगे
Ruling from Govt. should be obtained	: सरकार से व्यवस्था प्राप्त की जाए
Running repairs	: छोटी मरम्मत
Running summary of facts	: तथ्यों का क्रमिक सार
Rural credit	: ग्राम-ऋण

■■

S

Safe and sure, conduct back : सुरक्षित और सुनिश्चित रूप से ले जाना
Safe conduct : सुरक्षित रूप से ले जाना
Safe keeping : सुरक्षा में रखना
Safe period : सुरक्षित अवधि
Safety and welfare : सुरक्षा और कल्याण
Safety appliance : सुरक्षा साधन
Said rule : उक्त नियम
Salaried class Scale of pay : वेतनभोगी कर्मचारी
Sale by description : वर्णन के अनुसार विक्रय
Sale of the attached property : कुर्क की गयी संपत्ति की बिक्री
Sale proceeds : बिक्री की रकम / बिक्री आय
Sale proclamation : विक्रय उद्घोषणा
Salient features : प्रमुख बातें
Salvation army : मुक्ति सेना
Same amount of : उतना ही
Same character : वाही हैसियत
Same consequences : वे ही परिणाम
Sampling procedure : नमूनाकरण की प्रक्रिया
Sanction has become inoperative : मंजूरी निष्प्रभावी हो गई है
Sanction of the competent authority maybe obtained : समर्थ प्राधिकारी की स्वीकृति ली जाए
Sanitary arrangements : सफाई व्यवस्था
Satellite township : उपनगरी
Satisfaction objective : वस्तुपरक समाधान
Satisfaction of claim : दावे की तुष्टि
Satisfaction of court, to the : न्यायालय को समाधानप्रद रूप से
Satisfaction of the decree : डिक्री की तुष्टि
Satisfaction subjective : व्यक्तिपरक समाधान
Satisfactory account : समाधानप्रद वृत्तांत / समाधानप्रद लेखा
Satisfy the justice of the case, to : मामले में न्याय की तुष्टि के लिए

Save after consultation with : से परामर्श किये बिना
Save as aforesaid : जैसा ऊपर कहा गया है उसके सिवाए
Save as otherwise prescribed : जैसा अन्यथा विहित है उसे छोड़कर
Save as provided hereafter : इसके आगे तथा उपबंधित के अतिरिक्त
Save in so far as : इसके अतिरिक्त
Save where : जहाँ ---- है वहाँ के सिवाए
Saving all just exceptions : सब न्यायसंगत अपवादों को छोड़कर
Scale of charges : प्रभारों का मापमान
Scarcity and relief : अभाव और सहायता
Scavenging Tax : सफाई कर
Schedule of charges : प्रभारों की अनुसूची
Scheduled area : नियत / अनुसूचित क्षेत्र
Scheduled banks : अनुसूचित बैंक
Scheme of arrangement : प्रबंध की स्कीम (रूपरेखा)
Scheme of arrangements : प्रबंध-योजना
Scope considerable : विचारणीय / दिए जा सकने योग्य समय
Score out : काटना
Scholar of repute : ख्याति-प्राप्त विद्वान
Scope of audit : संपरीक्षा / लेखा-परीक्षा की परिधि
Scope of authority, beyond the : प्राधिकार के विस्तार के परे
Scope of authority, within : प्राधिकार के विस्तार के अंतर्गत
Scope of grant : अनुदान की सीमा
Scope of the inquiry : जांच की परिधि
Score out whichever is not appropriate : जो उचित न हो उसे काट दें
Screen from punishment : दंड से बचाना
Screening committee : छानबीन समिति
Scrutiny is over : छानबीन समाप्त हो गई
Seal common : सामान्य मुद्रा
Seal of the cover : मुद्रा जो लिफाफे पर लगी हो
Sealed tender : मुहरबंद निविदा
Sealing is required : सील किया जाना जरूरी है
Search and seizure : तलाशी और जब्ती

Seasonal character : समय विशेष
Second instrument : दूसरी लिखत
Second proviso : दूसरा परन्तुक
Secondary evidence : गौण साक्ष्य
Secret cover : गुप्त लिफाफे
Secret most : अति गुप्त
Section has no comment to offer : अनुभाग की तरफ से कोई टिप्पणी नहीं है
Section may please see : अनुभाग कृपया देखें
Secular State : धर्मनिरपेक्ष राज्य
Secured debt : प्रतिभूति ऋण
Secured high rank : ऊँची श्रेणी प्राप्त की
Securing possession : कब्जा प्राप्त करना
Securing the objects : उद्देश्यों को प्राप्त करना
Security bond : प्रतिभूति बंध-पत्र
Security for appearance : हाजिरी के लिए प्रतिभूति
Security for good behaviour : सदाचार के लिए प्रतिभूति
Security of public peace : लोकशांति की सुरक्षा
See my note in the linked file : संलग्न फाइल में मेरी टिप्पणी देखिये
Seemingly correct : बाह्य रूप से ठीक
Seen file : देखा लिया गया अब फाइल करें
Seen thanks : देख लिया गया, धन्यवाद
Sees ahead : दूरदर्शी है
Seizure memo : जब्ती-पत्र
Select grade : प्रवरण श्रेणी / क्रम
Selection post : चयन पद
Semi-autonomous : अर्ध-स्वायत्त
Semi-nomadic population : अर्ध-यायावर जनसंख्या
Semi-permanent : अर्धस्थायी
Semi-skilled worker : अर्ध-कुशल कामगार
Semi-technical : अर्ध-तकनीकी
Senior administrative grade : वरिष्ठ प्रशासन
Senior time scale : वरिष्ठ समयमान

Seniority tempered by merit : वरिष्ठता प्रधान योग्यता गौण
Sense of duty : कर्तव्यबोध
Sense of guilt : अपराधबोध
Sense of proportion : अनुपात बोध
Sense of punctuality : समयनिष्ठता
Sense of purpose : उद्देश्यनिष्ठा
Sense of urgency : आवश्यकता के महत्त्व की समझ
Sent herewith as directed : आदेशानुसार साथ भेजा गया
Sentence to fine : जुर्माने की सजा देना
Sentenced to gallows : फांसी का दंड दिया गया
Sentenced to undergo rigorous imprisonment for : वर्षों के लिए सश्रम कारावास का दंड दिया गया
Separate possession : पृथक कब्जा
Separate revenue : पृथक आगम
Separately and distinctly : पृथकतः और सुभिन्नतः
Sequence of occurrence : घटनाक्रम
Serially numbered : क्रमांकित
Serious inconvenience : घोर असुविधा
Serious interference : गंभीर बाधा
Series of acts : कार्यों का क्रम
Series of occurrences : घटनाओं का क्रम
Serious offence : गंभीर अपराध
Serious repercussions : गंभीर प्रतिक्रिया
Serious thought : गंभीर विचार
Serve a notice : सूचना तामील करना
Serve and return : तामील के बाद लौटाइये / तामील करना और लौटाना
Serve legal notice to the borrower : ऋण-प्राप्त व्यक्ति को कानूनी नोटिस देना
Serve term of imprisonment : कारावास की अवधि काटना
Service conditions are not satisfactory : सेवा की शर्तें संतुष्टिजनक नहीं हैं
Service contract : सेवा अनुबंध

Service envelope : सरकारी लिफाफा
Service of process : आदेशिका की तामील
Service of the summon : समन की तामील
Service paid article : दत्तशुल्क सरकारी वस्तु
Service verification : सेवा सत्यापन
Serviceable material : काम का माल
Services lent to ...department : सेवाएँ -----विभाग को सौंपी गईं
Servicing of debts : ऋणशोधन कार्य
Set a drift : खोलकर छोड़ देना
Set apart : पृथक करना
Set apart the sum : धनराशि अलग करना
Set aside the dismissa : खारिज / अपास्त करना
Set back : धक्का / हानि / रुकावट / बाधा
Set down for hearing : सुनवाई के लिए रखा जाना
Set forth in : में वर्णित किया गया
Set in jurisdiction, original : न्यायाधिकार में लाना
Set of promises : वादे / वादों की सूची
Set out : दिए गए / उपवर्णित
Set over : उपरिस्थापित
Set tactfully : समझदारी से रखा
Set up a committee : कमिटी बनाना
Setting a scheme : योजना बनाना
Setting forth such other particulars : ऐसी अन्य विशिष्टियाँ उपवर्णित करना
Setting forth the grounds : आधारों को बताते हुए
Setting of one item against another : एक मद को दूसरी में से मुजरा करना
Setting out opinions : राय उल्लिखित करते हुए
Setting out the whole : संपूर्णतः उपवर्णित करते हुए
Setting up a title : हक जताना
Settle down to work : काम में जम जाना
Settle the account : हिसाब तय करना
Settled land : व्यवस्थापित भूमि
Settlement instructions : बंदोबस्त सम्बन्धी हिदायतें

Settlement of a dispute : झगड़े का निपटान
Settlement of issues : विवाद्यकों का स्थरीकरण
Settlement operations : बंदोबस्त-कार्य
Several distinct grounds : कई सुभिन्न आधार
Severally and jointly : अलग-अलग और मिलकर
Severe disciplinary action will be taken : अनुशासन की कड़ी कार्यवाही की जायेगी
Severe loss of life : अत्यधिक जनहानि
Severe punishment : कठिन दंड
Severed, to be : पृथक किया जाए
Severer in kind : कठोरतम किस्म का
Shake his credit : उसकी विश्वसनीयता को धक्का पहुँचाना
Shake the credit : विश्वसनीयता को धक्का पहुँचाना
Shall aid with his advice : अपनी सलाह देकर सहायता करेंगे
Shall also be laid on the table of parliament : संसद के पटल पर रखा जाएगा
Shall be at liberty to explain : स्पष्टीकरण देने के लिए स्वतंत्र होगा
Shall be binding upon : पर आबद्धकर होगा
Shall be bound to attend : हाजिर होने के लिए आबद्ध होगा
Shall be bound to state : कथन करने के लिए आबद्ध होंगे
Shall be construed accordingly : तदनुसार उसका अर्थ किया जाएगा
Shall be convened : बुलाये जायेंगे
Shall be deemed to be included : सम्मिलित समझा जाएगा
Shall be deemed to have the meaning : के वे ही अर्थ समझे जायेंगे
Shall be deemed to mean : से अभिप्रेरित समझा जाएगा
Shall be discontinued : समाप्त होगा
Shall be equal in number : बराबर संख्या में होगा
Shall be guided by principles : सिद्धांतों से मार्गदर्शित होगा
Shall be liable to account for : के लिए उत्तरदायी होगा
Shall be made available : उपलब्ध किया जाएगा
Shall be omitted from the list : सूची से हटाया जाएगा
Shall be personally liable : व्यक्तिगत रूप से देय होगा
Shall be prevented : निवारित रखा जाएगा

Shall be read over : पढ़कर सुनाया जाएगा
Shall be subject to inspection : निरीक्षण किया जाएगा
Shall be sworn : शपथ दिलाई जायेगी
Shall be taken down : लिखा जाएगा
Shall be treated as confidential : गोपनीय माना जाएगा
Shall be void : शून्य होगा
Shall bring the case before..... : मामले को --- के समक्ष ले जाया जाएगा
Shall cease to be a member : सदस्य नहीं होगा
Shall cease to have effect : प्रभावहीन हो जाएगा
Shall cease to hold office : पद पर नहीं रहेंगे
Shall come into force : लागू होगा
Shall form part of : का भाग होगा
Shall have the force of law : विधि का बल रहेगा
Shall hold good : प्रभावी होगा
Shall maintain proper accounts : उचित हिसाब रखेगा
Shall not be called in question on any ground : किसी भी आधार पर आपत्ति नहीं उठाई जायेगी
Shall otherwise act : कोई अन्य कार्य करेगा
Shall prejudice the determination : अवधारण पर प्रतिकूल प्रभाव डालेगा
Shall proceed to hear the complaint : परिवाद सुनने के लिए अग्रसर होगा
Shall record the reason of his inability : अपनी असमर्थता का कारण लिखेगा
Shall serve a notice of demand : मांग की सूचना की तामील कराएगा
Shall stand amended : संशोधित हो जाएगा
Shall stand vacated : रिक्त हो जाएगा
Share paid up : समादत्त शेयर पूँजी
Short notice question : अल्प सूचना प्रश्न
Short of details : बिना विवरण दिए
Shortages written off : बट्टे खाते में डाली हुई घटती
Shortly stating : थोड़े में कहते हुए
Show as above : जैसा कि ऊपर दिया गया है

Show of force : बल-प्रदर्शन
Show of hands, on a : हाथ उठाकर
Side by side : साथ-साथ
Sifting of evidence : साक्ष्य का सूक्ष्म परीक्षण
Sight after : दर्शन के बाद
Sign a receipt therefore : उसके लिए रसीद हस्ताक्षरित करना
Signed, sealed and delivered : हस्ताक्षर और मुहरबंद करके दिया गया
Significant increase : महत्त्वपूर्ण बढ़त / काफे बढ़त
Significantly different : काफी अलग
Signify approval : अनुमोदन संज्ञापित करना
Signify assent : अनुमति संज्ञापित करना
Signify willingness : सहमति संज्ञापित करना
Signing and verification : हस्ताक्षर तथा सत्यापन
Signing in blank : रिक्त स्थान को छोड़कर हस्ताक्षर करना
Silent worker : शांत कार्यकर्ता
Silver jubilee : रजत जयंती
Simple minded : सरल स्वभाव का
Simultaneous agreement in writing : लिखित में समसामयिक करार
Sincerity is transparent : सच्चाई सुस्पष्ट है
Sine die : अनिश्चित काल के लिए
Sine qua non : अनिवार्य शर्त
Single consideration : एकल प्रतिफल
Single tender : एकल संविदा
Single transferable vote : एकल संक्रमणीय मत
Singly or taken together : अकेले या साथ मिलकर
Sit down strike : बैठे रहो हड़ताल
Sit in strike : हाजिर हड़ताल
Sitting member : वर्तमान सदस्य
Sitting over the papers : कागज दबाकर बैठना
Situation, responsible : उत्तरदायित्वपूर्ण ओहदा
Skilled work : कौशलपूर्ण कार्य
Slightly affected : थोड़ा-सा प्रभावित

Slip of pen : लेखन में त्रुटि
Slow but sure forted : सुस्त किन्तु सुदृढ़
So and so : अमुक
So appearing in evidence : इस प्रकार साक्ष्य में दर्शित होने पर
So as to ensure : ताकि यह सुनिश्चित किया जा सके
So as to have retrospective effect : कि उसका भूतलक्षी प्रभाव हो
So as to readily accessible : कि उन तक आसानी से पहुँच हो सके
So far : अब तक
So far as consistent with the provisions of... : जहाँ तक वह ------ के उपबंधों से संयत हों
So far as may be : जहाँ तक हो सके
So far as they are applicable : जहाँ तक वे लागू हो सकते हैं
So long as : जब तक
So often as : अधिकांशतः
Soberising influence of age : आयु-सुलभ गाम्भीर्य
Sociability fair : कुछ मिलनसार
Social adjustment : सामाजिक सामंजस्य
Social disparity : सामाजिक विषमता
Social evil : सामाजिक बुराई
Social institution : सामाजिक संस्था
Soft currency : सुलभ मुद्रा
Soft currency area : सुलभ मुद्रा क्षेत्र
Soft loan : सुलभ ऋण
Soil conservation : भूमि संरक्षण
Soil erosion : मिट्टी का कटाव
Sole and regular employment : अनन्यतः और नियमित रूप से नियोजित
Sole arbitrator : एकमात्र मध्यस्थ
Sole benefit of persons : व्यक्तियों का ही फायदा
Sole office : एकमात्र कार्यालय
Solely of money : एकमात्र धन के रूप में
Solely or mainly : केवल या मुख्य रूप से
Solely responsible : अकेले ही उत्तरदायी

Solemn affirmation : सत्यनिष्ठा से प्रतिज्ञान
Solemn declaration : सत्यनिष्ठ कथन
Solemnly affirm : सत्यनिष्ठा से प्रतिज्ञा करता हूँ
Soliciting the vote : मत की याचना करना
Solitary case : अकेला मामला
Solitary confinement : एकांत कारावास
Soon after receipt : प्राप्त होते ही
Sound and reasonable : ठीक और युक्तियुक्त
Sound and thorough : ठोस और पक्का
Sound mind Man, sane : स्वस्थचित्त
Sound on paper : कागजी काम में ठोस / कागज पर ठीक
Sound practice : ठीक चलन
Sound understanding : स्वस्थ समझ
Sovereign authority : प्रभुतासंपन्न प्राधिकारी
Sovereign power : प्रभुत्वसंपन्न शक्ति
Sovereignty and integrity : प्रभुता और एकता
Speak with papers to clay : दस्तावेज लेकर आज ही बात करें
Speaking deferred annuity : विशेष आस्थगित वार्षिकी
Speaking enactment : विशेष अधिनियमिति
Speaking form of procedure : प्रक्रिया का विशेष रूप
Speaking jurisdiction of powers : विशेष अधिकारिता या शक्ति
Speaking knowledge and experience : विशेष ज्ञान और अनुभव
Speaking leave to appeal : अपील करने की विशेष अनुमति
Speaking means of knowledge : जानकारी में विशेष साधन
Speaking order : कारण देते हुए आदेश
Speaking reasons to be recorded : लेख बड़े किये जाने वाले विशेष कारण
Speaking resolution : विशेष संकल्प
Speaking well of : प्रशंसा करना
Specially empowered : विशेष रूप से सशक्त किया गया
Specific denial : स्पष्ट खंडन

Specific fact : विनिर्दिष्ट तथ्य
Specific proposals : विशेष प्रस्ताव
Specification according to : विशेष निर्देश के अनुसार
Specified combination : उल्लिखित संयोजन
Specified date : उल्लिखित तिथि
Specified in the certificate : प्रमाणपत्र में उल्लिखित
Specified limit of error : बताई गई गलतियों की सीमा
Specifying the time, without : समय निर्दिष्ट किये बिना
Speedy remedy : शीघ्र उपचार
Spin over schemes : आगे लाई गई योजनाएँ
Splendid piece of work : शानदार कार्य
Split duty : विभाजित कर्तव्य काल
Spot delivery contract : हाजिर सौदा संविदा
Spread over : विस्तृत
Spurious document : नकली दस्तावेज
Squaring up : ठीक-ठीक करना / ठीक-ठीक बनाना
Stabilization of prices : कीमतों में स्थिरता लाना
Staff are being instructed to adhere to instructions rigidly : कर्मचारियों से कहा जा रहा है कि निर्देशों का कड़ाई से पालन करें
Staff at fault maybe, taken up as per rules : दोषी कर्मचारियों पर नियमानुसार कार्यवाही की जाए
Staff strength is not adequate : कर्मचारियों की संख्या पर्याप्त नहीं है
Staff strength needs to be augmented : कर्मचारियों की संख्या बढ़ाने की आवश्यकता है
Staff will be considered for compensatory off' : कर्मचारियों को एवजी छुट्टी दी जायेगी
Stand committed : वचनबद्ध होना
Stand still agreement : यथास्थिति समझौता
Stand together, cannot : एक साथ नहीं रह सकते
Standard error : मानक दोष
Standard form : मानक प्रारूप
Standard formula : मानक सूत्र
Standard head : मानक शीर्ष

Standard method : मानक विधि
Standard of decency : शिष्टता का स्तर
Standard of instruction : शिक्षण का स्तरमान
Standard of quality : गुणवत्ता का मानक
Standardisation committee : समिति मानकीकरण समिति
Standing guard file : स्थायी गार्ड फाइल
Standing instructions : स्थायी निर्देश
Standing order : स्थायी आदेश
Stands so declared : ऐसी घोषणा की जाती है
State a case : मामले का कथन
State enterprise : राजकीय उद्यम
State government are pleased to sanction... : राज्य शासन ----- की मंजूरी देता है
State government observe that... : राज्य शासन का मत है कि -----
State government regret that : राज्य शासन को खेद है कि ----
State its/one's finding : अपना निष्कर्ष देना
State of affairs : कामकाज की स्थिति / परिस्थिति
State of health : स्वास्थ्य की स्थिति
State of uncertainty : अनिश्चितता की स्थिति
Statement of allegations : आरोपों का विवरण
Statement of facts : तथ्यों का विवरण
Statement of material facts : वास्तविक तथ्यों का कथन
Statement of outstanding cases : बकाया मामलों का विवरण
Statement of solemn affirmation : सत्यनिष्ठापूर्ण प्रतिज्ञान से कथन
Statement of the cases : मामलों का कथन
Stationery and printing : लेखन सामग्री तथा मुद्रण
Statistics of growth and yield : वृद्धि और उपज के आंकड़े
Status quo : यथास्थिति
Statute book : कानून की किताब
Statutory body : कानूनी निकाय
Statutory declaration : कानूनी घोषणा

Statutory orders : कानूनी आदेश
Statutory power : कानूनी शक्ति
Statutory report : कानूनी रिपोर्ट
Statutory requirement : कानूनी आवश्यकता
Statutory rights : कानूनी अधिकार
Stay of execution : निष्पादन का रोका जाना
Stay of proceedings : कार्यवाही स्थगित रखना
Stay of recovery : वसूली रोक रखना
Steady decline : लगातार कमी
Step in aid : सहायक उपाय
Steps have already been taken : कदम पहले ही उठाये जा चुके हैं
Stereotyped reply : बँधा बँधाया उत्तर
Stipulated date, future : नियत तारीख
Stipulated specification : नियत विवरण
Stipulation as to time : समय के बारे में अनुबंध
Stipulation according to : शर्त के अनुसार
Stock verification : स्टॉक सत्यापन
Stood up : साहस दिखलाया
Stoppage at efficiency bar : दक्षतारोध पर रुकना
Stoppage in transit over rule the plea : अभिवहन में रोकना
Straight and popular : खरा और लोकप्रिय
Straight dealings : खरा व्यवहार
Straightness of conduct : आचरण में खरा
Strategic points : रणनीतिक बिंदु
Stratum size : स्तर का आकार
Strengthening of administration : प्रशासन का सुदृढ़ीकरण
Strenuous work : कष्टसाध्य कार्य
Stress of weather : मौसमजन्य कठिनाई
Strict control : कड़ा नियंत्रण
Strict custody : कड़ी अभिरक्षा
Strict discipline : कड़ा अनुशासन

Strict in his dealing : व्यवहार में कड़ा
Strict vigilence : कड़ी नजर
Strictest standard, by the : कड़े से कड़े मानदंड के अनुसार
Strictly adhere to : ठीक-ठीक पालन करना
Strictly justifiable by law : विधि के अनुसार सम्मत
Strictly speaking : यथार्थ रूप में
Strike off : काट दिया जाना
Strike off the name : नाम काट देना
Strike out : काट देना
Strike pay : हड़ताल का वेतन
Strike pen down : कलम रोको हड़ताल
Strike work to rule : नियमानुसार कार्य हड़ताल
Stringency in the money market : मुद्रा बाजार में टंगी
Stringent qualification : कड़ी शर्तें
Strive hard : जीतोड़ प्रयास करना
Strive one's best : भरसक प्रयत्न करना
Strong evidence : सशक्त साक्ष्य
Strong with his subordinates : अधीनस्थों के प्रति कड़ा
Study interdisciplinary : अंतर्विषयक अध्ययन
Stunted growth : अवरुद्ध विकास
Sub-contract : उपसंविदा
Sub-head of account : लेखा उपशीर्ष
Sub-lease : उप पट्टा / शिकमी पट्टा
Sub-paragraph : उप-अनुच्छेद
Sub-rule : उप-नियम
Subduced officer : निष्प्रभ अधिकारी
Subject is still under reference : विषय पर अभी पत्र-व्यवहार हो रहा है
Subject is treated as closed : यह विषय समाप्त समझा जाए
Subject matter of a suit : वाद की विषयवस्तु
Subject noted above : उपर्युक्त विषय
Subject of inquiry : जाँच का विषय
Subject to a condition : शर्त से जुड़ा हुआ

Subject to agreement : करार के अधीन
Subject to appeal : अपील की जा सकेगी
Subject to approval : अनुमोदन किया जा सकेगा
Subject to approval of : के अनुमोदनार्थ
Subject to audit : लेखा हेतु
Subject to conditions : शर्तें लागू हैं
Subject to confirmation : पुष्टि होने पर
Subject to imprisonment : कारावास से दंडनीय
Subject to jurisdiction : क्षेत्राधिकार होने पर
Subject to mortgage : बंधन के अधीन
Subject to privilege : विशेषाधिकार के अधीन
Subject to scrutiny : जाँच के अधीन
Subject to such special conditions : ऐसी विशेष शर्तों के अधीन रहते हुए
Subject to the previous approval of the Govt. : सरकार के पूर्व अनुमोदन के अधीन
Subject to the provisions of any law : किसी विधि के उपबंधों के अधीन
Subject to the provisions of this act : इस अधिनियम के उपबंधों के अधीन
Subject to the rules : नियमों के अधीन रहते हुए
Subject to the terms there of : उसमें दी गई शर्तों के अधीन
Subject to time and circumstances permitting : यदि उस समय और परिस्थितियों में ऐसा करना संभव हो तो
Subject to unnecessary pain or suffering : अनावश्यक पीड़ा या यातना पहुँचाना
Subject to unnecessary restraint : अनावश्यक रूप से अवरुद्ध करना
Submerged area : डूबा हुआ क्षेत्र
Submission regarding : के विषय में निवेदन
Submission to the custody : अभिरक्षा में समर्पित होना
Submission to the order : आदेश मानना
Submit before issue : भेजने से पहले प्रस्तुत
Submit the case : मामले को भेज देना / प्रस्तुत करना
Submit to test : परीक्षण कराना

Submitted for approval : स्वीकृति हेतु प्रस्तुत
Submitted for consideration : विचार हेतु प्रस्तुत
Submitted for favour of sympathetic consideration : सहानुभूतिपूर्ण विचार हेतु प्रेषित
Submitted for information : सूचना हेतु प्रस्तुत
Submitted for orders : आदेशों के लिए प्रस्तुत
Subscribe to : ग्राहक बनना / समर्थन करना
Subsequent act : पश्चातवर्ती अधिनियम
Subsequent addition : वाद की अभिवृद्धि
Subsequent conduct : पश्चातवर्ती आचरण
Subsequent proceedings become void : वाद की कार्यवाहियाँ रद्द की जाती हैं
Subsequent sitting : वाद की बैठक
Subsequent grant : पाश्चिक अनुदान
Subsidiary employment : सहायक नौकरी
Subsidiary register : सहायक रजिस्टर
Subsistence allowance : जीवन-निर्वाह भत्ता / गुजारा भत्ता
Subsistence grant : जीवन-निर्वाह अनुदान
Substance of statement : कथनों का सार
Substance of the order : आदेश का सार
Substantial cause : सारवान हेतुक
Substantial damage : भारी हानि
Substantial evidence : महत्त्वपूर्ण साक्ष्य
Substantial injustice : बहुत अन्याय
Substantial part : पर्याप्त भाग
Substantially identical : काफी एक सा
Substantiate by the evidence : साक्ष्य द्वारा सिद्ध करना
Substantiate the charges : आरोपों की पुष्टि कीजिये
Substantive appointment : मूल नियुक्ति पद
Substantive pay : मूल पद वेतन
Substantive post : मूल पद
Substitute maybe appointed as an interim arrangement : अंतरिम व्यवस्था के रूप में एवजी नियुक्त किया जाए
Substitute the following for : निम्नलिखित प्रतिस्थापित किया जाए

Subtle sense of humour : सूक्ष्म हास्यबोध
Subversive activities : तोड़फोड़ की कार्यवाही
Succeeding paragraph : आगे का पैरा
Succeeding year : अगला वर्ष
Succession, perpetual : शाश्वत उत्तराधिकार
Successor interest : हित उत्तराधिकारी
Such action, as maybe deemed necessary : ऐसी कार्यवाही जो आवश्यक समझी जाए
Sue in the court : मुकदमा चलाना
Suffer from sense of frustration : कुंठा से पीड़ित होना
Sufficient proof is not forthcoming : पर्याप्त साक्ष्य प्रकाश में नहीं आ रहा है
Sufficiently evident : पर्याप्त साक्ष्य
Suggestion Sui juris : विधि की दृष्टि से सक्षम
Suit in question : प्रश्नगत वाद
Suit of civil nature : सिविल प्रकृति का वाद
Summarily dealt with : सरसरी तौर पर निपटाया हुआ
Summarily reject : सरसरी रूप में अस्वीकार करना
Summary disposal : सरसरी तौर पर निपटान
Summary of the case : प्रकरण का सार
Summary rejection of appeal : अपील का संक्षेपतः खारिज होना
Summary way, try in a : संक्षेपतः विचारण करना
Summon is granted : सम्मन अनुदत्त कर दिया गया
Summon received back : सम्मन वापस मिला
Sundry charges : फुटकर प्रभार
Superannuation age : अधिवर्षिता आयु
Superannuation allowance : अधिवर्षिता भत्ता
Superannuation benefit : अधिवर्षिता प्रसुविधा
Superannuation gratuity : अधिवर्षिता उपदान
Supernumerary post : अधिसंख्य पद
Supersession of, in : का अधिक्रमण करते हुए
Supervisory instincts : पर्यवेक्षण वृत्ति
Supplementary agenda : अनुपूरक कार्यसूची

Supplementary award	: अनुपूरक अधिनिर्णय
Supplementary budget	: अनुपूरक बजट
Supplementary demand	: अनुपूरक मांग
Supplementary grant	: अनुपूरक अनुदान
Supplementary proceedings	: अनुपूरक कार्यवाहियाँ
Supplementary question	: अनुपूरक प्रश्न
Supplementary rule	: अनुपूरक नियम
Supplies and disposal	: पूर्ति और निपटान
Supply does not conform to the approved sample	: पूर्ति अनुमोदित नमूने के अनुरूप नहीं है
Support has been sought	: समर्थन माँगा गया है
Support price	: समर्थन मूल्य
Suppression of civil liberties	: नागरिक स्वतन्त्रता का दमन
Surcharge on	: पर अधिभार
Surrender of grants	: अनुदानों का समर्पण
Surrender value	: अभ्यर्पण मूल्य
Surreptitious inspection	: प्रच्छन्न निरीक्षण
Suspended credit	: निलंबित जमा
Suspense account	: उचंत लेखा
Suspense and reminder diary	: निलंबित मामलों और स्मरण-पत्रों की डायरी
Suspense to keep in	: अनिश्चय की दशा में रखना
Suspension of licence	: लाइसेंस का निलंबित किया जाना
Suspension order issued	: जारी किये गए आदेशों का निलंबन करना
Suspicious attention without delay	: अविरत ध्यान
Sustained loss	: उठाई गई हानि
Swearing in ceremony	: शपथ समारोह
Symbol of unity	: एकता का प्रतीक
System of proportional representation	: आनुपातिक प्रतिनिधित्व का तंत्र
Systematic variation	: व्यवस्थित भिन्नता

■■

T

Table of contents : विषय-सामग्री सूची
Table of the house : सदन का पटल
Table of the legislature : विधानमंडल-पटल
Tabular form : सारणीबद्ध रूप
Tabular presentation : सारणीबद्ध प्रस्तुति
Tabulation of infomation received : प्राप्त सूचना का सारणीकरण
Tacit consent : मौन स्वीकृति
Tackle the complex problem : जटिल समस्या का निपटान
Tag these papers : इन कागजात को नत्थी करें
Take advantage of : का फायदा उठाना
Take all reasonable steps : सभी युक्तियुक्त कदम उठाएँ
Take big strides towards progress : तेजी से उन्नति की ओर अग्रसर होना
Take cognizance of : पर ध्यान देना
Take/receive evidence : साक्ष्य प्राप्त करें
Take hold of : ग्रहण करना
Take in good spirit : स्वस्थ रूप में समझना / लेना
Take into account : हिसाब में लेना
Take levels of lend : भूमि को समतल करना
Take measures for : के लिए कदम उठाना
Take notice : ध्यान दें
Take off the file : फाइल से निकाल दिया जाए
Take over charge : कार्यभार ग्रहण करना
Take recourse : का सहयोग लें
Take round and report : जानकार देखिये और रिपोर्ट दीजिये
Take stock of the situation : स्थिति को समझें
Take such measures : ये कदम उठाएँ
Take the chair : कुर्सी लें / बैठें
Take under control : नियंत्रण में लें
Take up : ले लें

Tamper with : के साथ गड़बड़ करना
Tangible assets : मूर्त परिसंपत्ति
Tangible results : मूर्त परिणाम
Task work allowance : उजरती भत्ता
Tax assessment : कर-निर्धारण
Tax evasion : कर-चोरी
Tax exemption : कर से छूट
Tax liable to : कर योग्य
Tax revenue : राजस्व कर
Technical appraisal : तकनीकी मूल्यांकन
Technical know-how : तकनीकी जानकारी
Technical viability : तकनीकी व्यावहारिक संभावना
Telegraphic address : तार का पता
Temperamental trails : स्वभावगत लक्षण
Temperately worded : संयत शब्दों में
Temporal nature : ऐहिक प्रकृति
Temporarily incapable : अस्थायी रूप से असमर्थ
Temporary advance : अस्थायी अग्रिम
Temporary diversion : अस्थायी पथांतर
Temporary injunction : अस्थायी आदेश
Tenancy right : कृषक अधिकार
Tend to prejudice : प्रतिकूल प्रभाव डालने वाली
Tender sample : निविदा नमूना
Tenders have been invited : निविदा आमंत्रित की गई है
Tenure basis, appointment on : सेवानिवृत्ति के आधार पर नियुक्ति
Tenure post : सावधिक पद
Term of years : वर्षों की अवधि
Terminable annuity : समाप्य वार्षिकी
Terminable of one month's notice : एक महीने की नोटिस पर समाप्य
Terminal tax : सीमा कर
Terminate the appointment : नियुक्ति समाप्त करना
Terminated by dismissal : पदच्युति द्वारा समाप्त

Termination of lien : धारणाधिकार का पर्यवसान
Termination of time observe punctuality : समय आधारित अनुशासन का समापन
Terminus a quo : आरम्भ स्थल
Terms of reference : सौंपे गए काम / विचारार्थ विषय
Terms used in estimation : अनुमान में प्रयोग की गयी शर्तें
Territorial army : प्रादेशिक सेना
Test audit : नमूना लेखा परीक्षा
Test certificate : परीक्षा प्रमाणपत्र
Test charges : परीक्षा प्रभार
Test relief work : प्रायोगिक सहायता कार्य
Testamentary disposition : वसीयती निपटान
Testing report : प्रायोगिक जानकारी / परीक्षण रिपोर्ट
Text authoritative : प्राधिकृत पाठ
The bill is under fire : विधेयक की कड़ी आलोचना की गई
The case is under submission : मामला पेशी में है
The draft may be amended accordingly : प्रारूप को तदनुसार संशोधित कर लिया जाए
The fact stands as follows : तथ्य इस प्रकार है
The file in question is placed below : आक्षेपित फाइल नीचे रखी है
The issue is being re-examined : मामले की फिर से जाँच की जा रही है
The matter has been badly delayed : प्रकरण काफी विलंबित हो गया है
The mistake is much regretted : भूल के लिए बहुत खेद है
The proposal is quite in order : यह प्रस्ताव बिलकुल ठीक है
The relevant file is not readily available : सम्बन्धित फाइल सम्प्रति उपलब्ध नहीं
The year under review : पुनरावलोकन का वर्ष
There is no cause to modify : संशोधन की आवश्यकता नहीं है
There is no distinction : कोई भिन्नता नहीं है
There is no obligation for : के लिए बाध्यता नहीं है
There is no point in pursuing the case further : यह प्रमाणित करने के लिए कोई रिकार्ड नहीं है

Thereabout	:	उसके विषय में
Thereafter	:	उसके बाद
Thereby	:	उसके द्वारा
Therein	:	उसमें
Thereunder	:	उसके अधीन / उसके नीचे
Thereupon	:	उस पर / तत्पश्चात्
Therewith	:	उसके साथ
These views are endorsed	:	इन विचारों का समर्थन किया जाना है
Think fit	:	उपयुक्त समझना
This being, his first offence, he maybe dealt with leniently	:	यह उसका पहला अपराध है इसलिए कार्यवाही करते समय मुलायम रहा जाए
This can not be allowed	:	इसकी अनुमति नहीं दी जा सकती
This case relates to...	:	यह मामला ----- से सम्बन्ध रखता है
This does not concern office	:	इसका कार्यालय से कोई सम्बन्ध नहीं है
This has already been replied to	:	इसका पहले ही उत्तर दिया जा चुका है
This has crossed our letter as	:	इसके यहाँ प्राप्त होने से पहले ही क्रम संख्या --- का पत्र भेजा जा चुका है
This has reference to	:	के सन्दर्भ में
This is as per your verbal instructions	:	यह आपके मौखिक आदेशानुसार है
This is entirely within the competence of	:	यह पूर्णरूप से ---- के अधिकार में है
This is in accordance with the existing rules	:	यह वर्तमान नियमों के अनुसार है
This is not admissible under rule	:	नियमों के अनुसार इसे स्वीकार नहीं किया जा सकता
This is receiving attention	:	इस पर ध्यान दिया जा रहा है
This is to bring it to your kind notice	:	यह आपकी जानकारी में लाया जा रहा है
This may please be approved	:	कृपया इसका अनुमोदन किया जाए
This may please be regularised	:	कृपया इसे नियमित किया जाए

This may please be suitably amended : कृपया इसमें उपयुक्त संशोधन किया जाए

This may please be treated as urgent : कृपया इस पर तुरंत कार्यवाही की जाए

This office has no information in respect : इस सम्बन्ध में कार्यालय को कोई जानकारी नहीं है

This requires administrative approval : इसे प्रशासनिक अनुमोदन की आवश्यकता है

This should be approved by competent authority : इसका अनुमोदन समर्थ प्राधिकारी द्वारा होना चाहिए

This will take effect from... : यह ---- से लागू होगा

Thorough going : सम्यक रूप से काम करने वाला

Thorough going officer : सम्यक रूप से काम करने वाला अधिकारी

Thoroughfare : आम रास्ता

Thoroughly competent : पूर्णतः समर्थ

Thought and vision : विचार और दृष्टि

Through inadvertence : असावधानी से

Throw light upon : पर प्रकाश डालना

Till after the warrant is executed : वारंट निष्पादित होने के बाद तक

Till further orders : अगले आदेश तक

Till such time as : जब तक ---- तब तक

Time limited, by law : विधि द्वारा परिसीमित समय

Time scale of pay : काल वेतनमान

Time schedule maybe adhered to : समय सूची का पालन किया जाए

Time wages : अमानी

Timed programme : समयबद्ध कार्यक्रम

Timed compliance maybe ensured : समय पर पालन सुनिश्चित कर लिया जाए

Title adverse to the or someone : किसी व्यक्ति के हक के प्रतिकूल हक

Title deed : हक विलेख

Title of honour : मान की उपाधि
Title, official : पदाभिधन
To adjourn sine die : अनिश्चितकाल के लिए स्थगित करना
To assume management : प्रबंध हाथ में लेना
To be dealt with severely : कड़ाई से कार्यवाही करना
To be defended : बचाव करना
To be heard in public : सार्वजनिक रूप से सुनवाई हेतु
To be held responsible : जिम्मेदार ठहराना
To be incumbent upon : आवश्यक होना
To be levied : वसूल किये जाने वाले
To be readily accessible : तुरंत पहुँच होना
To be returned in original : मूल प्रति लौटाई जाती है
To compound offences : अपराधों का निपटान करना
To concert the offence with : अपराध की मिलकर योजना बनाना
To confer rights : अधिकार प्रदान करना
To connive at : जानकर उपेक्षा करना
To convince Shall be satisfied : संतुष्ट करना
To date : की तारीख तक
To deal exclusively... : केवल ---- लेन-देन करना
To designate : नामित करना
To discuss at length : सविस्तार चर्चा करना
To evoke against : के विरुद्ध भड़काना
To exercise jurisdiction not vested in it : निहित न किये गए क्षेत्राधिकार का प्रयोग न करना
To exercise option : विकल्प का प्रयोग करना
To expedite : शीघ्रता करना
To express the concern : चिंता जाहिर करना
To fill the office : पद को भरने के लिए
To fix up : निश्चित करना
To give effect : को प्रभावी करना
To have recourse to : के शरण लेना / की सहायता प्राप्त करना
To impose restrictions : निषेधाज्ञा जारी करना

To initiate action : कार्यवाही प्रारम्भ करना
To launch a scheme : योजना प्रारम्भ करना
To monitor intelligence branch : आसूचना प्रसारण
To operate simultaneously : एक साथ चलाना
To pay damages : नुकसान की भरपाई करना
To put in abeyance : स्थगित करना
To reconcile : समाधान करना
To release on a bond a person arrested : गिरफ्तार व्यक्ति को बंधपत्र पर रिहा करना
To snatch by force : बलपूर्वक छीनना
To speed up disposal : व्यवस्था से शीघ्रता करना
To take early steps : शीघ्र कदम उठाने हेतु / शीघ्र कदम उठाना
To that effect : उस उद्देश्य का
To the best of his belief : उसके सर्वोत्तम विश्वास के अनुसार
To the best of his judgement : उसके सर्वोत्तम निर्णय के अनुसार
To the best of my knowledge and belief : मेरी सर्वोत्तम जानकारी और विश्वास के अनुसार
To the effect that : इस आशय का
To the exclusion of : को छोड़कर
To the extent of : उस विस्तार तक / उस सीमा तक
To the following effect : नीचे दिए गए आशय का
To the fullest extent possible : अंतिम संभव सीमा तक
To the prejudice of : के प्रतिकूल प्रभाव डालने के लिए
To the satisfaction of : के समाधन / पर्यन्त
Token cut : सांकेतिक कटौती
Token cut motion : सांकेति कटौती प्रस्ताव
Token grant : सांकेतिक अनुदान
Token strike : सांकेतिक हड़ताल
Toll house : पथकर गृह / टोल घर
Took the initiative : सूत्रपात किया
Total brought forward : आगे लाया गया कुल जोड़
Total carried over : आगे ले जाया गया जोड़

Touching the matters : विषयों से सम्बंधित
Town planning : नगर आयोजन
Trace out the previous papers : पहले की कागजात का पता लगाइये
Traffic in human beings : मार्ग पर जनभीड़
Transaction of business : व्यावसायिक आदान-प्रदान
Transfer adjustment : अंतरण समायोजन
Transfer debit : अंतरण नामे
Transfer entry : अंतरण प्रविष्टि
Transfer memorandum : अंतरण ज्ञापन
Transfer of case : मामले का अंतरण
Transfer, absolutely : पूर्णरूपेण अंतरण
Transit duty : पारवहन शुल्क
Transit office : पारवहन कार्यालय
Transit pass : रवाना / पारगमन पास
Transmitting station : प्रसारण केंद्र
Transportation for life : आजीवन निर्वासन
Treasury accounts : कोषागार लेखे
Treasury benches : मंत्रीपीठ / राजपीठ
Treasury voucher : खजाना / कोष वाउचर
Treat cordially : सौहार्दपूर्ण व्यवहार करना
Treated alike : एक जैसा व्यवहार किया गया
Treated unfairly : दुर्व्यवहार किया गया
Treating, bribery by : सत्कार के रूप में रिश्वत
Treatment of a subject : विषय का प्रतिपादन
Trial balance : कच्चा-चिट्ठा
Trial cannot be had : विचारण नहीं हो सकेगा
Trial de novo : नए सिरे से न्याय-जाँच
Tribute land : खिराजी भूमि
Triennial report : त्रैवार्षिक रिपोर्ट
Trifling amendment : नगण्य संशोधन
Tripartite agreement : त्रिपक्षीय करार
Triplicate in : तीन प्रतियों में
Triplicate of a bill : बिल की तीसरी प्रति

True account	: सच्चा लेखा / सही वृत्तान्त
True allegiance	: सत्यनिष्ठा
True and correct view	: सच्चा और ठीक रूप
True and faithful account	: सही और यथार्थ लेखा
Trunk call	: ट्रंक काल
Trust funds	: न्यास निधि
Trustworthy hand	: विश्वसनीय व्यक्ति
Truthfully, interpret	: ठीक-ठीक भाषांतरण करना
Try to stand by	: साथ तैयार रहने का प्रयास करना
Turbulent agitation	: उपद्रवकारी आन्दोलन
Twofold action	: दोतरफा कार्यवाही
Type script	: टाइप प्रति
Typed letter is put up	: टाइप की गई प्रति प्रस्तुत है
Typographical error	: मुद्रण त्रुटि

■■

U

Ugly situation : खराब परिस्थिति
Ulterior motive : गुप्त अभिप्राय / अप्रत्यक्ष आशय
Ultimate objective : अंतिम / मुख्य उद्देश्य
Ultimate control : पूर्ण नियंत्रण
Ultimate cost : अंतिम / मूल लागत
Ultimate responsibility : अंतिम / असली दायित्व
Ultimate unit : अंतिम इकाई
Ultimately this has to be done : कुछ भी हो ये तो करना ही पड़ेगा
Ultimo : पिछले महीने का
Ultra vires : अधिकार से बाहर / शक्ति के परे
Unanimous decision : सर्वसम्मत निर्णय
Unassuming : सीधा सरल
Unauthorised action has been regularised : अनधिकृत कार्यवाही का नियमन कर दिया गया है
Unauthorised hours : अनधिकृत समय
Unauthorised interference : अनधिकृत हस्तक्षेप
Unauthorised occupation : अनधिकृत कब्जा
Unavailed leave : न ली गई छुट्टी
Unavoidable cause : अपरिहार्य कारण
Unbecoming his position : उसके पद की दृष्टि से अशोभनीय
Unbiased opinion : निष्पक्ष राय
Uncalled for : अकारण / अनपेक्षित / अनाहूत
Uncalled liability : अनाहूत दायित्व
Unceasing efforts : अनवरत प्रयास
Uncertain future extent : अनिश्चित भावी घटना
Unclassified categories : अवर्गित श्रेणियाँ
Unclassified posts : अवर्गित पद
Unconditional surrender : बिना शर्त समर्पण
Unconstitutional and void : असंवैधानिक और शून्य
Uncovered demand : अपूरित मांग

Under a mistake : भूल के कारण
Under advice to us : हमें सूचित करते हुए
Under charge : कम किराया या शुल्क देना / के अधीन / के प्रभार में
Under duress : दबाव में आकर
Under his hand and seal : उसके हस्ताक्षर और मुद्रा सहित
Under his patronage : उसके संरक्षण में
Under his signature : उसके हस्ताक्षर में
Under intimation to this office : इस कार्यालय को सूचना देते हुए
Under my hand : मेरे हस्ताक्षर से
Under my occupation : मेरे कब्जे में
Under protest : आपत्ति के साथ
Under reference : प्रसंगाधीन / निर्देशाधीन
Under the auspices of : के तत्वावधान में
Under the rules thereunder : तदधीन नियमों के अंतर्गत
Under various heads of accounts : विभिन्न लेखा शीर्षों के अधीन
Undergo a change : परिवर्तन होना / परिवर्तन के दौर से गुजरना
Undergo a sentence of imprisonment : कैद की सजा भुगतना
Underground : भूमिगत
Underhand dealings : कपट व्यवहार
Underlying assumptions : अन्तर्निहित धारणा / पूर्वानुमान
Underlying idea : अन्तर्निहित विचार
Undermine the administration : प्रशासन को कमजोर बनाना
Undersigned is directed to : निम्न हस्ताक्षरी को निर्देश दिया जाता है कि
Undertaking given : दिया गया विचार
Undertaking in writing : लिखित वचनबंध
Undertaking should be obtained : वचन लिया जाना चाहिए
Undervaluation should not be restored to : अवमूल्यन नहीं किया जाना चाहिए

Undignified behaviour : अभद्र व्यवहार
Undisbursed balance : अवितरित रकम
Undue hardship : अनुचित कष्ट
Undue influence : अनुचित प्रभाव
Undue interference : अनुचित हस्तक्षेप
Undue pressure : अनुचित दबाव
Unduly long period : असाधारण लम्बी अवधि
Undutiful act : कर्तव्य विरुद्ध कार्य
Uneconomic holding : अलाभकर जोत
Uneconomical method : घाटे का तरीका
Unexpired portion : असमाप्त भाग
Unfavourable balance : प्रतिकूल नियंत्रण / अर्थहीन नियंत्रण
Unforeseen charges : अदृष्ट प्रभार
Unforeseen circumstances : अप्रत्याशित परिस्थितियाँ
Unforeseen developments : अदृष्ट घटनाएँ
Unforeseen future contingency : अकल्पित भावी परिस्थिति
Ungentlemanly behaviour : अभद्र व्यवहार
Unhampered action : अबाध कार्यवाही
Unified scales : एकीकृत वेतनमान
Uniform increase : समान वृद्धि
Uniform procedure : एक-सी प्रक्रिया
Uniform process : एक समान प्रक्रिया
Uniform satisfactory : एक-सा संतोषजनक
Uniformity in procedure : प्रक्रिया में एकरूपता
Uniformly applicable : समान रूप से लागू
Unilateral action : एकतरफा कार्यवाही
Union list : संघ सूची
Union Public Service : संघ लोकसेवा आयोग
Union territories : संघशासित क्षेत्र
Unit of appropriation : विनियोजन इकाई
Unlawful assembly : गैरकानूनी जमावड़ा
Unlawful purpose : गैरकानूनी उद्देश्य
Unless otherwise agreed : जब तक अन्यथा सम्मत

Unless otherwise provided	:	जब तक अन्यथा उपबंधित न हो
Unless otherwise specified	:	जब तक अन्यथा स्पष्ट निर्देश न हो
Unless sooner dissolved	:	यदि पहले ही विगठित न कर दी जाए
Unless the context otherwise requires	:	जब तक प्रसंग से अन्यथा अपेक्षित न हो
Unlimited power	:	असीम अधिकार
Unnecessary stigma	:	अनावश्यक लांछन
Unqualified apology	:	बिना शर्त क्षमायाचना
Unrealisable sum	:	अप्राप्य राशि
Unreasonable delay	:	अनुचित विलम्ब
Unrestricted interpretation	:	अनियंत्रित निर्वचन
Unsound mind	:	विकृत चित्त
Unspent balance	:	अव्ययित / बिना खर्च हुआ शेष
Unstarred question	:	विशेष रूप से ध्यान न दिया जाने वाला प्रश्न
Until otherwise provided for	:	जब तक ---- अन्य उपबंध न हो
Until provision in that behalf is made	:	जब तक इसके लिए उपबंध न किया जाए
Until the contrary is proved joint lives, during their	:	जब तक विपरीत सिद्ध न हो जाए
Untiring efforts	:	अथक प्रयास
Untoward incident	:	अप्रिय घटना
Upgraded post	:	उच्चीकृत पद
Upgrading of posts	:	पद बढ़ाना / पद ऊँचा करना
Uphold the dignity of	:	की मर्यादा बनाए रखना
Uphold the lower authority's decision	:	नीचे की प्राधिकारी के निर्णय की पुष्टि
Upkeep the building	:	इमारत का रखरखाव
Upon supposition	:	अनुमान पर
Upto and including	:	तक तथा सहित
Upward tendency	:	ऊपर की तरफ जाने वाली प्रवृत्ति
Urgent call	:	तुरंत बुलावा
Urgent slip	:	आवश्यक पर्ची

Use, right of intended to be used : उपयोग का प्राधिकार

Use utmost endeavour : अधिकतम प्रयास

Utmost care : अधिकतम देखभाल / अधिकतम सावधानी

Utmost endeavour : अधिकतम प्रयास

Utmost good faith : परम सद्भावपूर्वक

Utmost secrecy : परम गोपनीयता

■■

V

Vacate the office as such : उस हैसियत का पद रिक्त करना
Vacate the order : आदेश रद्द करना
Vacation of appointment : पद रिक्त होना
Vacation of seats : स्थानों का रिक्त होना
Vague objections : अस्पष्ट आपत्तियाँ
Valid and effectual : विधिमान्य और प्रभावी
Valid discharge : विधिमान्य उन्मोचन
Validate the title : हक को विधिमान्य बनाना
Validly made : विधिमान्य बनाए गए
Valuation date : मूल्यांकन की तारीख
Value of benefit : फायदे का मूल्य
Value of consideration : प्रतिफल का मूल्य
Value rights for : मूल्य देकर अधिकार
Variable control limits : अस्थिर नियंत्रण सीमा
Variance ratio : परिवर्तनशील अनुपात
Variation in figures is due to : घट-बढ़ का कारण यह भी है कि
Variety of causes : कारणों की विविधता
Variety of subject : विषय की विविधता
Various subgroups : विभिन्न सह-समूह
Verbatim report : शब्दशः सूचना / शब्दशः रिपोर्ट
Verification is required from : से सत्यापन की आवश्यकता है
Verification of antecedents : पूर्ववृत्त का सत्यापन
Verification of cash balance : रोकड़ शेष का सत्यापन
Verification of stores : माल का सत्यापन
Verified and found correct : जाँच की और सत्य पाया गया
Verified claim : सत्यापित दावा
Verified copy : सत्यापित प्रति
Verify the accuracy : शुद्धता को सत्यापित करना
Vesting of management : प्रबंध में निहित करना
Vesting order : निहित करने वाला आदेश

Veto power : वीटो की शक्ति / निषेधाधिकार
Vexatious search : त्रासदायक तलाशी
Vexed question : जटिल प्रश्न
Via media : मध्य मार्ग
Vide endorsement above : उपर्युक्त पृष्ठांकन देखिये
Vide file attached : संलग्न फाइल देखिये
Vide folio flagged : पर्ची लगा पृष्ठ देखिये
Vide letter no . ... : पात्र क्रमांक ----- देखिये
Vide linked case : सम्बद्ध फाइल देखिये
Vide note on the order sheet : आदेश-पत्र की टिपण्णी के अनुसार
View the place : स्थान का अवलोकन करना
Vigilant control : सतर्क नियंत्रण
Vigorous campaign : जोरदार अभियान
Vigorous efforts : जोरदार प्रयत्न
Violate condition : शर्त का उल्लंघन करना
Virtue of office, by : पद के आधार पर
Virulent epidemic : घातक महामारी
Visible representation : दृश्य रूपण / दृश्य प्रतिनिधित्व
Visual publicity : दृश्य प्रचार
Vital question : महत्त्वपूर्ण प्रश्न
Vital service : अत्यावश्यक सेवा
Vital statistics : जन्म-मरण के आंकड़े / जीवन-मरण का प्रश्न
Vital to the needs of the economy of the country : देश की अर्थव्यवस्था की आवश्यकताओं के लिए अहम
Vivid account : विशद / सजीव विवरण
Void agreement : शून्य करार / प्रभावहीन समझौता / अर्थहीन समझौता
Void and of no effect : शून्य और प्रभावहीन
Void contract : शून्य ठेका / प्रभावहीन संविदा
Void for uncertainty : अनिश्चितता के कारण प्रभावहीन
Voluntarily and in good faith : स्वेच्छा और सद्‌भावपूर्वक

Voluntarily causing grievous hurt	: जानबूझकर बुरी तरह से चोट पहुँचाना
Voluntarily executed	: स्वेच्छापूर्वक निष्पादित
Volunteered to forgo	: स्वेच्छा से छोड़ दिया है
Votable expenditure	: मतदान के योग्य व्यय
Vote by proxy	: परोक्षी द्वारा मतदान / प्रतिपुरुष मतदान
Vote on account	: लेखानुदान

■■

W

Waive the recovery : वसूली छोड़ देना
Waive the restrictions : पाबंदियाँ हटा लेना
Waive the right : अधिकार छीन लेना
Waived his rights : उसने अपने अधिकार छोड़ दिए
Waiving of maximum age limit : अधिकतम आयुसीमा में छूट देना
Wandering at large : स्वच्छंद विचरण
Want of capacity : क्षमता का अभाव
Want of due precaution : उचित सावधानी की कमी
Want of execution : निष्पादन न किया जाना
Want of form : प्रारूप का अभाव
Want of jurisdiction : अधिकारिता का अभाव
Want of proper caution : उचित सावधानी का अभाव
Want of title : हक का अभाव
Warned to be careful in future : भविष्य में सावधान रहने की चेतावनी दी जाती है
Warrant of attachment of movable property : चल संपत्ति की कुर्की का वारंट
Warrant of committal : सुपुर्दगी का वारंट
Warrant of precedence : अग्रता अधिपत्र
Wasteland : बंजर भूमि
Watch and ward : पहरा और निगरानी
Watched, progress maybe : प्रगति पर निगरानी रखी जाए
Waterworks : जलप्रदाय कार्य / जलप्रदाय केंद्र / पानीघर
Way of penalty, by : शास्ति-स्वरूप
Ways and means committee : अर्थोपाय समिति
We are pleased to inform you : हम आपको सहर्ष सूचित करते हैं
We have carefully considered your request : हमने आपके निवेदन पर पूर्ण विचार किया है
We have no remarks to offer : हमारे पास इस पर कोई टिप्पणी नहीं है

We need not pursue the matter further : हम इस विषय को अब आगे नहीं बढ़ाना चाहते

We propose the following course of action : हम दिए गए अनुसार आगे की कार्यवाही का प्रस्ताव रखते हैं

We regret : हमें खेद है

We shall be glad : हमें प्रसन्नता होगी

Weaker sections of the society : समाज का कमजोर वर्ग

Wear and tear : टूट-फूट

Weeding of records : अभिलेखों की छँटाई

Welfare state : कल्याणकारी राज्य

Well-balanced : संतुलित / समझदार

Well-discussed : अच्छी तरह विचार-विमर्श किया गया / विवेवचनापूर्ण

Well-founded : सुआधारित

Well-meaning : सदाशय

Well-mentally : मानसिक गुणों से संपन्न

Well-read : सुपठित / अच्छी तरह से पढ़ा हुआ

Well-delays : देरी क्यों हो रही है ?

Well so ever : जो भी / जो भी हो

Whatever maybe the circumstances : चाहे जो भी परिस्थितियाँ हों

When called upon : अपेक्षा किये जाने पर

When occasion arises : जब अवसर आये

Whereabouts : पता-ठिकाना

Whereas it was his duty to attend : जबकि उपस्थित होना उसका कर्तव्य था

Whereby : जिससे / किस तरह / किस प्रकार

Whether incorporated or not : चाहे निगमित हो या न हो

Whether of law or fact : चाहे विधि सम्बन्धी हो या तथ्य सम्बन्धी

Which must happen : जो अवश्यम्भावी है

Which will have the effect : जिसका प्रभाव होगा

While in transit : अभिवहन के दौरान

While trying a suit : विचारण करते समय

White paper : श्वेतपत्र
Whoever does it : जो भी इसको करे
Whole of India : सारा भारत
Whole of the remaining : बचा हुआ सारा
Wholly absorbed : पूर्णतः अवशोषित
Wholly and exclusively : पूर्णतः एवं अनन्यतः
Wholly or in part : पूर्णतः अथवा अंशतः
Wide and precise knowledge : अतिसूक्ष्म ज्ञान
Wide knowledge : अत्यधिक ज्ञान
Widely read : पूर्णरूप से पढ़ा हुआ
Wilful absence from duty : जानबूझकर कर्तव्य से अनुपस्थित
Wilful act : जानबूझकर किया जाने वाला कार्य
Wilful concealment of a material fact : तात्त्विक तथ्य जानबूझकर छुपाना
Wilful contempt : जानबूझकर किया गया अपमान
Wilful disobedience : जानबूझकर की गई अवज्ञा
Wilful disregard : जानबूझकर अवहेलना करना
Wilful falsehood : जानबूझकर मिथ्या कथन
Wilful negligence : जानबूझकर की गई उपेक्षा
Wilfully absent : जानबूझकर अनुपस्थित रहना
Will be reckoned : गणना की जायेगी
Will be spared by : तक भारयुक्त कर दिया जाएगा
Will render the defaulter liable for punishment : गलती करने वाले को दंड का भागी बना देगा
Will you please refer to ... : कृपया ----- के बारे में देखें
Will you please state : कृपया बताएँ
Will, rational : तर्कसंगत इच्छाशक्ति
Willing worker : रुचिपूर्वक कार्य करने वाला कर्मचारी
Wind up the affairs : कार्यकलापों का परिसमापन
Wire is put up for signature : हस्ताक्षर हेतु तार प्रस्तुत है
With all convenient despatch : सुविधानुसार शीघ्रता से
With certainty : निश्चयपूर्वक
With diverse circumstances : विभिन्न परिस्थितियों सहित

With due deligence : सम्यक तत्परता से
With due regard to : का यथोचित ध्यान रखते हुए
With effect from : से प्रभावी / से लागू
With firm determination : दृढ़संकल्प के साथ
With full particulars : पूर्ण विवरण के साथ
With great vigour : बड़े उत्साह से
With his own hand : स्वयं अपने हाथ से
With immediate effect : तत्काल प्रभाव से
With intent to annoy : तंग करने के अभिप्राय से
With more promptness : और भी शीघ्रता से
With reasonable accuracy : यथोचित शुद्धता के साथ / जितना हो सके सही
With retrospective effect : पूर्वव्याप्ति सहित / भूतलक्षी प्रभाव से
With strong hand : सख्ती से
With the connivance of : की मौन सहमति से
With the like power : वैसी ही शक्ति से रहते हुए
With the previous consent of : की पूर्व सहमति से
With the remark that : की अभ्युक्ति के साथ
With this end in view : इस उद्देश्य को ध्यान में रखते हुए
Withdrawal of recognition : मान्यता वापस लेना
Withdrawing the approval : अनुमोदन वापस लेना
Withhold assent : अनुमति रोकना
Withhold refund : प्रतिदाय रोकना
Within reasonable time : यथोचित समय के भीतर
Within stipulated period : नियत अवधि के भीतर
Within the jurisdiction of : के क्षेत्राधिकार में
Within the local limits : स्थानीय सीमाओं में
Within the meaning of : के अर्थ में / के अर्थ के अंतर्गत
Within the purview : क्षेत्र के भीतर
Without affecting the substance : सार पर प्रभाव डाले बिना
Without airy further reference : बिना किसी और निर्देश के
Without assigning any reason : बिना कोई कारण बताये

Without detriment : को हानि पहुँचाए बिना
Without deviation : विचलन के बिना
Without due care : सम्यक सतर्कता के बिना
Without due cause : यथोचित कारण के बिना
Without fail : निश्चित रूप से
Without fear or favour : भय या पक्षपात के बिना
Without further proof : अतिरिक्त साक्ष्य के बिना
Without good and sufficient reasons : अच्छे और पर्याप्त कारणों के बिना
Without hinderance : बेरोकटोक
Without jurisdiction : अधिकारिता के बिना
Without payment of : के भुगतान के बिना
Without permission to prefix and suffix : पहले और बाद में जोड़ने की अनुमति के बिना
Without recording reasons : बिना कारण अभिलिखित किये हुए
Without recourse to : दायित्वरहित / का सहारा लिए बिना
Without reference to : के सन्दर्भ के बिना / से सम्बन्धित किये बिना
Without specifying time : समय विनिर्दिष्ट किये बिना
Without sufficient excuse : पर्याप्त प्रतिहेतु के बिना
Witness in attendance : हाजिर गवाह / उपस्थित साक्षी
Witness produced : गवाह पेश किये गए
Word and figures : शब्द और अंक
Word of mouth : मौखिक रूप से
Work charged : कार्य प्रभारित
Work execute the : कार्य निष्पादित करना
Work going on smoothly : काम अच्छा चल रहा है
Work indefatigably : अथक काम करना
Work needs further watching : काम पर आगे भी नजर रखने की जरूरत है
Work order : कार्य आदेश
Work to rule strike : नियमानुसार कार्य हड़ताल
Work with determination : दृढसंकल्प के साथ काम करना

Workable and sound : व्यावहारिक और ठीक
Workable knowledge : कामचलाऊ ज्ञान
Working arrangement : कामचलाऊ प्रबंध
Working balance : कामचलाऊ अतिशेष
Working capital : कार्यशील पूँजी
Working funds : कार्यशील धन
Working knowledge : कार्यसाधक ज्ञान
Working pattern : कार्यशैली
Working plan : कार्ययोजना
Working results : कार्य परिणाम
Working unit : इकाई
Workout cost : लागत निकालना
Works of public utility : लोकोपयोगी कार्य
Works outlay : निर्माण लागत
Writ of execution : निष्पादन याचिका
Writ of habeas corpus : बंदी प्रत्यक्षीकरण याचिका
Writ of mandamus : परमादेश याचिका
Writ of quo warranto : अधिकार पृच्छा याचिका
Write off an account : किसी लेखे के बट्टे खाते
Write off the irrecoverable amount : वसूल न होने पर रकम को बट्टे खाते में डाला जाए
Writing, in : लिखना / लिखकर मतदान करना
Written authority : लिखित प्राधिकार
Written instrument : लिखित पत्र
Wrong decided : गलत निर्णय लिया गया
Wrongful act : अनुचित कार्य
Wrongful confinement : सदोष परिरोध
Wrongful dismissal : सदोष पदच्युति
Wrongfully conceal : सदोष छिपाना
Wrongfully deferred : गलत तौर पर आस्थगित
Wronglly rejected : गलत तौर पर नामंजूर

■■

Y

Yardstick : मानदंड

Year ending on : को समाप्त होने वाला वर्ष

Year to year : वर्ष-प्रति-वर्ष

Year under report : रिपोर्ट गत वर्ष / आलोच्य वर्ष

Year under review : पुनरावलोकन वर्ष

Yellow dog contract : हड़ताल न करने का अनुबंध

Yield income : आय प्राप्त होना

Yield table : उपज सारणी

Yield to treatment : उपचार से अच्छा होना

You are called upon to show cause : आपसे कारण बताने की अपेक्षा की जाती है

You are hereby authorised to : एतद्द्वारा आपको यह अधिकार प्रदान किया जाता है

You are hereby informed : एतद्द्वारा आपको सूचित किया जाता है

You are suspended : आपको निलंबित किया जाता है

You can meet him by appointment : आप उनसे समय लेकर मिल सकते हैं

You may kindly report for duty on : आप कृपया अपने कर्तव्य (कार्य) पर ----- उपस्थित हों

You may like to discuss : संभवत: आप विचार-विमर्श करना चाहें

You may take necessary action accordingly : आप आवश्यक कार्यवाही करें

You will appreciate : आप सराहना करेंगे

Your attention is drawn : आपका ध्यान आकर्षित किया जाता है

Your attention is invited to para... : अनुच्छेद ----- पर आपका ध्यान दिलाया जाता है

Your Excellency : महामहिम

Your Excellency presumption is correct : आपकी धारणा ठीक है

Your Excellency reply should reach this office by...	: आपका उत्तर ----- तारीख तक इस कार्यालय में पहुँच जाना चाहिए
Your Excellency representation is untenable	: आपका अभ्यावेदन मान्य नहीं है
Your Excellency request cannot acceded to	: आपकी प्रार्थना स्वीकार नहीं की जा सकती
Your Majesty	: महागरिमामय
Yours obediently	: आपका आज्ञाकारी
Youth conference	: युवक सम्मलेन
Youth welfare activities	: युवक कल्याण गतिविधियाँ

■■

Z

Zeal and jest	: उत्साह और उमंग
Zero hour	: शून्यकाल
Zero option	: विकल्पहीनता
Zero rate	: शून्य दर (ब्याज की)
Zonal Manager	: क्षेत्रीय प्रबंधक / आंचलिक प्रबंधक

■■